the

GREAT

LAKES

REGION

in

CHILDREN'S

BOOKS

the GREAT LAKES REGION in CHILDREN'S BOOKS

ILLINOIS INDIANA MICHIGAN MINNESOTA OHIO ONTARIO WISCONSIN

A SELECTED
ANNOTATED
BIBLIOGRAPHY

THE GREAT LAKES REGION — ILLINOIS INDIANA MICHIGAN MINNESOTA OHIO ONTARIO WISCONSIN

EDITED BY **DONNA TAYLOR**

compiled by **ELVIA CARLINO**
LOIS CURTIS
DIANE M. GUNN
ERNESTINE MOKEDE
MARILYN SOLT
GRACE STAGEBERG SWENSON
PAT TOMEY

GREEN OAK PRESS ° Brighton, Michigan °

ILLINOIS INDIANA MICHIGAN MINNESOTA OHIO ONTARIO WISCONSIN

THE GREAT LAKES REGION IN CHILDREN'S BOOKS

A SELECTED ANNOTATED BIBLIOGRAPHY

edited by DONNA TAYLOR

Library of Congress Cataloging in Publication Data
Main entry under title:

The Great Lakes region in children's books.

   Includes indexes.
   SUMMARY: An annotated guide to works about the Great Lakes region including hard and soft cover books, pamphlets, and magazines.
   1. Great Lakes region—Juvenile literature—Bibliography. [1. Great Lakes region—Bibliography]
I. Taylor, Donna, 1921-   II. Carlino, Elvia.
Z1251.G8G73 [F551]   016.977   80-13746
ISBN 0-931600-01-4

Manufactured in the United States of America

Published by GREEN OAK PRESS
9339 Spicer Rd., Brighton, Michigan 48116

To no one person or group can this book be more appropriately dedicated than to all the Children of the Great Lakes Region.

CONTENTS

PREFACE

*The five interconnecting lakes, lying
in the heart of the North American
continent . . . are great in size,
great in commerce, great in engineering, great in history and romance,
great in cities and industry along
their shores, great in their interest
and their beauty . . . The Lakes form
the boundary between the United States
and Canada. The border is real
enough, of course, but on the Great
Lakes it is only an imaginary dotted
line cutting across the blue water.
It does not so much separate as join
together two great peoples. Since
the War of 1812 they have lived as
neighbors in peace on these shores
with the Lakes as a common waterway
free of warships and fortifications.*[1]

PURPOSE

The Great Lakes Region in Children's Books grew
out of the realization that librarians, students and
teachers are frequently frustrated in their search
for appropriate resources to help develop appreciation and a better understanding of the discovery,
and social, political and economic evolvement of the
vast international land mass encompassing Lakes
Michigan, Superior, Huron, Erie and Ontario. Conse-
quently, the intent of the compilers has been to

---

[1]Harlan Hatcher, *The Great Lakes*. New York: Oxford
University Press, 1944, pp.vii, viii.

create a selective, annotated listing of curriculum oriented children's books about Illinois, Indiana, Michigan, Minnesota, Ohio, Ontario and Wisconsin, as well as their bordering Lakes. Because their historical development is closely associated with the eastern portion of the continent, two other Great Lakes areas, Pennsylvania and New York, were considered inappropriate for a Great Lakes regional source list.

This bibliographical tool fulfills several functions. It is designed to serve as a foundation for building a library collection for learning about the heartland of the North American continent. Titles which will help to balance the present collection can be identified for future purchase. Knowledge of the existence of similar or better books may also influence librarians' decisions regarding rebinding, discarding or replacing the worn or damaged copies already in the collection. In addition, teachers, librarians and students will consult the comprehensive Subject index and the annotations to make decisions about the suitability of various books for reaching current curriculum goals.

SELECTION OF TITLES

The titles selected for *The Great Lakes Region in Children's Books* support the curriculum and provide for leisure pursuits, while appealing to a wide range of reading levels in Grades K-8, including reluctant, average and advanced. The latter level may supply background materials suitable for teachers.

Over-all selection criteria:
1) Contents have definite allusion to one or more areas or people within the Great Lakes region. Magazines demonstrate a consistent editorial policy for this subject specialization.
2) Conform to recognized critical standards in regard to style, characterization, plot, setting, theme, accuracy, point of view, tone, organization of contents, and physical format.

XII

3) Suitable for children in Grades K-8, including some adult books of interest to advanced readers and teachers for reference.
4) Print medium in paper or hard cover bindings, including full-length books, pamphlets and magazines.

   With these criteria in mind, the compilers found a wide range, from excellent to poor, in the quality and appropriateness of the printed materials available for examination. All suitable titles were examined critically, and those selected reflect the expertise of the individual compilers with children as well as with the books used by students, teachers and librarians in schools located within the Great Lakes region. The result is a highly selective bibliography, rather than an exhaustive one.

   In some instances, two compilers selected and annotated the same book because it contributes to an understanding of both geographical areas. Since there was no attempt to standardize the annotations in style or approach, each compiler indicates the special features in content or format which establish the book's value for a specific area. Although some duplication was necessary to assure the completeness of the bibliography in each area, only 62 (4.34%) of the 1428 numbered entries appear in more than one area.

   The dearth of quality materials has required the inclusion of some out-of-print books which the compilers found still available in libraries and new and used bookstores. Unfortunately, it appears that publishers do not find it economically expedient to continue selling many recently copyrighted books, and to reprint valuable older titles, or to replace them with newer ones offering similar learning experiences.

   While all the titles listed are recommended, some included for a particular contribution may also have certain deficiencies. They do, nevertheless, uniquely contribute local color, atmosphere, or information otherwise unavailable for the reading level represented. The weakness is clearly indicated so that decisions may be made regarding the suitability of the books for a particular library, and for the needs and abilities of individual readers.

To augment the area collections, a limited number of adult books are included because of their appropriateness for upper level readers, their value as reference sources, and as background material for teachers. Some of these books may be enjoyable and informative for all levels of readers by reason of their handsome pictorial content.

Additional valuable resources became available for selection because of the broad interpretation of the term "book" to include printed materials in any format. Both hard and soft cover books and pamphlet-type bindings were examined.

Another such resource is magazines, which have a special appeal to many children. Primarily for use by the individual child as a tool of enjoyment and learning, these magazines feature literature, informative articles valuable for their currency, and games and activities on the Great Lakes region. Although high quality juvenile magazines exist, those consistently featuring the Great Lakes region in literature and fact are relatively few. The single exception to this is Ontario, which has many excellent juvenile magazines devoted exclusively to that Canadian province.

BIBLIOGRAPHY
ARRANGEMENT. The bibliography is divided into eight major sections. These include the alphabetically arranged geographic areas of Illinois, Indiana, Michigan, Minnesota, Ohio, Ontario and Wisconsin, followed by Great Lakes – General, which was jointly contributed by the compilers. The latter contains valuable resources with a scope too broad for inclusion in one specific area.

Each of the major sections is sub-arranged alphabetically either by author, editor, compiler, or corporate body. If none of these is responsible for the creation of the work, the title is the alphabetizing factor. Joint authors are noted in the annotated entry. The second author is also in the alphabetical sequence, unnumbered, with a "see" reference to the joint entry. Both authors' names are in the Author Index with a coding reference to the annotated entry. Two or more titles by the same author are alphabetized under his name, except for a few books in series which are listed sequentially, as they were intended to be read. Annotations may contain references to other books with similar appeal, or other titles in a series. These additional titles are not numbered as bibliographic entries, but they do appear in the Title Index.

ENTRIES. The bibliographic format of the 1428 entries is consistent throughout. Numbered consecutively within each section, each entry includes author, title, illustrator, publisher, date, in-print status, reading level, awards, outstanding designations, and annotation.

Within those bibliographic elements, the in-print status was determined through one or more of the following sources: direct contact with authors and/or publishers, *Books in Print, Children's Books in Print,* and *Paperback Books in Print.* Another element is the approximate grades for which materials are suitable. In the experience of the compilers, many children in those grades have enjoyed reading the book independently, or profit from hearing it read aloud. Those gradings and the awards and outstanding designations are identified in the "Key to Abbreviations." A common bibliographic element, prices, is omitted from the entries because of their frequent and drastic changes. Before ordering any material, it is advisable to obtain a current price from a jobber or publisher.

SPECIAL FEATURES

MAGAZINES. To facilitate identification of their unique format, 27 magazines are annotated in a separate section. The basic arrangement follows that of the main bibliographic sections: alphabeticized geographic areas sub-arranged alphabetically by magazine titles. Identification numbers accompanying the titles correspond with their coding in the Magazine Index.

DIRECTORY OF PUBLISHERS. The availability of a book or magazine for purchase can be determined by contacting the publisher whose name appears in an abbreviated form in each bibliographic entry. Complete names and addresses obtained from publishers' current catalogs and numerous other sources are alphabetically arranged in the Directory. Included are major and minor publishers, self-published authors, and magazine publishers. Because many publishers have merged or vanished, a "see" notation directs the reader to the new organization if known. When no address was available, that is indicated.

INDEXES

Each index entry is followed by locator codes which identify both the geographic areas and the numbers of the bibliographic entries (*e.g.,* MN 64; WI 21, 42). The examples refer to the Minnesota section, 64th entry, and Wisconsin section, 21st and 42d entries. No page numbers are used in the indexes.

AUTHOR INDEX. All authors included in the eight sections of the bibliography are listed alphabetically. The bibliographic entries for books by each author are identified by the codes.

TITLE INDEX. All titles included in the eight sections of the bibliography are listed alphabetically. Although most have but one code, a few titles occurring in more than one list carry multiple codes to indicate the various locations of the bibliographic entries.

SUBJECT INDEX. All subjects are arranged alphabetically, followed by the codes identifying the location of the bibliographic entries. Unwanted areas can easily be eliminated without needless search through the bibliography.

Sears List of Subject Headings, 11th edition, was an invaluable aid in establishing subject index terms familiar to librarians, teachers and students. For topics relating to Canadian research, however, Sears has a limited usefulness. Unique indexing terms for Ontario subjects were provided by *Canadiana,* the authority used by the National Library of Canada. In the few instances that the two standard authorities offered insufficient guidance, the compilers drew upon their own experiences in the field to supply appropriate index terminology.

MAGAZINE INDEX. Magazines are indexed separately from books to facilitate the identification of this unique material which might conceivably have a totally different use by teachers, librarians and students. The ephemeral nature of magazine contents prohibits indexing their subjects. Each magazine title is listed in alphabetical order, followed by its location code for the magazine section.

ACKNOWLEDGMENTS

The regional study, *The Southwest in Children's Books,* edited by Mildred Priscilla Harrington (Louisiana State University Press, 1952), was the model used for development of a group of Library Science Masters Essays at Wayne State University. Dr. Robert E. Booth, Director of the Division of Library Science, guided Lois Curtis and Ernestine Mokede in their midwest regional bibliographies on children's books in Indiana and Wisconsin, respectively. From those beginnings, the editor of this volume expanded the model concept to the geographical entity of the Great Lakes Region, adding the international aspect.

Unquestionably, the development of *The Great Lakes Region in Children's Books* would have been impossible without the generous assistance of the many librarians in each area who made children's book collections readily available to the compilers in both their local libraries and through inter-library loans.

Donna Taylor

KEY TO ABBRE·VIATIONS

assoc.	association
B	Biography
Co.	company
Comp(s).	compiler(s)
ed(s).	editor(s)
enl.	enlarged
F	Fiction
illus.	illustrated
NA	Newbery Award for outstanding children's book.
o.p.	out of print (no longer available from publisher, but may be obtainable from used book stores and remainder sales).
P	important pictorial matter, such as plates, etc.
paper	paperback binding

XVIII

pseud.	pseudonym
pub.	publishing
repr.	reprint (not an original publication, but frequently a facsimile of an earlier publication).
rev.ed.	revised edition (changes made, usually to up-date information).
Soc.	Society
St.	saint
vol(s).	volume(s)
#	same title is in another area list; see Title Index for its location.
*	Outstanding for quality of style, characterization, or wealth of information.
(K-3)	Approximate reading level: Kindergarten through 3rd grade.
(5-7)	Approximate reading level: 5th through 7th grade.

NOTE: Non-fiction is not designated; this includes all titles classified by Dewey in small libraries.

CODING

GL	Great Lakes - General
IL	Illinois
IN	Indiana
MA	Magazines
MI	Michigan
MN	Minnesota
OH	Ohio
ON	Ontario
WI	Wisconsin

ILLINOIS

compiled by ELVIA CARLINO

Changes that took place over a span of billions of years have made Illinois what it is today. Because of the primeval seas which once lay over the land, the bedrock of Illinois is limestone, but again and again over unimaginably long periods of time the lands rose and the seas receded; the land sank and the seas rose again over the land. The climate was very different from the climate of today. When the land was exposed, lush vegetation grew, which, in turn, sank under the encroaching seas to be buried under tons of sediment. In that long ago time were formed the oil fields and coal beds that underlie the surface of the state.

Long after the last of the seas had ebbed away and the climate had changed drastically, the coming of the ice age brought further changes to the surface of Illinois. Four times great masses of ice moved down from the north, and four times it melted away leaving the surface changed each time. Great quantities of soil were moved from one place to another. The basins of the Great Lakes were gouged out and filled with water by the melting glaciers. Quantities of rich black soil were deposited on most of the northern two-thirds of the state. Great rivers were formed to drain away the waters of the melting ice masses. So the scene was set for the successful agricultural and transportation systems of Illinois.

At some time during the advance of the last glacier ancient primitive big game hunters roved over the land. As years passed, different groups of Indians made their appearance. Some reached a fairly high degree of cultural achievement, developed farming and left behind many interesting artifacts. At some period before the arrival of the white man the Illini (Ill' i nee) Confederacy became a powerful nation, but had already started to decline by the time the French explorers arrived.

Marquette, Joliet, and La Salle explored the Great Lakes region and Mississippi River. The Illinois country was claimed by the French, taken over ty the British after the French and Indian War, and finally was won for the Americans by George Rogers Clark. The first American settlers in Illinois came down the Ohio River by flatboat from the southern states to Southern Illinois. Later, the northern part of the state was settled by people who came by way of the Great Lakes water system or overland from the northeastern states, or from Europe. As a result of this conglomeration of settlers the Civil War period brought discord to the state as well as the nation.

However, two citizens of Illinois, President Abraham Lincoln and General Ulysses S. Grant, were highly responsible for holding the Union together. Illinois can lay claim to many other fine citizens, among them Jane Addams, proponent of social justice and help for the poor. The state has also had its share of not-so-fine citizens. Most notorious of those were probably the river pirates of Cave-in-Rock on the Ohio River and the Chicago gangsters of prohibition times.

Illinois is both an agricultural and an industrial state. Its central location with access to the Great Lakes and the Mississippi River, together with its many railway lines, have made it an important transportation center.

Children's books have been written about many aspects of Illinois. If it seems that books about Abraham Lincoln overshadow all the rest, it is perhaps because Lincoln the man overshadows all the rest. Some areas seem to have been neglected. Among the many books written about Indians, few are about Illinois Indians. Books about farm life and modern day life in general are **scarce**. There are other gaps and many of our Illinois books are out of print. Perhaps the time is ripe for budding authors to write some new books about life in Illinois past and present.

1 ADLER, IRVING and ADLER, RUTH. *The "Reason Why"
Books, Coal;* illus. Rev. ed. New York: John
Day, 1974. (4-6)
How coal was formed, early history of mining,
dangers of mining, safety measures, kinds of coal,
by-products, pollution problems are covered in this
book. Applies to Illinois as well as other coal producing areas. Earlier edition 1965.

— ADLER, RUTH. *The "Reason Why" Books, Coal.* See IL 1

2 ALLEN, JOHN. *Legends and Lore of Southern Illinois.*
Carbondale, Ill.: Southern Illinois University,
1963. (7-8)
A great deal of material is crowded into the
pages of this book. Unfortunately the print is quite
small, but children who are curious and interested in
facts and stories of Illinois will find much to satisfy
them. People, origin of names, folklore, Indians,
institutions, travel, places, and other subjects are
included. Perhaps the best use is by teachers and
parents with children. Index is helpful for finding
specific material.

3 ALLEN, MERRIT. *The Wilderness Way;* illus. by Larry
Toschik. New York: Longmans, Green, 1954.
(6-8) F
This is the story of La Salle's exploration of
the Mississippi River as seen by Laurent Delair, a
young man newly arrived from France, who shared the
hardships and miseries of the exploring party and witnessed the unending schemes that were hatched against
La Salle. Only his indomitable spirit and perseverance
against all odds enabled La Salle to continue to the
mouth of the Mississippi. Laurent's story woven into
La Salle's narrative has its own exciting episodes.

4 ANDERSON, A. M. *Wild Bill Hickok;* illus. by Jack
Merryweather. Chicago: Wheeler Publishing Co.,
1947. o.p. (4-6) B
This biography does not have much material on
Illinois. However, it gives a brief picture of life in
Illinois in the 1850's, and Illinois boys will probably

4

feel some pride in learning that Wild Bill Hickok was also an Illinois boy.

5   ANDERSON, LAVERE. *Mary Todd Lincoln, President's Wife;* illus. by Cary. Champaign, Ill.: Garrard Publishing Co., 1975. (3-5) B
    This biography begins with Mary Todd's girlhood in Kentucky and ends with her death in Springfield, Illinois. It is simply and clearly written giving high-lights of Mary Lincoln's life in Springfield and Washington, D.C. Springfield with its wooden sidewalks and muddy streets in which pigs wallowed, had its drawbacks in Lincoln's time, but political activities, debates, and especially Lincoln's election to the presidency made it an interesting place to live.

6   ANTHONY, BARBARA and BARNES, MARCILLENE. *Americans All: A Pageant of Great Americans;* illus. by Kreigh Collins. Grand Rapids, Mich.: Fideler, 1941. o.p. pp. 30-32, 63-65. (3-5)
    Of the 23 Americans included in this book two are from Illinois, Abraham Lincoln and Jane Addams. Both accounts are so brief they should perhaps be used merely as an introduction. Possibly the best use would be reading orally to young children.

7   AYARS, JAMES. *The Illinois River;* illus. by Lili Réthe. Chicago: Holt, Rinehart & Winston, 1968. o.p. (7-8) *
    The history of the Illinois River and its sur-rounding area from the Cambrian period to 1968. Geology, geography, wildlife, people (both individuals and groups) are all considered. Of special interest are the uses and abuses the river has suffered from the activities of people, and the changes that have come to the river and its environs as a result. An interesting, informative, and well-written account. Illustrations and map add to the value of the material.

8   BAILEY, BERNADINE. *Picture Book of Illinois;* illus. by Kurt Wiese. Chicago: Whitman, 1949. (4-5)
    Very brief accounts of Illinois beginning with the Illinois Indian tribe and naming other Illinois

tribes. Joliet, Marquette and La Salle are mentioned. A small amount of historical material is included. Chicago has more coverage than any other aspect of Illinois. Illustrations and map add interest to the book. Worthwhile though dated.

9 BAILEY, BERNADINE. *Puckered Moccasins, A Tale of Old Fort Dearborn;* illus. by Woodring Coons. Chicago: Laidlaw, 1938. o.p. (6-8) F
   This story of Fort Dearborn dwells on life in the fort preceding the ill-fated march toward Fort Wayne which resulted in the massacre. Fifteen-year-old Dave Rogers arrives at Fort Dearborn with a message for Captain Heald, a strict army man who never failed to carry out the orders of his superiors, no matter how unwise. Dave awaiting the arrival of his injured father is caught up in the life of the fort, but escapes during the massacre. A good account of life and anxieties in the fort.

10 BAKER, ELIZABETH. *Fire in the Wind;* illus. by Robert McLean. Boston: Houghton Mifflin, 1961. o.p. (5-8) F
   Life in Chicago in 1871 is well depicted in this story which revolves about the character Jeff Bellinger whose adventures, while not always believable, are exciting enough to keep children interested. The events during and results of the Chicago fire are described at the end of the book.

11 BAKER, NINA. *Ten American Cities, Then and Now;* illus. by Josephine Haskell. New York; Harcourt, Brace, 1949. o.p. pp. 204-225. (6-8)
   This account of Chicago includes a brief history of early people in the area, the Fort Dearborn massacre and the rapid development of the city. Most of the story is devoted to a vivid description of the Chicago fire and its aftermath. The Columbian Exposition, Mrs. Potter Palmer, the Haymarket Affair, and prohibition gangs conclude the narrative.

— BAKER, W. C. *Famous Railroad Stations of the World.*
      See IL 143

12 BARE, MARGARET. *John Deere Blacksmith Boy;* illus.
    by Robert Doremis. Indianapolis: Bobbs-Merrill,
    1964. o.p. pp. 167-192. (3-5) B
    Although only a few pages in this book cover the
fifty years that John Deere spent in Illinois, it is
useful because it relates the problems that Illinois
farmers had with the prairie soil which stuck to their
plows. Deere developed a steel plow which moved
through the soil without sticking.

— BARNES, MARCILLENE. *Americans All; A Pageant of
    Great Americans.* See IL 6

13 BAXTER, ERIC. *The Study Book of Coal;* illus. by
    Donald Green. London: The Bodley Head, 1959.
    o.p. (3-4)
    This is a simply written account of how coal was
formed, how it has been mined past and present, inventions which helped miners, how the miner gets into the
mine, how coal is brought to the surface, and products
made from coal. Terms used in the coal mining operation are italicized and explained. Though this book is
not written about Illinois, it applies to Illinois as
well as other areas.

14 BEALS, FRANK. *Chief Black Hawk;* illus. by Jack
    Merryweather. Evanston, Ill.: Row, Peterson,
    1943. o.p. (4-6) B
    This is the story not only of Black Hawk's life,
but also of the conflict which arose when the coming of
white settlers forced the Indians from their land. It
is made clear that there were self-seeking Indians as
well as white people; white people as well as Indians
of good will; and a lack of understanding between
Indians and white settlers. A map of the Sauk village,
Saukenuk, and the routes followed by the Sauks is
included.

15 BEATTY, JOHN. *The River Book;* illus. Chicago:
     Beckley-Cardy, 1942. **o.p.** (4-6)
     By means of a power boat, two boys with their
uncle explore the Fox River and discover many facts
that apply to all rivers; the kinds of life on the
river, in the river and near the river. They also
learn about river power, locks, dams, source of a river,
geology, and other fields of science in a river bed.
Specific material concerns mostly the Fox River, but
pages 229-232 relate to the Illinois River. Index, but
no maps.

16 BENÉT, LAURA. *Famous Poets for Young People;* illus.
     New York: Dodd, Mead, 1964. pp. 82-90, 104-112,
     148-151. (6-8) B
     Three of the poets in this collection were resi-
dents of Illinois for a part of their lives. Children
will be interested in learning that Eugene Field was a
mischievous little boy who became studious only when he
became a man; Vachel Lindsay was more interested in
being a wandering troubador than in being a medical
doctor; and Carl Sandburg was called "that terrible
Swede" by his college mates. Poems and photographs of
the poets are included.

17 BENÉT, ROSEMARY and BENÉT, STEPHEN. *A Book of
     Americans;* illus. by Charles Child. New York:
     Rinehart, 1933. pp. 83-84, 87. (4-8)
     Two poems, in this book, concern people of
Illinois, Abraham Lincoln and Ulysses S. Grant. There
is more substance to the poem about Lincoln than the
one about Grant. However, the Grant poem is a brief
crystallization of Grant's character and deeds; while
the Lincoln poem is a description of Lincoln and
summary of the way he was regarded by his Springfield
neighbors.

— BENÉT, STEPHEN. *A Book of Americans.* See IL 17

18 BENNET, ROWENA. *Creative Plays and Programs for Holidays.* Boston: Plays, 1966. pp. 29-36. (3-6)

A group of short poems about Lincoln, including a choral reading, "A Bit of Book Earning". The other poems are entitled "Prairie Growth", "A Boy's Wish", "The Strong Man", "The Nickname", "Lincoln", and "The Shovel Slate". All of the poems have the pioneer flavor of the prairies, as well as some aspect of Lincoln's character.

19 BLAIR, WALTER. *Tall Tale America; A Legendary History of Our Humorous Heroes;* illus. by Glen Rounds. New York: Coward-McCann, 1944. pp. 34-48. (5-8)

Along with Mike Fink's bragging, strutting, whooping and fighting, an account of keelboating on the Ohio and Mississippi Rivers is included in this tale. It also explains words used by the rivermen, such as, poling, bushwhacking, cordelling, and patroon.

20 BLANKMEYER, HELEN. *The Sangamon Country;* illus. by Harriet Cantrall. Springfield, Ill.: Phillips Brothers, 1965. paper. (Reprint under auspices Sangamon County Historical Society) (5-7)

Originally published in 1935 by the Board of Education District #186 Springfield and printed by the Illinois State Register, this book gives a brief survey of the Sangamon Country from 1673-1935. There are interesting bits about people, weather, animals, and other subjects. In spite of some personal bias, the book is useful for children studying Illinois history.

21 BLATCHFORD, FRANCES and ERMINGER, LILA. *Illinois Grows Up;* illus. by Louise Parsons. Chicago: A. C. McClurg, 1941. o.p. (4-6)

Arranged in alphabetical order beginning with the Algonquin Indians, this book deals mostly with historical material. There is a section on Abraham Lincoln, and another on "Verses of Our Poets" which includes poems that children have written as well as mention of the adult poets, including Carl Sandburg and Vachel Lindsay. Maps and a guide to pronunciation add value.

22 BLISS, GORDON. *Land of Lincoln, Our Illinois;* illus. St. Louis: State Publishing Co., 1968. (4-6)
Brief accounts of Indians, early explorations, settlements, and statehood give children some historical background. Modern Illinois subjects include communities, industry and resources, transportation, communication, education and government. A short biography of Lincoln is included, as well as a chapter on animals, birds and plants of Illinois. Concludes with recreation and places to visit in Illinois. Facts are presented prosaically, but illustrations in black and white add interest.

23 BORLAND, KATHRYN and SPEICHER, HELEN. *Allan Pinkerton, Young Detective;* illus. by Nathan Goldstein. New York: Bobbs-Merrill, 1962. (3-5) B
Only pages 147-167 deal with Pinkerton's life in Illinois. However, the background of his boyhood is an aid to understanding his later life as a detective. One of the most exciting parts of the book is Pinkerton's help in preventing the assassination of Lincoln in Baltimore on his way to the White House.

24 BOYNICK, DAVID. *Pioneers in Petticoats.* New York: Crowell, 1959. o.p. pp. 121-149. (6-8)
This book tells the stories of women who were pioneers in occupations that were normally considered for men only. Includes the story of Alice Hamilton, the first pioneer of either sex in the field of industrial disease in the United States. She taught at Northwestern University, did research at the University of Chicago, and was active at Hull House. She was instrumental in helping Illinois to become the first state to enact a workmen's compensation law. Index.

25 BRANDT, SUE. *Facts About Our Fifty States;* illus.
New York: Franklin Watts, 1970. (4-6)
The organization of this book makes it necessary
to read the whole book in order to sift out the facts
for any state. Some of the facts, such as how the
states received their names, and how the state capitals
were named are interesting and may be hard to find elsewhere. Maps, charts, and index are included.

26 BRITT, ALBERT. *The Boys' Own Book of Frontiersmen.*
New York: Macmillan, 1924. o.p. pp. 47-66,
145-160. (6-8) B
The story of "Peter Cartwright, the Frontier
Preacher," is interesting not only because it tells of
Cartwright's life as a pioneer preacher, but also pic-
tures religion on the frontier. It was a rough, ready,
and sometimes violent religion for which Peter
Cartwright fought with "ready wit and a sharp tongue,"
and sometimes his fists, for more than fifty years.
The story of George Rogers Clark is better written and
more interesting than some short versions of his life.

27 BROOKS, GWENDOLYN. *Bronzeville Boys and Girls;*
illus. by Ronni Solbert. New York: Harper,
1956. (2-4)
These poems for children about children catch a
moment of a child's feelings about things to do, dreams,
secret places, being sick, snow, and many other facets
of a child's activities and thoughts in the big city of
Chicago.

28 BRYANT, LORINDA. *The Children's Book of American
Landmarks;* illus. New York: Appleton-Century,
1933. o.p. pp. 24-25. (4-6)
Includes two photographs: one of Lincoln's tomb
in Springfield. There is a short discussion of
Lincoln's trip to Washington, D.C. as president, the
Lincoln-Douglas debates and Lincoln's inauguration as
president.

29 BUEHR, WALTER. *The French Explorers of America;*
       illus. by author. New York: Putnam's, 1961.
       o.p. pp. 63-78. (5-7)
       Included in this book are Marquette, Joliet, and
La Salle. The material on Marquette and Joliet is
brief, but more space is devoted to La Salle.
Describes problems and hardships he encountered while
exploring the Mississippi. A travel map of La Salle's
route and an index are included.

30 BUEHR, WALTER. *Underground Riches, the Story of*
       Mining; illus. by author. New York: William
       Morrow, 1958. o.p. (4-6)
       Coal mining and oil production are only a part
of this book on mining. Formation and composition of
coal, mining methods, types of coal, locations of coal
beds, uses of coal, by-products, industrial uses are
included. Index.

31 BULLA, CLYDE. *Lincoln's Birthday;* illus. by Ernest
       Criclow. New York: Crowell, 1965. (3-4) B
       This short summary of Lincoln's life includes
mention of New Salem, the Black Hawk War, life in
Springfield, term in Congress, election as president,
the Civil War, and the assassination.

32 BURT, OLIVE. *Old America Comes Alive;* illus.
       New York: John Day, 1966. (6-8) #
       "The Lincoln Heritage Trail" is not just a land-
mark. It passes through three states following the
route first taken by Tom Lincoln from Kentucky, where
Abraham was born, to Indiana where he grew up, and then
on to Illinois, where Abraham spent all of his adult
life except for the presidental years. While in
Illinois he left his family and moved to New Salem, and
finally to Springfield. Shrines all along the Lincoln
Trail mark the places where Lincoln lived. Includes
directions for reaching the shrines.

33 CARMER, CARL. *A Cavalcade of Young Americans;*
    illus. by Howard Simon. New York: Lothrop, Lee,
    & Shephard, 1958. o.p. pp. 202-209. (4-6)
    Although Grace Bedell did not live in Illinois,
this is the appealing story of the girl who wrote to
Lincoln in Springfield after his election to the presidency, advising him to grow a beard.

34 CARPENTER, ALLAN. *Illinois from Its Glorious Past
    to the Present;* illus. by Phil Austin. Chicago:
    Childrens Press, 1963. (5-8)
    Very useful as reference material this book
briefly presents historical material covering geologic
history, Indians, explorers, colonial control, territory
and state government, the Civil War, Chicago, and the
period of and between the two World Wars. Included
also, are natural resources, important people of
Illinois, modern Chicago, and places of special interest. Illustrations in color add interest. Index.

35 CARPENTER, ALLAN. *Illinois Land of Lincoln;* illus.
    Chicago: Childrens Press, 1968. (7-8)
    More detailed than the preceding book by the
same author, this book for slightly older children
includes interesting diagrams, maps, and illustrations.
Although largely historical, it includes government,
transportation, communication, conservation, manufacturing, mining, and education.

36 CHURCHILL, WINSTON. *Heroes of History;* illus. by
    Robert MacLean. New York: Dodd, Mead, 1968.
    pp. 139-156. (7-8)
    Although material relating to Lincoln in
Illinois is brief in this account, the powerful language
of Churchill makes it a worthwhile contribution. It
deals entirely with the question of slavery and seces-
sion; the conduct and end of the Civil War.

37 COLBY, C. B. *Historical American Landmarks;* illus.
New York: Coward, McCann & Geoghegan, 1968.
p. 28. (5-7)
Stagg Field at the University of Chicago is the
only Illinois landmark included. Under this stadium
the first sustained nuclear chain reaction was achieved.
Includes a photograph of the stands of the stadium,
which no longer exists, and another of a model of the
sculpture marking the spot.

38 COLVER, ANNE. *Abraham Lincoln for the People;*
illus. by William Moyers. Champaign, Ill.:
Garrard, 1960. (3-5) B
This simply written biography takes Lincoln from
boyhood to his return to Springfield after the assassination. The main facts of Lincoln's life are covered
briefly, including an incident of the Black Hawk War
and the finding of Blackstone's Commentaries, which led
to the study of law.

39 CONDIT, CARLTON. *The Fossils of Illinois; A Brief*
Guide to the More Common Fossils in the Rocks of
Illinois; illus. Springfield, Ill.: State of
Illinois, Dept. of Registration and Education—
Illinois State Museum, 1957. (7-8)
Information about what fossils are, and about
collecting, cleaning and labeling fossils is followed
by a section entitled, "A Brief Classification of
Fossils," accompanied by diagrams. The last section is
devoted to fossils of Illinois divided by geologic
periods. Following the text are 15 pages of illustrations of animal fossils. Includes a map showing distribution of bedrock strata.

40 COOKE, DAVID. *Behind the Scenes in an Oil Field;*
illus. New York: Dodd, Mead, 1959. o.p.
(5-7)
While not specifically about Illinois, applies
to it as well as other areas, except for off shore
drilling. Gives information about how and where oil is
found, how it is brought to the surface, how it is then
handled, stored and refined. Also describes products
of oil, research and development, and fighting oil
fires.

14

41 COOLIDGE, OLIVIA. *The Apprenticeship of Abraham
    Lincoln*. New York: Scribner's, 1974. (8) * B
    Not for faint hearted or reluctant readers, this
book traces the development of Lincoln from a raw backwoods farm boy to his election as president. The
emphasis is on Lincoln's political growth and education.
The point is made that Lincoln's education consisted
not only of reading, which was considerable, but also
making use of every contact with people and every
experience, to further his knowledge and understanding.
The description of the Republican convention in Chicago
that nominated Lincoln as a candidate for president is
especially interesting and revealing.

42 COOPER, ALICE, ed. *Poems of Today; A Collection of
    Contemporary Verse of America and Great Britain.*
    Chicago: Ginn, 1924. o.p. pp. 158-159,
    184-186. (7-8)
    Includes "Across Illinois" by John Stoltze, an
impression of Illinois while crossing the state on a
train at night. Also, Edwin Markham's powerful poem,
"Lincoln, the Man of the People."

43 COOPER, KAY. *"C'mon Ducks!";* illus. by Janet
    D'Mato, photos by Alvin Staffan. New York:
    Julian Messner, 1978. (3-5)
    When Ann and Susie receive four Muscovy ducks
for Christmas, they learn much about them and also
mallards, pintails, wood ducks and wigeons which live
near their home on Lake Springfield. They also learn a
few things about people. Ann's perceptive duck diary
is the basis for this book embellished with excellent
photographs and delightful drawings. Glossary and index.

44 CROSBY, ALEXANDER. *Go Find Hanka;* illus. by Glen
    Rounds. San Carlos, Cal.: Golden Gate Junior
    Books, 1970. (4-6) F
    This brief but dramatic glimpse of pioneer life
on the Illinois praire is a vivid picture of what
prairie grass was really like. The hunting dog, Phil,
provides the excitement in the hunt for a five-year-old
boy lost in the tall prairie grass where no guiding
landmarks could be seen.

45 CRUMP, IRVING. *Mog the Mound Builder*. New York:
Grosset & Dunlap, 1931. o.p. (6-8) F
This story goes back to the Mound Builders of
prehistoric times. Mog-an-ah has some narrow escapes in
his search for his father who disappeared on a mission
for his village. He befriends a boy of the Long Heads,
continue their adventure together, find Mog-an-ah's
father and rescue him. Eventually they arrive home
only to find a serious situation that ends in a desperate battle. The setting is not exactly specified, but
Mound Builders lived in Illinois.

46 CURTIS, MARY. *Our State Birds*; illus. by Julia
Morrison. Chicago: Lyons & Carnahan, 1947.
o.p. pp. 31-34. (3-4)
Black and white sketches illustrate this article
about the cardinal. Description of the songs and
physical appearance of both male and female, the eggs,
habits and food preferences.

47 DAUGHERTY, JAMES. *Abraham Lincoln*; illus. by
author. New York: Viking, 1942. o.p.
(6-8) * B
The outstanding features of this book are the
big, bold, striking illustrations, the forceful writing
style which has the strength to match both the illustrations and the Lincoln character, and the portrayal of
Lincoln as a listening, thinking man who had the
courage to act resolutely on the principles in which he
believed. Quotations from Walt Whitman and the inclusion of the Gettysburg Address are valuable additions.
Index.

— D'AULAIRE, EDGAR. *Abraham Lincoln*. See IL 48

48 D'AULAIRE, INGRI and D'AULAIRE, EDGAR. *Abraham
Lincoln*; illus. by authors. New York:
Doubleday, 1939; 1957. (3-5) CA B
The D'Aulaires' colorful illustrations make this
biography especially good for younger children. Text
is simply and clearly done. Includes the main events
of Lincoln's life, but stops short of the assassination.
Humorous episodes of special interest ot children.

49 DE LEEUW, ADELE. *George Rogers Clark, Frontier Fighter;* illus. by Russ Hoover. Champaign, Ill.: Garrard, 1967. o.p. (3-5) B #
Beginning with George Rogers Clark in Virginia as a youth to the frontier, he soon finds himself embroiled in the colonists' cause against the British, and secures the Illinois Country for the colonists. Easy reading for older reluctant readers.

50 DOBLER, LAVINIA and TOPPIN, EDGAR. *Pioneers and Patriots; The Lives of Six Negroes of the Revolutionary Era;* illus. by Colleen Browning. Garden City, N.Y.: Doubleday, 1965. (5-8)
In this short sketch of Jean Baptiste Pointe De Sable's life it is stated that there is much disagreement about his early life, but these facts are certain—he was a Negro, he was friendly with the Indians, he established a successful trading post at the present location of Chicago, and so became the "Father of the City."

51 EARLE, OLIVE. *State Birds and Flowers;* illus. New York: Morrow, 1951. (4-8)
Begins with the national bird, the bald eagle, then describes state birds and flowers alphabetically by states. If birds or flowers have been chosen by more than one state, all the states having that particular bird or flower are listed with the first state. Since the index at the front of the book lists birds and flowers but omits names of states, young children may have some difficulty in locating material. Sketches of birds and flowers included.

52 EARLE, OLIVE. *State Trees;* illus. by author. Rev. ed. New York: Morrow, 1973. (4-8)
Because the trees are arranged in alphabetical order, it is necessary to use the index located in the front of the book, to find the tree for a specific state. The trees, rather than the pages, are numbered. Two pages are devoted to each tree. For Illinois, the description includes sketches of leaves, bark and shape of the bur oak tree.

53 EIFERT, VIRGINIA. *Exploring for Mushrooms;* illus.
by author. Springfield: Illinois State Museum,
1945. Paper. (6-8)
The story of mushrooms is narrated. Also,
methods of handling and cooking are explained. More
than thirty types of mushrooms, both poisonous and
edible are specifically described and illustrated
(black and white). The author constantly admonishes
that if there is a doubt, do not gather the mushrooms.

54 EIFERT, VIRGINIA. *Flowers That Bloom in the Spring;*
illus. by author. Springfield: Illinois State
Museum, 1952. Paper. (5-7)
The brief foreword in this paperback booklet
explains how different types of soils developed in
Illinois, and how that soil affected the type of wild-
flowers that grew there. Thirty seven wild flowers are
interestingly described and well illustrated in black
and white. The native violet, the state flower, is in
color.

55 EIFERT, VIRGINIA. *Invitation to Birds; A Few
Common Birds of Illinois;* illus. by author.
Springfield: Illinois State Museum, 1948.
Paper. (5-8)
The first section discusses changes in the ways
people have looked upon birds, various kinds of birds
in different environments of Illinois, attracting birds
with feeders, bird baths. In the last section characteristics of 53 birds are clearly and interestingly
described and illustrated in black and white.

56 EIFERT, VIRGINIA. *Three Rivers South; The Story of
Young Abe Lincoln;* illus. by Thomas Benton.
New York: Dodd, Mead, 1953. o.p. (6-8) F
This is not only the story of young Abe Lincoln,
but also the story of transportation of goods by river
in the 1830's. The Sangamon, Illinois and Mississippi
Rivers are the highways used by Lincoln to transport
Offutt's goods to New Orleans. This short period in
Lincoln's life is used as the basis for a fine piece of
fiction, as well as a report on the problems and perils
of flat boat travel down the three rivers.

57 EIFERT, VIRGINIA. *With a Task Before Me: Abraham Lincoln Leaves Springfield;* illus. by Manning De V. Lee. Rev. ed. New York: Dodd, Mead, 1966. o.p. (7-8) * F
Well written story of Lincoln's New Salem and Springfield years sticks to basic facts but enhances them with imaginary conversations and incidents that might have happened. The real life characters are very well portrayed. Lincoln's character traits and political ideas are particularly well done.

58 EIFERT, VIRGINIA and THOMPSON, MILTON. *Birds in Your Backyard;* illus. by author and Robert Larson. Rev. ed. Springfield: Illinois State Museum, 1967. (6-8)
More than two hundred birds are discussed. One page is devoted to excellent description of the bird, habitat, habits and Illinois status. On the adjoining page is the equally good black and white illustration. General information about attracting birds and recognizing them, as well as lists of birds to be found in the Springfield area. At the back is a diary "The Year of Birds." Index of birds.

— ERMINGER, LILA. *Illinois Grows Up.* See IL 21

59 FANNING, LEONARD. *Fathers of Industry;* illus. by Albert Orbaan. New York: Lippincott, 1962. pp. 104-113. (6-8)
Cyrus Hall McCormick is the only industrialist in this book connected with Illinois. His life and work are briefly but effectively covered. The author notes that McCormick did more than invent a machine. He was instrumental in settling the "breadbasket of the world," and in helping Chicago become an important manufacturing and transportation center.

— FELTON, ELIZABETH. *The United States Book, Facts and Legends About the 50 States.* See IL 175

60 FERMI, LAURA. *The Story of Atomic Energy.*
    New York: Random House, 1961. pp. 80-91,
    149-150. (6-8)
    Traces atomic energy from its beginning with the
theory introduced by John Dalton, an Englishman born
in 1766. Development of the idea of splitting the atom
was slow but gained impetus in the 1930's, and the
success of a chain reaction was realized in the
University of Chicago experiment December 2, 1942. The
atomic power plant at Dresden, Illinois, 50 miles southwest of Chicago is also mentioned.

61 FISHER, AILEEN. *Plays About Our Nation's Songs.*
    Boston: Plays, 1962. o.p. pp. 103-130.
    (6-8)
    The play entitled "Sing the Songs of Lincoln,"
begins in the Kentucky log cabin and continues with
action and songs until Lincoln's death. A Reader provides the historical information between the dramatic
parts of the play, giving continuity to the life story
of Lincoln. The section of the play which takes the
Lincolns to Illinois begins on page 118. The play provides for a large cast plus an off stage chorus. Useful for music programs or a Lincoln's birthday presentation, providing both entertainment and information.

62 FLEMING, ALICE. *America Is Not All Traffic Lights:*
    Poems of the Middle West; selected by Alice
    Fleming; illus. Boston: Little, Brown, 1976.
    (6-8)
    Scattered throughout the book, the poems about
Illinois range from Chicago's steel, cement, and ceme-
teries to the prairie and small towns, where "America
is not all traffic lights". The poems chosen are
verbal pictures of a place, a thought or a feeling.
Brief notes on the poets are included.

63 FOSTER, GENEVIEVE. *Abraham Lincoln: An Initial*
    Biography; illus. New York: Scribner's, 1950.
    o.p. (4-6) B
    This well written condensed biography covers
Lincoln's life from his birth in Kentucky to his death
in Washington, D.C. The basic facts of his life are

included, but some omissions might lead children to erroneous conclusions. Lincoln's farewell speech at Springfield and the Gettysburg Address are included.

64 FOX, MARY. *Ambush at Fort Dearborn;* illus. by
Lorence Bjorklund. New York: St. Martin's
Press, 1962. o.p. (6-8) F
The Malen family arrive in the area of future Chicago only to find their relatives leaving because of danger from the Indians. Tom befriends an Indian boy, nursed during an illness by his mother. After Tom is captured by the Indians, he escapes, and also escapes the massacre at Fort Dearborn with his family. Good description of travel conditions and life at the fort, including the constant fear of Indian attack.

65 FRADIN, DENNIS. *Illinois in Words and Pictures;*
illus. by Robert Ulm. Chicago: Childrens Press,
1976. (2-4)
Colored illustrations, photographs, and drawings add interest to this book for younger children. Brief historical material; a rather full story of Chicago, past and present; brief information on Lincoln and Grant. Facts about Illinois are added at the end of the book. Clearly and simply, but not smoothly written. Maps and index add to the usefulness.

66 FRANCHERE, RUTH. *Hannah Herself.* New York:
Crowell, 1964. (6-8) F
Hannah visits her sister and brother-in-law who have started an academy in pioneer Illinois. She finds many unexpected situations and problems both in living conditions, and education. Runaway slaves are also part of the story. Hannah does not find answers to all the problems, but does find herself. The hardships of living among and attempting to educate the pioneers is well depicted. The story line is better than many fiction books on pioneer life.

67 FRANCHERE, RUTH. *The Travels of Colin O'Dae;* illus.
     by Lorence Bjorklund. New York: Crowell, 1966.
     o.p. (6-8) F
     This story of Colin O'Dae and a family of actors
begins in Chicago. Colin joins the Flower family to
escape working on the Illinois and Michigan Canal.
What follows is the story of transportation in the
1830's overland and down the Illinois River. Mr. Flower
turns a flatboat into a showboat. The problems with
paper money, land speculation, Irish immigrants and
ague are all included.

68 FRAZIER, CARL and FRAZIER, ROSALIE. *The Lincoln
     Country in Pictures;* illus. New York: Hastings
     House, 1963. (4-8) #
     Photographs in black and white with brief nota-
tions for each picture. Included are monuments; buildings, both inside and out; landscape scenes; and
Lincoln shrines.

— FRAZIER, ROSALIE. *The Lincoln Country in Pictures.*
     See IL 68

69 FRIERMOOD, ELISABETH. *Head High, Ellen Brody.*
     Garden City, NY: Doubleday, 1958. o.p.
     (7-8) F
     Most of the action takes place in northern
Indiana, but Jane Addams and Hull House are mentioned
throughout. Two chapters deal entirely with Chicago.
When Ellen visits that city she witnesses a fire at the
Iroquois Theatre. The plight of factory workers in the
early 1900's is made very real. The value of settlement houses in the mill areas becomes evident, but they
are not enough.

70 FRISKEY, MARGARET. *Tad Lincoln and the Green
     Umbrella;* illus. by Lucia Patton. New York:
     Oxford Univ. Press, 1944. o.p. (4-6) B
     A glimpse of the Lincoln family life in Spring-
field and Washington. The irrepresible Tad Lincoln,
his anxious, sometimes overwrought mother, and his
patient, forbearing father are caught up in the toils

of politics, war, and childish escapades. Tad and
Willie get evidence to clear their mother of the
accusation of treachery.

71 GARST, SHANNON and GARST, WARREN. *Wild Bill Hickok.*
New York: Julian Messner, 1952. o.p. (6-8) B
The first 18 pages deal with Illinois. Includes
a good description of life in a pioneer Illinois community, the Underground Railway, and the building of
the Illinois-Michigan Canal. The excitement of Hickok's
life is sustained throughout.

— GARST, WARREN. *Wild Bill Hickok.* See IL 71

· 72 GILBERT, MIRIAM. *Jane Addams World Neighbor;*
illus. by Corrine Dillon. New York: Abingdon,
1960. o.p. (4-6) B
After Jane's battle to win a college degree,
Rockford Seminary became Rockford College. Jane's
battles against the inequities and injustices of life
continued with Hull House. The outcome of this settlement in Chicago was for immigrants and the poor who
lived in desperate circumstances. A clearly and simply
written account of Jane Addams' life and work.

— GILFORD, HENRY. *Red Grange, Football's Greatest
Halfback.* See IL 172

73 GRAHAM, ALBERTA. *La Salle, River Explorer;* illus.
by Avery Johnson. New York: Abingdon, 1954.
o.p. (4-6) B
This prosaic story of La Salle's exploits in the
New World lacks the excitement of other accounts, but
contains information easily read by younger children.
Pages 68-110 tell the story of La Salle in Illinois,
but the whole book should be read to fully understand
La Salle's explorations.

74 GRAHAM, SHIRLEY. *Jean Baptiste Pointe de Sable, Founder of Chicago.* New York: Messner, 1953. o.p. (7-8) * B

A well-written biography of de Sable portrays the the circumstances surrounding the founding of Chicago and the Indian way of life. Depicts the English and the French exploitation of the Indians for their own purposes, and how the new United States government deprived the Indians of their lands, forcing them to move to other areas.

75 GRANT, BRUCE. *American Forts Yesterday and Today;* illus. by Lorence Bjorklund. New York: Dutton, 1965. o.p. pp. 165, 174-178. (5-8)

With the exception of Fort Dearborn the forts of Illinois are given one paragraph. Useful only as a reference for names, locations and reasons for building the forts of Illinois. The map on page 165 and index add to the usefulness.

76 GRANT, MATTHEW. *Jane Addams Helper of the Poor;* illus. by John Keely and Dick Brude. Mankato, Minn.: Creative Education, 1974. (3-4) B

A brief summary of Jane Addams' life. Some of the spirit that moved Jane Addams manages to shine through the bare bones of the facts of her life work in Hull House and her efforts to promote social legislation and world peace.

77 GRANT, MATTHEW. *Ulysses S. Grant, General and President;* illus. by John Nelson. Mankato, Minn.: Creative Education, 1974. (3-4) B

This short, sketchy biography is probably best suited for reluctant readers, rather than very young children, since the vocabulary might pose problems. It does, however, give the highlights of Grant's life.

78 *The Great Seal of Illinois and Other Official State Symbols.* Springfield: State of Illinois, Secretary of State. (4-8)

Useful as a reference source, this pamphlet describes and illustrates the Seal of Illinois, the state flag, the state tree and flower, and the state bird. The adoption of the state slogan is included, as well as a copy of the state song.

79 GRIDLEY, MARION. *Indian Tribes of America;* illus. by Lone Wolf. Northbrook, Ill.: Hubbard Press, 1940 , 1973. pp. 10-27. (5-7)
The discussion of the life of the Woodland Indians includes the Indians of Illinois, although they are not treated separately as some other groups are. A list of tribes on page 10 identifies the Woodland Tribes, the places where they lived, and where they are now living. Of all the Indians who lived in Illinois none now live here as a tribal group, and the Illiniwek are extinct.

80 HAMILTON, ELISABETH, ed. *How They Started.* illus. New York: Harcourt, Brace, 1937. o.p. (6-8) B
The biographical segment entitled "Abe Lincoln Starts Out" was taken from Carl Sandburg's *Abraham Lincoln: The Prairie Years.* The record of Lincoln's life from age 16 to 25 years of age shows his progress from pioneer farm boy to state legislator. Sandburg's story tells, with the flavor of pioneer speech and sometimes a poetic flow of word, how Lincoln got his start in politics in New Salem.

81 HANSEN, HARRY. *The Story of Illinois;* illus. by John Barron. Garden City, NY: Garden City Books, 1956. o.p. (6-8)
This historical account of Illinois is more detailed and more interesting than some. It does, however, err in stating that the Piasa bird painted by the Indians on a rocky cliff near Alton has been carefully restored. It has, in fact, been blasted away, and repainted in a different location with funds provided by Alton. One chapter is devoted to modern times.

82 HARNSBERGER, CAROLINE, comp. *The Lincoln Treasury;*
   illus. by Harold Hoopes and William Marsh.
   Chicago: Wilcox and Follett, 1950. o.p.
   (6-8)
   Lincoln's quotations from one sentence to
speeches, ranged in alphabetical order by subject, from
abolition to wrong. Because of the arrangement, it is
easy to find a Lincoln quotation for any subject upon
which he made a comment that was recorded.

83 HASTINGS, ROBERT. *A Nickel's Worth of Skim Milk;*
   A Boy's View of the Great Depression; illus. by
   Steve Kerr. Carbondale, Ill.: University
   Graphics and Publications, Southern Illinois
   University, 1972. (7-8) B
   Bob Hastings relates his family's experiences
during the depression in Marion, Illinois, from 1930 to
1938. Day by day life at home, school and church in
this coal mining area is vividly depicted. The hardships, the government programs, the struggles to make a
little go a long way, and the simple pleasures are all
aspects of life in Illinois that will be new to many
children.

84 HAVIGHURST, WALTER, ed. *Midwest and Great Plains.*
   illus. Grand Rapids, Mich.: Fideler, 1974.
   (5-7)
   A map and geographical facts about Illinois are
found on pages 252 and 267. Other material under
topics: land and climate, people, earning a living.
Illustrations and maps add to the usefulness of this
general study of the midwest and plains area, with a
little specific information on each state. Glossary
and index.

85 HEIDERSTADT, DOROTHY. *Frontier Leaders and*
   Pioneers; illus. by Clifford Geary. New York:
   McKay, 1962. o.p. pp. 12-19. (4-6) B
   This brief biography of George Rogers Clark
lacks the spirit of adventure and excitement that
longer accounts achieve, but gives the facts of the
securing of the Illinois Country for the Americans.

86 HOLDEN, RAYMOND. *All about Fire;* illus. by
  Clifford Stead, Jr.; photos. New York: Random
  House, 1964. pp. 65-75. (5-7)
  This story of the Chicago fire emphasizes the
drought, the wind, the wooden buildings, and the
depleted condition of the Chkcago Fire Department. It
had lost 2 engines and 30 firemen in a fire which
destroyed four blocks immediately before the big fire.

87 HORGAN, PAUL. *Citizen of New Salem;* illus. by
  Douglas Borsline. New York: Farrar, Straus and
  Cudahy, 1961. (7-8) * B
  A full, lively, and well-written portrayal of
Lincoln as a flatboatman, wrestler, rail-splitter,
store clerk, Indian fighter (whose only contact with an
Indian was to rescue him from would-be killers),
student of Mentor Graham, store owner, postmaster,
surveyor, member of the state legislature, law student,
story teller, speaker, and above all as a compassionate
human being in tune with people and events.

88 HORN, MADELINE. *Log Cabin Family;* illus. by
  Frances McCroy. New York: Scribner's, 1939.
  o.p. (4-6) F
  A series of day by day experiences on the frontier in Illinois, rather than a story. Describes life
in a log cabin, and education in rural pioneer areas.
The heavy snow and extreme cold of one winter is
especially interesting. The children of the family
experience the changes in transportation as they take
their first train ride.

89 HORN, MADELINE. *The New Home;* illus. by Harve
  Stein. New York: Scribner's, 1962. o.p.
  (3-5) F
  Although this simply written book suffers from
the stilted style, it presents a good picture of life
on the northern Illinois prairie in pioneer times. The
prairie grass fire in the fall and the heavy snow in
the winter add a bit of excitement, as do bumble bees
and a runaway horse.

27

90 HUME, RUTH. *Great Women of Medicine;* photos.
    New York: Random House, 1964. o.p.
    pp. 252-256. (6-8)
    A brief account of Dr. Alice Hamilton's work
with industrial diseases, and Illinois as the first
state to enact Workmen's Compensation. Index.

91 HUNT, IRENE. *Across Five Aprils.* Chicago:
    Follett, 1964. (6-8) * F
    A well-written story about the effect of the
Civil War on a Southern Illinois family, from just
before the armed conflict to the death of Lincoln.
Characterization, battles and the reactions of the
people are excellently portrayed. The problems of
Young Jethro and his family are especially poignant,
with one brother in the Confederate Army and the rest
of the family supporting the North. The family
suffered not only because of divided loyalties, but
also from ill-considered violence committed against
them by neighbors. Newbery Award runner-up.

92 *Illinois at War.* Springfield: State of Illinois.
    Office of Superentendent of Public Instruction,
    1968. (6-8)
    Most of the material in this booklet was taken
from Doctor Victor Hicken's book, *Illinois and the
Civil War,* covering the year 1861-1865. Summarizing
the part Illinois citizens played in the Civil War,
specific military units, battles and generals are
mentioned, as well as Illinois on the home front.
Useful for older children.

93 JACOBS, WILLIAM. *Robert Cavelier de La Salle;*
    illus. New York: Watts, 1975. (5-7) B
    This biography of La Salle emphasizes his
driving ambition and determined will to explore the
Mississippi to its mouth and claim it and all the lands
it drained for the King of France. The schemes of his
enemies, Indian problems, problems with the men of his
own expedition, attempts on his life did not deter him
from his goal. Illustrations include authentic prints,
documents and maps.

28

94 JAGENDORF, MORITZ. *Sand in the Bag and Other Folk Stories of Ohio, Indiana and Illinois.* New York: Vanguard Press, 1952. pp. 135-184. (5-8) #
These folk tales told in the folksy manner of the pioneer story teller, include real people and real places. Ranging in area from Cairo to Chicago and in type from serious to slapstick humor, most have the rough and ready spirit of the frontier.

95 JONES, HELEN. *Over the Mormon Trail;* illus. by Carol Rogers. Chicago: Childrens Press, 1963. o.p. pp. 9-14, 26-28. (4-6) F
While only a small portion deals with Illinois, it gives a good account of Nauvoo and the shameful manner in which the Mormons were treated by their neighbors in Illinois. Map.

96 JUDSON, CLARA. *City Neighbor, the Story of Jane Addams;* illus. by Ralph Roy. New York: Scribner's, 1951. o.p. (5-7) B
A well-written story of Jane Addams' childhood, travel, and life work at Hull House in the section of the immigrant poor of Chicago. Mentions many others who gave time and possessions, including Helen Culver owner of Hull House.

97 JUDSON, CLARA. *The Green Ginger Jar; A Chinatown Mystery;* illus. by Paul Brown. Boston: Houghton Mifflin, 1949. (5-7) F
Chicago's Chinatown of 1935 sets the stage for this intriguing mystery. Chinese customs, as well as problems which immigrants and their children face, add depth to the story. An injured dog, a boys' club, three small boys trapped as sand caves in on them, Lee's heroic actions and ambitions, added to Ai-mei's problems concerning the ginger jar, provide enough action to sustain interest throughout.

98 JUDSON, CLARA. *The Lost Violin: They Came from Bohemia;* illus. by Margaret Pradfield. Chicago: Follett, 1947, 1958. o.p. (6-7) F
Problems and prejudices which immigrants faced in the city of Chicago at the time of the World's Columbian Exposition in 1893, are woven into the story of Anna Kovec's lost violin. Some of the characters were real people, Jane Addams, and the Bohemian composer, Dvorac, among others. Hull House also has an important role in the story.

99 JUDSON, CLARA. *Reaper Man, the Story of Cyrus McCormick;* illus. by Paul Brown. Boston: Houghton Mifflin, 1948. o.p. pp. 93-156. (6-8) B
While Cyrus McCormick began and perfected his work on the reaper on his family's farm in Virginia, he built his factory and lived most of his adult life in Chicago. Includes the growth and development of Chicago, other pioneer reaper inventors, the fire, and merging of five leading manufacturers of farm machinery to form the International Harvester Company after McCormick's death.

100 KAY, HELEN. *Abe Lincoln's Hobby;* illus. by William Hutchinson. Chicago: Reilly & Lee, 1961. o.p. (3-4) B
According to this book, Lincoln's hobby was cats. It is evident, although not stated, that telling funny stories was another. Relates several episodes about the experiences the Lincoln family had with cats and other animals. A delightful book for young children.

101 KAY, HELEN. *Lincoln a Big Man;* illus. by Arthur Polonsky. New York: Hastings House, 1958. (4-6) B
Lincoln's life in Springfield and riding the circuit to Illinois courts. Special emphasis is placed upon his love for children, his humor, and his size, which so impressed some of the residents of Springfield that they had a special nine foot long bed made for his use in the White House.

102 KEATING, BERN. *Famous American Explorers;* illus.
by Lorence Bjorklund. Chicago: Rand McNally,
1972. pp. 37-41. (5-8)
Colorful full page illustrations add interest to
the accounts of explorers. Mentions Marquette and
Joliet's exploration of the Mississippi, La Salle and
Tonti. Information is brief, but the style is inter-
esting. A glimpse of the struggle among the French,
British, and Spaniards for the Great Lakes and
Mississippi Valley.

103 KELLY, REGINA. *Beaver Trail;* illus. by Carl Junge.
New York: Lothrop, Lee & Shephard, 1955. o.p.
(5-7) F #
Begins at Fort Mackinac where Jimmy Russell and
his Uncle must stop on their way to Fort Dearborn.
They move on to Fort Dearborn where Uncle James buys a
farm near the fort. John Jacob Astor and his Fur
Trading Company, Tecumseh and the Indian uprising, as
well as the Fort Dearborn massacre are part of the
story. Much detail about fur trading and its effect
upon the Indians.

104 KING, MARTHA. *The Key to Chicago;* illus. New York:
Lippincott, 1961. o.p. (5-8)
How Chicago came to be called the Windy City is
explained in the first chapter, which describes the
location, buildings, weather and the activities of the
people of Chicago. Following chapters discuss jobs,
institutions, Jane Addams and recreation. After back-
tracking through historical events, Chicago's quick
growth, fire and rehabilitation are recounted. Much
interesting information, plus photographs.

105 KJELGAARD, JIM. *The Coming of the Mormons;*
illus. by Stephen Voorhies. New York: Random
House, 1953. pp. 3-32. (5-8)
The story of the Mormons begins with trouble in
Illinois. Although only a few pages are given to the
life of the Mormons in Nauvoo, Illinois, the brief
account does show the prejudice, lack of understanding
and violence which was a part of Illinois pioneer life

in the 1840's. The description of Nauvoo and the
Mormons indicate that many of them were people of great
faith, determination, education and refinement. A map
shows Nauvoo and routes followed in Illinois.

106 KJELGAARD, JIM. *The Explorations of Pére Marquette;*
       illus. by Stephen Voorhies. Yew York: Random
       House, 1951. (5-7) B #
       A clear, concise account of life and work of
Marquette in the Great Lakes Region and of his explora-
tion of the Mississippi River. Although most of the
Indians are portrayed as unsavory and most of the
French as exemplary, the characters of Marquette and
Joliet appear to be realistically depicted, although
Marquette is the more important of the two. Maps aid
in locating areas.

107 *Know Your U.S.A.;* illus. Chicago: Rand McNally,
       1954. pp. 16-17. (3-5)
       Begins with illustrated statistics about the
U.S. and continues alphabetically with the same treatment for each state, except for Alaska and Hawaii which
are added at the end. Illinois is one of the few
states with a full page color illustration (of Abraham
Lincoln, with a quote from the Gettysburg Address).
Included are nicknames, boundaries, largest cities,
time zone, state song and origin of state name.

108 LAIR, JOHN. *Songs That Lincoln Loved;* illus.
       New York: Duell Sloan & Pearce, 1954. o.p.
       (7-8)
       Deals with a phsse of Lincoln's life that has
been given very little space in other books. Music had
a deep effect on Lincoln. It could plunge him into
melancholy, or restore him to gaiety. Some of Lincoln's
favorite songs are included, along with biographical
notes relating to the songs. This is the book to use
with Fisher's *Plays About Our Nations's Songs.*

109 LAUBER, PATRICIA. *The Mississippi: Giant at Work;*
      illus. Champaign, Ill.: Garrard, 1961. o.p.
      (4-7)
      Since the Mississippi is the longest river in
the United States, this book includes areas other than
Illinois. Useful in the study of Illinois because much
of its early history and transportation were affected
by the Mississippi River. Much of the book deals with
the flood waters of the river and how the floods have
been handled. Since Illinois is bounded on the west by
the Mississippi, the flooding river has grave conse-
quences for the state. Maps and photographs add to the
usefulness.

110 LAWSON, ROBERT. *The Great Wheel;* illus. by author.
      New York: Viking, 1957. o.p. (6-8) F
      This story about the building of the Ferris
wheel for the World's Columbian Exposition, 1893, in
Chicago, takes Conn Kilroy from Ireland to New York and
then on to Chicago. He traveled with his Uncle Patrick
to help build the Ferris wheel, then Conn acted as
guard in Car No. 1 for the duration of the Fair. The
building of the Ferris wheel is described in interesting detail and the reader is also given a good view of
the fair grounds.

111 LEACH, MARIA. *The Rainbow Book of American Folk
      Tales and Legends;* illus. by Marc Simont.
      Cleveland, Ohio: World, 1958. o.p. (4-6)
      This Mike Fink legend states that Mike was a
real person, gives factual information, about keelboats,
trips on the Ohio and Mississippi and relates Mike's
last escapade when he shot his friend Carpenter. In
the "State Lore" section, information about the name of
the state, nicknames and an anecdote about Sangamon
County are included.

112 LENGYEL, CORNEL. *Presidents of the United States;*
      illus. New York: Golden Press, 1961. o.p.
      pp. 50-55, 58-60. (6-8) B
      The short biographical stories of Abraham
Lincoln and Ulysses Grant are more detailed and

complete than in some collections. Illustrations for these two presidents include photographs and paintings in black and white.

113 LE SUEUR, MERIDEL. *Sparrow Hawk;* illus. by William Moyers. New York: Knopf, 1950. o.p. (6-8) F #

This story of Sparrow Hawk, his white friend, Buck, and the Sauks who followed Black Hawk is laced throughout with pathos and tragedy. Life in the village of Saukenuk, the destruction of the village, the flight of the Sauks, the slaughter at the river crossing, the capture of Black Hawk are portrayed vividly. The importance of corn to the Indians is pointed out in Sparrow Hawk's personal story.

114 LINDSAY, VACHEL. *Johnny Appleseed and Other Poems;* illus. by George Richards. New York: Macmillan, 1913. (4-7)

Poems which refer definitely to Illinois are "Abraham Lincoln Walks at Midnight" (in Springfield Illinois) pp. 101-102, and "The Litany of Heroes" section on Lincoln p. 11. "The Ghost of the Buffaloes" applies to Illinois, as well as other states where the buffalo roamed. The poems of Lindsay have a haunting quality.

115 LYBACK, JOHANNA. *Indian Legends of Eastern America;* illus. by Dick West and Alexander Key. Chicago: Lyons and Carnahan, 1963. o.p. pp. 161-171. (4-6)

The Illinois Indian legends are "The Piasa," the monstrous bird whose likeness was painted on the cliff near Alton; "The Evil Spirit at Starved Rock"; "The Story of Lolomi," who threw herself from Starved Rock when she learned that her suitor had married another; "The Legend of Rock Island"; and "The Legend of the Mastodon," the story of the destruction of the mastodon and the coming of the cranberry.

116 MC CAGUE, JAMES. *Flatboat Days on Frontier Rivers;*
illus. by Victor Mays. Champaign, Ill.:
Garrard, 1968. o.p. (4-6) #
Description of flatboats, methods of propelling,
hazards of the journey are well depicted. Flatboats
were much the same on all frontier rivers, but Illinois'
Shawneetown and Cave-in-Rock presented dangerous problems: Shawneetown because of the treacherous river and
outlaws, and Cave-in-Rock because of menacing river
pirates. Glossary and index.

117 MC CAGUE, JAMES. *Mississippi Steamboat Days;* illus.
by Paul Frame. Champaign, Ill.: Garrard, 1967.
o.p. (4-5)
Travel on the Mississippi by steamboat is
covered quite well. It does not mention Illinois particularly, but descriptions of the steamboats, accounts
of how rich and poor passengers were accommodated, fuel,
dangers and length of time for journeys on the
Mississippi, applies as well to the ships north of
St. Louis as south. Glossary and index.

118 MC CALL, EDITH. *Men on Iron Horses;* illus. by
Carol Rogers. Chicago: Childrens Press, 1960.
o.p. pp. 42-56. (4-7) F
Only one chapter of this book about the beginning and growth of railroad travel in the United States
concerns Illinois. It tells the story of the "Pioneer,"
a locomotive which came to Chicago in 1848 after
seeing service in the East and in Detroit. Now, not
only waterways, but also the railroads would "make
Chicago great."

119 MC GOVERN, ANNE. *If You Grew Up with Abraham
Lincoln;* illus. by Brinton Turkle. New York:
Four Winds Press, 1968. (3-4) B
Although the 45 pages of this book covers
Lincoln's life in Kentucky and Indiana, the frontier
living described would have been similar in Illinois.
Lincoln's life in New Salem, a frontier village, is
contrasted with his life in Springfield, which had gone
beyond the frontier stage. Growth of the city and the

effect of machines on the lives of both urban and rural people is ably portrayed.

120 MC NEER, MAY. *America's Abraham Lincoln;* illus. by Lynd Ward. Boston: Houghton Mifflin, 1957. (6-8) * B

Well-written book includes the important events in the life of Lincoln, and also the burning political disagreements over the questions of abolition and the spread of slavery. Mentions the repeal of the Missouri Compromise, the Dred Scott Decision, the Lincoln-Douglas debates, and other political concerns of the time. Quotes Lincoln's farewell speech to Springfield citizens. Of special interest are the illustrations, many of them full page in vibrant color.

121 MC NEER, MAY and WARD, LYND. *Armed with Courage;* illus. New York: Abingdon, 1957. pp. 57-68. (5-7) B

Condensed version of Jane Addams life and work includes her childhood, education, and foreign travel which helped her form the plan for Hull House. Describes her work for labor and social laws to improve the lot of immigrants and poor working people. Excellent introduction to Jane Addams.

122 MC NICOL, JACQUELINE. *Elizabeth for Lincoln;* illus. by Tom O'Sullivan. New York: Longmans, Green, 1960. o.p. (4-6) F

Elizabeth Shires quite unexpectedly found herself in Springfield, November 1860, when Lincoln was elected president. She shared in the excitement that swept the city and was instrumental in helping prevent an "accident" aimed at ending Lincoln's presidency before it began.

123 MALCOMSON, ANNE. *Yankee Doddle's Cousins;* illus. by Robert McCloskey. Boston: Houghton Mifflin, 1941. pp. 129-137. (4-7)

Mike Fink legend tells about his trickery. Not being a common thief, he obtained some sheep by trickery, but was brought before the court. He came in his keelboat which was mounted on wheels and pulled by oxen. This allowed him to escape before the trial ended.

124 MARTIN, PATRICIA. *Abraham Lincoln;* illus. by Gustan Schrotter. New York: Putnam's, 1964. (2-3)   B

Simply written, sketch of Lincoln's life, includes some of the highlights of his Illinois life. Written for primary children, the style is not distinguished. Illustrations on every page add interest for young children, but one picture misleads by showing Lincoln playing on the floor with four little boys. Never were four boys together in the family at the same time.

125 MEADOWCROFT, ENID. *By Secret Railway;* illus. by Henry Pitz. New York: Crowell, 1948. (5-7)   F

Excellently pictures the working of the Underground Railway. Includes many exciting adventures of fictional characters in 1860 Chicago, as well as mentioning Stephen Douglas, Allan Pinkerton and Abraham Lincoln. Daily living conditions and Lincoln's nomination by the Republican Convention are a part.

126 MEIGS, CORNELIA. *Jane Addams, Pioneer for Social Justice;* illus. Boston: Little, Brown, 1970. (7-8)   * B

Excellent biography delves into every aspect of Jane Addams life and work. The far reaching influence of Hull House and the people who so ably assisted Jane, not only at Hull House, but also in the fight for social justice, is clearly evident. Presents the ceaseless activities for child labor laws; decent living and working conditions, and wages; and the elimination of many other ills. That Jane did not always meet with success failed to discourage her, although the abuse heaped upon her at times must have hurt.

127 MELIN, GRACE. *Carl Sandburg, Young Singing Poet;*
illus. by Robert Doremus. Indianapolis: Bobbs-
Merrill, 1973. (3-5) B
Much of every day living in Galesburg, Illinois,
in the late 1800's, such as, getting water from the
stove reservoir for Saturday night baths, milk deliver-
ies, cleaning the cistern, repairing the well. In one
glaring error, the author states that Sandburg was
christened Charles, later deciding to call himself Carl.
According to Sandburg's own account, he was "solemnly
christened Carl" and decided to call himself Charles
while in the first or second grade.

128 MERWIN, BLANCHE; NICKELL, VERNON and MERWIN, BRUCE.
Illinois, Crossroads of a Nation; illus. by
Mildred Hetherington. Chicago: Lyons and
Carnahan, 1943. o.p. (4-6)
Mostly historical, the facts are sometimes
presented in story form. The first two chapters on the
Indians and pioneer days are examples of this format.
Includes sketchy maps and illustrations, some photo-
graphs and drawings. Nine chapters discuss Illinois
today, but that was more than thirty years ago. Final
chapter lists interesting facts not mentioned elsewhere
in the book.

— MERWIN, BRUCE. *Illinois, Crossroads of a Nation.*
See IL 128

129 MEYER, EDITH. *Champions of the Four Freedoms;*
illus. by Eric von Schmidt. Boston: Little,
Brown, 1966. o.p. pp. 28-43, 165-177.
(7-8) B
Elijah Lovejoy, shot in Alton, Illinois, defending his printing press against proslavery troublemakers,
died defending the freedom of the press to speak out
against slavery. Julia Lathrop, a colleague of Jane
Addams at Hull House, spoke out against corruption in
Illinois politics and the indifference of the citizens
toward social injustice. As a result of her efforts,
Illinois set up the first clinic anywhere for psycho-
pathic children, later the Illinois Institue for
Juvenile Research.

130 MIERS, EARL. *Our Fifty States;* illus. by Eleanor
        Mill. New York: Grosset & Dunlap, 1961. o.p.
        pp. 144-149. (6-8)
        Brief summary of "Illinois Land of Lincoln"
begins with the arrival of the Lincoln family in
Illinois and ends with a comment on modern Chicago.
Compressed into the account are Marquette's explora-
tions, the Black Hawk War, Lincoln's activities, Civil
War, industrial growth. Useful for a quick survey of
Illinois. Map included.

131 MILLER, HELEN. *First Plays for Children: a
        Collection of Little Plays for the Youngest
        Players.* Boston: Plays, 1960. pp. 158-166.
        (4-6)
        Play based on a club formed by ten children (the
cast of characters), is a meeting of the Rail Splitters
who earn ten pennies for Lincoln doing something
Lincoln might have done, or something connected with
his life. Ends with the singing of two songs, words of
which are included, the pledge of allegiance and the
singing of "America." Suitable for a Lincoln's birthday program.

132 MILLER, HELEN M. *George Rogers Clark, Frontier
        Fighter;* illus. by Albert Orbaan. New York:
        Putnam's, 1968. (4-6) B #
        Biography for young children is action filled
and fast moving enough to hold their interest.
Concerned mostly with Clark's military actions in the
area bounded by the Ohio, Wabash and Mississippi Rivers.
Taking forts at Kaskasia, Cahokia and Vincennes, and
marching to Vincennes a second time through flooded
plains, he secures the territory for the Americans.
Map and Index.

133 MILLER, OLIVE. *Heroes, Outlaws and Funny Fellows
        of American Popular Tales;* illus. by Richard
        Bennett. New York: Doubleday, Doran, 1939.
        pp. 89-115. (8-)
        Mike Fink tangles with the river pirates at
Cave-in-Rock on the Ohio River in Southern Illinois.

He rescues a bride in his usual rip-snorting style and ends the piracy at Cave-in-rock. The second Illinois legend is the story of a French girl and her beloved in Cahokia in the days when French settlements were part of the Illinois scene.

134 MILLER, WALTER. *Lincoln Lived Here: Lincoln Heritage Trail;* illus. Williamsburg, Va.: Walter H. Miller & Co., Inc., 1971. (4-6)
Both the text and a map trace the Lincoln Heritage trail from Lincoln's birth place in Kentucky at the Sinking Spring farm, to Indiana, to Illinois and finally to Washington, D.C. The map stops in Illinois, but text and photographs include points of interest concerning Lincoln in Washington. The photographs in color are an attractive and important part of the booklet.

135 MONGHAN, JAY. *This Is Illinois: A Pictorial History;* illus. Chicago: University of Chicago Press, 1949. o.p. (5-8)
Primarily pictures with captions. Photographs, paintings, lithographs about a variety of subjects from Indians, explorers, and early settlers to industry, agriculture, and architecture. Provides a quick, easy survey of Illinois.

136 MOONEY, ELIZABETH. *Jane Addams;* illus. Chicago: Follett, 1968. o.p. (4-6) B
A clear, rather full account of Jane Addams' life from early childhood to death. Covers how Jane became interested in being of service to the poor, how she decided to implement her desire to be helpful, and how successful her efforts were. Space is also given to some of the people who helped her achieve success.

137 MYERS, ELISABETH. *George Pullman, Young Sleeping Car Builder;* illus. by Al Fiorentino. Indianapolis: Bobbs-Merrill, 1963. pp. 173-182, 184-192. (4-6) B
After a night trip on an Erie Canal packet, the boy, George Pullman, began to think of better sleeping

accommodations while traveling. In Chicago, after raising buildings from the marshy mud and putting them on
firm foundations, he went to work in earnest to perfect
a good sleeping car. Not until Mary Lincoln made the
trip back to Springfield after the assassination, was
Pullman able to convince the railroads that using his
car was feasible.

138 NADEN, CORINNE. *The Chicago Fire 1871; The Blaze
That Nearly Destroyed a City;* illus. New York:
Watts, 1961. o.p. (6-8)
Full and lively account not only tells of the
Chicago fire, but also mentions other disastrous fires
in the United States. Concludes with a chapter
entitled, "The Lessons Learned," which tells of the
impact of the Chicago fire on building codes, fire
fighting equipment, fire prevention efforts. As a
result of the fire we have Fire Prevention Week every
year in October. Index, photographs, and a number of
maps add to the usefulness.

139 NADEN, CORINNE. *The Haymarket Affair; Chicago 1886*
illus. New York: Watts, 1968. (7-8)
The effects of the bomb thrown in the Haymarket
which resulted in a riot leading to the death of six
policemen. The riot and resulting trials of the sus-
pects had a far-reaching effect on the labor movement,
political careers, and reactions of citizens toward all
people considered radicals. Worthwhile in helping
children understand the beginnings of the labor movement, and the reactions of laborers and others.

140 NADEN, CORINNE. *The Mississippi; America's Great
River Systems;* illus. New York: Watts, 1974.
(4-6)
While this book emphasizes the Mississippi as a
river system in which the Missouri and Ohio Rivers are
important tributaries, it is an aid in understanding
the part played by the Mississippi in the settling and
development of Illinois, as well as other parts of the
country. Black and white sketches and maps.

141 NATHAN, ADELE. *Lincoln's America;* illus. New York: Grosset & Dunlap, 1961. o.p. (7-8) B

With the focus more on Lincoln's political than on his personal life, much of the book is devoted to the Civil War, and the verbal battle concerning slavery prior to the war. Full page portraits of Lincoln, Mary Lincoln, Lee and Grant, as well as many other illustrations, add much to this well-written book. Lincoln in Illinois is confined to pp. 22-29, 37-48.

142 NATHAN, ADELE. *Wheat Won't Wait;* illus. by Millard McGee. New York: Aladdin, 1952. o.p. (4-6) F

An interesting story of Cyrus McCormick and his reaper. There is almost as much excitement in some of the field tests of the reaper as in a horse race. The description of the Chicago that McCormick saw on his first visit to the city is particularly well done.

143 NATHAN, ADELE and BAKER, W. C. *Famous Railroad Stations of the World;* illus. by Graham Bernbach. New York: Random House, 1953. o.p. pp. 75-79. (5-7)

Worthwile, although old, because it explains so well how Chicago became the greatest railroad junction in the whole world, in spite of being built on a marsh. Grand Central Station is described, and other Chicago railroad stations are mentioned.

144 NEYHART, LOUISE. *Henry's Lincoln;* illus. by Charles Wilson. New York: Holiday House, 1945. o.p. (4-6) F

Entire book revolves around the Lincoln-Douglas debate at Freeport. Henry Oaks is excited about going to the debate, and is not disappointed by the debate itself. The enthusiasm of the crowd, main points of the debate, some of the personal qualities of the debaters are made very real. The illustrations, especially the last one, add much.

— NICKELL, VERNON. *Illinois, Crossroads of a Nation.*
See IL 128

145 NOLAN, JEANNETTE. *Abraham Lincoln;* illus. by Lee
Ames. **New** York: Messner, 1953. o.p. (6-8) B
Sketches of Lincoln from boyhood to the White
House years, which are to be found at the beginning of
each chapter, add an interesting visual dimension to
this well-written book. Especially well-handled are
the Lincoln-Douglas debates and the controversy over
the spread of slavery into new territory.

146 NOLAN, JEANNETTE. *The Gay Poet, the Story of
Eugene Field;* illus. by Robert Robison. New
York: Messner, 1940. o.p. (7-8) B
Because of today's deplorable usage, the title
is unfortunate, but the book sparkles with Eugene
Field's youthful, mischievous pranks, gentle courtesy,
loving kindness, and boundless humor. After growing up
in New England, spending a year at Knox College in
Galesburg, time in St. Louis, and St. Joseph, Missouri,
and in Denver, Colorado, Eugene settled with his family
in Chicago where he spent the remainder of his life
writing a column, "Sharps and Flats," for *The Daily
News*. It was at this time that he began publishing his
books, and bought a home in Buena Park, a Chicago
suburb.

147 NOLAN, JEANNETTE. *George Rogers Clark;* illus. by
Lee Ames. New York: Messner, 1954. o.p.
(6-8) B #
Well-written story of the hardships that Clark
endured in carrying out his plans of wresting the
Illinois country from the grasp of the British during
the Revolutionary War. Tells of his unfulfilled dream
of capturing Detroit in order to end the British-
inspired Indian raids.

148 NOLAN, JEANNETTE. *Hobnailed Boots;* illus. by
Charles Hargens. Chicago: Winston, 1939. o.p.
(6-8) F
Dan Ballard and John Sanders became members of
George Rogers Clark's expeditionary force on its way to
capture Kaskaskia. Their adventures began when they
were captured by two members of the expedition who

suspected them of being spies because of Dan's newly
acquired hobnailed boots. Plenty of action and narrow
escapes keep interest from flagging during the march to
Kaskaskia.

149 NOLAN, JEANNETTE. *The Little Giant: The Story of
Stephen A. Douglas and Abraham Lincoln;* illus.
by Monte Crews. New York: Messner, 1942.
(7-8) B
A very well-written story of the colorful, vigorous, courageous Douglas whose successes were phenomenal,
his failures few. He collided with Lincoln politically,
but both had integrity and adhered to the principles
they really believed in. The Lincoln-Douglas debates
were so noteworthy that they brought Lincoln the nation-
wide attention that finally took him to the presidency.

150 NOLAN, JEANNETTE. *The Victory Drum;* illus. by
Lorence Bjorklund. New York: Messner, 1953.
(4-6) F
Another story of George Rogers Clark and the
conquest of the Northwest Territory. Benny Lemoyne of
Kaskaskia goes as a drummer boy with Clark's regiment
to recapture Fort Sackville at Vincennes. In spite of
the hardships of travel in the "Drowned Lands" and
near-starvation, Benny has some exciting adventures,
and with the help of his drum revives the flagging
spirits of the regiment.

151 NORTH, STERLING. *Abe Lincoln; Log Cabin to White
House;* illus. by Lee Ames. New York: Random
House, 1956. (5-8) * B #
A short quotation from Lincoln's sayings or
writings is used at the beginning of each chapter of
this biography which covers his mid-western years
rather fully. How the books Lincoln read influenced
his character, education, and political beliefs is
noted throughout. This well-written book presents a
good picture of Illinois as well of Lincoln.

152 ORRMONT, ARTHUR. *Master Detective, Allan Pinkerton.*
New York: Messner, 1965. o.p. (7-8) B
Pinkerton's life in Glasgow is covered briefly,
but the major portion of the book is devoted to his
adult life in Illinois. Although he established detective offices elsehwere, the first, and the one from
which he operated personally, was in Chicago. His
work for railroads and banks took him frequently from
Illinois, but his most outstanding job, historically,
was the prevention of the assassination of Lincoln in
Baltimore before he ever reached Washington.

153 OSTENDORF, LLOYD. *Abraham Lincoln, the Boy and the
Man;* illus. by author. New York: Lamplight,
1962. (4-8) B
This book is primarily pictorial. Each page
consists of a short anecdote concerning the photograph
and drawing included. This is not a study in depth,
but is useful for the pictures and bits of information
which may encourage children to delve more deeply into
an interesting aspect of Lincoln's life. Some of the
information is unusual, for instance, Lincoln was the
only president who ever received a patent. Apparently,
Jefferson did not patent his inventions.

154 PARKER, BERTHA. *The 50 States;* illus. New York:
Golden Press, 1959. o.p. (5-6)
After a short introduction of the United States
as a whole, the individual states are covered alphabetically. Two pages are devoted to each state, one
mostly text, the other has a map, illustrations, and
statistical material. For Illinois this includes eleva-
tion, area, state seal, bird, flower. A legend
explains the pictures on the map. The text briefly
tells of the settlement of Illinois, and provides facts
about Chicago, industry and farming.

155 PARMALEE, PAUL. *Amphibians of Illinois;* illus.
Springfield: State of Illinois, Dept. of Registration and Education-Illinois State Museum,
1954. (6-8)
This booklet includes a section on collecting
and preserving specimens, and also caring for live ones.

Descriptive terminology is explained with the use of a
diagram. Salamanders, toads and frogs of Illinois are
described and illustrated with photographs. Facts of
natural history, distribution, the common and scientific name are given for each.

156 PETERSHAM, MAUD and PETERSHAM, MISKA. *Story of the
Presidents of the United States of America;*
illus. by authors. New York: Macmillan, 1953.
(4-6)
Includes presidents from Washington to Eisen-
hower. The oath of office is printed at the front of
of the book. A brief summary of Lincoln's life and
presidency is found on pages 40-43, and of Grant's,
pages 46-47. Included are drawings of Lincoln as rail-
splitter, as flatboatman, and saying farewell to the
citizens of Springfield. Grant is shown as a boy with
a horse, and as a soldier.

— PETERSHAM, MISKA. *Story of the Presidents of the
United States of America.* See IL 156

157 PETERSON, HAROLD. *Forts in America;* illus. by
Daniel Feaser. New York: Scribner's, 1964.
(5-8)
Fort Dearborn is the only Illinois fort included.
The illustration and description of the fort is very
good. Index, but no map of the Illinois area.

158 PETERSON, HELEN. *Jane Addams, Pioneer of Hull
House;* illus. by Hobe Hays. Champaign, Ill.:
Garrard, 1965. o.p. (2-4) B #
A simply and clearly written account of Jane
Addams' life and work among the poor in the settlement
house that she established in Chicago. The work she
did to bring about child labor laws, and the resistance
she met in her efforts, should be especially interesting to children who have not encountered child labor
problems.

— PRATER, JOHN. *Exploring Illinois.* See IL 160

159 PRATT, HARRY. *The Illinois Story;* illus.
Springfield: State of Illinois, Illinois State
Historical Library, 1956. (6-8)
Covered in this booklet is the location of
Illinois, history from 1673-1953, and brief accounts of
agriculture, manufacturing, labor, coal mining, oil
production, transportation, education, literature and
art for this period. Pictures, maps and graphs.

160 PYGMAN, CLARENCE and PRATER, JOHN. *Exploring*
Illinois; illus. Chicago: Follett, 1955. o.p.
(4-6) R
This text book devotes two pages to Illinois
Indians, and twelve to Illinois before statehood. It
is a combination of factual material and little stories.
Farming, coal mining, oil, manufacturing industries are
included in the economic area. Government, state parks,
cities of Illinois are other aspects of the state
covered. A brief story of Lincoln, and a fairly complete account of Chicago are included. Best used as a
reference for material not likely to be out-dated.

161 RANDALL, RUTH. *I, Mary: A Biography of the Girl*
Who Married Abraham Lincoln; illus. Boston:
Little, Brown, 1959. (7-8) B
Mary Lincoln steps out of the mists of half-
truths and falsehoods to become a real person with
virtues as well as faults, joys and sorrows, hopes and
fears, but most of all as the loving wife of Abraham
Lincoln. Especially interesting is the account of the
Lincoln's life in Springfield, both social and domestic.
Description of the house on Eighth Street and Mary's
interest in furnishing adds historical interest. It is
good to learn that Mary's life was not all headaches
and temper tantrums.

162 RANDALL, RUTH. *Lincoln's Animal Friends;* illus. by
Louis Darling. Boston: Little, Brown, 1958.
o.p. (5-7) B
Animals that touched his life are only a small
part of the incidents about Lincoln recorded in this
book. New Salem seems most important as the place

where his education was improved. Here he became an
independent adult, and decided to become a lawyer. His
day by day life in Springfield, including his relationship with his children, citizens of the town, and animals, make interesting reading for children.

163 RAUCH, MABEL. *The Little Hellion, a Story of
"Egypt" (Southern Illinois).* New York: Duell,
Sloan and Pearce, 1960. o.p. (5-8) F
   A good picture of life in Southern Illinois in
the 1890's. Sally, who is just thirteen at the end of
the book, recounts episodes of family feuds, horse
racing, gypsies, and the still rankling disagreements
over the split in Southern Illinois as a result of the
Civil War.

164 RAUCH, MABEL. *Vinnie and the Flag-Tree: a Novel
of the Civil War in Southern Illinois—America's
Little Egypt.* New York: Duell, Sloan and
Pearce, 1959. o.p. (7-9) F
   Since many of the people of Southern Illinois
were from regions of the South, sympathies were divided.
Not only communities, but also families were split by
the upheaval which resulted in the Civil War. The
author has used this historical fact, and both historical and fictional characters, to bring a picture of
the times to young people.

165 RICH, LOUISE. *The First Book of the New World
Explorers;* illus. by Cary. New York: Watts,
1960. (5-6)
   The explorations of Marquette and Joliet and
La Salle are briefly treated. Line drawings add inter-
est, and maps are useful aids.

166 ROSS, GEORGE. *Know Your Presidents and Their Wives;*
illus. by Seymour Fleishman. Chicago: Rand
McNally, 1960. o.p. (4-6)
   Limited to the main facts of the lives and public careers—given in statistical form for both Lincoln
and Grant. One page writeups of the presidents' wives
on the page adjoining the information on their husbands

is the most useful part of the book. While material for Mrs. Lincoln is easily available, information about Mrs. Grant is more scarce.

167 SANDBURG, CARL. *Prairie-Town Boy;* illus. by Joe
    Krush. New York: Harcourt, Brace, 1952.
    (6-8) B
    This autobiography, covering the period from 1878-1898, is the story of Sandburg's boyhood and youth in Galesburg, Illinois. Though not easy, life for the townspeople and the Swedish immigrants had a rather even tenor, especially during the depression following the Panic of 1893. Ably describes Galesburg life between pioneer times and the days when modern conveniences became common. Includes food, furnishings, such as, corn husk mattresses, transportation and recreation.

168 SANDBURG, CARL. *Windsong;* illus. by William Smith.
    New York: Harcourt, Brace, World, 1953.
    (5-8)
    Selections in this book of poetry referring directly to Illinois are "Corn Belt," parts of "Night," "Winds of the Windy City," and "Children of the Wind." The poems have a realistic and earthy quality very unlike the mystic quality of Vachel Lindsy's poems.

169 SANFORD, ANN. *Lincoln Plays.* New York: Dodd,
    Mead, 1933. o.p. (5-8)
    This selection of plays includes a wide variety, thirteen in number, suitable for use in elementary schools. Two may be performed without royalty payment. Information about permission to perform and royalty payments are given on the first page of each play.

170 SANFORD, ANN. *Pageants of Our Nation: Central
    States Ohio, Indiana, Illinois, Michigan.* New
    York: Dodd, Mead, 1929. o.p. (7-8)
    The Illinois section includes "The Pageant of the Illinois Country" with six scenes, "The Courage of Tonty," "The Freeing of Illinois," "Battling Against Slavery," "The Fringe of Fame," The West's First Shot," and a final scene from local history to be written by

members of the community. There are several other pageants, all of which require large casts.

171 SATTLEY, HELEN. *Annie;* illus. by Katherine Monroe. New York: Dodd, Mead, 1961. o.p. (6-8) F

An English family, mother and six children, join the father in Chicago immediately after the Chicago fire. Their experiences include watching the rebuilding of Chicago, and Halloween and Thanksgiving celebrations. The story points out the contributions that other cultures have made to American life. In this case, English Christmas customs and the celebration of May Day.

172 SCHOOR, GENE with GILFORD, HENRY. *Red Grange, Football's Greatest Halfback.* New York: Messner, 1952. o.p. (7-8) B

The gridiron feats of Red Grange, the Galloping Ghost of the Fighting Illini are exciting for young football fans. Well known Big Ten coaches of their time, Bob Zuppke, Alonzo Stagg, Fielding Yost, and sports writers like Grantland Rice add glamour, just as Red Grange's spectacular playing and the excitement of the football games add zest.

173 SECHRIST, ELIZABETH. *Poems for Red Letter Days;* illus. by Guy Fry. Philadelphia: Macrae Smith, 1951. (4-8)

The poem entitled "Illinois," by C.H. Chapman, is the official song for the state. Also included are nine poems about Lincoln. Among them are Whitman's "O Captain! My Captain!" and "This Dust Was Once the Man," Markham's "Lincoln Triumphant," and Lindsay's "Abraham Lincoln Walks at Midnight."

174 SEVERN, BILL. *Adlai Stevenson, Citizen of the World;* illus. New York: McKay, 1966. (8-) B

This is a rather full account of Stevenson's life with emphasis on his political life, views on foreign policy, and nuclear explosives. His early life in Bloomington, later life in Chicago and Libertyville, and also his life as governor of Illinois, give glimpses of life in these Illinois cities and of the events that happened while he lived in them. Photographs in black and white. Index.

175 SHORT, MAX and FELTON, ELIZABETH. *The United States Book, Facts and Legends about the 50 States;* illus. Minneapolis: Lerner, 1975. (3-4)

After a one page introduction, the states are treated alphabetically. Each has one page with an outline map of the United States defining the boundaries of the state, and another map showing the state's two major cities. Illinois cities are Springfield and Chicago. On the adjoining page a few important facts about the state are listed. Useful as an introduction to Illinois for younger children.

176 SICKELS, EVELYN. *The School Bell Rings;* illus. by Sandra James. New York: Scribner's, 1952. o.p. (4-6) F

A collection of stories about early schools, two of which, "The Blab School, On the Plains 1825" and "Pert-Miss-Prat-a-Pace, Illinois 1830" concern Illinois. Both stories seem to indicate that more mischief then learning was afoot in some of the pioneer schools.

177 SIMON, CHARLES. *Lays of the New Land: Stories of Some American Poets and Their Work;* illus. by James MacDonald. New York: Dutton, 1943. o.p. (6-8)

Three Illinois poets, Edgar Lee Masters, Carl Sandburg, and Vachel Lindsay are introduced with some samples of their work. More concerned with their writings, than with the personal side of their lives.

178 SMITH, EUNICE. *High Heels for Jennifer;* illus. by author. Indianapolis: Bobbs-Merrill, 1964. o.p. (6-8) F

Jennifer Hill devotes most of her time to her art, horses—especially a friend's horse High Heels— and to romantic fantasies. Some of the fantasies revolve around books she has read, and some around a friend of her brother. The horseshow in Aurora, Illinois, is the highlight.

179 SMITH, EUNICE. *The Jennifer Gift;* illus. by author. Indianapolis: Bobbs-Merrill, 1950. o.p. (5-7) F

Life in rural setting has many pleasures and some problems for the Hill family who moved to the country from Aurora, Illinois. Much of the story revolves around Jennifer's plan for a Christmas gift to her whole family, but Christmas brings an unexpected situation that changes her plan. Although many phases of life were different, such as school, transportation, lighting, and heating, Christmas was as full of anticipation and surprises in 1908 as it is today.

180 SMITH, EUNICE. *The Jennifer Prize;* illus. by author. Indianapolis: Bobbs-Merrill, 1951. o.p. (4-6) F

Jennifer and the other Hill children have many pleasures, adventures, and some unpleasant experiences during their first winter of rural living on a farm near Aurora, Illinois. Jennifer's prize in an essay contest turns out to be a heifer, but not a tractable cow. She refused to be domesticated until her calf was born on Easter Sunday. Jennifer's friend Sarabeth regains the use of her legs.

181 SMITH, EUNICE. *The Jennifer Wish;* illus. by author. Indianapolis: Bobbs-Merrill, 1949. o.p. (4-6) F

Family life in Illinois during the early 1900's is portrayed in this story of Jennifer and her comfortably-off family. The move from town to country life, the acquisition of pets, the excitement of a runaway horse, rescue from drowning, and finding a lost child add interest. Young readers will discover how children found recreation, fun, and entertainment before the days of movies, television, radio, and automobiles.

182 SMITH, FREDRIKA. *The Fire Dragon, a Story of the Great Chicago Fire;* illus. by Ray Naylor.
Chicago: Rand, McNally, 1956. o.p. (6-8) F
Andy Williams befriends a newly arrived Irish boy, Terry, who is set upon by a bully and his friends. In spite of the wide difference in their backgrounds, the boys become fast friends, and are together in the midst of the Chicago fire. Their experiences in the conflagration in the business district and later escaping the fire are realistically portrayed. Includes the aftermath of the fire, the aid from other countries, as well as from areas in the U.S.

183 SMUCKER, BARBARA. *Wigwam in the City;* illus. by Gil Miret. New York: Dutton, 1966. o.p. (5-8) F #
The problems of today's Indians are seen through the eyes of Susan (Little Flower), a Chippewa girl who leaves the reservation at Lac du Flambeau, Wisconsin, to be relocated with her family in Chicago. The move was necessary for Susan's father to find a job, but once in Chicago there were many unexpected problems to be faced, for instance, how to light the gas stove.

— SPEICHER, HELEN. *Allan Pinkerton, Young Detective.* SEE IL 23

184 SYME, RONALD. *La Salle, of the Mississippi;* illus. by William Stobe. New York: Morrow, 1953. (5-7) B #
La Salle's burning desire to know more about the Great Lake area and what lay south of it, not only gets the biography off to a good start, but takes La Salle to the New World where he meets exciting adventures and a number of scoundrels in his explorations. La Salle's dream of French colonies prospering along both sides of the Mississippi was not to be realized. Syme's account is lively and adventurous.

185 TAYLOR, FLORANCE. *Jim Long-Knife;* illus. by Dirk
      Gringhuis. Chicago: Whitman, 1959. (5-7) F
    A young boy, Jim Hudson, and his family are cap-
tured by Indians as they leave their Kentucky cabin for
the safety of a fort. Jim is separated from his family
in Illinois when the chief of the Potawatomi tribe
makes a trade for Jim and his drum. Jim escapes from
the Indians, joins the forces under George Rogers Clark,
is present at the capture of the forts in Illinois, and
is finally re-united with his parents at Vincennes.

186 TAYLOR, FLORANCE. *Owen of the Bluebird;* illus. by
      Harve Stein. Chicago: Whitman, 1942. o.p.
      (6-8) F
    Owen Pryce and his mother move from Wales to an
Illinois coal mining community where Owen finds work
with the help of his mother's brother. Poor working
conditions and low pay in the mines finally leads to a
strike which causes increased hardship. Owen is instrumental in bringing about a satisfactory conclusion to
the strike (a bit far fetched, perhaps), but the portrayal of life in an Illinois coal mining district in
the 1890's is valid.

187 TAYLOR, FLORANCE. *Vermilion Clay;* illus. by
      Eleanor Young. Chicago: Whitman, 1937. o.p.
      (4-6) F
    An injured Miami Indian boy, Ahmik, is rescued
from freezing by Elizabeth Grigsby's father. The
family cares for the boy at the site of a salt lick on
Saline Creek, near the Vermilion River, where Mr.
Grigsby produces salt from the salt wells. After
Ahmik's unexpected departure, Elizabeth is captured by
the Potowatomies and is later abandoned on the prairie
to die because the Indians believe she has brought them
bad luck. After further adventures, she is returned to
her family. The importance of salt to pioneers and
Indians is made clear.

188 TEMPLE, WAYNE. *Indian Villages of the Illinois Country;* illus. Springfield: State of Illinois, Dept. of Education and Registration-Illinois State Museum, 1966. (Rev. ed.) (7-9)

A thorough and well-documented study of the Indians of Illinois during the historical period. The main concern is locations of Indian villages inhabited by the various tribes that lived in Illinois, and their contacts with white explorers, settlers, and governments, rather than their day by day living.

189 THOMAS, BENJAMIN. *Lincoln's New Salem;* illus. by Romaine Proctor. Springfield: Abraham Lincoln Association, 1934. (7-8)

A detailed account of life in New Salem. Illustrations in black and white help children visualize the interiors and furnishings of the log cabins. Divided into three parts, "New Salem," "Lincoln at New Salem," and "New Salem Restored," the book has a wealth of information on the settlement. Unfortunately, the very small print may deter some children who might otherwise find the book interesting.

190 THOMAS, HENRY. *Ulysses S. Grant.* New York: Putnam's, 1961. o.p. (7-8) B #

A well-written account of Grant's failures and triumphs before, during and after the Civil War. Grant remains a heroic character beset by ill fortune and betrayed by self-seeking men. While only a little of Grant's life was spent in Illinois, his home in Galena is a point of historical interest. He was living in Illinois when he entered the army during the Civil War, and also when he was elected president.

— THOMPSON, MILTON. *Birds in Your Backyard*
    SEE IL 58

— TOPPIN, EDGAR. *Pioneers and Patriots; The Lives of Six Negroes of the Revolutionary Era.* SEE IL 50

— WARD, LYND. *Armed with Courage.* See IL 121

191 WARD, MARTHA. *Adlai Stevenson, Young Ambassador;*
    illus. by Nathan Goldstein. Indianapolis:
    Bobbs-Merrill, 1967. (4-6) B
    Though this biography has much fictional conver-
sation, it does give a good account of Stevenson's life
in Bloomington, Illinois, and of farming conditions in
the surrounding area in the early 1900's. Also
included are incidents that occurred in Springfield
while Adlai's father was Secretary of State, and he,
himself was governor. Adlai's work in national politics and his peace efforts are included.

192 WEISBERGER, BERNARD. *Captains of Industry;* illus.
    New York: American Heritage, 1966. o.p.
    pp. 31-43. (6-8)
    Cyrus McCormick and Philip Armour are two men
working in Chicago who made "Fortunes from the Farm,"
McCormick with the reaper and Armour in meat packing.
Chicago's location on Lake Michigan, with access to the
Mississippi River system and also the center of railroad activity, made possible the quick growth of both
industries.

193 WHITNEY, PHYLLIS. *Willow Hill.* New York: McKay,
    1947. (7-8) F
    The action centers around the racial problems,
most of which were more feared than real, that existed
in a town close to Chicago. Although similar incidents
are unlikely to recur (hopefully), it provides a picture of a situation that existed in the recent past,
and also shows how fear causes people to act in unrea-
sonable and unfortunate ways. In this story it was the
students who worked out the solutions to the problems
fomented by their elders.

194 WILKIE, KATHERINE. *Mary Todd Lincoln, Girl of the
    Bluegrass;* illus. by Harry Lees. Indianapolis:
    Bobbs-Merrill, 1954. (3-5) B
    Only pages 166-192 deal with Mary's life in
Illinois. The scene on election day, November 6, 1860,

56

is the best picture of Illinois presented in the book,
which is mostly a fictionalized account of Mary Todd's
girlhood in Kentucky.

195 WOLFE, ANYA. *It Happened in Illinois*. Decatur:
House of Illinois, 1975. (4-6)
The scraps of interesting and sometimes little
known historical information may whet the appetite of
curious students to learn more about the topics that
appeal to them. Others will be informed about events
they otherwise might never have known at all. The book
is a hodgepodge of factual material with no organization.

196 WOOD, FRANCES. *Enchantment of America: Lakes,
Hills and Prairies; The Middlewestern States;*
illus. by Tom Dunnington. Chicago: Childrens
Press, 1962. o.p. (5-7)
The first 65 pages of this book are devoted to
the entire Great Lakes area including formation, climate, people, life today, historical information, and
other aspects of living in the area. Material on
Illinois includes a pictorial map, important dates in
Illinois history, a brief account of geographical features, agriculture, and information on Chicago. Index.

197 WRIGHT, GILBERT. *Common Illinois Insects and Why
They Are Interesting;* illus. Springfield:
State of Illinois, Dept. of Registration and
Education-Illinois State Museum, 1951. (5-8)
After a general discussion of insects, this
booklet has sections on names and classifications of
insects, insect growth and transformation, kinds of
insects that are benefactors, kinds that cause trouble,
common butterflies of Illinois, common Illinois moths,
and common Illinois beetles. Numerous black and white
photographs.

198 YOUNG, BEN. *Rock River Ranger;* illus. by Nils
    Hogner. New York: Abelard, 1953. o.p. (6-8) F
    The story revolves around a boy of "almost
fifteen" who has the responsibility of caring for his
mother and small sister during the Black Hawk War, in
the vicinity of Rock Island. The fear and foolish
actions of the frontier settlers, as well as the desperate plight of the Indians, are shown. Based on historical fact, with several well-known historical figures
included. A map increases the value.

INDIANA

compiled by **LOIS CURTIS**

Indiana was early called the "Land of the Indians," which perhaps was how the state was named. This land was a battleground for more than a hundred years. The Miamis, Chief Pontiac, Tecumseh, and the French and English did battle in the early days of the pioneers. Indiana proved to be an Eden for many early settlers, though the work was hard and the going rough. As a part of the Old Northwest Territory, Indiana carved for herself a notable niche in American History. Heroes, such as George Rogers Clark and William Henry Harrison, have "written" pages of Indiana history. Pioneers, Quakers, Amish, farmers and industrialists form a background of heritage for which every Hoosier is proud.

"Hoosier" is a term known far and near. Many tales of the origin of "Hoosier" are recounted but the one most favored seems to be the answer to a knock on the door. "Who's there?" was called out and the caller thought "Hoosier" was the reply. Next day the caller came back and hallooed "Hoosier!". At any rate, the nickname has become a famous nomenclature—one of which to be proud!

The quotation "Ain't God Good to Indiana," from the poem by William Herschell, comes to mind when subject matter and literary topics are reviewed. From the tip of Lake Michigan to the flowing waters of the Ohio, over sand dunes, lakes and swampland to the beautiful hill country, Brown County, we sweep with our mind's eye and touch a panoramic view of background locale and people that here have mingled as the crossroads of America converge geographically.

Indiana continued for many years as the center area of population for the United States and was aptly called "The Crossroads of America." She is considered a typical American state. "Her people have the courage and inventiveness, the friendliness and good humor that are thought to be truly American."* Indiana writers are popular because they express the thoughts and feelings of the people everywhere.

Not only was Indiana's pioneer period noteworthy; in later years other names stand out: New Harmony—the Robert Owen dream of peaceful living through love and cooperation; the Indianapolis Motor Speedway—famed 500 Mile Race; Gene Stratton Porter—whose book sales were greater than any other writer in her time. Notable, too, is Notre Dame University; Hoosier basketball; "On the Banks of the Wabash"; and Wallace's *Ben Hur*. The latter has reputedly sold more copies than any other book except the Bible!

Imagination and literary skill have unfolded the rich background and traditions of the state of Indiana and her people in a vast collection of children's literature created by many noteworthy authors. They have described the lives and deeds of native sons and daughters—both great and small—who have made history. To know a state's traditions, monuments, names, places, local color and to travel in time from today to yesteryear is the privilege of every reader. Students can glean much information—historical and modern, factual and fictional—from the following materials, perhaps even pricking some other literary appetite and kindling a flame to enjoyment and knowledge.

---

*Bernadine Bailey, *Picture Book of Indian* (Chicago: Whitman, 1950), p. 25.

1   ADE, GEORGE. *Forty Modern Fables*. New York:
R. H. Russell, 1902. o.p. (7-) F
A rich heritage of modern fables written at the
turn of the century, the morals of which are still
modern today. Humor and satire by an able writer whose
locale was Indiana with her friendly people.

2   ALDIS, DOROTHY. *Lucky Year*; illus. by John Dukes
McKee. Chicago: Rand McNally, 1951. o.p.
(4-6) F
The White family activity in Madison, Indiana, a
few blocks from the Ohio River, centers around hog
raising, the "annual drive" and river traffic. The
highlight of the story is the preparation for, and the
performance of, the famous singer, Jenny Lind.

3   ALLEE, MARJORIE HILL. *Ann's Surprising Summer*;
illus. by Maitland De Gogorza. New York:
Houghton Mifflin, 1933. o.p. (6-8) F
The Indiana sand dunes on the shores of Lake
Michigan are the site of the strange and happy country
to which Ann and her family escape for the summer.
Ann's scientific experiments and the mysterious ranger
add excitement to their meager living in a lonely ramshackle cabin.

4   ALLEE, MARJORIE HILL. *A House of Her Own*; illus.
by Manning de V. Lee. Boston: Houghton Mifflin,
1934. o.p. (7-8) F
The hardships and rewards of a pioneer school-
mistress in a Quaker settlement in Indiana are revealed.
The romance of the teacher and "biggest" schoolboy adds
interest and suspense.

5   ALLEE, MARJORIE HILL. *Judith Lankester*; illus. by
Hattie Longstreet Price. New York: Houghton
Mifflin, 1930. o.p. (6-8) F
Judith Lankester proves herself to be a worthy
Indiana pioneer in a Quaker household though she had
been reared on a southern plantation in luxury and
wealth.

61

6   ALLEY, HARTLEY and ALLEY, JEAN. *Southern Indiana.*
    Photographed by Hartley Alley. Bloomington,
    Ind.: Indiana University Press, 1965. (4-8)
    * P
    A photographic study of Indiana covering the
complex combination of rural Americana and modern
industry and locales. Places and events, both historical and modern, makes this photo history delightful
reading and viewing, adding a humanistic approach.

—   ALLEY, JEAN. *Southern Indiana.* See IN 6

7   ANKENBRUCK, JOHN. *The Voice of the Turtle;* illus.
    Fort Wayne, Ind.: News Publishing Co., 1974.
    Paper. (7-8) B
    A mature, fast-moving biography of the fascinat-
ing, many talented Miami Indian war chief, Little Turtle.
For almost a generation he beat off the American westward movement with his scheming war strategy and
cruelty.

8   ARBUCKLE, DOROTHY FRY. *The After-Harvest Festival;
    The Story of a Girl of the Old Kankakee;* illus.
    by Maurice Whitman. New York: Dodd Mead, 1955.
    o.p. (6-8) F
    The Kankakee River marshlands in northern
Indiana are the setting for Paris La Croixes' activities
and adventures. The daughter of a French fur trapper
isolated by his work, she is devoted to her family and
animal friends. To attend the harvest festival is her
big dream.

9   ARBUCKLE, DOROTHY FRY. *Andy's Dan'l Boone Rifle;*
    illus. by author. Lake Village, Ind.: The
    Villager, 1966. (6-) F
    The setting is Northwest Indiana in the early
1800's. The Ritter family homesteaded in Indiana and
wove a tale of pioneer hardship and neighborliness.
Indians and pioneers were friendly and helpful to each
other. Andy Ritter, the young son, finally received
his Dan'l Boone rifle as a gift from his best friend,
Little Wolf.

10 BAILEY, BERNADINE. *Picture Book of Indiana;* illus.
   by Kurt Wiese. Rev. ed. Chicago: Whitman,
   1966. (3-8) *
   A succinct history of Indiana covering the territorial beginning and its becoming the 19th state to
enter the Union, up to date when book written. Land
use, topography, industry, and highlights of people,
places, and Hoosier events make this enlarged edition
an in depth study. Illustrations and index increase
usefulness.

11 BAILEY, BERNADINE. *Picture Book of Indiana;* illus.
   by Kurt Wiese. Chicago: Whitman, 1950. (2-3)
   P *
   A simplified panoramic view of Indiana's history
from its beginning down to the present in a manner
interesting to all ages. Despite its date, much helpful and useful information is given in words and pictures of the state's scenery, commerce, natural
resources and accomplishments.

12 BAKER, RONALD and CARMONY, MARVIN. *Indiana Place
   Names.* Bloomington, Ind.: Indiana University
   Press, 1976. (4-8) R
   An alphabetical listing of Indiana place names
with pronunciation guide. Includes counties, cities,
towns and villages, plus some streams. Also includes
historical data as well as linguistic, geographic, and
folkloristic information. An interesting (word study)
reference tool for pupil and teacher.

13 BALL, CABLE G., ed. *The Journals and Indian
   Paintings of George Winter, 1837-39;* illus.
   Indianapolis: Indiana Historical Society, 1948.
   o.p. (6-8) P *
   Outstanding color and black and white reproductions of George Winter's paintings from life as he
lived with the Indians along the Wabash, near Logans-
port and Vincennes, Indiana in 1837-39. Included are a
biographical sketch of Winter, and two journals relating extensive details concerning the Indians and their
customs.

14 BARNHART, JOHN D. and CARMONY, DONALD F. *Indiana, The Hoosier State;* illus. Chicago: Wheeler, 1959. o.p. (6-8) R
A complete and well-balanced history of Indiana from the French explorers to the present time for use as a text in Junior High School. Pictures, maps, and chapter aids for study are included. Useful as a reference source.

15 BLOEMKER, AL. *500 Miles to Go;* photographs. New York: Coward-McCann, 1966. (4-8) * R
This is the history of the Indianapolis Motor Speedway from Ray Harroun's victory in 1911, to 1965 with Jim Clark the victor. The tragedy, success and failure of racing heroes in their quest for speed has made exciting history in Speedway. Story and photos picture the racing careers of many, and the drastic changes in motors, cars, and the track that have made the 500 Mile Race one of the world's spectacular sports events. Appendix of race summaries, one lap records, official photographs, and index made this an Indiana "must" for reference.

16 BURCHARD, S. H. *Bob Griese;* photographs and drawings by Paul Frame. New York: Harcourt, Brace, Jovanovich, 1975. (3-6) B
An easy to read biography of the football star, Bob Griese. Bob grew up in Evansville, Indiana, where he first played football in high school. Purdue University saw Bob as a good student and excellent football player. Later, as a pro, he played outstanding football and led the Miami Dolphins to a world championship. A Hoosier son.

17 BURNET, MARY Q. *Art and Artists of Indiana;* illus. New York: Century, 1921. o.p. (4-) P
Discussion of artists and their work; photo plates illustrate important and typical work.

18 BURRIS LABORATORY SCHOOL. *Let's Re-Discover Indiana.*
    Vol. I: *Northwest Indiana;* illus. Muncie, Ind.:
    Ball State University, 1975. Paper. (4-)
    A booklet created to develop an awareness of his-
tory past and present within the state of Indiana, and
to make history fun, alive, and "in our own backyard."
Part of a state-wide program under the auspices of the
Indiana Junior Historical Society. Also available is
a coordinated colored slide set with accompanying tape
narration.

19 BURRIS LABORATORY SCHOOL. *Let's Re-Discover Indiana.*
    Vol. II: *Southeast Quadrant;* illus. Muncie,
    Ind.: Ball State University, 1976. Paper.
    (4-)
    Vol. II is another booklet to help children be-
come aware of their heritage and realize that today's
happenings are history in the making. Especially useful to make local history come alive for children in
the Southeast Quadrant of Indiana. Coordinated colored
slide set and accompanying tape narration also available.

20 BURT, OLIVE. *The National Road;* maps and photo-
    graphs by Ellen Viereck. New York: Day, 1968.
    (5-8) R
    How America's vision of a transcontinental high-
way grew through the centurees to become a reality.
The National Road—later U.S. 40—dissects the state
and brought the people of the westward movement to and
through Indiana. A connecting link between East and
West, the road by 1850 passed through the heart of
Indianapolis, the state capital and "crossroad of America." The meager index lacks details, but book supplies
information difficult to find elsewhere.

21 BURT, OLIVE. *Old America Comes Alive;* illus.
    New York: Day, 1966. (4-8) P #
    Restored villages from colonial Williamsburg to
Dodge City are pictured in words and photos. In chapter 13 the Lincoln Heritage Trail helps us visualize
the early life of Abraham Lincoln. The Lincoln Memor-
ial Pioneer Village at Rockfort, Indiana is one site
re-created.

22 CARMER, CARL. *The Boy Drummer of Vincennes;* illus.
by Seymour Fleishman. Irvington-on-Hudson, N.Y.:
Harvey House, 1972. (2-5)
The colorful story of the little French boy who
accompanied George Rogers Clark on his march from Kaskaskia to Vincennes is told in verse with "strong
rhythms." A great read-aloud poetic story in history.
The illustrations tell the story again in memorable
drawings—even to the drummer boy beating the drum on
which he is floating across the Little Wabash.

— CARMONY, DONALD F. *Indiana, the Hoosier State.*
See IN 14

— CARMONY, MARVIN. *Indiana Place Names.* See IN 12

23 CARPENTER, ALLAN. *Indiana: From Its Glorious Past
to the Present;* illus. by Phil Austin. Chicago:
Children's Press, 1966. (4-8) R *
A succinct history of Indiana from the "lay of
the land"—as it was—to today. A well-rounded story
of Indiana heritage including Indian and pioneer life,
manufacturing, mineral wealth, outstanding political
figures, musicians, inventors and many other interesting Hoosiers. A "Handy Reference Section" provides
lists of dates, facts, events, governors, and "thinkers,
doers and fighters." An excellent index and detailed
Table of Contents add value to this definitive "state"
book. *Enchantment of America* series.

24 CARPER, JEAN and DICKERSON, GRACE L. *Little Turtle:
Miami Chief;* illus. by Grace Leslie Dickerson.
Chicago: Whitman, 1959. (3-6) #
Biography of the Indian leader whose home was at
Kekionga—which is now Fort Wayne, Indiana. Little
Turtle, Miami Indian Chief, fought brilliantly to save
his people's land and way of life. He also helped them
settle into farming when he was defeated—like a great
warrior.

25 CARSON, JOHN F. *The Coach Nobody Liked: A Basketball Story.* New York: Farrar, Straus & Giroux, 1960. (6-8) F

A basketball story set in Indiana where the hero, Sid Hawkes, has a problem. The new coach shifts emphasis from winning every game to playing good basketball and developing character. Excitement comes both on and off the basketball court.

26 CAVANAH, FRANCES. *Abe Lincoln Gets His Chance;* illus. by Paula Hutchison. Chicago: Rand McNally, 1959. (4-6) B

Abe Lincoln's childhood and his friends are emphasized in this biography which takes him up to his election for the Presidency. A chapter is devoted to Abe's life at Pigeon Creek Farm, Indiana. Available in paper, Starline edition, Scholastic Book Service.

27 CHAPPELL, CARL L. *Virgil I. Grissom, Boy Astronaut;* illus. by Robert Doremus. Indianapolis: Bobbs-Merrill, 1971. (3-6) B

An interesting and inspiring early childhood biography of Gus Grissom, one of the original seven U.S. astronauts. His childhood ambition to become a pilot was realized through hard work, and his contributions to the U.S. space program will be long remembered. Grissom grew up in Mitchell, Indiana and attended Purdue University.

28 CLIFFORD, ETH. *The Year of the Three-Legged Deer;* illus. by Richard Cuffari. Boston: Houghton Mifflin, 1972. (5-8) F

A warm sensitive story combining the lives of pioneers, blacks, and Indians and half-breeds. The Jesse Benton family (a combination of all) weaves a story of love, strenth and courage as the characters face dangers, family problems and love of children and animals. A poignant story with authentic historical happenings in Indiana near the present site of Noblesville. Also available in paper, Dell, 1973.

29 CLIFFORD, ETH; KIRK, RICHARD E. and ROGERS, JAMES.
*Living in Indiana History: A Story of People
from Many Lands;* illus. Rev. ed. Indianapolis:
David-Stewart, 1973. (4-8) *
A comprehensive history of the land and people
of Indiana, beginning with the pre-historical Ice Age
and ancient Indians. Includes changes in agriculture,
settlement, industry and people—the political scene
and equal rights of races and women. Indiana's natural
treasures of animals, birds, parks, forests and natural
resources weave a rich background knowledge for all
Hoosiers. Index and glossary.

30 COOPER, JAMIE LEE. *The Horn and the Forest.*
Indianapolis: Bobbs-Merrill, 1963. (7-8) F
The main locale of the story is along the Wabash,
Salamonie and Mississinewa Rivers in northern Indiana.
The Indiana frontier is a difficult life for the son of
a white physician and a half-breed Indian woman.

31 CROUT, GEORGE and MC CALL, EDITH S. *Where the Ohio
Flows;* illus. by Berthold Tiedemann. Chicago:
Benefic, 1960. o.p. (4-6) R #
Indiana history as it happened along the Ohio
River country, and the men who made it possible. Study
questions for use as a text for intermediate grades.
Our Growing America series.

32 DALEY, ARTHUR. *Knute Rockne, Football Wizard of
Notre Dame;* illus. with photographs. New York:
Kenedy, 1960. (6-8) P B
Rockne's college career at Notre Dame and his
coaching prowess there are set forth to depict his
struggle, will power, nerve and character. A tribute
to Rockne after his death. *American Background Books.
Lives of Catholic Heroes and Heroines in American History* series.

33 DEAM, CHARLES C. and SHAW, THOMAS EDWARD. *Trees of Indiana;* illus. Indianapolis: Bookwalter, 1953. o.p. (4-) P
A scientific study of trees growing in Indiana; with plates, maps and index.

34 DE LEEUW, ADELE. *George Rogers Clark: Frontier Fighter;* illus. by Russ Hoover. Champaign, Ill.: Garrard, 1967. (2-5) B #
An easy to read biography written about George Rogers Clark to interpret history to young people. His boyhood and young adult independence, courage and prowess as an American frontiersman and military leader tell us of a great American. Colorful pictures enhance the story.

— DICKERSON, GRACE L. *Little Turtle; Miami Chief.* See IN 24

— DONALDSON, LOIS. *Abigail.* See IN 138

35 DOUGLAS, EMILY TAFT. *Appleseed Farm;* illus. by Anne Vaughan. New York: Abingdon, 1958. (3-6) F
The story of the beginning of a pioneer Indiana farm: family life, hardships, struggle, and their happiness partly due to "apple seeds." Johnny Appleseed's visit, his seeds, and his brotherly love help turn the tide for this family.

36 EGGLESTON, EDWARD. *The Hoosier School-Boy;* illus. New York: Scribner, 1936. (c1882 by Edward Eggleston) o.p. (6-8) F *
A vivid picture of the trials, teaching and learning, that faced the school boy in the 1800's in the villages of Indiana where beatings from a cruel master were commonplace. Learning could and did take place for those who cared, amidst games, trickery and spelling matches.

37 EGGLESTON, EDWARD. *The Hoosier School Master;*
    illus. by Frank Beard. New York: Orange Judd,
    1871. o.p. (7-) F *
    Demonstrates some of the problems and struggles
of a young intellectural whose career was to be a Hoosier schoolmaster in a rough and rugged community in
early pioneer days in Indiana. Indiana hill dialect.
A classic.

38 EGGLESTON, EDWARD. *The Hoosier Schoolmaster;* sim-
    plified and adapted by Robert J. Dixon. New
    York: Regents, 1973. Paper. (7-8) F
    A simplified and adapted edition of the classic
story of a one room school master, Ralph Hartsook, in
Indiana in the mid-1800's. Exercises for conversation
and vocabulary drill are included. An excellent study
tool which could lead to further reading and research.

39 EMERY, ANNE. *Sweet Sixteen.* Philadelphia: Macrae
    Smith, 1956. (7-8) F
    An Indiana farm is the setting for a sixteen-
year-old girl's activities. Jane Ellison thinks this
will be her most important year, but becomes bogged
down with disappointments and seeming failures. The
turn of events and unexpected surprises coupled with
good philosophy hold the reader's interest.

40 *Encyclopedia of the United States—Indiana;* illus.
    St. Clair Shores, Mich.: Somerset, 1976.
    (6-) R
    This Indiana volume contains essays on the state
as a whole, and a concise dictionary of every important
political, historical, and geographical unit of Hoosier-
land. A section of biographies of famous Hoosiers,
photographs, and a chronology of Indiana history augment the volume. Index.

70

41 ENGEL, LYLE KENYON. *The Incredible A. J. Foyt;*
    illus. New York: Arco, 1970. (6-8) B
    An exciting biography of an equally exciting
personality—A. J. Foyt—enthusiastic race driver and
possibly the greatest driver in racing history. Racing
from age five (his father built him a car at age three),
his brilliant career and sometimes obnoxious personality
come through the printed page to throw light on his
tremendous accomplishments. One chapter is devoted to
the "statistical side of A. J. Foyt" to reveal more
"racing honors" than ever recorded for one man. His
greatest honors and spectacular victories were at the
Indy 500.

42 ENGEL, LYLE KENYON and THE EDITORS OF *AUTO RACING*
    MAGAZINE. *The Indianapolis "500";* illus. New
    York: Four Winds, 1970. (6-7) R *
    Excellent pictorial coverage of 1911-1969.
Short paragraph annotations to explain both history and
photos. Complete statistical charts for each race and
drivers. A great reference browsing volume.

43 ERVIN, JANET HALLIDAY. *The Last Trip of the Juno;*
    illus. by Eric Von Schmidt. Chicago: Follett,
    1970. (3-6) F
    The tale of Juno, a steamboat on the Wabash
River in Indiana that was built and run by two brothers
who couldn't agree. The fatal demise of the steamboat
was caused by their arguments of speed vs. safety.
Thus, the legendary tale has been preserved for
posterity.

44 ERVIN, JANET HALLIDAY. *More Than Halfway There;*
    illus. by Ted Lewin. Chicago: Follett, 1970.
    (4-8) F
    A fictionalized story of Albert Long whose
chance meeting and day spent with Abraham Lincoln in
Gentryville, make it the most eventful day in his life.
Albert's dream of school and need for an education,
though discouraged by his father, is re-inforced in
several interesting incidents during his day with
Lincoln. Albert is reminded by Lincoln that "once a
person makes up his mind, he's more than half way there."

45 EWEN, DAVID. *The Story of Cole Porter*. New York:
Holt, Rinehart & Winston, 1965. (6-) B
A musical genius, Cole Porter was born to wealth
in Peru, Indiana. His childhood was spent in the rural
atmosphere, but dominated by his mother's love of music
and theater. His ultimate success as a song writer is
history as we recognize musical comedies, Broadway hits,
and Hollywood movies for which Cole wrote the brilliant
music. An inspirational biography for the music lover.
Appendixes: Porter's stage productions, greatest songs,
and selected recordings. Index.

46 FISHER, AILEEN. *My Cousin Abe;* illus. by Leonard
Vosburgh. New York: Nelson, 1962. o.p.
(6-) B
A folksy, fictionalized biography of Abraham
Lincoln told in a "you were there" format. Conversation, Hoosier speech and colloquialisms paint a vivid,
intimate picture of young Abe—his pioneer Indiana home
and surroundings, his family and their influence on his
life. Dennis Friend Hanks, Abe's cousin and close boyhood friend (though ten years his senior) recounted by
interview and letter his vivid recollections of their,
and particularly Abe's, boyhood. Part II is "Indiana."
Bibliography.

47 FITZPATRICK, BEATRICE B. *Indiana Through the Years;*
illus. by John C. Bigham. Indianapolis: E. C.
Seale, A Jonathan Press Book, 1962. (4-8)
Short vignettes acquaint the reader with Indiana
history and reveal how very interesting is the Hoosier
heritage. This is the story of Indiana—yesterday and
today.

48 FRAZIER, CARL and FRAZIER, ROSALIE. *The Lincoln
Country in Pictures;* illus. New York: Hastings
House, 1963. (2-8) P * #
Lincoln's birth, life and heritage is photograph-
ically presented to help us relate to the environment
in which Lincoln spent most of his formative years. It
was this heritage that helped Lincoln acquire the compassion, courage and understanding that fostered his
great humanitarism. A brief chronology is included.

— FRAZIER, ROSALIE. *The Lincoln Country in Pictures.*
See IN 48

49 FRICK, C. H. *Tourney Team.* New York: Harcourt,
Brace, Jovanovich, 1954. (6-8) F
The locale is Indiana—the basketball state—
written by a Hoosier to help instill fair play and
respect for the other fellow, as well as skill in a game.
Rocky Ryan learns the meaning of the team's philosophy
the hard way. A story of integrated teams and equality
to all.

50 FRIERMOOD, ELISABETH HAMILTON. *Focus the Bright
Land.* Garden City, N.Y.: Doubleday, 1967.
(6-8) F
In reliving the "summer photography pilgrimage"
on which Victoria Bodkin accompanied her brother in
their horse-drawn studio, we see the Indiana corn fields,
and the rural and city life of the 1880's. While Vicky
plies her trade as a photographer, she captures unfor-
gettable images of this rich mid-western setting—people
and locale. Charming story of a spunky only sister
determined to "be something" when girls were supposed
to only do housework and sewing.

51 FRIERMOOD, ELISABETH HAMILTON. *Hoosier Heritage;*
illus. by Robert Hallock. Garden City, N.Y.:
Doubleday, 1954. o.p. (7-) F
The Jonathan Edwards' family story of rural life
in Indiana in the late 1800's. Julia, middle daughter
showed courage and spunk to lead her life in great
independence for those times. A love story—locale
near Wabash, Indiana.

52 FRIERMOOD, ELISABETH HAMILTON. *The Watch Knows the
Secret;* illus. by Grace Paull. Garden City,
N.Y.: Doubleday, 1951. o.p. (6-8) F *
Henrietta Hale, eldest daughter of a teacher
turned farmer to support his family, has a deep love
for the aesthetic qualities of the Wabash River. For
two generations the mystery of her great grandfather's
murder and hidden "wheat" money has prompted search of

the river's banks. "The Wabash knows the secret" is the clue left behind by great grandfather William's day books. The events of Henrietta's life at home, school, church, and by the river weave an interesting tale and lead up to the solving of the mystery. Excellent philosophy of living and treatment of fellowmen are subtly revealed.

53 FRIERMOOD, ELISABETH HAMILTON. *The Wild Donahues.* Garden City, N.Y.: Doubleday, 1963. o.p. (5-8) F
Sycamore Park, northern Indiana, is the setting for an exciting story of suspense, love and intrigue. The "underground railway system of pre-Civil War days" and "money making the law" help relive history in a vivid, dramatic way. Meg Donahue experiences the excitement of life in Indiana in the late 1850's.

54 GODFROY, CHIEF CLARENCE. *Miami Indian Stories;* comp. & ed. by Martha Una McClurg. Winona Lake, Ind.: Light & Life, 1961. (6-8)
Central northern Indiana is rich in Miami Indian lore. The interesting stories, traditions, and legends of these Indians are preserved for us in this writing of places, events, peoples and animals of Indiana. An appendix of Indian names is included.

55 GREEN, MADGE MILLER. *Through the Years in Indiana;* illus. Oklahoma City, Okla.: Harlow, 1954. o.p. (4-6) R
This book was written to be used as a text in Indiana schools at the intermediate level. Carefully chosen vocabulary, many illustrations, maps and frequent paragraph headings aid the reader. Activity questions appear at the end of each chapter.

56 HADLEY, ALDEN H. *Birds of Indiana; Permanent Resident;* illus. Indianapolis: Indiana Department of Conservation, Divison of State Parks, 1959. o.p. (4-) F
Forty-eight birds described here in prose and picture are found in some part of Indiana at all

74

seasons of the year. Illustrations taken from the late
Major Allen Brook's true-life color paintings.

57 HALLIDAY, WILLIAM R. *Depths of the Earth: Caves
and Cavers of the United States;* illus. Rev. ed.
New York: Harper & Row, 1976. (6-) R
This revised volume is an excellent in-depth
account of the adventures and history of American caves.
Chapter 12, "The Story of Indiana Caves," is sure to
appeal to those delving in Hoosier geology and spele-
ology. Photographs add interest and information. Index.

58 HAMILTON, DOROTHY. *Anita's Choice;* illus. by Ivan
Moon. Scottdale, Pa.: Herald, 1971. Paper.
(5-8) F
A sensitive poignant story of Mexican-Americans
in the migrant camp of Springvale, Indiana (near New-
castle). Anita's father has a year round job and she
feels a part of and happy to be in Indiana. Mrs. Her-
nandez, however, laments her family in Texas, making
Anita feel torn. The school and friends help to bridge
the cultural gap by helping children and adults feel
needed and wanted—not like rubber balls bouncing
between two worlds.

59 HAVIGHURST, WALTER. *The Heartland: Ohio, Indiana,
Illinois;* illus. by Grattan Condon. New York:
Harper & Row, 1962. (6-) R * #
The history and life pulse of America's heartland—including Indiana—is revealed in a scholarly
blending of history, people, and times. Included are
Indiana novelists who around the turn of the century
enjoyed popular success as no other single state. The
definitive table of contents and index make it useful
for young history buffs and teachers.

60 HAYS, WILMA PITCHFORD. *Abe Lincoln's Birthday;*
illus. by Peter Burchard. New York: Coward-
McCann, 1961. (3-6) F
Early pioneer story of Abe Lincoln's life in
southern Indiana, confined to a short period of time
around Abe's twelfth birthday. Reveals his tasks and
ambitions.

61 HIGDON, HAL. *Thirty Days in May: The Indy 500;*
    illus. with photographs. New York: Putnam,
    1971. (6-8)
       This is the exciting story of the 1970 race run
on the Indianapolis Motor Speedway multimillion dollar
track. All eyes in the racing world are on the Indy
500 during the 30 days of May. Here drivers and mechan-
ics and owners live for the time trials, mechanical
problems and the race itself. Each year repeats itself.

62 HUBBARD, FRANK MC KINNEY (KIN). *Abe Martin's Back
    Country Sayings;* illus. Indianapolis: Abe
    Martin, (n.d.) o.p. (6-8) F
       A book of backwoods sayings of "A land of a
comical mixture of hoss-sense and no sense at all,"
compiled, revised and edited by the author from his
writings for the *Indianapolis News.* (For heritage.)

63 HUFFARD, GRACE THOMPSON. *When Rebels Rode;* illus.
    by Reisie Lonette. Indianapolis: Bobbs-Merrill,
    1963. (4-8) F
       The Civil War times brought changes to farm
life in southern Indiana. The entire family's involve-
ment in war and intrigue are interesting reading.
Rebels, including Morgan's Raiders, add excitement to
this saga.

64 HUNT, MABEL LEIGH. *Better Known as Johnny Apple-
    seed;* illus. by James Daugherty. Philadelphia:
    Lippincott, 1950. (6-) B #
       The legends and true life of Johnny Appleseed,
including his Indiana wanderings, written for older
youth.

65 HUNT, MABEL LEIGH. *The Boy Who Had No Birthday;*
    illus. by Cameron Wright. New York: Stokes,
    1935. o.p. (6-8) F
       A heart-warming story of David, an orphan boy
who grew up along the Tollroad near Marbury, Indiana,
in the 1880's. He aspired to be a doctor, and gained
a family and a birthday when he became a foster son to
Doctor Carlisle.

66 HUNT, MABEL LEIGH. *Cupola House;* illus. by Nora S.
      Unwin. Philadelphia: Lippincott, 1961. o.p.
      (6-8) F #
      The heart-warming story of a closely knit family
based on real happenings during the youth of our author
in Greencastle and Plainfield, Indiana. The doctor
moves his family to a college town for better education.
Their new home, near-tragic events and family growth
make a rich, humorous story of family devotion.

67 HUNT, MABEL LEIGH. *Little Girl with Seven Names;*
      illus. by Grace Paull. Philadelphia: Lippincott,
      1936. (3-5) F
      Melissa-Louisa was happy to start with two of
her seven names for her new twin sisters. Those seven
names were fun, but also a problem at school. Quaker
girl of Indiana.

68 HUNT, MABEL LEIGH. *Lucinda, A Little Girl of 1860;*
      illus. by Cameron Wright. New York: Stokes,
      1934. o.p. (5-7) F
      Pioneer Quaker life depicted through Lucinda's
activities on the family farm near New Bethel, Indiana.
Her life is full and exciting. On one visit to Indianapolis she meets Mr. Merrill, the publisher. Her kindness in tending a grave is rewarded by a gift which
enables her to get a higher education.

69 HUNT, MABEL LEIGH. *Matilda's Buttons;* illus. by
      Elinore Blaisdall. New York: Lippincott, 1948.
      o.p. (4-6) F
      Matilda Foster was so generous that her family
thought she would surely become a missionary. She decided to find another life's mission because she felt
she couldn't give up her pretty clothes. However,
Matilda's urge and love to give "presents" gets her
into many merry escapades, narrow escapes, and brings
her a foster sister. The story is laid in Indianapolis
at the turn of the century.

70 HUNT, MABEL LEIGH. *Susan, Beware!;* illus. by
　　Mildred Boyle. New York: Stokes, 1937. o.p.
　　(5-8) F
　　Susan, a tomboy, has many an adventure with her
brother and boy cousins. Yet after a visit to New
Orleans, she was willing to grow up and become a lady.
The locale is Indianapolis in the 1870's, and Susan
is in part a real descendant of Samuel Merrill, publisher.

71 ICENHOWER, JOSEPH B. *Tecumseh and the Indian Con-
　　federation: The Indian Nations East of the
　　Mississippi Are Defeated;* illus. New York:
　　Watts, 1975. (6-) #
　　The history of Indiana is part of the history
of the old Northwest Territory. Tecumseh, a chief of
the Shawnee tribe, struggled to unite the tribes east
of the Mississippi into a strong confederation. The
author traces the events leading up to the defeat of
Tecumseh and his forces in their bid for an Indian
nation in the early 1800's. The Wabash River territory,
Vincennes and Tippecanoe all played a dramatic role in
this struggle.

72 JACKSON, ROBERT B. *Championship Trail: The Story
　　of Indianapolis Racing;* illus. with photos.
　　New York: Walck, 1970. (3-8)
　　The story of the highly competitive 500 mile
race—before, during and after May 30th. The competition of men, cars, and equipment is vividly portrayed
to give the layman a better understanding of automobile
racing as a sport and profession. "Championship trail"
is a series of races (of which the "500" is one) held
to determine a national driving champion.

73 JACOBS, HARVEY. *We Came Rejoicing: A Personal
　　Memoir of the Years of Peace.* Chicago: Rand
　　McNally, 1967. o.p. (4-8)
　　Indiana local color is recaptured through the
spirit of that vanished era of the years between the
two World Wars on the rural farm lands of Indiana. The
time of sugaring, one room schoolhouse, the huckster,

threshing hay, "crystal sets," "Saturday Night," and more. The nostalgia of times vanished is revealed to become history to our modern generation. A glimpse into this more recent past is as important as the Indian days. Useful as reference or read-aloud for local history.

74 JAGENDORF, MORITZ A. *Sand in the Bag and Other Stories of Ohio, Indiana and Illinois;* illus. by John Moment. New York: Vanguard, 1952. (6-) F #
A collection of folk stories of Ohio, Illinois and Indiana. Colorful legends and enduring tales of the great Midwest.

75 JUDSON, CLARA INGRAM. *Bruce Carries the Flag: They Came from Scotland.* New York: Follett, 1957. o.p. (6-8) F
Bruce MacGregor came with his family from Scotland to join their pioneer relatives in Indianapolis, Indiana. Because the relatives have moved on, many exciting events occur to the entire family and especially Bruce, including mystery, daring and intrigue.

— KIRK, RICHARD. *Living Indiana History.* See IN 29

76 KOHLER, JULILLY H. *Harmony Ahead;* illus. by Peter Burchard. New York: Aladdin, 1952. o.p. (6-8) F
The account of the exciting voyage of the famous Boatload of Knowledge down the Ohio River to the newly planned City of New Harmony, Indiana. As the story unfolds, Alan Ward, a rebellious problem child, changes to an eager and idealistic student under the influence of these future leaders.

77 LACEY, JOY MUCHMORE. *Living in Indiana;* illus. by George Jo Mess. Chicago: Wheeler, 1946. o.p. (4-6) R
This history of Indiana is on the intermediate level. Two divisions are studied: Living in Indiana Long Ago and Living in Indiana Today. An extensive

guide for study is included as well as study questions for each chapter.

78 LAMB, E. WENDELL and SHULTZ, LAWRENCE W. *Indian Lore*. Winona Lake, Ind.: Light and Life Press, 1964. (4-8) R *
A readable reference source on Indiana Indian customs, food, homes and language. The great contributions of Indians—namely Miami and Potawatomi—are made available by stories, poetry, songs, sign language, pictures and maps drawn from various sources. The story of Frances Slocum is recounted. An excellent Indian vocabulary (alphabetical) with both picture and word explanation. Miami Indian word list, glossary of Indian names, and detailed index make this an outstanding resource.

79 LAUTER, FLORA. *Indiana Artists (Active) 1940;* illus. Spencer, Ind.: Guard, 1941. o.p. (4-) P B
A valuable collection in prose and plates to provide general information and understanding of Indiana art—contemporary artists—1940.

80 LEARY, EDWARD A., ed. *Indiana Almanac and Fact Book, 1977-78.* Indianapolis: Sycamore Press, 1977. (6-) R
A special Indiana ready-reference book in the almanac format. Historical, political and statistical information is given pertinent to the Hoosier state and to the special interests of Hoosiers. (Re-introduced after ten years.)

81 LEARY, EDWARD A. *The Nineteenth State - Indiana.* Indianapolis: Ed Leary, 1966. (6-8) R
Sesquicentennial (1816-1966) report and concise history of the state of Indiana includes Indiana's statehood, wilderness, times of war and peace, and industrialization. Discusses modern Hoosier land from railroads, to Indy 500, to Burns Harbor. The appendix—statistical, historical, and factual—should be very beneficial to the student.

82 LE SUER, MERIDEL. *Little Brother of the Wilderness: The Story Johnny Appleseed;* illus. by Betty Alden. New York: Knopf, 1960. (2-7) B
    The story of Johnny Appleseed carrying apple seeds to Indiana and the middle western states to help pioneer Americans have a better life.

83 LEWIS, DOROTHY F. *The Indiana Story;* illus. by George Jo Mess. Chicago: Wheeler, 1951. o.p. (7-8) R
    This is designed as a text book to be used in Indiana schools in the junior high to supplement and expand the reading and understanding of Indiana's role as a state. Exercises for study, map work and outside reading are given at the close of each chapter.

84 LIBBY, BILL. *Parnelli, A Story of Auto Racing.* New York: Dutton, 1969. (6-) B
    A vivid, realistic biography of Parnelli Jones from boyhood through his moving, grinding career as a race driver. We feel Parnelli's hard driving single ambition—to be a winner. A moving account of car racing with Parnelli Jones the key personality. An appendix of Jones' record covering many races as well as the 500 mile.

85 LOCKRIDGE, ROSS F. *George Rogers Clark: Pioneer Hero of the Old Northwest;* illus. New York: World Book, 1927. o.p. (6-) B
    A biography of Clark told in authentic and dramatic style to honor him as pioneer, soldier, and patriot. During the last years of the revolution, he won for the nation the Old Northwest Territory, as is recounted in his daring deeds and dauntless heroism.

86 LOCKRIDGE, ROSS F. *The Story of Indiana;* illus. Oklahoma City, Okla.: Harlow, 1951. o.p. (7-) R
    This book was written for use as a text on the junior high school level in Indiana schools. The book tries to make the reading of history interesting and enjoyable, showing the important part Indiana played in

pioneer development of our country. It also acquaints children with men of valor, and helps them grow in Hoosier consciousness. Illus., maps, study questions.

87 LONG, LAURA. *Hannah Courageous;* illus. by Edward Caswell. New York: Longmans, Green, 1939. o.p. (6-8) F

Hannah Nicholson, a Quaker girl living in southern Indiana during Civil War times, goes to Washington to pursue study in her talent of art.

88 LONG, LAURA. *Without Valour;* illus. by Edward Caswell. New York: Longmans, Green, 1940. o.p. (7-8) F

The reader sees Richard Clayton, son of a mill owner, as he matures amid the activities before the Civil War reaches southern Indiana. There is a glimpse of Morgan's Raiders, Abraham Lincoln, pro and con of slavery among those who loved their country—during the conflict and also the aftermath of peace.

89 LUDWIG, CHARLES. *Levi Coffin and the Underground Railroad.* Scottdale, Pa.: Herald Press, 1975. (7-12) F

Levi Coffin was a Quaker whose family and life were devoted to improving the lot of the slave. He was known as the "President" of the Underground Railway. A span in our history—awesome, terrible and interesting— that is fascinating reading for both young and old. Among the experiences of Levi Coffin is his assistance to Eliza Harris, who became the leading character in *Uncle Tom's Cabin*. Fountain City, Indiana is the main locale of these experiences.

90 MC CAGUE, JAMES. *Flatboat Days on Frontier Rivers;* illus. by Victor Mays. Champaign, Ill.: Garrard, 1968. (4-8) #

Indiana farmers and frontiersmen built flatboats and took loads of cargo down the Wabash and Ohio Rivers— to the Mississippi and on to New Orelans. Though clumsy crafts to navigate through dangerous territory, they

were a vital part of river transportation and represented one facet of pioneer living.

— MC CALL, EDITH S. *Where the Ohio Flows.* See IN 31

91 MC ELFRESH, ADELINE. *Summer Change;* illus. by
Charles Greer. Indianapolis: Bobbs-Merrill,
1960. (7-8) F
Cathy Earl plans to "act" as if she is enjoying
her summer in a small town in Indiana, but finds real
enjoyment and needs no longer to act. Cathy's problems
of decisions about the future are typically teenage and
universal.

92 MC LAUGHLIN, ROBERT. *The Heartland: Illinois,
Indiana, Michigan, Ohio, Wisconsin.* New York:
Time-Life, 1967. (4-8) * #
A comprehensive view of the Heartland—a paradox—
from agricultural to urban regions; from the ice age to
present industrial greatness. Excellent illustrations—
many in color. The appendix provides reference for
tours, museums, local festivals and events, wildlife,
and statistical information. Bibliography and index.
Time-Life *Library of America.*

93 MAJOR, CHARLES. *The Bears of Blue River;* illus. by
A. B. Frost and Others. New York: Macmillan,
1963. (3-6) F
The setting is near Brookville, Indiana, on the
Whitewater River in the 1820's. Balser, a boy of fif-
teen, learns to hunt, fish and trap with his father.
The highlights of the story are Balser's escapades with
bears: shooting, running from, saving a little girl
friend and his brother in numerous exciting adventures.
Children's Classics series.

94 MALLETT, ANN. *A Child's History of Indianapolis;*
illus. by Wilma Brown. Indianapolis: Public
Schools, 1971. (3-8) *
This sesquicentennial edition of the history of
the capital of Indiana was written for study of third
and fourth graders. A chronological date list of

Indianapolis history and a supplement of interesting
facts add to the intrinsic value of this volume. Every
Hoosier (former or present) will gain knowledge and
pleasure from the reading and study of this definitive
yet easy history.

95 MANNING, LAWRENCE. *Indiana Festivals;* text by
　　 Morri Schieschel-Manning; photographs by Lawrence
　　 Manning. Bloomington, Ind.: Indiana University
　　 Press, 1976. (4-8) P *
　　 This is a pictorial presentation of description
and travel of Indiana festivals. The story is in pictures of small town festivals staged for the enjoyment
of others and for a good cause. Shows how smallness—
in a community celebration—can be a precious way of
life.

96 MASON, MIRIAM E. *A House for Ten;* illus. by Kate
　　 Seredy. Boston: Ginn, 1949. o.p. (4-6) F
　　 Another pioneer family story set at Smiling Hill
Farm on the Whitewater River in Indiana. The reader
sees large family cooperation, early one room school,
building of corduroy roads, and neighborly help and
friendliness.

97 MASON, MIRIAM E. *Little Jonathan;* illus. by George
　　 and Doris Hauman. New York: Macmillan, 1944.
　　 (2-4) F
　　 Jonathan Brown, a pioneer boy, lives in a big
house on the shores of the Ohio River in Indiana. He
regrets that he is the youngest, but children will enjoy his adventures as he tries to help out to prove
himself worthy.

98 MASON, MIRIAM E. *Sara and the Winter Gift;* illus.
　　 by Paul Frame. New York: Macmillan, 1968.
　　 (3-6) F
　　 A heart-warming story of Sara and her pet raccoon told in Indiana pioneer and nature setting. Everyday living reveals a girl's life in early Indiana—
tasks, pets, visitors and family life.

99 MASON, MIRIAM E. *Smiling Hill Farm*; illus. by Kate
Seredy. New York: Ginn, 1937. o.p. (3-6) F
An excellent picture of pioneer life—migration
to Indiana, log cabin and farming through successive
generations showing change and improvement in mode of
living, all with neighborly cooperation.

100 MASON, MIRIAM E. *Susannah, the Pioneer Cow*; illus.
by Maud and Miska Petersham. New York: Macmillan, 1941. (K-3) F
Indiana is used as the setting for a pioneer
story with Susannah, a cow, as the main character.

101 MIERS, EARL SCHENCK. *That Lincoln Boy*; illus. by
Kurt Werth. New York: World, 1968. (3-6) B *
An interesting account of Lincoln by the American author who is a leading Lincoln scholar. Abe's
schooling, his mother's influence and death, his sister's death, and his struggle to earn a living provide
little-known insights and details. Readers see Abe's
humor, his "fightings," his hatred of the idea of slavery, and how others respected him for his ideas and
integrity all his life.

102 MILLER, HELEN MARKLEY. *George Rogers Clark: Frontier Fighter*; illus. by Albert Orbaan. New York:
Putnam, 1968. (3-6) B #
George Rogers Clark, as an officer in the Virginia militia, led a handful of men on a frontier expedition to eventually capture the British outposts and
claim the land for the U.S. Clark accomplished the impossible by his courage, prowess, and ability to use
all the tricks of a frontier fighter. This biography
reveals the formidable fighter and statesman as he led
his men westward, capturing Kaskaskia and Vincennes,
and then his later years. An *American Pioneer Biography*.

103 MITCHELL, MINNIE BELLE. *Hoosier Boy: James Whitcomb Riley*; illus. by Syd Browne. Indianapolis:
Bobbs-Merrill, 1942. (4-6) B
James Whitcomb Riley began writing poetry at a
very early age about his home, family and environment.

His creativity and imaginative capabilities are revealed by his boyhood activities and escapades. Riley lived in the small town of Greenfield, Indiana, on the National Turnpike about 20 miles east of Indianapolis. This biography begins with his birth and goes through his family experiences during the Civil War and his father's homecoming. *Childhood of Americans* series.

104 NOBLE, IRIS. *Labor's Advocate: Eugene V. Debs.* New York: Julian Messner, 1966. (7-) B
A story of courage and compassion revealing Debs and the union organizer, political crusader and fighter for freedom of the individual and all working men. His life and work laid the basis for today's unions and our continuing efforts toward better working conditions for all. An inspiring story for today's youth. Index.

105 NOLAN, JEANNETTE COVERT. *George Rogers Clark: Soldier and Hero, November 10, 1752 - February 13, 1818;* illus. by Lee Ames. New York: Messner, 1954. (4-6) B #
Biography of George Rogers Clark beginning when he was a young man, 1772, continuing through his explorations and retirement. Exciting descriptions of Clark's real experiences and perilous dangers in the wilderness, and his wise, honest-yet-crafty handling of the Indians. A vivid account of his famous "March to Vincennes" in Indiana territory.

106 NOLAN, JEANNETTE COVERT. *Getting to Know the Ohio River;* illus. by Charles Sovek. New York: Coward, McCann & Geoghegan, 1973. (4-8) #
The Ohio River played an important role in the reaching and settling of its surrounding territory. Indiana, one of these heartland states, was and is a part of the Ohio River story. From Clark at Vincennes, to Morgan's Raiders, to Abraham Lincoln's boyhood in Indiana—the stories of the Ohio River and Indiana are bound together. A useful index is included.

107 NOLAN, JEANNETTE COVERT. *Hoosier City: The Story of Indianapolis;* illus. by George Jo Mess. New York: Messner, 1943. o.p. (6-) R
A detailed account of the plan, development and growth of the capital of Indiana, Indianapolis. Pioneer beginnings, growth and progress through World War II are recounted. *Cities of American Biography* series.

108 NOLAN, JEANNETTE COVERT. *Indiana;* illus. with photographs and maps. New York: Coward-McCann, 1969. (5-8) R *
The varied profile of Indiana—its outstanding citizens and noteworthy heritage—is written with vitality and authority. The crossroads of America, Indiana is primarily an agricultural state but has a large industrial sector of steel and other manufactured goods. A page "profile" includes general information, physical characteristics, climate, cities, waterways, products and government. An historical date line and important citizens listings plus an index make this volume a valuable reference tool. *States of the Nation* series.

109 NOLAN, JEANNETTE COVERT. *James Whitcomb Riley, Hoosier Poet;* illus. by Robert S. Robison. New York: Messner, 1941. o.p. (7-8) B *
Biography of James Whitcomb Riley written to endear him, his writings, and his personality to readers as in his lifetime he had affected people in person.

110 NORTH, STERLING. *Abe Lincoln: Log Cabin to White House;* illus. by Lee Ames. New York: Random, 1956. (4-8) B #
Biography of Lincoln recounting his boyhood on a farm in Indiana and his brief schooling there.

111 NORTH, STERLING. *Midnight and Jeremiah;* illus. by Kurt Wiese. Philadelphia: Winston, 1943. o.p. (4-6) F
Midnight, a black buck lamb, is raised by Jeremiah after being disowned by his mother. A rascal, Midnight's escapades go from butting in the General Store to winning first prize at the County Fair.

Midnight gets lost but returns to the town creche on Christmas eve. Indiana setting.

112 NORTH, STERLING. *So Dear to My Heart.* Garden City, N.Y.: Doubleday, 1947. o.p. (6-8) F
Jeremiah Tarleton, a ten-year-old orphan living with his grandmother, struggles with his love of his black lamb (a forbidden pet) and his loyalty to his grandmother. The flavor of Indiana hill country beliefs, superstitions, rural farm life and "dialect" converge to make this a story of courage, emotional depth and beauty. Indiana days of copper-toed boots and slat bonnets come alive in this nostalgic novel.

113 O'CONNOR, PATRICK. *Black Tiger at Indianapolis.* New York: Washburn, 1962. (5-8) F
An exciting story of a well-known road racer, famous for his success, who is challenged to compete at Indy 500. A colorful exposition of thrills on the gruelling, dangerous course at Indianapolis. Depicts the shift of technique, expertise in driving, mechanical details and human temperament required for Indy driving.

114 PEEK, DAVID T. *Indiana Adventure;* illus. by Jane Cooper. Indianapolis: Brand, 1962. (4-6) R
A text for Indiana schools written for intermediate grades—factual yet challenging. Well illustrated. Chapters also dealing with places, artists, writers, parks, memorials and the 500 Mile Race.

115 PEEK, DAVID T. *Once Upon a Time 150 Years Ago;* Berne, Ind.: Economy, 1966. (4-8) P
A large format pictorial reference bringing together Hoosier talent from stage, screen, radio, and television. Authors, tourist places of interest and highlights of Indiana's larger cities are noted with an informative essay.

116 PORTER, GENE STRATTON. *Freckles*; illus. by E. Stetson Crawford. New York: Grossett & Dunlap, 1904. o.p. (6-) F

Freckles, an orphan boy, gets a job in the Limberlost, a forest swamp in north central Indiana. By his sincere devotion to duty, he proves himself worthy to McLean, his boss and benefactor. Scientific nature pursuits add to his knowledge and self respect. A love story is woven into the intriguing and exciting narrative of life in days gone by.

117 PORTER, GENE STRATTON. *A Girl of the Limberlost*. New York: Grosset & Dunlap, 1909. o.p. (6-) F

The story of a young girl struggling to gain an education against the wishes of a disagreeable mother. She hunts, preserves and mounts moths in her Limberlost to sell to obtain money for her education. An inspiring story set in north central Indiana at the turn of the century.

118 PYLE, ERNIE. *Home Country*. New York: Sloane, 1947. o.p. (7-) R

Three chapters about Ernie Pyle's home life, background, philosophy of life, his parents: "Home in in Indiana," "Stopover at Dana," "Hoosiers." Also brings famous Indiana people to mind.

119 REED, EARL H. *The Silver Arrow and Other Indian Romances of the Dune Country*; illus. by author. Chicago: Reilly & Lee, 1926. o.p. (4-) F

Folk tales of the spirit and romance of the Indian life in the dune country along the shores of Lake Michigan in Indiana and the region immediately surrounding it.

120 RILEY, JAMES WHITCOMB. *The Book of Joyous Children*; illus. by J. W. Vawter. New York: Scribner, 1902. o.p. (3-8) *

Text and delightful illustrations of Riley's famous dialect poetry.

121 RILEY, JAMES WHITCOMB. *The Complete Poetical Works of James Whitcomb Riley.* New York: Grosset, 1916. o.p. (4-) *
Great poetry for all ages.

122 RILEY, JAMES WHITCOMB. *The Gobble-Uns'll Git You Ef You Don't Watch Out! James Whitcomb Riley's Little Orphant Annie;* illus. by Joel Schick. Philadelphia: Lippincott, 1975. (1-6)
A delightfully illustrated edition of an "old" monster tale—as told by Orphan Annie in Riley's classic children's poem. Illustrator's note on the author likens him to a pre-movie and TV entertainer. To be read aloud.

123 RILEY, JAMES WHITCOMB. *Joyful Poems for Children;* illus. by Charles Geer and Sally Tate. Indianapolis: Bobbs-Merrill, 1960. (3-8)
A selection of 95 of Riley's poems especially for children, with handsome illustrations. Fanciful and created to stimulate the imaginations of children, Riley's poems feature some dialect, some funny and some thought-provoking. To be read aloud as well as for individual reading.

124 RILEY, JAMES WHITCOMB. *Riley Child-Rhymes;* illus. by Will Vawter. Indianapolis: Bobbs-Merrill, 1920. o.p. (4-) *
A selected group of poems included in this volume—written especially for children.

125 RILEY, JAMES WHITCOMB. *While the Heart Beats Young;* illus. by Ethel Franklin Betts. Indianapolis: Bobbs-Merrill, 1887. o.p. (3-8) *
Favorite famous poems. Colorful illustrations.

—— ROGERS, JAMES. *Living Indiana History.* See IN 29

—— ROSENBERG, CLIFFORD. *War Paint and Wagon Wheels.* See IN 126

126 ROSENBERG, ETHEL; ROSENBERG, CLIFFORD and OTHERS.
War Paint and Wagon Wheels; illus. Indianapolis:
David Stewart, 1968. (4-8) *
Stories of Indians and pioneers told to whet the
reader's appetite for courage, bravery and knowledge of
early Indians and white men. Includes the Drummer Boy
of the Wabash, Frances Slocum, Ralph Hartsook, and
Lincoln. An excellent section describes how Indians
and pioneers worked and played, what their homes were
like and what they ate. Charts on Indian sign language,
trail signs, weapons, costumes, food and homes. Glossary and index.

127 ROSENUS, ALAN, ed. *Selected Writings of Joaquin
Miller;* drawings by Joaquin Miller. Eugene, Ore.:
Urion Press, 1976. (4-8)
Chapter II, "Life Among the Indians of Indiana"—
a chapter from Joaquin Miller's *Overland in a Covered
Wagon*—is included for the local color of an Indian
"trial" before a white man. Because Joaquin Miller, pen
name of Cincinnatus Hiner Miller, was born and lived
some childhood years in Indiana, he is considered a
Hoosier "son."

128 SANDBURG, CARL. *Abe Lincoln Grows Up,* reprinted
from *Abraham Lincoln: The Prairie Years;* illus.
by James Daugherty. New York: Harcourt, Brace,
1931. (4-8) B *
Lincoln's boyhood and youth in Kentucky and Indiana. Recounts his games, chores, and schooling until
age nineteen when he left home to make his way at New
Salem. Dramatic illustrations. Also available in
Harcourt, Brace, Jovanovich, Voyager Books, 1975. Paper.

129 SCHAAF, MARTHA E. *Lew Wallace: Boy Writer;* illus.
by Frank Nicholas. Indianapolis: Bobbs-Merrill,
1962. (3-6) B
A biography of Lew Wallace told in intimate detail for boys and girls. Beginning with Wallace's boyhood explorations along the Wabash River in Indiana to
his world famous responsibilities and noted writings,
including *Ben Hur*. *Childhood of Famous Americans*
series.

91

130 SCHRODT, PHILLIP. *George Rogers Clark: Frontier Revolutionary;* illus. by James Campbell. Bloomington, Ind.: Buffalo Wallow, 1976. (7-8) B

A relatively short, concise, yet complete biography of George Rogers Clark dealing with his early years, Kentucky life, Kaskaskia and Vincennes. His life after the Revolution and Clark's final days sum up the biography. Bibliography for further reading.

—— SCHULTZ, LAWRENCE W. *Indian Lore.* See IN 78

131 SELVIN, DAVID F. *Eugene Debs: Rebel, Labor Leader, Prophet.* New York: Lothrop, Lee & Shepard, 1966. (7-) B

As a young boy in Terre Haute, Indiana, Eugene V. Debs displayed tendencies which later surfaced in his great drive to help others. His early need to work to help his family led him to jobs as railroad car painter and fireman. Gene joined the Union—Brotherhood of Locomotive Firemen—to help them strive for better working conditions. This quest to help the people and our country to remedy the ills and injustices of the working man, brought dishonor, slander and even prison to Debs. He was labelled rebel, labor leader and prophet. Today, however, we reap benefits of his ground work. For mature readers.

132 SENTMAN, GEORGE ARMOR. *Drummer of Vincennes: A Story of the George Rogers Clark Expedition;* illus. by John Gretzer. Philadelphia: Winston, 1952. o.p. (5-7) B

The true story of the George Rogers Clark campaign to wrest control of the old Northwest Territory from first French-Indian and then British-Indian rule. Also, the little known story of the "Drummer of Vincennes" is told in this tale of heroic accomplishment against great odds: few men, little food, cold and icy waters, and Indians skilled in harrassing warfare.

133 SEVERN, BILL. *Toward One World: The Life of Wendell Willkie.* New York: Washburn, 1967.
(6-) B
Wendell Willkie, Indiana born and bred, made an outstanding contribution to United States philosophy and thinking. One World, Willkie's book and concept, served to focus the thinking of post-war goals on a community of nations. We relate to his small-town life boyhood, devoted parents (though individualistic beyond their times) and on to his defeat by F. D. Roosevelt for the Presidency. He was a successful businessman and a leader in world affairs, though not a politician.

134 SHAPIRO, IRWIN. *Tall Tales of America;* illus. by Al Schmidt. Poughkeepsie, N.Y.: Guild Press, 1958. o.p. (4-8) F
The story of Johnny Appleseed told as a folk tale—revealing his Indiana sojourn and death.

135 SHAW, THOMAS EDWARD. *Fifty Common Trees of Indiana;* illus. Lafayette, Ind.: State Department of Conservation and Purdue University, 1956. o.p. (4-) R
Description and illustrations of fifty important Indiana trees; for knowledge and enjoyment.

—— SHAW, THOMAS EDWARD. *Trees of Indiana.* See IN 33

136 SIEVERS, HARRY J. *Benjamin Harrison: Hoosier Warrior 1833-1865.* Chicago: Henry Regnery, 1952. (6-8) B R
A carefully researched biography which could serve as a reference tool for upper level elementary and junior high students. Table of contents and index render this a usable volume to research the accomplishments of a great warrior.

137 SNEDEKER, CAROLINE DALE. *The Beckoning Road;* illus. by Manning de V. Lee. Garden City, N.Y.: Doubleday, 1929. o.p. (7-8) F
The Tom Coffyns leave their home in Nantucket to join the New Society of Communal living founded by

Robert Owen at New Harmony, Indiana. Dencey, the eldest
daughter of the Quaker family, reveals to the reader
the activities, surprises and disappointments of their
trip west, their New Harmony home, and the failure of
the project. Dencey's seafaring lover returns after
being thought dead and adds intrigue and interest.

138 SPERRY, PORTIA HOWE and DONALDSON, LOIS. *Abigail;*
   illus. by Zabeth Selover. Chicago: Whitman,
   1938. (4-8) F
   The locale is Brown County in southern Indiana.
Abigail, Susan's new doll, is her companion as the family moves to Indiana and settles near Nashville in
southern Indiana. The events of preparing for the trip,
the journey itself and through the housewarming party
unfold in easy comfortable reading.

139 STEVENSON, AUGUSTA. *Tecumseh: Shawnee Boy;* illus.
   by Clotilde Embree Funk. Indianapolis: Bobbs-
   Merrill, 1955. (4-6) B #
   A biography of the boyhood details of Tecumseh's
life in the Shawnee tribe on the Little Miami River in
Indiana. His youthful training and prowess were a fore-
cast of his later ability as a great orator and chief.
Tecumseh was a boy and man of honor, truth and character. *Childhood of Famous Americans* series.

140 SWAYNE, SAMUEL F. and SWAYNE, ZOA. *Great-Grandfather in the Honey Tree;* illus. by the authors.
   New York: Viking, 1949. (2-6) F
   A delightful folk tale of a young pioneer couple
who settles in Indiana along the Wabash River. Samuel's
fabulous hunting trip will entrance the reader or young
listener.

—— SWAYNE, ZOA. *Great-Grandfather in the Honey Tree.*
   See IN 140

94

141 SWEENEY, MARGARET. *Fact, Fiction and Folklore of Southern Indiana.* New York: Vantage, 1967.
(6-) R
The author states that this is a blend of history and literature with the folklore of people whose names, tales and songs tell the story of Southern Indiana. People, places and events are revealed in poetry, song and prose. The main topics are: Old Vincennes, George Rogers Clark, Clarksville, Clark County, Jeffersonville, Shipbuilding (Jeffersonville), The Scribners Found New Albany, Washington County—County Seat Salem. Bibliography and comprehensive index.

142 TEALE, EDWIN WAY. *Dune Boy: The Early Years of a Naturalist;* illus. by Edward Shenton. Rev. ed. New York: Dodd, Mead, 1966. (6-) B *
Autobiography of Edwin Way Teale's childhood years. Summers on the Indiana Dune farm of his Way grandparents influenced him as a man and his life's profession.

143 THOMAS, LOWELL. *The Hero of Vincennes: The Story of George Rogers Clark;* illus. by F. C. Yohn. New York: Houghton Mifflin, 1929. o.p. (6-8) B
George Rogers Clark's biography from early childhood on his father's Virginia plantation to his daring feats as an explorer and Indian fighter. The life of the hero of Vincennes (Indiana Territory) is traced, revealing his prowess in dealing with the Indians as well as British and French, his disappointment in later life and final tribute to him by his countrymen.

144 THOMPSON, MAURICE. *Alice of Old Vincennes;* illus. by F. C. Yohn. Indianapolis: Bowen-Merrill, 1900. o.p. (6-) F
Alice, an orphan, grows up in old French Vincennes, Indiana, on the Wabash, as foster daughter to M. Roussillon. She is well-read though primitive in many ways. Alice's courage and forthrightness bring much trouble during the English occupartion of Vincennes, but when Gen. Clark recaptures the Fort—all is well

again. Alice's love affair with an army officer brings
suspense and a happy ending.

145 THOMPSON, MAURICE. *Stories of Indiana;* illus. New
York: American Book, 1898. o.p. (6-) *
Stories of actual life in Indiana portraying
correct traits and conditions to form an interesting
and instructive series of life sketches—early inhabitants, explorers, pioneers, New Harmony, and writers.

146 THRASHER, CRYSTAL. *The Dark Didn't Catch Me.* New
York: Atheneum, 1975. (6-8) F
Southern Indiana hill country is the new home of
a family who moved there to find work—hoping to "beat"
the Depression. Family troubles, endless back-breaking
work, illness and suicide add trauma to the lives of
young children. One daughter, Seely, is able to rise
above the everyday despair to hope and work for a better life. "The Dark Didn't Catch" her has several mean-
ings. Courage, humor and pathos are combined to form a
compelling story. *A McElderry Book.*

147 TOBIN, JACK. *John Wooden: They Call Me Coach.*
Waco, Tex.: Word Books, 1972. (7-) B
An inspirational biography of John Wooden, successful basketball coach at Purdue University and UCLA,
who built men as well as teams. Johnny's childhood
experiences occurred on farms and in Martinsville, Indiana. He was a small town boy whose work patterns and
morals were guided by his father. "The Pyramid of Success" created by Wooden is the frontis-piece and back
end page.

148 TUNIS, JOHN R. *Yea! Wildcats!* New York: Harcourt, Brace, 1944. (6-8) F
An Indiana small town basketball story of
thrills, disappointments and team spirit. Ingredients
of prejudice, adult interference and a sincere coach
are woven into an intriguing tale.

149 VAN RIPER, GUERNSEY, JR. *Knute Rockne, Young Athlete;* illus. by Paul Laune. Indianapolis: Bobbs-Merrill, 1959. (3-5) B
   Biography of Knute beginning with his swimming and skiing prowess in Norway. His family's move to the U.S. brought a change in sports for the boy, but his ability increased as he grew—especially in football. *Childhood of Famous Americans* series.

150 VOIGHT, VIRGINIA FRANCES. *A Book for Abe: A Lincoln Birthday Story;* illus. by Jacqueline Tomes. Englewood Cliffs, N.J.: Prentice-Hall, 1963. (3-6) F
   Abe's friends surprised him with a party and gifts because he always did kind things for them. Locale: near Pigeon Creek in southern Indiana.

151 WIBBERLEY, LEONARD. *Red Pawns.* New York: Farrar, Straus & Giroux, 1973. (6-) F
   An exciting adventure which illuminates a crucial period in American history—namely events leading up to the battle between General Harrison's militia and Tecumseh's forces. Manly Treegate and his young brother, Peter, travel to the frontier and become a part of the battle with the "red pawns"—thought to be the decisive factor in the struggle that was the War of 1812. Enough action and suspense in this historical fiction book to satisfy the most demanding reader.

152 WILKIE, KATHERINE E. *George Rogers Clark: Boy of the Old Northwest;* illus. by Paul Laune. Indianapolis: Bobbs-Merrill, 1958. (4-6) B
   George Rogers Clark's early childhood is told in exciting adventure episodes, showing how his boyhood training prepared him for his daring exploits and conquests of the Old Northwest. Clark's boldness and decisive capture of Vincennes won for the new nation this breat Middlewest.

153 WILLIS, PRISCILLA D. *Jory and the Buckskin Jumper;*
    illus. by Lorence Bjorklund. New York: St.
    Martin's, 1960. o.p. (6-8) F
    An Indiana farm is the scene for this fictional
depiction of farm life, including 4-H Club and how it
actually works. Pete was Jory Pinder's horse, a born
jumper, who with training finally made the Olympic
team—an exciting tale. Jory's problems and adjust-
ments have a universal appeal.

154 WILSON, ELLEN. *Ernie Pyle: Boy from Back Home;*
    illus. by Paul Laune. Indianapolis: Bobbs-
    Merrill, 1955. (3-6) B
    Human interest and local color biography of
Ernie Pyle's youth as he grew up in a small Indiana
town, to his high school graduation and the start of
his college career at Indiana University in Bloomington,
Indiana. Ernie's fame came as a journalist on the
battlefront in World War II. *Childhood of Famous Americans* series.

155 WILSON, WILLIAM E. *The Wabash;* illus. by John
    De Martelly. New York: Farrar & Rinehart, 1940.
    o.p. (7-) *
    A look at the Wabash River from its beginning;
the territory surrounding Indiana—early settlers,
river traffic, and life through the years around and
near the river. *The Rivers of America* series.

156 WINGER, OTHO. *The Lost Sister Among the Miamis;*
    illus. Elgin, Ill.: Elgin Press, 1936. o.p.
    (6-) B
    Frances Slocum was stolen by the Indians as a
young child. She spent her life as an Indian; later
married a Miami chief and lived in Indiana with the
Miamis. Though she had been sought by her family, no
trace had ever been found until a letter disclosed her
whereabouts. Reunited with her two brothers and a sister, Frances chose to remain with her Indian family.
Now elderly, she told her own life story to her nephew.

157 WOOD, FRANCES E. *Lakes, Hills and Prairies: The Middlewestern States;* illus. by Tom Dunnington. Chicago: Children's Press, 1962. (4-8) #

The Lakes states' background geology, explorers and early settlers, as well as modern life with its industry and natural resources, are explained for young people. A short chapter specifically discusses each state (Indiana, pp. 70-73), pinpointing important history and famous citizens. A detailed table of contents and glossary are helpful tools, but, unfortunately, no index is included. *Enchantment of America* series.

158 YATES, BROCK W. *The Indianapolis 500: The Story of the Motor Speedway;* illus. Rev. ed. New York: Harper, 1961. (6-8) P

An engrossing account of the founding and development of the Indianapolis Motor Speedway—home of the 500 mile auto race. Factual narration concerning the actual races, cars and drivers from the first race in 1911 to 1955.

159 YOUNG, STANLEY. *Tippecanoe and Tyler, Too!* illus. by Warren Chappell. New York: Random 1957. o.p. (4-6) B

The stirring story of William Henry Harrison from his childhood through his Indiana fighter adventures, Governor of Indiana and ninth president of the U.S. Harrison led the famous Tippecanoe battle that took place on that river in Indiana.

MICHIGAN

compiled by DIANE M. GUNN

The state which boasts in its motto, "If you seek a pleasant peninsula, look about you," is unique in its distinguishable shape and its possession of two separate land forms. Michigan has over 3,000 miles of shoreline, which is longer than any other inland state, and four of the Great Lakes surround it: Lakes Erie, Huron, Superior, and Michigan. The name Michigan comes from the Chippewa word, *Michigama*, meaning great or large lake.

One of the nation's leading manufacturing states, Michigan surpasses in the production of automobiles, steel, and food processing. The minerals, iron ore, copper and salt, are an important natural resource. Farming covers nearly forty percent of the state's land, with corn the leading crop, followed by wheat. More dry beans are grown than in any other state. Fruit growing is prevalent along the Lake Michigan shoreline, and that area leads nationally in the production of cherries. Tourism is a natural: lakes for fishing, boating and resorts; forests and wooded areas for hunters and campers; climate and terrain for summer and winter sports; and natural grandeur for sight-seeing. Ten million tourists visit Michigan each year.

Michigan is rich in history. Indians of Algonquian stock inhabited the area, probably for as long as a century before white settlers arrived. Algonquian tribes included: Chippewa (or Ojibwa), Ottawa, Potawatomi, Menominee, Miami, and Sauk. The Wyandot of the Iroquoian tribe settled near Detroit. French explorers traveled the Great Lakes: Brulé, Nicolet, Minard, Pere Marquette—founder of the first permanent settlement at Sault Ste. Marie—Joliet, La Salle, and Cadillac—founder of Fort Pontchartrain (Detroit). Disputes over control of the regions by French, British and Indians caused many altercations. The first of the anthropologists, Henry Rowe Schoolcraft, studied and recorded the Indian culture. By 1787, Michigan became part of the Northwest Territory; 1805 saw Michigan a Territory; and in 1837 Michigan became the twenty-sixth state of the United States.

Technology was instrumental in the further development of Michigan. The Soo Canal, completed in 1855, allowed for the shipping of mine output to industrial centers. Sawmills permitted the extensive lumbering throughout the state which some refer to as the rape of Michigan forests. Inventors, such as Henry Ford, a plethora of raw materials, and natural transportation facilities brought about the automobile industry and other manufacturing which centered in Detroit. The population grew, more roads were built, the number of canals at the Soo increased, and the Mackinac Bridge was touted as an engineering feat which links the five mile span between the Upper and Lower Peninsula.

Most importantly, Michigan is people. A diverse population brings an interesting ethnic blend to the state: Canadians, Polish, Italians, British, Germans, Russians, Scotch, Dutch and smaller samplings of many other nationalities. Michigan has produced representatives in all forms of the arts, the sports world, and world leaders—some as recent as Gerald Ford, our 38th president. Michigan abounds in Indian legends, marine lore, and tales of Paul Bunyan, the lumberjack. Fine museums and institutes preserve our physical history from Fort Michilimackinac to Greenfield Village; the literature records the history; and music ranges from the distinguished Detroit Symphony to Motown.

With the foregoing in mind, the following bibliography of children's literature provides sources for an entry into Michigan's diversified natural elements, history, personalities, and other glimpses of a unique state.

1   AARON, JAN. *Gerald R. Ford: President of Destiny;*
        illus. New York: Fleet Press, 1975. (5-8) B
        The story of Gerald Ford, 38th President of the
U.S., from boyhood through his first one hundred days
in office. Includes his Grand Rapids and University of
Michigan days.

2   ABBOTT, ETHELYN THERESA. *Abbott's Michigan History*
        Stories for Boys and Girls; illus. Hillsdale:
        Hillsdale Educational Pub., 1960. o.p. (3-5)
        Textbook. Simplified material on Michigan his-
tory and geography; much of the material from original
1930's printing.

3   AIRD, HAZEL and RUDDIMAN, CATHERINE. *Henry Ford,*
        Boy with Ideas; illus. Indianapolis: Bobbs-
        Merrill, 1959. (2-4) B
        Easy-reading biography of Henry Ford's child-
hood from the *Childhood of Famous Americans* series.

4   ARMER, ALBERTA. *Screwball;* illus. Cleveland:
        World, 1963. (4-6) F
        A move to Detroit gives a crippled boy a chance
to compete with his athletic twin brother when he
becomes involved in the Soap Box Derby.

5   ARMOUR, DAVID. *Fort Michilimackinac Sketch Book;*
        illus. by Dirk Gringhuis and Patricia Hogg.
        Lansing, Mich.: Mackinac Island State Park
        Commission, 1975. Paper. (1-3)
        A read-and-color book depicting Mackinac Island
scenes, life at the Fort.

6   BAILEY, BERNADINE. *Picture Book of Michigan;* illus.
        Chicago: Whitman, 1965. (3-5)
        Popular, brief history and geography of Michigan
from *The United States Books* series. Index.

7   BAIRD, WILLARD. *This Is Our Michigan;* illus.
        Battle Creek, Mich.: Federated Pub., 1954. o.p.
        (4-8)
        Brief sketches about interesting places, things,
and people in Michigan; dated, but useful if available.

8 BAKER, NINA BROWN. *Big Catalogue: The Life of Aaron Montgomery Ward;* illus. New York: Harcourt, Brace, 1956. o.p. (3-6) B
The biography of Montgomery Ward as he grew up in Niles, Michigan, and dreamed of starting a business where farmers could shop by mail for good merchandise at fair prices.

9 BALD, F. CLEVER. *Michigan in Four Centuries;* illus. New York: Harper, 1961. (5-) *
A comprehensive history of Michigan beginning with prehistoric times, and systematically recording the development of Michigan and its people. Published under direction of Michigan Historical Commission.

10 BANNON, LAURA. *Who Walks the Attic?;* illus. Chicago: Whitman, 1974. (2-4) F
Located along the bay shore from Traverse City, Michigan, is the small town of Acme where the author spent her childhood and used it as the setting for this story.

11 BARRY, JAMES P. *Henry Ford and Mass Production; An Inventor Builds a Car That Millions Can Afford;* illus. New York: Watts, 1973. (3-6) B
A *Focus Book* of the life of Henry Ford emphasizing the creation and growth of the Ford Motor Company and its impact on the American economy. Bibliography and index.

12 BATSON, LARRY. *Gordie Howe;* illus. Chicago: Children's Press, 1974. (2-5)
Up-to-date biography of one of the finest all-around hockey players the game has ever seen. Howe spent the main part of his career with the Detroit Red Wings.

13 BERNARD, JACQUELINE. *Journey toward Freedom: The Story of Sojourner Truth;* illus. New York: Norton, 1967. o.p. (5-8) B
The story of a valiant Negro woman sho settled

in Battle Creek, Michigan, in her later years. She was
the champion of anti-slavery, women's rights, prison
reform, and better conditions for the worker.

14 BIERHORST, JOHN, comp. *Songs of the Chippewa;*
      illus. New York: Farrar, Straus, and Giroux,
      1974. (4-8) #
      Songs adapted from collections of Frances
Densmore and Henry Rowe Schoolcraft, and arranged for
piano and guitar with sepia-toned illustrations.

15 BIRD, DOROTHY M. *Granite Harbor;* illus. New York:
      Macmillan, 1967. (4-8) F
      Story of a young girl from Texas who has to
acclimate herself to a sudden change of life style.
She learns to take pride in the new skills she acquires
for winter sports in a small town on Lake Superior.

16 BIRD, DOROTHY M. *Mystery at Laughing Water;* illus.
      New York: Macmillan, 1963. (4-6) F
      Story of life in a girl's summer camp near
Copper Harbor, Michigan, which furnishes a realistic
picture of the Lake Superior region.

17 BISCHOFF, JULIA BRISTOL. *A Dog for David;* illus.
      New York: W. R. Scott, 1966. (2-4) F
      David yearns for a dog while living on a farm in
the "thumb" area of Michigan in 1905.

18 BISCHOFF, JULIA BRISTOL. *Great-Great Uncle Henry's
      Cats;* illus. New York: Young Scott Books, 1965.
      o.p. (2-4) F
      Even cats had to work on the farm many years ago
in Michigan.

19 BISCHOFF, JULIA BRISTOL. *Paddy's Presposterous
      Promises;* illus. New York: Young Scott Books,
      1968. o.p. (2-4) F
      Amusing story of a hired man's unorthodox
methods for getting work done on a farm in Michigan
sixty years ago.

106

20 BLEEKER, SONIA. *The Chippewa Indians; Rice Gather-
    ers of the Great Lakes;* illus. New York:
    Morrow, 1955. 3-6) #
    Provides the everyday life of this Great Lakes
tribe.

21 BRILL, ETHEL CLAIRE. *Copper Country Adventure;*
    illus. New York: Whittlesey House, 1949. o.p.
    (4-6) F
    As an heir to a share in a copper mine, a young
man learns much about the geology and copper mining in
Michigan; includes mystery.

22 BUEHR, WALTER. *Through the Locks: Canals Today
    and Yesterday;* illus. New York: Putnam, 1954.
    (2-4)
    Succinct explanation of the workings of canals
and locks; includes Sault Sainte Marie Locks. Dated in
that the *proposed* St. Lawrence Seaway is mentioned.

23 BURGOYNE, LEON E. *State Champs;* illus.
    Philadelphia: Winston, 1951. o.p. (4-8) F
    Basketball story written by an ex-coach using
St. Joseph, Michigan, as the setting.

24 BURT, WILLIAM H. *Mammals of the Great Lakes Region;*
    illus. Ann Arbor, Mich.: University of
    Michigan, 1972. (6-) R #
    Valuable reference tool for identification and
distribution of species.

25 BUTLER, HAL. *Al Kaline and the Detroit Tigers;*
    illus. Chicago: Regnery, 1973. o.p. (6-8) B
    Story of the Detroit Tigers' infielder; concen-
trating on his twenty-year career on that team. Now
retired.

26 BUTLER, HAL. *The Willie Horton Story;* illus. New
    York: Messner, 1970. o.p. (5-8) B
    Story of the hometown Detroit Tigers' outfielder
and how he reached the top from his beginnings in a
Negro ghetto, overcoming personal tragedies and
physical injury.

107

27 CALDWELL, CY. *Henry Ford;* illus. New York:
    Messner, 1947. (4-8) B
    A biography of Henry Ford's life, his genius and
his biases.

28 CARPENTER, JOHN ALLAN. *Michigan: From Its Glorious
    Past to the Present;* illus. Chicago: Children's
    Press, 1964. (3-8)
    One of the *Enchantment of America* series which
briefly tells the story of Michigan; its formation and
its people.

29 CARR, HARRIETT H. *The Mystery of Ghost Valley.*
    New York: Macmillan, 1962. o.p. (5-8) F
    Young Detroit boy becomes interested in his
Pennsylvania-Dutch heritage.

30 CARR, HARRIETT H. *Where the Turnpike Starts.* New
    York: Macmillan, 1955. o.p. (5-8) F
    Young girl is caught up on the exciting and tur-
bulent years of Michigan's fight for statehood.

31 CHAFFEE, ALLEN. *Story of Hiawatha;* illus. New
    York: Random House, 1951. o.p. (1-4)
    Simple, illustrated adaptation from Longfellow's
poem with occasional quotes from original wording.

32 CHAPUT, DONALD. *The Cliff; America's First Great
    Copper Mine;* illus. Kalamazoo, Mich.: Sequoia
    Press, 1971. (5-8) P
    Story of the Pittsburgh and Boston Copper Mining
Company and their most famous property, the Cliff Mine
of Lake Superior; how mining communities developed,
patterns for shipping and marketing, and the impact on
national and international trade networks.

33 CHAPUT, DONALD. *Michigan Indians: A Way of Life
    Changes;* illus. Hillsdale, Mich.: Hillsdale
    Educational Pub., 1970. (3-6) *
    Graphically depicts Indian life before the White
man and how Europeans changed the Michigan Indians'

ways. Indian homes, clothing, food, games, hunting and fishing, travel, and religion.

34 CHASE, LEAH MAY HOWLAND. *The Song of the Maples.*
New York: Exposition Press, 1958. o.p.
(6-8) F
A novel of a Michigan farm girl and the difficulties she faced in attempting to be an artist; appeal will be limited.

35 CLOUTIER, HELEN H. *Isle Royale Calling;* illus.
Grand Rapids: Eerdmans, 1967. o.p. (4-6) F
Life of a ranger in Isle Royale National Park combined with author's interest in ham radio operation.

— CLUTE, TOM. *Champion Dog Prince Tom.* See MI 69

36 CONRADER, CONSTANCE STONE. *Blue Wampum;* illus.
New York: Duell, Sloan, and Pearce, 1958. o.p.
(5-8) F #
The young son of a French-Indian fur trader and his American wife, must choose between two ways of life while growing up near Fort Detroit.

37 COOKE, DAVID C. *How Automobiles Are Made;* illus.
New York: Dodd, Mead, 1972. (3-6)
Using words and pictures, the production of a car is outlined from engineers and stylists designing a new model, how ideas are tested, and, finally, how it is put together on the production line.

38 DAVIS, VERNE. *The Runaway Cattle;* illus. New York: Morrow, 1965. o.p. (2-4) F
Teenagers attempt to recapture a runaway herd in western Michigan in 1890. .

39 DAVIS, VERNE. *The Time of the Wolves;* illus. New York: Morrow, 1962. o.p. (2-4) F
Realistic story of two resourceful boys alone in the wilds, protecting eight head of cattle from starvation and wolves during a late 19th century Michigan winter.

40 DE ANGELI, MARGUERITE. *Copper-Toed Boots;* illus.
by author. Garden City, NY: Doubleday, 1938.
(3-6) F
The author combined her father's description of
his prized red leather-topped, copper-toed boots and
Michigan summer activities, to create a lovely and realistic story of family and community life in the 1880's.

41 DERLETH, AUGUST. *Captive Island;* illus. New York:
Aladdin Books, 1952. (3-6) F
Exciting, factual story of how Culver and his
son, John, help American forces during the British
siege of Mackinac Island in 1812.

42 DERLETH, AUGUST. *Empire of Furs: Trading in the
Lake Superior Region;* illus. New York: Aladdin,
1953. o.p. (3-6) F
Adventure story of a Mackinac Island youth's
encounters with danger and hardship on a fur trading
voyage.

43 DERLETH, AUGUST. *Land of the Blue Sky Waters;*
illus. New York: Aladdin, 1955. o.p. (3-6) F #
Fictionalized story of Henry Schoolcraft's
search for the source of the Mississippi, and his fasci-
nation with the life style of the Indians.

44 DERLETH, AUGUST. *Sweet Land of Michigan.* New York:
Duell, Sloan and Pearce, 1962. (6-8) F
Young settler is enamored with adventure and
joins the militia to fight for the Toledo territory.
He takes part in a spying mission and is given the
opportunity to survey unknown and dangerous parts of
Michigan territory.

45 DUNBAR, WILLIS FREDERICK. *All Aboard: A History
of Railroading in Michigan;* illus. Grand Rapids:
Eerdmans, 1969. o.p. (6-)
Comprehensive history of Michigan railroading
from the first struggling in 1837, through the troubled
growth across the state. For the special assignment or
railroad buff.

46 DUNBAR, WILLIS FREDERICK. *Michigan: A History of the Wolverine State;* illus. Grand Rapids: Eerdmans, 1965. (6-) R *
Comprehensive history of Michigan that can be used as a reference tool by older students. Bibliography and Index.

47 DYE, JACOB. *Lumber Camp Life in Michigan; An Autobiographical Account;* illus. Hicksville, NY: Exposition Press, 1975. (4-8)
A brief eyewitness record of the life and activities in the early days of Michigan lumber camps.

48 EAST, BEN. *The Last Eagle, the Story of Khan;* illus. New York: Crown, 1974. (6-8) F
Life story of an American bald eagle in northern Michigan woods.

49 EBERLY, CAROLE. *Michigan Cooking . . . & other Things.* (self-published) 1977. (5-)
All recipes are based on the state's agricultural products with Michigan sketches and tales.

50 EDWARDS, AUDRY and WOHL, GARY. *The Picture Life of Stevie Wonder;* illus. New York: Watts, 1977. (K-3) B
A *Picture Life Book* biography of the Black from Michigan who is the leading figure in popular music.

51 ELLIOTT, FRANK N. *When the Railroad Was King: The Nineteenth-century Railroad Era in Michigan.* Lansing: Michigan Historical Commission, 1966. (6-8)
A brief account of the high point of Michigan's railroading history.

52 EMBERLEY, BARBARA. *Story of Paul Bunyan;* illus. by Ed Emberley. Englewood Cliffs, N.J.: Prentice-Hall, 1964. (K-3)
Striking book of the deeds of Paul Bunyan in the singing prose of Barbara Emberley, and the giant woodcuts of Ed Emberley.

53 EMERY, ANNE. *Spy in Old Detroit;* illus. Chicago.
Rand McNally, 1963. o.p. (5-8) F
Paul becomes a spy for the English during the
Detroit seige in 1763, but has to wrestle with conflict-
ing emotions about the French, English and Indian
hostilities.

— EPSTEIN, BERYL. *Dr. Beaumont and the Man with the
Hole in His Stomach.* See MI 54

54 EPSTEIN, SAM and EPSTEIN, BERYL. *Dr. Beaumont and
the Man with the Hole in His Stomach;* illus.
New York: Coward, McCann & Geoghegan, 1978.
(2-6) B #
Story of curious army surgeon at the Fort in
the wilderness of Mackinac Island, and the unusual
patient who enabled him to carry out experiments concerning digestion.

55 FARLEY, CAROL. *The Bunch on McKellahan Street.*
New York: Watts, 1971. (5-8) F
Story set in Piney Ridge, Michigan, in 1945,
which involves a group of troublemakers from the tough
side of town.

56 FARLEY, CAROL. *The Garden is Doing Fine;* illus.
New York: Atheneum, 1975. (5-8) F
Carrie refuses to believe her father is dying;
dying as his garden had died. Set in the Lake Michigan
area in 1945.

57 FARLEY, CAROL. *Loosen Your Ears;* illus. New York:
Atheneum, 1977. (4-6) F
Although Josh is an old man, the memories of his
childhood on a farm in Michigan are very clear, the
more so because his family included so many people.
Sequel: *Settle Your Fidgets,* Atheneum, 1977.

58 FARLEY, CAROL. *Mystery of the Fog Man;* illus. New
        York: Watts, 1966. (4-6) F
        Mystery, which takes place in Ludington,
involves the car ferry that crosses Lake Michigan.
        Additional mystery in similar setting: *Mystery in*
the Ravine, Watts, 1967. o.p.

59 FARLEY, CAROL. *Sergeant Finney's Family;* illus.
        New York: Watts, 1969. (5-8) F
        Young girl must get used to a new school in
Michigan as well as adjust to life without Dad, who was
assigned to a year in Vietnam.

60 FERNALD, HELEN. *The Shadow of the Crooked Tree.*
        New York: McKay, 1965. (6-8) F
        The story of a young school teacher, whose first
assignment was in the homeland of the Ottawa Indians in
Northwestern Michigan, in 1900.

61 FERRY, CHARLES. *O Zebron Falls.* Boston: Houghton
        Mifflin, 1977. (6-8) F
        A story which blends the nostalgic tone of the
early 1940's in a small Michigan town (Rochester), with
the realism of the Detroit Riot and its impact upon the
town's only Black. An unresolved conflict with her
father, imminent high school graduation, and World
War II complicate Lukie's struggle to shape her life.

62 FISCHLER, STAN. *Gordie Howe;* illus. New York:
        Grosset & Dunlap, 1973. (4-8) B
        Full-length account of Gordie Howe's amazing
career in professional hockey as a great scorer and
most honored player. Major part of his career was as a
Detroit Red Wings player.

63 FISHER, AILEEN LUCIA. *Timber! Logging in Michigan;*
        illus. New York: Aladdin, 1955. o.p. (3-6) F
        Young boy works in lumber camp in Escanaba and
becomes involved in more aspects of forestry than
logging.

113

64 FORD, R. CLYDE. *Heroes and Hero Tales of Michigan;*
illus. Milwaukee, WI: E. M. Hale, 1930. o.p.
(4-6)
Twelve biographical and historical sketches from
Marquette to Henry Ford concerning the emerging of
Michigan from the wilderness. Useful despite publishing date.

65 FORD, R. CLYDE. *My Michigan.* Delaware, Ohio:
Gateway Publishing Co., n.d. o.p. (4-6)
The book in the format of individual sketches
discusses cities, area, and details of Michigan history.

66 FORD, R. CLYDE. *Sandy MacDonald's Man;* illus.
Lansing: Michigan School Service, 1929. o.p.
(4-8) F
A tale of the Mackinac fur trade. A valuable
book for the details of the life at that time in spite
of extremely old publishing date.

67 FOX, FRANCES M. *Little Mossback Amelia;* illus.
Traverse Bay, Mich.: Little Traverse Regional
Historical Society, 1969. o.p. (3-5) F
True story of a little girl and her family
pioneering in the northern Michigan woods near Petoskey.
First published in 1870.

68 FRAZIER, NETA LOHNES. *Little Rhody;* illus. New
York: Longmans, 1953. (3-6) F
The story of Rhody and family life on a Michigan
farm near Owosso in the 1870's.
Continuation of Rhody's adventures:
Somebody Special, Longmans, 1954. o.p.
Secret Friend, Longmans, 1956. o.p.
The Magic Ring, Longmans, 1959. o.p.

69 FRITZ, JEAN and CLUTE, TOM. *Champion Dog Price Tom;*
illus. New York: Coward-McCann, 1958. o.p.
(3-6) F
True story of a boy and his cocker spaniel which
takes place near Adrian, Michigan.

70 GEORGE, MARY KARL (Sister). *The Rise and Fall of
    Toledo, Michigan... .The Toledo War!;* illus.
    Lansing: Michigan Historical Commission, 1971.
    (4-8) #
    Cartographical errors and the belief that Toledo
would become a leading city in the Old Northwest lead
to a bloodless war in 1835. Background and events are
presented in this book which describes "how to fight a
war without hurting anybody."

71 GEORGIADY, NICHOLAS P. and Others. *Michigan
    Historical Sights;* illus. Milwaukee, Wisc.:
    Franklin, 1967. o.p. (2-5)
    Brief sketches from the *State History* series of
highlights in Michigan's history. Contents: The Soo,
Straits of Mackinac, Pines, History comes to life, Land
of Hiawatha, Detroit River.

72 GEORGIADY, NICHOLAS P. and Others. *Michigan Men;*
    illus. Milwaukee, Wisc.: Franklin, 1967. o.p.
    (2-5) B
    Nine biographies of men of importance to
Michigan's history from the *State History* series.

73 GEORGIADY, NICHOLAS P. and Others. *Michigan Women;*
    illus. Milwaukee, Wisc.: Franklin, 1967. o.p.
    (2-5) B
    Short biographies in large print of seven women
instrumental in the history of Michigan. Contents:
Madame Cadillac, Katherine (Ojibway Squaw), Mary A.
Mayo, Lucinda Hinsdale Stone, Sarah Emma Seelve, Lizzie
Merrill Palmer, and Sojourner Truth. From *State
History* series.

74 GEORGIADY, NICHOLAS P. and Others. *Michigan's
    First Settlers—The Indians;* illus. Milwaukee,
    Wisc.: Franklin, 1967. o.p. (2-5)
    Relates the progress of Indians as they spread
throughout America, with emphasis on Michigan Indians.
From the *State History* series.

75 GILCHRIST, MARIE E. *Story of the Great Lakes;*
    illus. Harcourt, Brace, 1957. o.p. (3-6) #
    Still useful, simply written text of history and
geography of the Great Lakes; illustrated with lovely
lithographs.

76 GIRARD, HAZEL B. *A Giant Walked Among Them;* illus.
    Francestown, N.H.: Marshall Jones, 1977. (4-6)
    Half-tall tales of Paul Bunyan and his loggers;
a collection of warm stories.

77 GREENE, MERRITT. *Curse of the White Panther.*
    Hillsdale, Mich.: Hillsdale Educational Pub.,
    1960. o.p. (5-8) F
    Sequel to *The Land Lies Pretty.* Begins with
United States attempting to purchase Indian lands in
Michigan, and ends with the Toledo War.

78 GREENE, MERRITT. *The Land Lies Pretty.* Hillsdale,
    Mich.: Hillsdale Educational Pub., 1959. o.p.
    (5-8) F
    The story of the Great Sauk Trail in 1832 (now
U.S. 112 from Detroit to Chicago), with descriptions
of Potowatomi life style.

79 GREENMAN, EMERSON F. *The Indians of Michigan.*
    Lansing: Michigan Historical Commission, 1961.
    (6-8)
    Brief, but informative account of the various
tribes of Michigan.

80 GRIDLEY, MARION E. *Pontiac;* illus. New York:
    Putnam, 1970. (1-3) B #
    A *See and Read Beginning to Read* biography of
Pontiac's life which was spent trying to save the land
and culture of his people.

81 GRINGHUIS, DIRK. *The Big Dig;* illus. by author.
    New York: Dial, 1962. o.p. (2-6)
    The story of the reconstruction of Fort
Michilimackinac.

82 GRINGHUIS, DIRK. *Big Mac: The Story of the World's Biggest Bridge;* illus. by author. New York: Macmillan, 1959. o.p. (2-6)
The building of the longest, costliest, and safest bridge situated between Lake Michigan and Lake Huron, over the Straits of Mackinac.

83 GRINGHUIS, DIRK. *The Eagle Pine;* illus. by author. Hillsdale, Mich.: Hillsdale Educational Pub., 1970. Paper. (4-6) F
A boy's experiences while working in the woods and in logging camps in north central Michigan in the closing years of the 19th century.

84 GRINGHUIS, DIRK. *The Great Parade: Tall Tales and True of Michigan's Past;* illus. by author. Hillsdale, Mich.: Hillsdale Educational Pub., 1970. o.p. (3-5)
Text material which deals with the history, geography, economics, and legends of Michigan. Especially good on natural history.

85 GRINGHUIS, DIRK. *Let's Color Michigan;* illus. by author. Hillsdale, Mich.: Hillsdale Educational Pub., 1971. Paper. (1-3)
A read and color paperback book depicting famous Michigan sights or historical events. Text vocabulary controlled. Simple introduction to the state.

86 GRINGHUIS, DIRK. *Lore of the Great Turtle;* illus. by author. Mackinac Island, Mich.: Mackinac Island Park Commission, 1970. Paper. (2-4)
Retold Indian legends of Mackinac revolving around animals, places, and other folklore.

87 GRINGHUIS, DIRK. *Michigan's Indians;* illus. by author. Hillsdale, Mich.: Hillsdale Educational Pub., 1972. (1-3)
A read and color book which serves as an introduction to Michigan Indians and how they lived. Deals simply with the Ottawa, Chippewa and Potawatami Tribes.

88 GRINGHUIS, DIRK. *Moccasin Tracks: A Saga of the Michigan Indian;* illus. by author. East Lansing: Museum, Michigan State University, 1974. o.p. (5-8)
A brief account of archaeologists' reconstruction of the Indian migration and culture in Michigan.

89 GRINGHUIS, DIRK. *Mystery at Skull Castle;* illus. by author. New York: Reilly & Lee, 1964. o.p. (3-5) F
Two young boys use an abandoned castle on the outskirts of a Dutch village on Lake Michigan as a hiding place for their valuables. Suspense and humor in the folk tale tradition.

90 GRINGHUIS, DIRK. *Open Door to the Great Lakes;* illus. by author. New York: Duell, 1966. o.p. (4-8) #
A comprehensive survey of the Great Lakes and the surrounding areas. The author traces their history through prehistoric times to present; includes their lore and legends.

91 GRINGHUIS, DIRK. *Saddle the Storm;* illus. by author. Indianapolis, Ind.: Bobbs, 1962. o.p. (4-6) F
Story of a Beaver Island resident's love of a horse. This enables him to overcome his fear of the hardships of winter on deserted High Island in order to protect the horse.

92 GRINGHUIS, DIRK. *Tulip Time;* illus. by author. Chicago: Whitman, 1951. o.p. (1-3) F
Delightfully illustrated account of the famous annual Tulip Festival held each Spring in Holland, Mich.

93 GRINGHUIS, DIRK. *Were-Wolves and Will-O-the-Wisps;* illus. by author. Mackinac Island, Mich.: Mackinac Island State Park Commission, 1974. (2-4)
French fur traders' tales of Mackinac retold. Deal with ghosts, goblins, and other creatures of folklore.

94 GRINGHUIS, DIRK. *The Young Voyageur: Trade and Treachery at Michilimackinac;* illus. by author. Lansing, Mich.: Mackinac Island State Park Commission, 1969. Paper. (4-8) F
Story of a young boy in Fort Detroit in 1762 who is hired by a French trader for a trip to Fort Michilimackinac, and suffers the hardships of the wilderness.

95 GROSS, STUART D. *Indians, Jacks, and Pines;* illus. Midland, Mich.: Pendell Pub., 1976. (4-6)
Interesting documentary of Saginaw history, which is typical of much of Michigan.

96 HALL, E. LORENE and KURETH, ELWOOD J.C. *Hi! I'm Michigan;* illus. Hillsdale, Mich.: Hillsdale Educational Pub., 1976. Paper. (1-2)
An elementary social studies text dealing very simplistically with the history, geography, and economics of Michigan.

97 HAMIL, FRED C. *Michigan in the War of 1812.* Lansing: Michigan Historical Commission, 1960. (6-8)
Brief, but informative account of an important event in the history of Michigan.

98 HATHAWAY, ELLEN C. *Your Capital and Mine;* illus. Lansing: Michigan Historical Commission, 1953. o.p. (3-5)
The story of Michigan's government for young readers which deals primarily with historical aspects: Michigan as a territory, building of the capital.

99 HAYS, WILMA PITCHFORD. *Pontiac, Lion in the Forest;* illus. Boston: Houghton Mifflin, 1965. o.p. (3-5) B #
Author presents the story of a skilled political chieftain; an example of personal integrity and leadership.

100 HEINRICH, EBERHARDT WILLIAM. *Mineralogy of Michigan;* illus. Lansing: Michigan Department of Natural Resources, Geology Division, 1977. (6-8)
A complete reference for minerals of Michigan. Although scholarly in nature, this volume will acquaint the layman mineral collector with geological character- istics of the types of mineral deposits in Michigan, and record the significant mineral occurrences in the state. Bibliography.

101 HERBERT, PAUL A. *Great Lakes Nature Guide;* illus. Lansing: Michigan United Conservation Clubs, 1975. (4-8)
Guide to Michigan animals, birds, fish, flowers, insects, shrubs, snakes, trees, and weeds. Provides sketch, identifying marks, and brief description of each in an inexpensive and useful publication.

102 HOEHLING, MARY. *Girl Soldier and Spy: Sarah Emma Edmundson.* New York: Messner, 1959. o.p. (4-6) B
Girl disguised as a boy fights as private in the Civil War. As a volunteer in the Michigan infantry, she perpetuated this herioc hoax for three years.

103 HOLLING, HOLLING C. *Paddle-to-the-Sea;* illus. Boston: Houghton Mifflin, 1941. (3-6) F * #
Beautifully illustrated story of the travels of a toy canoe through the Great Lakes and the St. Lawrence River to the Atlantic Ocean.

104 HOLLMAN, CLIDE. *Pontiac: King of the Great Lakes.* New York: Hastings House, 1968. (6-8) B
Chief Pontiac, a legend in his time, was a stout- hearted fighter for the rights of his people.

105 HOLMAN, J. ALAN. *Michigan's Fossil Vertebrates;* illus. East Lansing: Museum, Michigan State University, 1975. (4-8)
Scholarly, but readable and interesting material that answers such questions as: Whales in the Great

Lakes?, No dinosaurs?, or Beavers impounded tremendous bodies of water?

106 HOLMAN, J. ALAN. *Mystery Mammals of the Ice Age; Great Lakes Area;* illus. by Dirk Gringhuis. Hillsdale, Mich.: Hillsdale Educational Pub., 1972. (4-8)
Describes the characteristics and habits of pre-historic mammals inhabiting the Great Lakes region during the Ice Age, and some of their present-day descendants. Tries to explain why the mammals disappeared such a short time ago.

107 HOWARD, ELIZABETH. *Candle in the Night.* New York: Morrow, 1952. o.p. (5-8) F
Early interest is created by Tamsen's arduous stagecoach journey from Albany to Buffalo, and the dangerous boat trip across Lake Erie to Detroit, with two storms and a shipwreck. Despite the antagonism of her new sister-in-law, Tamsen proves herself during the British occupation of Detroit and Indian attacks. Well-written, 1812 historical romance.

108 HOWARD, ELIZABETH. *A Girl of the North Country.* New York: Morrow, 1957. (6-8) F
A 16 year old girl has to adjust to northern Michigan pioneer life in a one-room cabin in a tiny settlement. Romance and mystery.

109 HOWARD, ELIZABETH. *North Winds Blow Free.* New York: Morrow, 1949. (5-8) F
Michigan farm girl assists runaway slaves to safety in Canada through the Underground Railroad.

110 HOWARD, ELIZABETH. *Peddler's Girl.* New York: Morrow, 1951. o.p. (5-8) F
Story of Lucy and Elijah as they travel in their uncle's peddler wagon throughout Michigan in the 1840's.

111 HOWARD, ELIZABETH. *Wilderness Venture.* New York:
Morrow, 1973. (5-8) F
A young adult novel in which sixteen-year-old
Delia and her three brothers set out to claim land in
the Michigan wilderness that their widowed mother
bought sight unseen along the St. Clair River in 1825.

112 ICENHOWER, JOSEPH B. *Tecumseh and the Indian Confederation: 1811-1813; The Indian Nations East
of the Mississippi Are Defeated;* illus. New
York: Watts, 1975. (5-8) #
A *Focus Book* which traces the events of the
defeat of Tecumseh's efforts to build a confederated
Indian nation in the early 1800's.

113 JACKSON, C. PAUL. *Match Point.* Philadelphia:
Westminster, 1956. o.p. (4-6) F
Small boy qualifies for the National Boys'
Tennis Tournament at Kalamazoo College's Stowe Stadium.

114 JACKSON, C. PAUL. *Rose Bowl All-American.* New
York: Crowell, 1949. o.p. (5-8) F
Follows the University of Michigan Football team
from season's start to an exciting climax at the Rose
Bowl tournament in California.

115 JOHNSON, IDA AMANDA. *The Michigan Fur Trade.*
Grand Rapids, Mich.: The Black Letter Press,
1971. (6-8)
Story of the rise and growth of various fur
trading posts and outposts within Michigan borders;
first printed in 1919.

116 JUDSON, CLARA INGRAM. *Mighty Soo; Five Hundred
Years at Sault Ste. Marie;* illus. Chicago:
Follett, 1955. o.p. (4-6)
The history of one square mile of land and
water and resultant Michigan history influenced by the
Soo.

117 KELLER, MARTHA V. and WEAVER, JOAN S. *Where to Go and What to Do with the Kids in Detroit;* illus. Los Angeles: Price, Stern, Sloan, 1974. o.p. (K-8) R
Attractions, camps, parks, tours, and exhibits in metropolitan Detroit area of interest to children.

118 KELLY, REGINA Z. *Beaver Trail;* illus. New York: Lothrop, Lee and Shepard, 1955. o.p. (4-6) F #
In 1811, Jimmie spent three months on Mackinac Island sorting furs for John Jacob Astor's warehouse, but rumors of Indian uprisings meant he had to journey to Fort Dearborn.

119 KELLY, REGINA Z. *Henry Ford;* illus. Chicago: Follett, 1970. o.p. (3-8) B
Biography of a man remembered as "father of the assembly line production" and innovator of labor practices. Bibliography and Index.

120 KERLE, ARTHUR G. *Whispering Trees; A Tale of Michigamaw;* illus. St. Cloud, Minn.: North Star Press, 1971. (4-8) F
A young Ojibway boy, longing to grow to manhood in the wilderness as his father had, watches his best friend, a white boy, join the lumber crews that are slowly destroying the Ojibway land and way of life.

121 KJELGAARD, JAMES A. *Explorations of Pere Marquette;* illus. New York: Random House, 1951. o.p. (3-6) B
This *Landmark* biography covers Marquette's missionary work and life among the Indians, as well as his search with Joliet for the Big River to the West.

122 KJELGAARD, JAMES A. *Spell of the White Sturgeon.* New York: Dodd, Mead, 1953. o.p. (6-8) F #
An action-packed story of Lake Michigan commercial fishing and of the great white sturgeon who can cast a spell of fear over the sturdiest of fishermen.

123 KLOSE, NORMA CLINE. *Benny; The Biography of a Horse;* illus. New York: Lothrop, Lee and Shepard, 1965. (4-6)
True story of a horse on a farm near Grand Blanc. Tells of the fun and excitement of the Cline family.

124 KUBIAK, WILLIAM J. *Great Lakes Indians: A Pictorial Guide;* illus. by author. Grand Rapids, Mich.: Baker Book House, 1970. o.p. (4-8) P #
Informative volume and striking graphic portrayal of the Indians of the Great Lakes area. Interesting aspects of Indian life, brief surveys of tribal history. Bibliography, index of tribal names, and general index. Reprint by Bonanza Books, division of Crown Publishers, may be available.

125 KUMIN, MAXINE W. *Paul Bunyan;* illus. New York: Putnam, 1966. (1-3)
From the *See and Read Beginning to Read Book* series, tall tales of the famous lumberjack for the very young.

126 KURELECK, WILLIAM. *Lumberjack;* illus. Boston: Houghton Mifflin, 1974. (3-6) #
The author's paintings of Canadian lumber camp accompany his first-hand observation of the life of a lumberjack. Actual lumbering experiences of the author while earning money for college and a trip to Europe to further his career.

—— KURETH, ELWOOD J. C. *Hi! I'm Michigan.* See MI 96

127 LARRIE, REGINALD. *Black Experiences in Michigan History;* illus. Lansing: Michigan History Division, Michigan Department of State, 1975. Paper. (6-8)
Collection of actual black experiences in Michigan is an attempt to expose some of the myths of black history.

128 LAWRENCE, MILDRED. *Crissy at the Wheel;* illus.
New York: Harcourt, Brace, 1952. o.p. (4-6) F
Story of a young girl who helps her father, the
best carriage salesman in Granite City, Michigan, to
sell horseless carriages.

129 LAWSON, H. L. *Pitch Dark and No Moon.* New York:
Crowell, 1958. o.p. (6-8) F
A mystery involving the Coast Guard along
Saginaw Bay.

130 LEEKLY, THOMAS B. *The World of Manabozho: Tales
of the Chippewa Indians;* illus. New York:
Vanguard, 1965. o.p. (4-8) #
The author retells Manabozho stories of the
Chippewa and Ottawa tribes with whom he lived. Tales
reflect their beliefs, fears, and aspirations.

131 LENSKI, LOIS. *We Live in the North;* illus. by
author. Philadelphia: Lippincott, 1965. o.p.
(3-4) F
Three short stories of Michigan families: an
auto worker in Hamtramck, cherry pickers in Traverse
City and Muskegon Heights, and Christmas tree growers.

132 LENT, HENRY B. *Men at Work in the Great Lakes
States;* illus. New York: Putnam, 1958. o.p.
(3-6) #
Discusses the major industries and products of
the Great Lake states, including Michigan. Includes
farming, milling, scientific research, mining, manufacturing, etc.

133 LEWIS, FERRIS E. *Learning About Michigan's Government;* illus. Hillsdale, Mich.: Hillsdale Educational Pub., 1973. (4-6)
Elementary text covering state, county, and
local government in Michigan. Color pictures of the
Capitol, state flag, stone, flower, tree, fish and bird.
Index.

125

134 LEWIS, FERRIS E. *Michigan Yesterday and Today;*
illus. Hillsdale, Mich.: Hillsdale Educational
Publ., 1975. (6-)
Michigan's geological and geographic background
and how it has affected Michigan's economic and social
development. Covers the Indians, the pioneer days,
early settlements, the formation of the state, up to
the present day. Index.

135 LEWIS, FERRIS E. *My State and Its Story;* illus.
Hillsdale, Mich.: Hillsdale Educational Pub.,
1972. (6-)
Textbook oriented history and geography of
Michigan; stressing development of industry, transpor-
tation and resources. Index.

136 LEWIS, FERRIS E. *Our Own State: Michigan History
and Geography Workbook;* illus. Hillsdale, Mich.:
Hillsdale Educational Pub., 1978. Paper. (6-8)
Combination text and workbook on Michigan history, Indians, geography, resources, and people. More
inclusive than similar text by George Hall.

137 LEWIS, FERRIS E. *State and Local Government in
Michigan.* Hillsdale, Mich.: Hillsdale Educational Publ., 1974. (6-8)
Descriptions of the workings of the Michigan
governments: state, city, county, village, and township. Describes legislative, executive, and judicial
branches. Index and Constitution.

138 LEWIS, FERRIS E. *Then and Now in Michigan;* illus.
Hillsdale, Mich.: Hillsdale Educational Pub.,
1950. o.p. (3-5)
Historical and present-day Michigan; dated but
useful. Index.

139 MASON, F. VAN WYCK. *The Battle of Lake Erie;* illus.
Boston: Houghton Mifflin, 1960. (3-6)
Vivid account of the Battle of Lake Erie during
the War of 1812. Has biographical information of Oliver
Hazard Perry, one of the great naval heroes of the
United States.

140 MASON, MIRIAM E. *Caroline and Her Kettle Named Maud;* illus. by Kathleen Voute. New York: Macmillan, 1951. (2-4) F
Story of pioneer life in Michigan centering on an eight year old girl. A farewell gift of a copper kettle proves more valuable to her than a gun during dangerous times.

141 MAY, GEORGE S. *Pictorial History of Michigan: The Early Years;* illus. Grand Rapids, Mich.: Eerdmans, 1967. (5-)
Carefully researched text with photographs and illustrations to document Michigan's first three centuries. Useful for reference work.

142 MAY, GEORGE S. *Pictorial History of Michigan: The Later Years;* illus. Grand Rapids, Mich.: Eerdmans, 1969. (5-)
A continuation of a graphic history of Michigan dealing with the 20th century. Profusely illustrated with photographs, drawings, maps and documents.

143 MAY, GEORGE S. *War of 1812;* illus. Lansing, Mich.: Mackinac Island State Park Commission, 1962. (5-8)
Brief account of the surprise attack and capture of Mackinac Island without firing a shot.

144 MAYBEE, ROLLAND HARPER. *Michigan's White Pine Era, 1840-1900;* illus. Lansing: Michigan Historical Commission, 1964. Paper. (6-8)
Brief, but informative, account of the lumbering industry in Michigan's history.

145 MC CORMICK, DELL. *Paul Bunyan Swings His Axe;* illus. by author. Caldwell, Idaho: Caxton, 1964. (3-6) #
Tall tales about this giant woodsman from his boyhood days in Maine through the western adventures with his Blue Ox.

146 MC CORMICK, DELL. *Tall Timber Tales;* illus. by
author. Caldwell, Idaho: Caxton, 1966. (3-6) #
More Paul Bunyan stories.

147 MC GUIRE, FRANCES. *Indian Drums Beat Again;* illus.
New York: Dutton, 1953. o.p. (4-6) F
A story of a summer spent on Mackinac Island
which develops into an adventure and friendship.

148 MEEKS, ESTHER K. *The Hill That Grew;* illus.
Chicago: Follett, 1959. o.p. (K-2) F
Story is based on a real event which took place
in Oak Park, Michigan. One child's sled for Christmas
resulted in a coaster hill being built by the community.

149 MERCER, CHARLES. *Gerald Ford;* illus. New York:
Putnam, 1975. (1-4) B
From the *See and Read Biography* series. A
United States President who grew up in Grand Rapids,
Michigan, and was the first to take office as the
result of a presidential resignation.

150 MICHIGAN AUDUBON SOCIETY. *Enjoying Birds in
Michigan;* illus. Rev. ed. Lansing, Michigan:
The Society, 1971. Paper. (4-8)
A useful guide and resource for finding, attract-
ing, identifying, and studying 100 species of birds in
Michigan. Line drawings, photographs and maps.

151 MICHIGAN. DEPARTMENT OF CONSERVATION. *Michigan
Whitetails;* illus. Lansing: The Department,
1959. o.p. (4-8)
Assorted facts on the Michigan deer; article
format.

152 MICHIGAN. DEPARTMENT OF CONSERVATION. *Michigan Wildlife Sketches,* by Glenn W. Bradt; illus. by Charles E. Schafer. 5th ed. Hillsdale, Mich.: Hillsdale Educational Pub., 1967. Paper. (4-8) *
Information on the native mammals of Michigan's forests, fields and marshes. Accurate sketches of many animals, as well as their tracks.

153 MICHIGAN. DEPARTMENT OF NATURAL RESOURCES *Michigan Trees Worth Knowing,* by Norman F. Smith; illus. by Charles E. Schafer and photographs by author. Rev. ed. Hillsdale, Mich.: Hillsdale Educational Pub., 1970. (4-8) *
A useful guide for the identification and study of Michigan trees.

154 MICHIGAN. DEPARTMENT OF NATURAL RESOURCES. *Mother Nature's Michigan,* by Oscar Warbach; illus. by author. Hillsdale, Mich.: Hillsdale Educational Pub., 1976. Paper. (4-8)
Humorous, but accurate illustration on a variety of Michigan wildlife subjects. Designed to create environmental awareness and concern.

155 MICHIGAN. DEPARTMENT OF NATURAL RESOURCES. *Rocks and Minerals of Michigan,* by O. F. Poindexter, H. M. Martin and S. G. Bergquist; illus. Rev. ed. Hillsdale, Mich.: Hillsdale Educational Pub., 1971. Paper. (4-8)
A useful guide and resource for the identification and studying of rocks in Michigan. Origin, location and basic uses of rocks and minerals.

156 MICHIGAN HISTORICAL COMMISSION. *Michigan Historical Markers.* Lansing: The Commission, 1967. o.p. (5-)
Markers and descriptions are reproduced with location. Listings are consecutive, beginning with first to be erected in 1955.

157 *Michigan Statistical Abstract*. Lansing: Michigan
State University Press, 1977. R
Wealth of information includes: population,
industry, employment, government, etc.

158 MISTELE, LORNA DEE. *I Sing of Michigan;* illus.
The author, 1962. o.p. (K-6)
Collection of Michigan songs with words, music
and block prints.

159 MONTGOMERY, ELIZABETH RIDER. *Henry Ford: Auto-
motive Pioneer;* illus. Champaign, Ill.:
Garrard, 1969. (2-5) B
A brief biography, from the *Americans All* series,
of a farm boy whose desire to tinker led to the design
of the horeseless carriage.

—— NEVILL, JOHN T. *Miracle Bridge at Mackinac.*
See MI 201

160 NEWCOMB, DELPHINE. *Exploring Michigan;* illus.
Chicago: Follett, 1963. o.p. (3-5)
Simplified study of Michigan history and
geography. Index and now-dated bibliographies.

161 NEWTON, STANLEY. *Mackinac Island and Sault Ste.
Marie;* illus. Grand Rapids, Mich.: Black
Letter Press, 1976. (6-8)
Collection of historical facts and stories;
first published in 1923.

162 NEWTON, STANLEY. *The Story of Sault Ste. Marie and
Chippewa County.* Grand Rapids, Mich.: Black
Letter Press, 1975. (6-8)
This small volume, first published in 1923, was
written to honor the Homecoming year in Sault Ste.
Marie. Valuable for the facts that are not found
elsewhere.

163 NEYHART, LOUISE A. *Henry Ford, Engineer;* illus.
Boston: Houghton Mifflin, 1950. o.p. (5-8) B
Worthwhile biography of Henry Ford and the step-
by-step development of his famous car.

164 NYE, RUSSELL BLAINE. *Michigan;* illus. New York:
Coward-McCann, 1966. o.p. (4-6)
Michigan today and the explanation of its
development by exploring geography, history, industry,
people, and recreation. Strong on Indian tribal background and Douglass Houghton. Excellent photographs.

165 OBERREICH, ROB. *Blood Red Belt;* illus. Garden
City, N.Y.: Doubleday, 1961. (3-6) F
Peter Casson and his Indian friend defend the
trading post against enemy attack. Setting near the
Soo.

166 OLDENBURG, E. WILLIAM. *Potawatomi Indian Summer;*
illus. Grand Rapids, Mich.: Eerdmans, 1975.
(2-6) F
Children entering a cave along Lake Michigan
find themselves 300 years back in time, and learn much
about the Potawatomi tribe and culture.

167 OLSON, SIDNEY. *Young Henry Ford: A Picture
History of the First Forty Years;* illus.
Detroit: Wayne State University, 1963. o.p.
(5-8) B
Pictorial biography of little known facts of
this unique, original inventor of automobiles prior to
1901.

168 ORTIZ, VICTORIA. *Sojourner Truth, a Self-made
Woman;* illus. Philadelphia: Lippincott, 1974.
(5-8) B
A biography of a former slave who became a
fighter for black's and women's rights after gaining
her freedom. Sojourner Truth made her home in Battle
Creek, Michigan, after the Civil War.

169 ORTON, HELEN F. *Secret of the Rosewood Box;* illus.
    Philadelphia: Lippincott, 1965. (3-6) F
    A mystery, plus historical tale of pioneer life
in the 1880's. Takes place during the journey of the
King family from New York State to Michigan. A lost
hat box with something precious under the lining helps
to create and sustain interest.

170 OSOLINSKI, STAN. *Michigan;* illus. Portland, Ore.:
    Graphic Arts Center Pub., 1977. (All ages) P
    Expensive, but spectacular publication of photo-
graphs of Michigan's natural grandeur, with seven pages
of text.

171 PARADIS, ADRIAN A. *Henry Ford;* illus. New York:
    Putnam, 1968. (1-2) B
    A *See and Read Beginning to Read* biography of
Henry Ford's dream and achievement of making a better
engine.

172 PATTERSON, LILLIE. *Lumberjacks of the North Woods;*
    illus. Champaign, Ill.: Garrard, 1967. o.p.
    (2-4) #
    Authentic account of life in a logging camp in
the Great Lakes region.

173 PECKHAM, HOWARD. *Pontiac, Young Ottawa Leader;*
    illus. Indianapolis, Ind.: Bobbs, 1963.
    (2-5) B
    Easy-reading biography from the *Childhood of
Famous Americans* series. More fictional than biograph-
ical, the emphasis is on the growing-up period of
Pontiac's life. Much dialogue; story moves quickly.

174 PETERSEN, EUGENE T. *Conservation of Michigan's
    Natural Resources.* Lansing: Michigan Histor-
    ical Commission, 1960. (6-8)
    Brief, but informative account of Michigan's
natural resources; their history, their usefulness,
the need for conservation.

175 PETERSEN, EUGENE T. *Mackinac Island: Its History in Pictures;* illus. Mackinac Island, Mich.: Mackinac Island State Park Commission, 1973. (4-8) P
A series of photographs chronologically records the history of Mackinac Island since 1780. Over 275 pictures, maps and sketches.

176 PETERSON, HELEN S. *Sojourner Truth: Fearless Crusader;* illus. Champaign, Ill.: Garrard, 1972. (2-5) B #
A brief biography of the former slave who became the first Black woman to give antislavery lectures in the United States, and who lived her later years in Battle Creek. *Americans All* series.

177 PRAEGER, ETHEL M. *Michigan—Land of the Big Water;* illus. Chicago: Follett, 1965. o.p. (4-6)
Textbook containing simplified material of a survey of Michigan. Index.

178 PRESCOTT, JOHN B. *Beautiful Ship: A Story of the Great Lakes;* illus. New York: Longmans, 1952. o.p. (4-6) F #
An adventure revolving around the fishing industry in Lake Michigan.

179 PRIESTLEY, LEE. *A Teacher for Tibby;* illus. New York: Morrow, 1960. (4-5) F
Eight-year-old girl and her mother concoct a plan to get a school built in Michigan forest country 100 years ago.

180 RANDALL, KENNETH CHARLES. *Wild Hunter;* illus. New York: Watts, 1951. o.p. (4-6) F
In the Michigan thumb area, a guide and young boy find a fine hunting dog.

181 RANDALL, RUTH PAINTER. *I, Elizabeth.* Boston: Little, Brown, 1966. o.p. (6-8) B
A biography of the girl who married George Armstrong Custer to become an Army wife and leave Michigan "society" to travel with her husband.

182 RANKIN, CARROLL W. *Dandelion Cottage;* illus.
Marquette, Mich.: Marquette County Historical
Society, 1977. (3-5) F
Four little girls in northern Michigan keep
house in a tiny cottage one summer. Original book
published in 1904.

183 RATIGAN, WILLIAM. *The Blue Snow;* illus. Grand
Rapids, Mich.: Eerdmans, 1958. o.p. (3-5)
Retelling of the blue snow of Paul Bunyan fame.

184 RATIGAN, WILLIAM. *Tiny Tim Pine;* illus. Grand
Rapids, Mich.: Eerdmans, 1958. o.p. (3-5)
The retelling of the Paul Bunyan tale of a tiny
pine ridiculed by larger trees.

185 RATIGAN, WILLIAM. *Young Mr. Big.* Grand Rapids,
Mich.: Eerdmans, 1955. o.p. (4-6) B
The biography of Charles T. Harvey, builder of
the Sault Ste. Marie canal.

186 REEDER, RED (COLONEL). *Attack at Fort Lookout;*
illus. New York: Duell, 1959. o.p. (5-8) F
The adventures of a young officer at a small
fort north of Detroit prior to the War of 1812.

187 REYNOLDS, QUENTIN. *Custer's Last Stand;* illus.
New York: Random House, 1951. o.p. (4-6) B
A *Landmark* book telling of the Monroe Indian
fighter and the massacre of his command.

—— RITZENTHALER, PAT R. *The Woodland Indians of the
Western Great Lakes.* See MI 188

188 RITZENTHALER, ROBERT E. and RITZENTHALER, PAT R.
The Woodland Indians of the Western Great Lakes;
illus. Garden City, N.Y.: Natural History
Press, 1970. o.p. (6-8) #
A factual book about the culture of the Woodland
Indians, including Michigan Indians. Bibliography.

189 ROBERTSON, KEITH. *In Search of the Sandhill Crane;*
illus. New York: Viking Press, 1973. (4-8) F
• During a summer in the Michigan wilderness in
the Upper Peninsula, Link discovers that he can be
still and silent, and not bored. The friendship of
Aunt and Charley Horse transcends age, race and backgrounds.

190 ROUNDS, GLEN. *Ol' Paul the Mighty Logger;* illus.
by author. New York: Holiday, 1976. (2-4) #
Easy-to-read stories of the exploits of Paul
Bunyan. First published in 1936.

191 ROWE, VIOLA. *A Way with Boys;* illus. New York:
Longmans, 1957. o.p. (3-5) F
Novel of young teen-age girl and her coming of
age in present-day Upper Peninsula. Other titles in
the same setting:
Oh, Brother, 1955.
Girl in a Hurry, 1956.
Free for All, 1959.

192 RUBIN, LAWRENCE A. *Mighty Mac: The Official
Picture History of the Mackinac Bridge;* illus.
Detroit: Wayne State University, 1958. o.p.
(4-8) P
The story of the world's greatest bridge project
to date told through photographs. Demonstrates feats
of engineering and construction to connect two
peninsulas.

—— RUDDIMAN, CATHERINE. *Henry Ford, Boy with Ideas.*
See MI 3

193 SANDBURG, HELGA. *Blueberry;* illus. New York:
Dial, 1963. o.p. (4-6) F
Story of a mare purchased at the county fair by
fourteen year old girl, and the training, schooling and
enjoyment of the horse. Setting is along Lake Michigan
shoreline and includes many references to Michigan.

194 SANDBURG, HELGA. *Gingerbread;* illus. New York:
   Dial, 1964. o.p. (4-6) F
   Blueberry's young foal, Gingerbread, is struck
by lightning and blinded. Sequel to *Blueberry*.

195 SCHOOLCRAFT, HENRY R. *The Fire Plume Legends of
   the American Indian;* illus. New York: Dial,
   1969. (3-6)
   Ten legends collected in the Lake Superior
region of the Chippewa Indians; edited by John
Bierhorst.

196 SCHOOLCRAFT, HENRY R. *The Indian Fairy Book: From
   the Original Legends;* illus. New York: Stokes,
   1916. o.p. (4-8)
   Indian lore from the stories gathered by Schoolcraft as he lived among the Indians around the Great
Lakes. Publication is dated, but still useful.

197 SEVERANCE, CHARLES L. *Tales of the Thumb.* Phila-
   delphia: Dorrance, 1973. (4-6)
   Collection of stories with their setting in the
"Thumb"of Michigan, which consists of five counties
nearly equal in size; thereafter all similarity ceases.
Written by a story teller of the area.

198 SLOTE, ALFRED. *Hang Tough, Paul Mather;* illus.
   Philadelphia: Lippincott, 1973. (4-6) F
   Little Leaguer who develops leukemia, moves to
Ann Arbor for treatment at the University of Michigan
hospital. Honest discussion of death.

199 SOMMERS, LAWRENCE M., ed. *Atlas of Michigan;* illus.
   Lansing: Michigan State University Press, 1977.
   (4-8) R *
   Complete and up-to-date Michigan atlas containing: natural environment, people and society, history
and culture, economy, recreation, transportation and
communication, and selected statistics by county.
Bibliography and Index.

200 SPIER, PETER. *Tin Lizzie;* illus. Garden City,
N.Y.: Doubleday, 1975. (4-5) F
Story of a series of owners—from 1909 to the
present day—of a 1909 Model T touring car, fondly
referred to as a "Tin Lizzie".

201 STEINMAN, DAVID B. and NEVILL, JOHN T. *Miracle
Bridge at Mackinac;* illus. by Reynold H.
Weidenaar. Grand Rapids, Mich.: Eerdmans, 1957.
o.p. (6-)
Complete information on the construction of the
great Straits of Mackinac bridge told in non-technical
language by the engineer shose design made the "impossible" bridge a reality. Includes photographs taken
during construction and a short summary of "Interesting Facts" regarding the numbers of rivets and bolts,
cables, concrete, important dates, etc.

202 STEVENS, JAMES. *Paul Bunyan;* illus. New York:
Comstock Edns., 1975. (5-8) #
Collection of legends about this lumberjack hero
in mill towns and lumber woods.

203 STONE, CAROLINE R. *Clorinda of Cherry Lane Farm;*
illus. New York: Liveright Pub., 1945. o.p.
(5-8) F
Story of the daughter of a migratory family and
their arrival in the Saginaw, Michigan, area to work on
the beet crop.

204 STONE, CAROLINE R. *Inga of Porcupine Mine;* illus.
New York: Holiday House, 1942. o.p. (4-6) F
The story describes the life style typical of a
mining company town in the Upper Peninsula.

205 STONE, NANCY. *Whistle up the Bay;* illus. Grand
Rapids, Mich.: Eerdmans, 1966. (5-6) F
Three young sons of a Swiss immigrant are
orphaned in 1870 near the "boom town" of Antrim City,
Michigan. They are forced to make their own way,

struggling with the farm, working in lumber camps, and loading ships. Points up the boys' determination and courage, and the kindness of the community members.

206 STONE, NANCY. *The Wooden River;* illus. Grand Rapids, Mich.: Eerdmans, 1973. (5-6) F
Story of a young girl and her life in a lumber-ing camp near Saginaw, Michigan.

207 STUART, DONNA VALLEY. *Michigan Undiscovered; A Guide to the Great Lake State.* Grosse Pte. Woods, Mich.: Michigan Ventures, 1973. Paper. (4-6)
A guide to natural attractions throughout the state with emphasis on things to do and see which are free or inexpensive. Approximately one-third deals with Upper Peninsula.

208 SWARTHOUT, GLENDON F. *Melodeon.* Garden City, N.Y.: Doubleday, 1977. (6-8) F
Adult fiction of an incident in the life of the author who grew up near Howell, Michigan.

209 SWARTHOUT, GLENDON and SWARTHOUT, KATHRYN. *The Ghost and the Magic Saber;* illus. New York: Random House, 1963. (3-5) F
Humorous story of a boy who must spend the summer on a Michigan farm. He also has to practice a flute daily, and finds that his chief companion is a girl.

—— SWARTHOUT, KATHRYN. *The Ghost and the Magic Saber.* See MI 209

210 SYME, RONALD. *LaSalle of the Mississippi;* illus. by William Stobbs. New York: Morrow, 1953. (3-6) B #
Forceful account of the difficulties and suc-cesses of Robert LaSalle as he explored the lower Great Lakes, and established French forts in Michigan and along the Mississippi River valley.

211 SYME, RONALD. *Marquette and Joliet: Voyagers on the Mississippi;* illus. New York: Morrow, 1974. (2-4) B
Easy reading biography of two 17th century explorers who first charted the course of the Mississippi River. Bibliography.

212 TEFFT, BESS HAGAMAN. *Ken of Centennial Farm;* illus. Chicago: Follett, 1959. o.p. (3-5) F
Eleven-year-old Ken is happy when his father lets him run the tractor and do some of the more important work on a Michigan farm. Present-day setting.

213 THAYER, MARJORIE. *The Christmas Strangers;* illus. by D. Freeman. Chicago: Childrens Press, 1976. (2-5) F
An endearing story of an old-fashioned Christmas in the Michigan territory.

214 VOIGHT, VIRGINIA F. *Pontiac: Mighty Ottawa Chief;* illus. Champaign, Ill.: Garrard, 1977. (2-4) F
Fast-moving story of Pontiac, the famous Great Lakes region Indian leader. The dramatic scenes are full of colorful action in this introduction to American history from the Indian's point of view. Checked for factual accuracy by anthropologists Alice Marriott and Carol K. Rachlin.

215 WADSWORTH, WALLACE. *Paul Bunyan and his Great Blue Ox;* illus. by Enrico Arno. Garden City: Doubleday, 1964. o.p. (4-6) #
Stories of the legendary lumberjack retold for children.

216 WAH-BE-GWO-NESE (Little Flower). *Ojibwa Indian Legends;* illus. Marquette, Mich.: Northern Michigan University Press, 1972. (4-6)
Beautifully illustrated Algonquian legends retold by author: How the Robin Came to Be King, and the tale of the Origin of Indian Corn.

217 WALKER, LOUISE JEAN. *Legends of Green Sky Hill;*
illus. Grand Rapids, Mich.: Eerdmans, 1959.
o.p. (4-6)
A collection of Chippewa Indian legends retold.
Depiction of Indian life and customs.
Additional titles by author on same subject:
Woodland Wigwams, Hillsdale, 1964.
Beneath the Singing Pines, Hillsdale, 1971.

—— WEAVER, JOAN S. *Where to Go and What to Do with
the Kids in Detroit.* See MI 117

218 WHITNEY, PHYLLIS. *Mystery of the Gulls;* illus.
Philadelphia: Westminster, 1949. (4-8) F
A story of mystery and adventure on Mackinac
Island. Junior Literary Guild selection.

219 WILLIAMS, FREDERICK D. *Michigan Soldiers in the
Civil War.* Lansing: Michigan Historical
Commission, 1960. (6-8)
Brief, but informative, account of the men from
Michigan who fought in the Civil War.

220 WILSON, HOLLY. *Double Heritage.* Philadelphia:
Westminster, 1971. o.p. (5-8) F
Story of an intercultural marriage between a
half-Chippewa girl and the son of one of Detroit's
aristocratic French families. The Black Hawk War and a
cholera epidemic in 1832 provide the exciting background.

221 WILSON, HOLLY. *Snowbound in Hidden Valley;* illus.
New York: Messner, 1957. o.p. (4-6) F
A story of adventure and mystery concerning the
Chippewas during a Michigan blizzard. Jo Shannon,
snowbound at the home of her Indian classmate, Onota
Leroy, was surprised by a way of life which combined
native Chippewa customs with modern living.

222 WILSON, HOLLY. *Stranger in Singamon;* illus. New
York: Messner, 1959. o.p. (3-5) F
The story of a young girl living with relatives
in the lumber town of Singamon, Michigan, where she is
miserable until she finds surprise and suspense.

223 WITHERIDGE, ELIZABETH. *Never Younger, Jeannie;*
illus. by Virginia Lee Bates. New York:
Atheneum, 1963. o.p. (4-6) F
In 1914 eleven-year-old Jeannie comes from California to stay for a year with grandparents on a
Michigan farm, and finds many new experiences.
Jeannie matures as she faces her fears for the safety
of her vacationing parents, who were trapped in Europe
at the beginning of World War I.

—— WOHL, GARY. *The Picture Life of Stevie Wonder.*
See MI 50

224 WRIGHT, ZITA. *Danger on the Ski Trails.* New York:
Lothrop, 1965. (5-8) F
Mystery of iron miner's daughter and her activities in skiing and working on a small town weekly newspaper. "Ghost skier" provides mystery.

225 WUNSCH, JOSEPHINE. *Flying Skis;* illus. New York:
McKay, 1962. o.p. (4-8) F
Story of Nikki Jorgenson who makes skiing a
career. Training in the Upper Peninsula helps her get
a chance to try her skill in the State Races. Another
title by the author set in a resort area of Michigan
involves a summer romance:
Summer of Decision, McKay, 1963.

226 YORTY, JEANE. *Far Wilderness;* illus. Grand
Rapids, Mich.: Eerdmans, 1966. o.p. (6-8) F
Adventures of a family traveling from New York
to the Michigan Territory in 1835.

MINNESOTA

compiled by GRACE STAGEBERG SWENSON

Much of the colorful past and promising future of
Minnesota, the North Star State, is tied to its abundant water supply. Called the "land of 10,000 lakes",
Minnesota actually contains 15,291 official lakes, tens
of thousands of ponds and hundreds of rivers and streams.
Over five percent of Minnesota's 84,068 square miles is
covered by inland water, and the state is bordered on
three sides by lakes and rivers. During the Ice Age,
glaciers moved south from Canada and carved out most of
the water basins that exist in Minnesota today.

Prehistoric peoples who settled the area left more
than 10,000 burial mounds near those rivers and lakes.
The state's first recorded inhabitants were the Dakota,
or Sioux, Indians. They were largely a peaceful people,
who called their land "minisota", meaning "sky-tinted
waters." In later years the Dakota were driven from
their lands by the more militant Ojibwe, or Chippewa,
nation. Ultimately, both tribes lost their territories
to the white man through treaty and exploitation.

143

The first Europeans to reach Minnesota in the late 1600's were French traders and missionaries. In time, a lively fur trade developed as the French-Canadian voyageurs transported the valuable beaver pelts down from north along the boundary waters canoe routes.

As exploration and settlement continued, the region was claimed in turn by four governments—France, Spain, England and ultimately, the United States. In 1819 the U. S. government established Fort Snelling at the strategically located confluence of the Minnesota and Mississippi Rivers. In 1849 Minnesota became a U. S. Territory and in 1858, the thirty-second state in the Union.

After the Civil War, free or cheap land attracted many homesteaders from eastern states and Europe, and the economy flourished. The abundant forests were logged to supply much of the nation's lumber. In the 1880's iron ore was first shipped from Minnesota's Iron Range, the world's largest supply of high-grade iron ore. By that time Minnesota wheat had made Minneapolis the nation's leading flour milling center.

In the first half of the 20th century Minnesota experienced great industrialization and growth. By the late 1970's over two-thirds of its 3,805,000 people were living in urban areas, with 434,000 in Minneapolis, the state's largest city. The Twin Cities area—Minneapolis, St. Paul (the capital), and suburbs—has become a sprawling megalopolis which supports a wide variety of industry, business, medical care, education, culture and recreation. Rochester, in southeastern Minnesota, boasts the world-renowned Mayo Clinic, and smaller cities around the state contribute to a diversified economy. On the Iron Range the mining of taconite, a low-grade iron ore, has become an important industry.

Agriculture, however, remains one of Minnesota's leading single industries. In the early 1970's the state ranked among the nation's leaders in the production of hogs, turkeys, cattle, dairy products, and corn and peas for canning. Wheat is still a major crop in the fertile Red River Valley, but the farmers in southern Minnesota have turned to the more profitable crops of corn, soybeans and oats.

As in years past, the state's abundant water supply
sustains a variety of industrial and recreational activities. The mighty Mississippi River, which begins as a
small northern Minnesota stream, is an important commercial waterway. Along Lake Superior's scenic North Shore,
visitors can view this awesome inland sea which holds
approximately ten percent of the world's fresh water.
Duluth, the western terminal of the St. Lawrence Seaway,
is one of the ten busiest ports in the country.

The million-acre Boundary Waters Canoe Area on
Minnesota's northeastern border is the largest and most
popular wilderness area east of the Rockies. Here
canoeists can paddle through 150,000 acres of water in
over 1000 crystal-clear lakes, bordered by rugged
glacial rocks. And across the state, fishing, boating
and swimming are favorite pastimes.

Minnesota today embraces many ethnic groups, but
the descendents of the Scandinavian and German immigrants who arrived in the last half of the 19th century,
are still in the majority. Politically, the state has
been a maverick, supporting independent and protest
parties as well as Republicans and a combined Democrat-
ic-Farmer-Labor Party. Modern Minnesota politicians
Eugene McCarthy, Hubert Humphrey and Walter Mondale are
well-known across the nation.

Today Minnesota faces the same problems that
beset the nation. Energy supplies are dwindling, and
Minnesota's lakes, streams and rivers are becoming pol-
luted as industry and the population grow. Taconite
tailings must be filtered from the once pure Lake
Superior drinking water. Yet the state still contains
a sizeable portion of unspoiled natural beauty. With
far-sighted leadership and bold conservation measures,
future generations will be able to enjoy this priceless
heritage.

145

1   ADAMSON, WENDY WRISTON. *Saving Lake Superior: A
    Story of Environmental Action.* Minneapolis:
    Dillon, 1974. (5-9)
       An overview of environmental problems facing
Lake Superior. Adamson cites geographical, geological
and historical background of the lake, industrial
development, politics involved and threats of pollution.
She tells of attempts by the courts and people to stop
Reserve Mining, on the North Shore, from discharging
67,000 tons of taconite tailings daily into the lake,
a procedure since 1947. Citizens, particularly the
young, are urged to become involved. A level-headed,
well-organized approach to a difficult problem which
has no easy answers. Youthful readers can easily com-
prehend this simplified, concise argument for activism.
Photographs, maps, glossary and bibliography.

2   ADAMSON, WENDY WRISTON. *Who Owns a River? A Story
    of Environmental Action.* Minneapolis: Dillon,
    1977. (5-9) #
       Adamson's second environmental book deals with
the St. Croix River which marks 127 miles of the
Minnesota-Wisconsin boundary. After general historical
and geographical background, the author tells of the
construction of the Northern States Power plant at Oak
Park Heights, Minnesota, despite protest of many citizens. Environmentalists lost the fight, but the controversy led to the passing of federal laws to protect
natural resources and the designation of the St. Croix
as a "wild river." A simplified, readable account of a
complex issue. Photographs, maps, glossary and bibliography.

3   ADRIAN, MARY. *The North American Wolf;* illus. by
    Genevieve Vaughan-Jackson. New York: Hastings,
    1965. (3-5)
       An easy-to-read account of one year in the life
cycle of a male timber wolf, his mate and their four
pups as they struggle to survive in northern Minnesota.
The wolves in turn are both predators and prey.
Adrian's sympathetic and sensitive true story gives

young readers basic concepts of nature's system of balance. Realistic black and white drawings complement
the text. Short bibliography.

— AKERS, SAM. *The Game Breaker.* See MN 4

4 AKERS, TOM and AKERS, SAM. *The Game Breaker: The
Story of Bruce Smith.* Wayzata, Minn.: Turtinen,
1977. (8-) B
Bruce Smith, a modest unassuming young man, captured attention in the state and nation when he was
named America's Heisman Award Winner in 1941. Smith
played with the Minnesota Gophers under Bernie Bierman
during the team's golden years. He symbolized courage,
even at his death at the age of 47 when he lost the
battle against cancer. Much of the book relates highlights of Smith's football career, but there are glimpses of his remarkable life. Football fans in particular will enjoy this detailed personal account.

5 ALLEN, GEORGE and ROSSMAN, BOB. *Bald Eagles of the
Chippewa Forest.* Grand Rapids, Minn.: Grand
Rapids Herald-Review, 1971. Paper. (4-)
A small attractive booklet on the bird which has
been an endangered species since 1967. The Chippewa
National Forest in north central Minnesota is one of
the most concentrated eagle breeding areas in the
country. Information from ornithologists includes the
eagle's features and habits, its life cycle, banding
and field techniques and a table of data covering a
9-year period which shows an increase in eagle population. Well-organized, easily-understood information
with numerous color photographs, a map of the Chippewa
Forest and suggested readings.

6 ALLEN, GEORGE and ROSSMAN, BOB. *The Loon: Minnesota's State Bird.* Grand Rapids, Minn.: Grand
Rapids Herald-Review, 1967. Paper. (4-8)
A booklet on the Minnesota state bird, the
common loon. Information on the loon's appearance,
habits, life cycle and migration pattern is included as
well as explanations of the loon's four basic calls.

147

Although loons still are abundant in remote lakes in
northern Minnesota, they are threatened in more populated areas by botulism, insecticides and chemicals.
Ten frames from a 16mm motion picture show a sequence
of a loon's dive. Small, compact, readable, non-
technical book for the young reader as well as for the
adult.

7 AMB, THOMAS M. *The Voyageurs: Frontiersman of the
Northwest;* illus. by Louis R. Thompson.
Minneapolis: Denison, 1973. Paper. (4-8)
A publication in paper format designed to
acquaint readers with the Voyageurs National Park in
northern Minnesota. The three sections include a brief
history of early fur trade from the 1600's through the
mid-1800's, information on the voyageurs who once travelled the early canoe routes and details on the establishment of the park. A map shows points of interest
in the park. Despite lifeless watercolor illustrations
the book is useful introduction to a unique area with
historical significance.

8 ANTELL, WILL. *William Warren;* illus. Minneapolis:
Dillon, 1973. (4-6) B
Will Antell, Ojibwe Indian from the White Earth
Reservation in Minnesota, has written a short, readable
biography of William Whipple Warren, Ojibwe Indian historian, author and legislator. Warren played an important role in the 1850 Sioux-Ojibwe Peace Council at
Fort Snelling and was a government representative to
the Territorial Legislature. Although the text is
uninspired, Antell displays a deep regard for the culture and heritage of his people. Old historical photographs add interest.

9 BAILEY, BERNARDINE. *Picture Book of Minnesota;*
illus. by Kurt Wiese. Rev. ed. Chicago:
Whitman, 1967. (3-5)
Although this book needs updating, there is useful information on Minnesota for beginning researchers.
Similar to the other state books in the "Picture Book"
series, there is first a brief history of the state

followed by geographical information, points of interest, major towns and cities, industrial development and
people who were important to the state. Kurt Wiese's
pictures in color and black and white decorate each
page. Index.

10 BAKER, LAURA NELSON. *Here by the Sea.*
Philadelphia: Lippincott, 1968. (7-9) F
In a first person story Stephanie Harris looks
back on her Senior year at Crowell High in Minneapolis
when her younger sister, Marise, met a tragic death in
a car accident at the hands of a boyfriend involved
with drugs. Stephanie draws apart in isolation until
she accepts the fact that life is sometimes unfair and
unpleasant. Although this story does not match the
realism of more recent publications, Baker does handle
the problems of youth with sensitivity and understanding. The setting in Minnesota has little significance
to the story.

11 BAKER, LAURA NELSON. *Somebody, Somewhere.* New
York: Knopf, 1962. (7-9) F
After Diane Edson moves from north Minneapolis
to the suburbs, she acquires new friends, among them a
boyfried, Bill Rumford, son of a policeman. Diane's
jealous former boyfriend, Chick West, is jailed by
Bill's father after creating a minor disturbance. The
story has a plausible, expected conclusion. Though not
of the recent genre of problem books for teen-age readers, this story is well-paced, has believable characters and natural dialogue.

12 BAKER, LAURA NELSON. *The Special Year.* New York:
Knopf, 1959. (7-9) F
An idealistic story of the 1950's set in a fic-
titious middle class suburb of Minneapolis. Scott
Wagner's senior year at Golden Prairie High School is
complicated by personal problems—temporary rejection
by his best girl, the accidental death of his friend,
Alec, and his increasing fondness for Alec's girlfriend.
His problems are resolved when he is forced to make
plans for college and a career. Baker's unsophisticated

story will please adolescents who desire uncomplicated romantic themes, believable characters and satisfactory conclusions.

13 BATSON, LARRY. *An Interview with Alan Page;* photographs by John Croft. Mankato, Minn.: Creative Ed. Soc., 1977. (4-6) B

A brief introduction to the person and thoughts of Alan Page, the former Minnesota Vikings defensive tackle. Page is a paradox—gentle, concerned father of four, industrious student seeking a law degree, firm believer in discipline and justice, yet on the football field an explosive, tough, temperamental competitor. High-quality color photographs with a large print text that looks deceptively easy. May interest reluctant readers.

14 BATSON, LARRY. *An Interview with Rod Carew;* photographs by John Croft. Mankato, Minn.: Creative Ed. Soc., 1977. (4-6) B

"It's not all bad, being a loner," says Rod Carew, baseball's No. 1 major league hitter. From his childhood in the Panama Canal Zone, through his youth in New York, to his position with the Minnesota Twins, Carew has fought shyness and loneliness. But being a loner gave him an all-consuming drive to make it to the top of the major leagues. In later years he found support from a few select friends, a loving wife and two daughters. This short, easy-to-read biography, enhanced by full page color photographs, captures some of the Carew philosophy and personality.

15 BIERHORST, JOHN, ed. *The Fire Plume, Legends of the American Indians;* pictures by Alan E. Cober. New York: Dial, 1969. (4-6)

Ten Indian legends from Chippewa, Ottawa, Menominee and other Algonquin tribes originally collected by Henry Schoolcraft in his travels through the Great Lakes and upper Mississippi region in the early 1800's. Includes unusual black and white illustrations and a glossary of Indian words. These campfire tales are of particular interest because of Schoolcraft's importance in Minnesota history.

16 BIERHORST, JOHN. *Songs of the Chippewa;* pictures
    by Joe Servello. New York: Farrar, Straus &
    Giroux, 1974. (5-) P #
    Seventeen Chippewa songs adapted from originals
collected by explorer Henry Schoolcraft in the 1850's
and musicologist Frances Densmore in the early 1900's
from the western shores of the Great Lakes. Bierhorst
has arranged the chants, lullabies and dream songs with
simple piano and guitar accompaniment. He identifies
the source of each song, suggests its background and
interpretation and gives proper pronunciation of
Chippewa words. Servello's full-page, brown-tone pictures are exceptionally appealing. A handsome book for
children to look at and for all ages to use.

17 BLACKLOCK, LES. *Meet My Psychiatrist;* photographs
    by the author. Bloomington, Minn.: Voyageur,
    1977. (6-) P
    Wherever he travels, whether to the Minnesota-
Ontario wilderness, Isle Royale, Yellowstone or the
Rockies, Minnesota's Les Blacklock, wildlife photographer and naturalist, collects pictures and adventures. Here his personal observations and experiences,
told with gentleness and warmth, alternate with four
galleries of superb full-color photographs, 54 in all.
And we meet Old Doc Log, his psychiatrist, on whose
couch most problems vanish. A high quality book to be
enjoyed and appreciated by nature lovers everywhere.

18 BLEEKER, SONIA. *The Chippewa Indians, Rice Gather-
    ers of the Great Lakes;* illus. by Patricia
    Boodell. New York: Morrow, 1955. (4-6) #
    The family life and culture of the Cranes, a
typical Chippewa Indian family living at Sault Ste.
Marie before the advent of white man. They gather
wild rice, make maple sugar, build canoes, train warriors and medicine, play games, tell stories and go to
war over disputed lands. In the last chapter Bleeker
tells of reservation life in Minnesota, Michigan, Wisconsin and North Dakota. In all of her books on Indian
tribes the author shares abundant information with dignity and skillful simplicity. Illustrations, a map of
reservations and index.

19 BOLZ, J. ARNOLD. *Portage into the Past;* drawings
     by Francis Lee Jaques. Minneapolis: University
     of Minnesota Press, 1960. (7-)
        A log of the author's canoe trip through the
Minnesota-Ontario Boundary Waters, a route taken by the
French-Canadian voyageurs from Grand Portage in Lake
Superior to Lake Namakan near Rainy Lake. In his day-
to-day diary Bolz interjects excerpts from old historical journals, some up to 250 years old, of those who
took the same journey. There are drawings, reproductions of historical paintings and maps, as well as a
bibliography and index. A unique blending of history,
travel and nature study and will interest a wide variety of readers.

20 BRADY, LILLIAN. *Aise-ce-bon, a Raccoon;* illus. by
     Jerome Connolly. New York: Harvey, 1971.
     (4-6) P *
        In Minnesota's northern wilderness area a female
raccoon, Aise-ce-bon, nurses her four coonlets through
a year of discipline and training to insure their survival. All of the wild creatures are given Chippewa
Indian names, which, along with other Indian words, are
listed in a glossary. Brady, who has a summer home in
this remote area, understands and loves wildlife. Her
beautifully-written nature story illustrated by Con-
nolly's meticulous life-like drawings make this a book
children will respect and enjoy.

21 BRAUN, THOMAS. *Football's Greatest Passer: Fran
     Tarkenton.* Mankato, Minn.: Creative Ed. Soc.,
     1977. (2-4)
        A brief summary of highlights of the football
career of Minnesota Viking's veterna quarterback, Fran
Tarkenton. Photographs in color and black and white
alternate with text printed on only half of each page.
The book has visual appeal, but its limited scope will
only whet the appetite of the young reader for more
information.

22 BRAY, EDMUND C. *Billions of Years in Minnesota:
    The Geological Story of the State.* St. Paul,
    Minn.: Science Museum of Minnesota, 1977. (8-)
    An expansion of an earlier publication, *A Million
Years in Minnesota,* which remains as Part III in this
edition. Covers geological areas beginning with the
Early Precambrian Period over four billion years ago.
Includes a tour guide to the state's rock formations, a
glossary of geological terms, numerous maps, illustrations and photographs. A carefully-researched, under-
standable text written for the lay person. Bibliography
and index.

23 BRECKENRIDGE, WALTER J. *Reptiles and Amphibians of
    Minnesota.* Minneapolis: University of Minnesota
    Press, 1944. (6-) R *
    A comprehensive guide to reptiles and amphibians
of Minnesota and adjoining states compiled by the former director of the University of Minnesota's Museum of
Natural History. In his introduction Breckenridge
includes the history of herpetology, its folklore, the
preservation of specimens, care for those in captivity
and avoiding and treating snake bites. Includes pictures of the reptiles and amphibians, their descriptions, habits, life cycles and habitats. For lay persons and professional naturalists. Glossary, bibliography and index.

24 BREINING, GREG and WATSON, LINDA. *A Gathering of
    Waters: A Guide to Minnesota's Rivers.*
    St. Paul: Minnesota Department of Natural
    Resources, 1977. Paper. (8-)
    An attractive book showing canoe and boating
routes on 18 of Minnesota's most scenic and popular
rivers. There are vivid descriptions, detailed maps
and inviting color photographs of each river. An additional section gives brief information on 25 other
rivers and streams in the state. Although this is a
guide primarily for canoeists, the book could be used
by hikers, fishermen and nature lovers. References for
additional reading.

25 BRILL, CHARLES. *Indian and Free: A Contemporary Portrait of Life on a Chippewa Reservation;* text and photographs by Charles Brill. Minneapolis: University of Minnesota Press, 1974. (6-) P
  The major impact of this book is in the 106   v black and white photographs portraying people and activities of the Red Lake Indian Reservation in northern Minnesota. Brill's accompanying text discusses the history of the reservation, customs and traditions of the Chippewa tribes and the problems attending their adaptation to modern life. For the young person who does not want to read the text, the pictures and captions tell a dramatic story.

26 BRINGS, LAWRENCE M., ed. *Minnesota Heritage.* Minneapolis: Denison, 1960. (6-)
  Subtitled "A panoramic narrative of the historical development of the North Star State." Leading authorities in various fields write on Minnesota's prehistoric period, Indian heritage, natural resources, business and industry, education, politics, art, music, humanities and what appears to be the state's future. A large impressive volume with well-presented historical information illustrated by numerous pictures, photographs and maps. Recent developments of the 1960's and 70's are missing. Unfortunately, the lack of an index limits the use of this volume.

27 BRO, MARGUERITTE HARMON. *Sarah.* New York: Grosset & Dunlap (Tempo), 1949. Paper. (8-11) F
  Before Sarah Duncan's father died, he hoped that Sarah would become "something grand . . . an artist, maybe." So Sarah diligently pursues art, then music. When her fiance dies in World War I, Sarah plunges into frenzied activity. Existence has little real meaning until a young serviceman, wounded in the war, turns her life around. Author Bro based her book on her own experiences as a minister's daughter in St. Paul in the 1900's. Her characters are believable, and dialogue flows naturally. Family relationships and personal philosophy are well-anchored in this warm story for older readers.

154

28 BROCK, EMMA L. *Drusilla;* illus. by author. New
     York: Macmillan, 1937. (3-5) F
     Drusilla, corn-husk doll, tells her own version
of pioneering in Minnesota. When Drusilla falls off
the Hodgett's covered wagon as they travel to their new
home on the Minnesota prairie, the doll is found and
loved by Moonflower, a young Indian girl. Drusilla's
fate is determined when the Hodgetts meet Moonflower's
family. Children will enjoy this humorous, fanciful,
yet historically-based story.

—   BROOKINS, JEAN A. *Minnesota's Major Historic Sites,
     A Guide.* See MN 78

29 BUCHANAN, JAMES W. *Minnesota Walk Book, Vol. I;*
     illus. by Marianne Lydecker. Reprint edition.
     Minneapolis: Nodin Press, 1978. **Paper.** (6-)
     This first volume of a series of guides for
hikers and backpackers covers over 500 miles of trails
in Minnesota's Arrowhead region and Isle Royale. Gives
a brief history of the area, tells how to plan a trip,
describes and maps out short and long hikes. Buchanan,
a veteran backpacker, planned this paperback book to
take along on the trail. He encourages keeping personal notes on the blank pages. A suggested reading list
and index make this a worthy reference book as well as
a valuable guidebook.

30 BUCHANAN, JAMES W. *Minnesota Walk Book, Vol. II;*
     illus. by Robert Negaard. Minneapolis: Nodin
     Press, 1977. (6-)
     This second volume in the series is guide to
hiking and backpacking in the Heartland of Minnesota,
a region running north and south in a central corridor
in the northern half of the state. Following a brief
geological survey of the area, there are tips for the
hiker. The trails are to be found in state forests and
parks, public campgrounds and private resorts. Attractive sketches, a reading list, glossary and index.
Another guide for hikers of all ages and abilities to
take along on the trail.

31 BUCHANAN, JAMES W. *Minnesota Walk Book, Vol. III;*
    illus. by G. Grindle. Minneapolis: Nodin Press,
    1978. (6-)
    A companion to the first two volumes, this is a
guide to the more populated area of Minnesota's agricultural Hiawatha Land in the southeastern corner of
the state. After an overview of the area there are
suggested hikes to take in state parks, forests, public
hiking areas and private resorts. New in this volume
are two trails to be found in underground caves.
Includes maps, subtle illustrations of scenery and wildlife, reading list, but no index.

32 BULLA, CLYDE ROBERT. *Down the Mississippi;* illus.
    by Peter Burchard. New York: Crowell, 1954.
    (3-6) F
    Thirteen-year-old Erick Lind realizes his ambi-
tion to be a riverman when he becomes a cook's helper
on a raft bringing logs down the Mississippi from
Minnesota to St. Louis. Erick soon discovers there is
more work than pleasure, and there are fights, storms,
Indian raids and exploding steamboats. But nothing
dampens Erick's love for the River. Indians in the
story are portrayed negatively as are some of the white
rivermen. This exciting vigorous story of the 1850's
moves quickly and can be read easily by young adventure
seekers.

33 BURCHARD, MARSHALL. *Fran Tarkenton.* New York:
    Putnam, 1977. (4-8) B
    Biography in the *Sports Hero* series of the
Viking's veteran quarterback from early childhood,
through his long career with the NFL as the star "Scrambler." Both triumphs and defeats are described, adding
a sense of reality. Although the large print format
gives a deceptive appearance of easy-reading, the book
should be of interest to a wide range of young sports
enthusiasts who want plenty of action and inside information.

34 CANTRELL, DALLAS. *Youngers' Fatal Blunder: North-field, Minnesota.* San Antonio, Tex.: Naylor, 1973. (7-)

The disastrous robbery and murders at Northfield, Minnesota, on September 7, 1876, by the James-Younger gang. Cole, Jim and Bob Younger were captured and imprisoned at Stillwater State Prison. Friends and sympathizers tried in vain to secure their parole after years of good conduct. The author, a Southerner before she moved to Minnesota, immersed herself in extensive research of old newspapers and records to prove that the long imprisonment of the Youngers was a result of Northern prejudice, politics and publicity. An intriguing and mature work by a 19-year-old author. Historical photographs and bibliography.

35 CARLEY, KENNETH. *Minnesota in the Civil War.* Wayzata, Minn.: Ross and Haines, 1961. (8-)

Although Minnesota achieved statehood only three years before the outbreak of the Civil War, she contributed from 22,000 to 25,000 men to fight. Of these, 2500 lost their lives. Historian Carley has researched extensively the participation of Minnesota's 11 infantry regiments and two light artillery batteries in some of the war's most crucial battles. There is a chronology of important events from 1861 to 1865. Six famous paintings are reproduced in color, as well as other black and white photographs and maps. A carefully-written history for all Civil War students. Bibliography and index.

36 CARLEY, KENNETH. *The Sioux Uprising of 1862.* 2d. ed. St. Paul: Minnesota Historical Society, 1976. (8-) *

An account of Minnesota's tragic and bloody Sioux War from its beginning on August 17, 1862, when five white settlers were killed in Meeker County, to December 26, when 38 Indians were hanged at Mankato. In this revised edition, Carley has expanded the text with newly-discovered information which explains the Indian viewpoint and examines the events that led to the war. The book features careful research, precise

documentation, unbiased writing and a provocative array
of photographs, maps and drawings. Includes an extensive bibliography and detailed index. Available in
hardcover or paperback.

37 CARPENTER, ALLAN. *Enchantment of Minnesota;* illus.
by Roger Herrington. Chicago: Childrens, 1966.
(4-6)
Similar to others in the *Enchantment of America*
series, this introduces young readers to the general
aspects of Minnesota's geology, geography, history and
present development. Tables of information, annual
events and lists of famous people are in the back of
the book. Watercolor illustrations in blue are appropriate for the state which advertises its 10,000 lakes.
State symbols are pictured on the cover. Children
should be advised of the age of this volume—the population is from the 1960 census. They will also have to
search for specific information. A good index.

38 CLARK, ANN NOLAN. *All This Wild Land.* New York:
Viking, 1976. (4-7) F
When 11-year-old Maiju and her parents come from
Finland to a Finnish settlement in Minnesota in 1876,
they struggle to build a home and earn a living in the
harsh and lonely wilderness. When hail destroys the
first crop and Maiju's father dies in a blizzard, Maiju
and her mother are sustained by the love of family and
friends and large amounts of *sisu* (Finnish word for
courage). Clark's research in Finland and in a Finnish
community in Minnesota provided material on customs and
traditions. Except for romanticized Indian characters,
this young people's novel is a perceptive and realistic
portrait of frontier living.

39 CLARKSON, EWAN. *Wolf Country: A Wilderness Pil-
grimage;* drawings by David K. Stone. New York:
Dutton, 1975. (6-)
An English author takes to the remote areas of
Isle Royale in Lake Superior, the Superior National
Forest and the Boundary Waters Canoe Area in northern
Minnesota to study the inter-relationships of the tim-
ber wolf to the other animals of the area. His search

for the wolf is never realized, but he learns to appreciate the wilderness and the natural order which maintains a balance between the wolves, moose and deer. A
perceptive and well-developed argument for the preservation of the wolf and the wilderness.

40 COATSWORTH, ELIZABETH. *Door to the North;* illus.
     by Frederick T. Chapman. New York: Holt, Rine-
     hart & Winston, 1950. o.p. (7-10) F
     A story of the Viking expedition of 1354 that
supposedly came to Minnesota via the Hudson Bay and Red
River in search of the lost colony of Greenlanders.
Young Olav Sigurdson goes on the dangerous journey, and
his adventures sustain the plot. Coatsworth bases the
story on the theory propounded by some Minnesotans that
Vikings "discovered" Minnesota and left their message
on the Kensington Runestone, a rock discovered near
Alexandria. A skillfully-written, intricate historical
novel that requires careful reading.

41 COEN, RENA. *Painting and Sculpture in Minnesota,*
     1820-1914. Minneapolis: University of Minne-
     sota Press, 1976. (6-) P *
     An outstanding pictorial history of art in
Minnesota from the establishment of Fort Snelling in
1820 to the beginning of World War I. The author, art
history instructor at St. Cloud State University, compiled the book for the University Gallery Bicentennial
exhibition, drawing on art collections across the
nation. Included are works of early recorder-artists
such as George Catlin and Seth Eastman, primitives by
folk artists, landscapes of Minnesota scenes by eastern
painters and the work of emerging Minnesota artists.
An articulate, well-researched text accompanies 37
beautifully reproduced color plates and over 100 black
and white illustrations. A superior book.

42 COHEN, PETER ZACHARY. *The Muskie Hook;* drawings by
     Tom O'Sullivan. New York: Atheneum, 1969.
     (6-9) F
     At a resort in northern Minnesota Aaron Rennin
helps his father run the lodge and guides eager fisher-

men to a good catch and possibly to the prize muskie.
When Aaron guides a party of three unusual men in a
search for the big muskie, they find more adventure
than fish. There is a surprising conclusion. Portions
of the story are told by the muskie as he contemplates
the fishermen from the bottom of the lake. Humorous,
sparse line drawings illustrate this tongue-in-cheek
fishing tale.

43 COMFORT, MILDREN HOUGHTON. *James J. Hill, Young*
     Empire Builder; illus. by William K. Plummer.
     Indianapolis: Bobbs-Merrill, 1968. (3-5) B
     A biography in the *Childhood of Famous Americans*
series covering primarily the childhood and youth of
the famous "Empire Builder." Even as a child in Ontario, James J. Hill was enterprising and precocious.
When he came to Pig's Eye (St. Paul), Minnesota, he was
penniless but ambitious. He seized opportunities as
they came, first with steamboats, then with railroads.
When he died, he was one of Minnesota's wealthiest and
most famous men. The book concludes with a chronology
of events, questions, activities, bibliography and
glossary. A fictionalized biography easily read by
children.

44 COMFORT, MILDRED HOUGHTON. *Treasure on the Johnny*
     Smoker; illus. by James MacDonald. New York:
     Morrow, 1947. (4-8) F
     A sequel to *The Winter on the Johnny Smoker,*
unfortunately out-of-print. When 15-year-old Timothy
Dustin stumbles on a valuable cache of stolen muskrat
pelts, he and his family become deeply involved in solving the theft and returning the furs to the rightful
owners. The pelts must be guarded until the family
side-wheeler, the *Johnny Smoker,* makes its first spring
trip from Reads Landing on Lake Pepin up the Mississippi to St. Paul. Minnesota author Comfort based this
story on her own family experiences at Reads Landing.
A fast-moving adventure full of the zest of rivertown
life in the mid-1870's.

45 CRAZ, ALBERT G. *Getting to Know the Mississippi River;* illus. by Nathan Goldstein. New York: Coward, McCann, 1965. (3-6)

In the *Getting to Know* series, this is a general introduction to the Mississippi, its history, legends, navigational facilities, river travel and the industries it supports. Includes information on the major river cities, among them St. Paul and Minneapolis. A brief, factual book with solid information and numerous illustrations, but one which should be up-dated. Index.

46 DAHL, BORGHILD. *Under This Roof.* New York: Dutton, 1961. (6-9) F

In a small Minnesota town in the early 1900's 16-year-old Kristine Romness resolves that she will keep her family together despite the tragic death of her parents. Relatives reluctantly agree to give her until Easter to prove that she can manage the household. If she fails, the children will be placed in separate homes. With the aid of a young minister, the five children struggle through the winter, growing closer and stronger with each difficulty. Minnesota author Dahl writes compassionately of young people caught in personal and religious conflict. A satisfying story with a hint of discreet romance.

47 DALGLIESH, ALICE. *Ride on the Wind;* pictures by Georges Schrieber. New York: Scribner, 1956. (3-5)

This simplified account is taken from Charles Lindbergh's *The Spirit of St. Louis.* Includes a brief over-view of Lindbergh's early life in Minnesota and his youthful experiences as a pilot. The major portion of the book relates the exciting and grueling 33-hour non-stop flight from New York to Paris in 1927. Schrieber's watercolor pictures are attractive but give a picture-book appearance to a story which could be enjoyed by older children.

48 DE LEEUW, ADELE. *Paul Bunyan Finds a Wife;* illus.
by Ted Schroeder. Champaign, Ill.: Garrard,
1969. (3-5)
Paul's ideal woman appears in the person of
Carrie, a lady of considerable size who can make large
pancakes. Paul marries her and puts her to work as
chief cook in his lumbercamp. When the King of Sweden
commissions Paul to clear trees in Minnesota to make
room for settlement by the Swedes, Paul and Carrie
finish the job in record time. The King rewards them
with gold, cheese, bacon and two cows. Schroeder's
humorous illustrations complement this tall tale which
is easy-to-read and provides good story-telling
material.

49 DENSMORE, FRANCES. *Chippewa Music.* Two Volumes in
One. Wayzata, Minn.: Ross and Haines, 1973.
(6-) R *
This famous study by Minnesota's ethno-musicolo-
gist, Frances Densmore, was originally published in two
volumes by the Bureau of American Ethnology of the
Smithsonian Institution in 1910 and 1913. Although it
is an extensive study of Chippewa music from Minnesota
Indian reservations, it also provides abundant information on Chippewa Indian culture and traditions. Numerous black and white photographs and song pictures accompany the detailed text and the musical notation. Each
volume has a complete index. Valuable for its auxiliary
information on Chippewa Indian life in the early 1900's.

50 DENSMORE, FRANCES. *Dakota and Ojibwe People in
Minnesota.* St. Paul: Minnesota Historical
Society, 1977. Paper. (4-6) *
Originally published in *Roots* magazine. Although
Densmore wrote many adult works, this is written specifically for children. For 70 years she travelled to
reservations interviewing Native Americans and recording their music. Densmore describes lcustoms, occupations and life-styles of Dakota and Ojibwe Indians in
the early 1900's. High quality photographs from the
author's own collection illustrate the readable text.
Valuable information drawn from primary sources.

51 DES JARLAIT, PATRICK. *Patrick DesJarlait: The Story of an American Indian Artist.* As told to Neva Williams. Minneapolis: Lerner, 1975. (4-6) B

Prior to his untimely death in 1972, DesJarlait gained distinction as an artist-interpreter of the Chippewa Indian life on the Red Lake Indian Reservation in northern Minnesota. In this short book he recounts his childhood and youth on the reservation, his education, military service and career in the Twin Cities. Although DesJarlait's unemotional story does not explore his real person, thoughts or feeling, it does reflect life on the reservation with its hunting, fishing, pow-wows, maple sugaring and wild ricing. Fortunately, seven of his paintings in color illustrate his stylized interpretation of Chippewa Indian life.

— DUNN, JAMES TAYLOR, ed. *Gopher Reader.* See MN 144

— DUNN, JAMES TAYLOR, ed. *Gopher Reader II.* See MN 145

52 EASTMAN, CHARLES E. *Indian Boyhood;* illus. by E. L. Blumenschein. New York: Dover, 1971. Paper. (6-)

A reprint of the original 1902 edition. Charles Eastman, or Ohiyesa, tells of his boyhood experiences in a Sioux camp on the shores of Lakes Calhoun and Harriet (in Minneapolis) in the 1870's and 80's. Left motherless at birth, Eastman was taught what every young brave needed to know by his grandmother and uncle. He learned to love the Indian way of life, their customs and traditions. But he also learned of war, hostility and white man's cruelty. At the appearance of his father, who had been reported dead, Ohiyesa reluctantly adopted the white man's ways as his father had. Valuable, authentic first-hand information.

53 ERVIN, JEAN ADAMS. *The Twin Cities Perceived;* drawings by Gemma Rossini Cullen, Robert Halladay, Heidi Schwabacher and Robert N. Taylor. Minneapolis: University of Minnesota Press, 1976. (8-) P *

Residents and visitors are treated to an out-of-the-ordinary tour of well-known and famous landmarks, as well as some of the little publicized buildings, neighborhoods and sites of Minneapolis and St. Paul. Gives historical background of each location and present status. Four Minnesota artists supply numerous black and white sketches. A wealth of information in a readable, entertaining text set in a handsome, graphic format. Map of area and index.

— EUBANK, NANCY. *Jeffers Petroglyphs.* See MN 109

54 EUBANK, NANCY. *The Lindberghs: Three Generations.* St. Paul: Minnesota Historical Society, 1975. Paper. (8-) B

This pamphlet from the *Minnesota Historic Sites* series gives the background of the famous flier and his family, beginning with his grandparents, the August Lindberghs and his parents, the Charles A. Lindberghs, Sr. Charles, Jr. spent his boyhood at Little Falls, Minnesota, and his home on the Mississippi River is now restored and preserved as an historic site. A short, factual presentation with numerous black and white photographs. Bibliography.

55 EUBANK, NANCY. *A Living Past: 15 Historic Places in Minnesota;* drawings by Ron Hunt. Rev. ed. St. Paul: Minnesota Historical Society, 1978. Paper. (6-) P

This booklet in the *Minnesota Historical Sites* series includes 15 historic places which have been at one time associated with people important in the development of the state. Included are the State Capitol, Fort Snelling, Alexander Ramsey House, Mille Lacs Lake Museum and others. Eubank's brief one-page history of each site is readable and enlightening. Hunt's full-page black and white drawings are meticulous in detail. An attractive guide for Minnesotans and visitors.

— FEERICK, EMALIE P. *The First Book of Vice-Presidents of the United States.* See MN 56

56 FEERICK, JOHN D. and FEERICK, EMALIE P. *The First Book of Vice-Presidents of the United States.* Rev. ed. New York: Watts, 1977. (4-6) B
Following an introduction to the office of the Vice President are brief biographies of the 42 men, many long forgotten, who have filled the post. Each sketch is accompanied by an engraving or photograph. Hubert Humphrey, the 38th Vice President, served with President Lyndon P. Johnson from 1964 to 1968 (pp. 86-87). Walter P. Mondale was elected as 42nd Vice President with President Carter in 1976 (p. 91). Both Humphrey and Mondale served as senators from Minnesota. A factual book of hard-to-find information. Index.

57 FISHER, MARK A. *North Country: The Scenery and Wildlife of the Quetico-Superior;* photographs by author. Winton, Minn.: Packsack, undated. Paper. (4-8) P
Over a period of 10 years the author-photographer took pictures of the canoe country in the Superior National Forest in Minnesota and the Quetico Provincial Park in Ontario. These are 50 of the best in full-page black and white reproductions, with alternating pages of text briefly describing each picture. There are artistic summer and winter scenes and unusual close-ups of wildlife. An attractive, easily-perused book with a glimpse of wilderness natural beauty that whets the appetite for further exploration.

58 FISK, NICHOLAS. *Lindbergh the Lone Flier;* illus. by Raymond Briggs. New York: Coward, McCann, 1968. (3-6)
During most of his youth Charles Lindbergh knew he wanted to fly. After varied experiences as a stunt flier, parachutist and airmail pilot, he went for the big prize--the $25,000 Orteig award given to the first pilot to fly non-stop across the Atlantic. Lindbergh won the prize and instant fame, but in so-doing spent 33 grueling hours flying alone over 3600 miles

of lonely ocean before landing in Paris. This short, dramatic book with bright illustrations and simplified text is attractive and exciting reading even for older children.

59 FLANAGAN, BARBARA. *Minneapolis*. New York:
   St. Martin's Press, 1973. (6-)
   Minneapolis columnist, Barbara Flanagan, takes a look at her town and likes what she sees. With her usual enthusiasm, she writes of the city's early history, its development, attractions and achievements. Her suggested downtown walking tour and the auto excursion to outlying places is useful for visitors and home folks. Old and recent photographs are sprinkled at random through the book. This is not a reference source since it has no formal chapters, page numbers or index. It does, however, provide fascinating reading about Minnesota's largest city.

60 FOSTER, JOHN T. *The Flight of the Lone Eagle*. New
   York: Watts, 1974. (4-8)
   A more specific and detailed account of Lindbergh's transatlantic flight than other books available for this age group. After careful preparation Lindbergh embarked on the grueling 3600 mile flight from New York to Paris. Following 33 hours in the air, he touched down at Paris, won the Orteig prize and was catapulted into world fame. Historical pictures of the times and the Lindbergh family, a bibliography and index add to the value of this book as a reference source.

61 FRESCHET, BERNIECE. *Year on Muskrat Marsh;* illus.
   by Peter Parnall. New York: Scribner, 1974.
   (3-6) *
   As seasons pass, life in Muskrat Marsh in Minnesota's northern wilderness is an ever-changing cycle. The marsh is home to the muskrat, water snake, bullfrog and a host of other water creatures. It also provides a rich hunting ground for owls and hawks and gives water to thirsty animals. To survive requires vigilance and ingenuity. Freschet's writing is colorful,

alive and sensitive to the wonders of nature. The deli-
cate, precise line drawings by Parnall complement the
text. A satisfying book in all respects.

62 GILL, BRENDAN. *Lindbergh Alone.* New York:
    Harcourt Brace, 1977. (8-) B
    The author's intent is not to write a biography
of Charles Lindbergh, but to view one young man and the
forces that made him a national hero. Drawing on Lindbergh's unpublished manuscript, *Autobiography of Values,*
Gill gives insight into the evolution of Lindbergh's
personality and ideology as he responded to the changing times in which he lived. Attractively illustrated
with 86 photographs, some never before published. For
the mature reader.

63 GOODSELL, JANE. *The Mayo Brothers;* illus. by Louis
    S. Glanzman. New York: Crowell, 1972. (3-5) B
    A biography of Will and Charles Mayo, Minnesota's
famous brother doctors. Stimulated by their father's
medical practice and their mother's interest in science,
the two brothers went on to pioneer advances in surgi-
cal medicine and establish the world-famous Mayo Clinic
in Rochester, Minnesota. The brothers, though differing in temperaments, remained a close medical team
until they both died in 1939. The illustrations are
attractive; the format of the book handsome. The text
is short enough to be easily read, but complete enough
to tell children of the highlights of the lives and
careers of these renowned men.

64 HAMBERGER, JOHN. *The Call of a Loon;* pictures by
    author. New York: Four Winds, 1969. o.p.
    (2-5) P
    A quiet, poetic nature story of the loon's
search for a mate in the wilderness of Canada's lake
country. The woodland animals hear the loon's haunting
call, and an answer comes back through the stillness.
But the answer is just an echo, and the loon continues
his lonely search. Hamberger's splendid black and
white illustrations fill the major part of every page
and tell the story of Minnesota's state bird as elo-
quently as the evocative text.

65 HAMMONTREE, MARIE. *Will and Charlie Mayo, Boy Doctors;* illus. by Shannon Stirnweis. Indianapolis: Bobbs-Merrill, 1962. (3-5) B

This fictionalized biography in the *Childhood of Famous Americans* series tells of the boyhood experiences and the forces that propelled the two famous Mayo brothers toward their distinguished medical careers. At the back of the book is a chronological list of important dates during their lifetime together with questions, suggested activities, further reading and a glossary. Children who have discovered this series will like this story-biography.

66 HANSEN, MARCUS L. *Old Fort Snelling 1819-1858.* Wayzata, Minn.: Ross and Haines, 1958. (8-)

A reprint of a 1918 account of Minnesota's first military post. In this edition Russell Fridley, Director of the Minnesota Historical Society, writes a long introduction detailing the fort's past and the restoration up to 1957. Hansen's topical account tells of construction of the original fort and its history through the years. Extensive notes and references, numerous historical pictures and a comprehensive index make this a valuable volume for research. Younger readers could read of the early life at the fort in preparation for a visit to the restored site.

67 HARTLEY, LUCIE. *Maria Sanford: Pioneer Professor.* Minneapolis: Dillon, 1977. (5-8) B

Biography of an extraordinary woman, the nation's first woman college professor. Her 54 years in education ranged from teaching in a one-room school to full professorship at Swarthmore and the University of Minnesota. Though highly respected and loved as a teacher and lecturer, she battled sex discrimination, jealousy, ridicule and threats of losing her job. Her life was one of poverty, self-sacrifice and dedication. After retiring from the University of Minnesota in 1909 at age 72, she supported herself by lecturing until her death in 1920. A direct, factual biography revealing personal qualities of a remarkable woman. Historical photographs.

68 HASSLER, JON. *Four Miles to Pinecone.* New York:
Warne, 1977. (5-8) F *
First-person narrative of Tom, Sophomore at a
St. Paul high school, who has to decide whether or not
to "squeal" on Mouse, his best friend, involved in
assault and robbery of elderly Mr. Kerr for whom Tom
works. Tom makes his decision when he finds himself a
victim of murderous outboard motor thieves at his
uncle's resort near Pinecone in northern Minnesota.
Hassler, English teacher at Brainerd (Minnesota) Community College, is an adept storyteller with a fine
sense of dialogue and an intuitive insight into the
adolescent psyche. Strong characterizations and satisfying portrayal of family and school relationships.

69 HEILBRON, BERTHA L. *The Thirty-Second State: A
Pictorial History of Minnesota;* illus. 2d ed.
St. Paul: Minnesota Historical Society, 1966.
(6-) P *
A picture presentation of 3 centuries of Minnesota history from 1654 to 1958. Nearly 500 photographs,
drawings and paintings with explanatory text tell the
story of the state in chronologically arranged chapters.
Heilbron believes in the value of pictures to tell history. This superior, oversized book is ideal for browsing, but the concise captions should not be ignored.
The index lists specific subjects and pictures. Valuable for all historical collections on Minnesota.

70 HOFSINDE, ROBERT (GRAY-WOLF). *Indian Costumes;*
illus. by author. New York: Morrow, 1968.
(4-6)
Hofsinde's interest in Indian culture began when
he came to Minnesota from Denmark in his late teens.
He was made a blood-member of the Chippewa tribe and
given the name Gray-Wolf when he saved the life of a
Chippewa boy. In this volume he writes of the wearing
apparel of ten tribes, two of which lived in Minnesota—
the Ojibwe (pp. 61-71) and Sioux, or Dakota (pp. 86-91).
Hofsinde's readable, well-presented text together with
his clear, uncluttered drawings make this and his other
Indian books sources of merit for children.

71 HOFSINDE, ROBERT (GRAY-WOLF). *The Indian Medicine
Men;* illus. by author. New York: Morrow, 1966.
(4-6)
The medicine man was a highly-respected individual in Indian cultures of the past. The author tells
of medical practices in 6 specific tribes, among them
the Sioux (pp. 21-32) and the Ojibwe (pp. 69-83). He
explains the training of the Sioux medicine man, the
treatment of the sick, the wearing apparel and the significance of the medicine bag. The Ojibwes had their
Midewiwin, whose members were trained and ceremoniously
installed into the Grand Medicine Society. An educational book on a little known, but important, aspect of
Indian culture. Illustrations but no index.

72 HOFSINDE, ROBERT (GRAY-WOLF). *Indian Music Makers;*
illus. by author. New York: Morrow, 1967.
(4-6)
Music has played an important role in Indian
life. From Frances Densmore's *Chippewa Music II,*
Hofsinde has transcribed and explained 10 Ojibwe songs
originating in Minnesota. There are original Ojibwe
words with English translations. He also describes
musical instruments of various tribes and gives directions for making them. A useful book with information
not often found for young readers and musicians. Index.

73 HOFSINDE, ROBERT (GRAY-WOLF). *Indian Warriors and
Their Weapons;* illus. by author. New York:
Morrow, 1965. (4-6)
Hofsinde tells of preparation for battle in 7
tribes. In the chapter on the Ojibwes (pp. 9-26) he
describes their war costumes, ceremonies and dances.
The chapter on the Sioux (pp. 35-56) tells of scouting
the enemy, weaponry, the attack, the victory dance and
honoring the brave and the dead. Young readers will be
interest in the elaborate battle rituals. No index.

74 HOFSINDE, ROBERT (GRAY-WOLF). *Indians at Home;*
   illus. by author. New York: Morrow, 1964.
   (4-6)
   Characteristic shelters of 6 major tribes. For
the Algonquian nation Hofsinde has chosen to describe
Ojibwe homes of the past (pp. 12-24). Throughout the
year the Ojibwe lived in 4 seasonal homes, the most
permanent being the domed winter wigwam. There are
details of constructing, arranging and furnishing the
wigwam, the duties and activities of family members. An
appendix lists the 6 major Indian liguistic groups and
the tribes belonging to each. Index.

75 HOLBERT, ALLAN. *How We Got Our Kicks;* illus.
   Wayzata, Minn.: Turtinen, 1976. (8-)
   When Jack Crocker, president of a grocery chain,
organized the Minnesota Kicks soccer team, no one expected the new professional team and sport to "catch on"
instantly with youthful fans. Holbert, Minneapolis
Tribune sports writer, tells how it happened, gives
sketches of the players and coach, a brief history of
soccer, the rules of the game, a glossary of terms and
the players" standings. A candid inside look at a new
American pastime—of interest mainly to sports fans.
Numerous photographs.

76 HOLLING, HOLLING CLANCY. *Minn of the Mississippi;*
   illus. by author. Boston: Houghton Mifflin,
   1951. (5-8) P * #
   Minn, the snapping turtle, hatches from her egg
in the headwaters of the Mississippi at Minnesota's
Lake Itasca. An Indian boy finds her, gives her a name
and releases her. She moves slowly downstream, arriv-
ing at St. Anthony Falls in Minneapolis after 10 years.
At Fort Snelling she explores the waters and moves on
to Hastings and Lake Pepin. When she finally reaches
the Gulf of Mexico, she is 25 years old. A wealth of
history and geography is packed into the superbly-
colored pictures, detailed marginal sketches and exciting text. A notable piece of research, writing and art.

77 HOLLING, HOLLING CLANCY. *Paddle-to-the-Sea;* illus.
by author. Boston: Houghton Mifflin, 1941.
(5-8) F P * #
Paddle-to-the-Sea, a carved wooden boy in a
canoe, journeys from Canada's Nipigon country to Duluth,
down the Great Lakes, through the St. Lawrence and to
the ocean. Along the way Paddle-to-the-Sea survives a
sawmill's blade, a forest fire, shipwreck, storm and a
dash over Niagara Falls. Holling's full-color paintings and detailed black and white sketches around each
page of text show remarkable artistry. His articulate,
well-researched writing embellishes history and geography in a palatable form for young readers. This book
could be used in conjunction with the film of the same
name.

78 HOLMQUIST, JUNE DRENNING and BROOKINS, JEAN A.
Minnesota's Major Historic Sites, A Guide; illus.
2d ed. St. Paul: Minnesota Historical Society,
1972. Paper. (6-) P R *
Information on 45 major historic sites and 14
others located in four geographical areas in the state.
The co-authors tell the historical significance of the
sites and give directions and maps to locate them. In
the introduction they make a case for preserving landmarks and explain the problems in establishing sites.
The most comprehensive guide available to Minnesota's
historic places, with over 150 illustrations and photographs. A major research effort that will be of value
to both residents and visitors. Bibliography and index.

79 HOOVER, HELEN. *Animals at My Doorstep;* illus. by
Symeon Shimin. New York: Parents, 1966. (3-5)
In 1954 Helen Hoover and her husband moved from
Chicago to the wilderness region in northern Minnesota
near the Canadian border. Here they observed nature
first hand. With sensitivity and scientific understanding Hoover writes of the animals, birds and insects
that surround them through the year. Symeon Shimin's
soft-toned illustrations are poignantly expressive.
Children will enjoy reading and looking at this attractive nature book.

80 HOOVER, HELEN. *The Gift of the Deer;* pen-and-ink
    drawings from life by Adrian Hoover. New York:
    Knopf, 1966. (6-) *
    When a starving, nearly-blind buck stumbles to
their cabin, the Hoovers begin a long friendship with
the animal. The next season Peter returns with his
mate, later brings in turn 3 sets of twins to the feeding station. The fourth year, when the aging buck does
not return, the Hoovers conclude that the wolf and deer
tracks indicate that nature's cycle is complete. Mrs.
Hoover's writing is unpretentious and homey, yet profound with the observations of a dedicated naturalist.
Mr. Hoover's drawings are in complete harmony with the
text. An emotional experience for readers.

81 HOOVER, HELEN. *The Long-Shadowed Forest;* illus. by
    Adrian Hoover. New York: Crowell, 1963.
    (6-) *
    Mrs. Hoover is a keen observer of life in the
northern Minnesota woods. She writes intimately of
trees, fungus, water creatures, hibernating animals,
birds and other components of the natural world. Her
knowledge is impressive, her viewpoint convincing, her
enthusiasm infectious, yet her writing is poetic,
simple and direct. There are detailed black and white
drawings, a bibliography and index. A book for adults
which can be read by younger readers who appreciate
nature.

82 HOOVER, HELEN. *A Place in the Woods;* pen-and-ink
    drawings by Adrian Hoover. New York: Knopf,
    1969. (6-) *
    When the Hoovers moved to their remote home 155
miles north of Duluth, they were novices at wilderness
living. They often made mistakes, but through the
experience they became increasingly fond of the beauty
of the region and the wildlife it supported. Mrs.
Hoover's account abounds with spirit, humor and sincerity. Her husband contributes full-page drawings.
Another adult book with broad appeal.

173

83 HOOVER, HELEN. *The Years of the Forest;* pen-and-ink
    drawings by Adrian Hoover. New York: Knopf,
    1973. (6-)
    A fitting last book that summarizes 16 years of
the Hoover's north woods experience. Part I, "The Inno-
cent Years," reviews the period from 1956 to 1961;
Part II, "The Years of Change," tells of 1961 to 1967.
In the "Epilogue" they have returned to their cabin
after a 4-year vacation of travel. Ending on a nostalgic note Mrs. Hoover writes, "I had found what all men
seek—my place in the world of my time." The Hoovers
have since moved to other parts, but their four adult
books will remain an inspiration to those who yearn for
a similar retreat.

84 HUNTINGTON, GEORGE. *Robber and Hero.* Wayzata,
    Minn.: Ross and Haines, 1962. (8-)
    This reprint of an 1895 book written 19 years
after the Northfield, Minnesota, robbery by the James-
Younger gang is said to be the most authentic account
available. Huntington chronicles the robbery and murder of a Northfield banker, the street battle and
deaths of two of the gang, the pursuit and capture of
all but Jesse and Frank James who escaped. There are
short biographies of people involved, numerous old
photographs and a bibliography. Though dated in style,
this captures the excitement of a first-hand account.

85 JACOBS, LINDA. *Cindy Nelson: North Country Skier.*
    St. Paul, Minn.: EMC, 1976. Paper. (4-6) B
    A brief biography in the *Women Who Win* series of
the U.S. champion woman skier from Lutsen, Minnesota,
who won the 1974 World Cup competition despite serious
injuries 2 years before. Unfortunately the book was
written before Nelson won the bronze medal in the 1976
Olympics. A compact and appealing personal glimpse of
a daring, disciplined athlete with numerous well-chosen
photographs of the skier and her family.

86 JAQUES, FLORENCE PAGE. *Canoe Country;* illus. by
Francis Lee Jaques. Minneapolis: University of
Minnesota Press, 1938. (5-)
A diary in words and pictures of a 3-week canoe
trip in the Boundary Waters Canoe area. Mrs. Jaques
records their daily experiences and the wildlife they
observe along the way. They marvel at the solitude and
harmony of the wilderness and capture the mood for the
reader both in text and pictures. A light-hearted,
personal account written with keen awareness of the
beauty of the natural world.

87 JAQUES, FLORENCE PAGE. *Francis Lee Jaques:
Artist of the Wilderness World.* New York:
Doubleday, 1973. (6-) P *
A beautiful book in all respects. When painter-
ornithologist-naturalist Francis Lee Jaques died in
1969, his wife wrote this book to memorialize his life,
share his art and preserve a personal record of their
remarkable life and work as a team. Included are reproductions of 64 full-color paintings, 100 drawings and
sketches, excerpts from 6 books they published together
and tributes from other artists and naturalists.
Though an expensive book its format is outstanding and
its content of high quality. It should have broad
appeal for those who appreciate art, skillful writing
and nature.

88 JAQUES, FLORENCE PAGE. *The Geese Fly High;* illus.
by Francis Lee Jaques. Minneapolis: University
of Minnesota Press, 1964. (6-)
A companion to *Canoe Country*. This finds the
Jaques following the migration route along the Mississippi flyway from the marshes of northern Minnesota to
Louisiana. As they travel, they observe, record and
sketch the wildlife and scenery. Another personal book
written with zest and illustrated with care.

89 JAQUES, FLORENCE PAGE. *Snowshoe Country;* illus. by
   Francis Lee Jaques. Minneapolis: University of
   Minnesota, 1944. (5-)
   The winter season comes to canoe country bringing a change in activities and wildlife. Canoes are
traded for dog-sleds and snow-shoes, and neighbors take
shortcuts across the frozen lakes instead of travelling
the longer route by road. The Jaques are as fond of
winter as they are of summer. The winter diary has the
same humor and enthusiasm found in Mrs. Jaques other
books. Her husband's drawings set the aesthetic mood.

90 JAQUES, FRANCIS LEE. *The Art of Francis Lee Jaques.*
   Minneapolis: J. F. Bell Museum, 1972. Paper.
   (4-) P
   An inexpensive gallery guide to 59 paintings and
drawings by Francis Lee Jaques, Minnesota's noted naturalist and artist, as exhibited at the Bell Museum of
Natural History in 1972. Unfortunately the black and
white reproductions lose the artist's mastery of color,
but they do show his craftsmanship and skill in portraying Minnesota scenery and wildlife. Included is a
short biography of the artist.

91 JOHNSON, H. NAT. *Minnesota Panorama, Saga of the
   North Star Empire;* illus. by Oz Black.
   Minneapolis: Denison, 1957. (4-7)
   Written for the Minnesota Centennial in 1958,
this covers highlights of the major historical events
in the state from the geological beginnings to modern
day development. Johnson's chronologically arranged
text is factual and concise. Oz Black, cartoonist for
the Minneapolis Sunday Tribune, adds numerous cartoon
illustrations in brown tones. A short, open-ended book
with graphic appeal. An index would be helpful.

92 JONES, THELMA. *Once Upon a Lake: A History of
   Lake Minnetonka.* Wayzata, Minn.: Ross and
   Haines, 1969. (6-)
   An account of the area around beautiful Lake
Minnetonka, near the Twin Cities. Jones writes of the
geology of the region, Gov. Alexander Ramsey's purchase

of land from the Dakota Indians, the first white
settlers, James J. Hill's enterprises, the era of luxury hotels and steamboats, and the growth in the early
1900's. Written with dramatic flair and a sense of
immediacy, this narrative history based on diaries,
journals, old records and interviews, is candid and
honest. Though an adult book young readers will be
interested in the stories of pioneers.

93 JORDAN, PHILIP D. *Fiddlefoot Jones of the North
Woods;* illus. by Hans Helweg. New York:
Vanguard, 1957. (5-7) F
The tales and nature lore of Fiddlefoot Jones,
or Plum Nelly, are preserved in this narrative of two
boys who vacation at Woman Lake in Minnesota's north
woods. Jordan, who once taught history at the University of Minnesota, has embellished Plum Nelly's humorous tall tales with a slight plot and a degree of
credible realism. Exaggerated fun.

94 JUDSON, CLARA INGRAM. *Sod-House Winter;* illus. by
Edward C. Caswell. Chicago: Follett, 1957.
o.p. (4-6) F
A Swedish immigrant family settles in Vasa,
Minnesota, near Red Wing, in 1856. With resourcefulness and faith in themselves and God, they set about
making the most of the opportunities in the new land.
Gustaf, the ambitious eldest son, quickly learns English and makes plans for a career in law. When a fire
breaks out in Red Wing, Gustaf's quick thinking makes
him a local hero. Young readers will learn of customs
and traditions of Swedish immigrants and the local feeling toward Indians at the time, but they will not be
exposed to the real rigors of pioneer life.

95 KATZ, JANE B. *We Rode the Wind: Recollections of
Nineteenth-Century Tribal Life.* Minneapolis:
Lerner, 1975. (6-9)
A collection of writings by eight American
Indian authors who belonged to tribes that inhabited
the Great Plains in the 19th century. There are two
excerpts from the autobiography, *Indian Boyhood,* written

177

by Charles A. Eastman, Indian historian from Minnesota
(pp. 17-26). A selection from *History of the Ojibway
Nation* by William Whipple Warren, Minnesota's first
Indian legislator, tells of hunting, recreation and
ritual in his tribal home in the Great Lakes area
(pp. 69-73). Reproductions of famous paintings illustrate various chapters. Authentic stories carefully-
selected to be of interest to the young reader.

96 KEATING, BERN. *The Mighty Mississippi;* photographs
    by James L. Stanfield. Washington, D.C.:
    National Geographic, 1971. (6-) P
    An overview of the Mississippi River from its
source at Lake Itasca to New Orleans. Keating followed
the river, learned of its history, people and places.
In the first two chapters he journeys from the headwaters in Minnesota to Dubuque, Iowa. The remaining
five chapters follow the river south to the Gulf of
Mexico. Written as a travelogue, enhanced by excellent
photographs, portraits, reproductions of historical
paintings and maps typical of National Geographic publications, this is to be looked at, if not read, by
adults as well as young readers.

97 KLOBUCHAR, JIM and TARKENTON, FRAN. *Tarkenton.*
    New York: Harper & Row, 1976. (8-) B
    If one wants to get acquainted with the Minne-
sota Vikings veteran quarterback, his career, background, philosophy and views on colleagues, coaches and
owners, this is the book to read. Through its 267
pages Minneapolis Star columnist Klobuchar writes alternate chapters with Tarkenton. They share many confi-
dences and personal glimpses of the "Scrambler", of
pro-football and those involved with it. A witty,
thoroughly enjoyable collaboration written for adults,
but one which will have wide appeal for younger readers
as well. Index.

98 KNAUTH, PERCY and THE EDITORS OF TIME-LIFE BOOKS. *The North Woods, The American Wilderness.* New York: Time-Life, 1972. (6-) P

An attractive book which surveys the geology, ecology, history, geography and natural beauty of the Quetico-Superior area of Canada and Minnesota. The author follows the canoe route of the old voyageurs from Grand Portage on Lake Superior north along the boundary waters. A high quality readable book with superb nature photography in color, many from Minnesota, and excellent reproductions of four Frances Anne Hopkins' paintings of the voyageurs. Recommended for all ages for reading and browsing.

99 KOSTICH, DRAGOS D. *George Morrison;* illus. Minneapolis: Dillon, 1976. (5-8) B

George Morrison's life is a success story because he made it so. Through his impoverished childhood in the dying village of Chippewa City on Lake Superior's north shore, he was acutely aware of his Chippewa heritage and inspired by the natural beauty surrounding him. After high school he studied art in Minneapolis, New York and Paris. He then taught at various art schools in the U.S. before instructing in American Indian studies and art at the University of Minnesota. A short, factual biography written with understanding and respect. There are family photographs and reproductions of Morrison's paintings, unfortunately none in color.

— KREUTER, GRETCHEN, ed. *Women of Minnesota.*
See MN 161

— KUBISTA, IVAN. *Minnesota.* See MN 171

100 KUNZ, VIRGINIA BRAINARD. *St. Paul, Saga of an American City.* Woodland Hills, Calif.: Windsor, 1977. (8-) P R *

A scholarly presentation of the history of Minnesota's capital city from the early days of exploration and settlement to the present as an industrial, business and government center. Young readers may find the text

too detailed, but the first chapter of St. Paul's colorful beginnings should be of interest. There is an
attractive array of old maps, historical pictures and a
section of color photographs. A superior reference
book, not only of St. Paul, but of the state. Handsome,
over-sized book with extensive bibliography. Index.

101 LASS, WILLIAM E. *Minnesota: A Bicentennial History;* photograph essay by Don Getsug. New York:
Norton, 1977. (8-)
This portrait of Minnesota is unlike most histories. The author, a qualified authority on the Midwest, sees influences which shaped the state—availability of abundant forests, rich iron deposits and fertile
land. He sees that in developing the state, there was
exploitation of the Indians, denuding of forests and
depleting of natural resources. A well-drawn composite
of the state, its significance in the nation and what
appears to be its future. Although written for adults,
this will show younger readers that there is more to
history than dates, facts and figures. Includes photographs, bibliography and index.

102 LE GARDE, AMELIA. *Aseban: The Ojibwe Word for
Raccoon;* illus. by Julie Borgren. Duluth, Minn.:
Duluth Indian Educ. Advisory Comm., 1978. Paper.
(K-3)
One of the *Anishinabe Reading Materials* publications featuring Native American culture. Nanaboujou,
hero of the Ojibwe Indians, travelled about Minnesota
and the Great Lakes helping people. After Raccoon had
tricked two old blind men, Nanaboujou pronounced that
the animal henceforth would wear a mask on his face and
rings on his tail. After the legend appears in English,
the author writes it in the original Chippewa language.
Bold, earthy illustrations complement this fireside
legend. An attractive book for beginning readers and
to be read aloud.

103 LETTERMANN, EDWARD J. *Farming in Early Minnesota.*
St. Paul, Minn.: Ramsey County Historical Soc.,
1969. Paper. (4-8) P *
A booklet that tells of pioneer farm life in
Minnesota with drawings and descriptions of tools,
machines and buildings typical of those found on Midwest farms in the second half of the 19th century.
Lettermann, former curator of the Gibbs Farm Museum in
St. Paul, has compiled the guide from the equipment on
display at the Farm. The hand-lettered text, the
detailed black and white sketches and the blue jeans
cover are attractively old-fashioned. A valuable
source of easy-to-read information as well as a useful
guide for a field trip.

104 LETTERMANN, EDWARD J. *From Whole Log to No Log.*
Minneapolis: Dillon, 1969. (6-)
History of the Indians who once lived where
Minneapolis, St. Paul and Bloomington now stand.
Inspired by stories told by a Dakota Indian who lived
at the Lake Harriet Mission in the 1830's, Lettermann
writes of the periods when the Indians originally
owned the "whole log", then had to "share the log" and
finally at the end of the 1800's had "no log." A well-
documented text with historical photographs, maps, a
list of Indian chiefs, chronology of significant dates,
bibliography and index. A scholarly book for studying
Indian heritage which can be read by mature young
people.

105 LIBBY, BILL. *Rod Carew: Master Hitter.* New York:
Putnam, 1976. (5-8) B
Sports writer Libby writes of one of baseball's
leading singles hitters, former Minnesota Twins controversial second-baseman, Rod Carew. He tells of Carew's
early life in Panama, his youth in New York and his
playing in the minor and major leagues. In his early
adult life Carew was often lonely and moody, but marriage and family life gave him maturity and stability.
Although this journalistic account is mainly of Carew
the pro-ball player, it does reveal something of the
sensitivity, sincerity, warmth and good humor of the
real person.

106 LIEBLING, JEROME and MORRISON, DON. *The Face of Minneapolis;* photography by Jerome Liebling, text by Don Morrison. Minneapolis: Dillon, 1966. (7-) P

The many facets of life in Minneapolis artfully presented in word and picture. Liebling's camera captures people and places in many moods and seasons, in broad panoramas and minute detail. Minneapolis columnist, Morrison, gives his personal opinions and observations of the history of the city, its government, people, architecture, business and education. A large, attractive book, but one that shows Minneapolis before the more recent changes in buildings, malls and freeways.

107 LIERS, EMIL E. *A Black Bear's Story;* illus. by Ray Sherin. New York: Viking, 1962. o.p. (4-6)

A two-year span in the life of a black bear family in the Gunflint area north of Duluth. Liers creates distinct animal personalities, identified with Indian names. Kabato, the stern but loving mother, disciplines and trains her two playful cubs, Anang and Anoki. Their father, Koda, remains aloof and alone. A wide range of information on bears and forest life in this palatable well-constructed nature story.

108 LINDBERGH, CHARLES A. *Boyhood on the Upper-Mississippi: A reminiscent Letter.* St. Paul: Minnesota Historical Society, 1972. (6-) B

In 1969 when the Minnesota Historical Society began restoring the Lindbergh home on the banks of the Mississippi at Little falls, Minnesota, they asked Charles Lindbergh to write them his detailed recollections of his boyhood home. In these letters written from all parts of the world, the famed flier vividly and precisely recalls an exciting childhood and youth in the early 1900's. The text is liberally infused with family photographs and personal correspondence. Index.

109 LOTHSON, GORDON A. and EUBANK, NANCY. *Jeffers Petroglyphs: A Journey Through Time.* St. Paul: Minnesota Historical Society, 1974. Paper. (6-)
This compact booklet in the *Minnesota Historic Sites* series directs visitors on a walking tour of the Jeffers Petroglyphs in southwestern Minnesota. Here prehistoric peoples etched a variety of human figures, animals and symbols into outcroppings of quartzite rock. There are photographs, drawings and explanations of the etchings, some estimated to date back to 3000 B.C. Although a guide to a specific site, the book has value for all students of prehistoric people and their art.

The following Betsy-Tacy books by Maud Hart Lovelace are arranged in the sequence of the series rather than in strict alphabetical order by title. Because the characters develop through-out the series, this arrangement should help readers to identify successive books.

110 LOVELACE, MAUD HART. *Betsy-Tacy;* illus. by Lois Lenski. New York: Crowell, 1940. (2-4) F
In the initial book of the *Betsy-Tacy* series, 5-year old Betsy Ray meets for the first time her new neighbor, Tacy, who has just moved to Hill Street in Deep Valley, Minnesota. Another friend, Tib, completes the trio that pursues adventure with youthful exuber-ance. Lovelace bases the entire series on her own childhood and youthful experiences in the early 1900's at Mankato, Minnesota. Lenski's carefully-drawn pic-tures illustrate the text. Today's youngsters will enjoy adventuring with Betsy.

111 LOVELACE, MAUD HART. *Betsy-Tacy and Tib;* illus. by Lois Lenski. New York: Crowell, 1941. (2-4) F
In the second book of the series, 8-year-olds Betsy, Tacy and Tib continue to find pleasure and excitement in a variety of experiences. One of their chief pastimes is listening to Betsy's imaginative stories.

112 LOVELACE, MAUD HART. *Betsy and Tacy Go Over the Big Hill;* illus. by Lois Lenski. New York: Crowell, 1942. (3-5) F
The third book in the series finds the three 10-year olds busy getting Tib chosen as the local Queen of the Summer. Their world expands to include and understand their new neighbors, and immigrant family from Syria.

113 LOVELACE, MAUD HART. *Betsy and Tacy Go Downtown;* illus. by Lois Lenski. New York: Crowell, 1943. (4-6) F
The 12-year old threesome discovers new excitement at the public library and the local theatre. Automobiles and new friends enter their young lives. Young fans hooked on this series will continue to read them, even though the books become longer and more difficult. Fourth in the series.

114 LOVELACE, MAUD HART. *Heaven to Betsy: A Betsy-Tacy High School Story;* illus. by Vera Neville. New York: Crowell, 1945. (6-9) F
The fifth book in the series. In 1906 Betsy and Tacy begin their freshman year at Deep Valley High School and are swept up in parties, crushes on boys and current fads.

115 LOVELACE, MAUD HART. *Betsy in Spite of Herself: A Betsy-Tacy High School Story;* illus. by Vera Neville. New York: Crowell, 1946. (6-9) F
In the sixth book of the series, a sophisticated newcomer joins "the crowd" and complicates life for sophomores Betsy and Tacy. Betsy journeys from home to visit Tib who has moved to Milwaukee.

116 LOVELACE, MAUD HART. *Betsy Was a Junior: A Betsy-Tacy High School Story;* illus. by Vera Neville. New York: Crowell, 1947. (6-9) F
Seventh in the series. As junior in high school, Betsy's social world expands to include dances, parties and football games. She also is faced with choices of boyfriends, social groups and careers.

117 LOVELACE, MAUD HART. *Betsy and Joe: A Betsy-Tacy High School Story;* illus. by Vera Neville. New York: Crowell, 1948. (6-10) F
The eighth book finds Betsy graduating from Deep Valley High School and entering a growing-up world of romance and courtship. Tib is fond of a football player, but unattached Tacy is a worry to the other two girls. As the series progresses, stereotyped sex roles current in the 1940's become more obvious, but the girls still emerge as strong, independent characters.

118 LOVELACE, MAUD HART. *Betsy and the Great World;* illus. by Vera Neville. New York: Crowell, 1952. (6-11) F
Betsy strives to put Joe out of her thoughts as she leaves Deep Valley to travel in Europe. Life takes a serious turn as World War I begins. The ninth book in the series.

119 LOVELACE, MAUD HART. *Betsy's Wedding;* illus. by Vera Neville. New YYork: Crowell, 1955. (6-12) F
In the tenth and last book newlyweds Betsy and Joe settle in an apartment in Deep Valley. Domestic responsiblities keep them busy at home, while World War I escalates abroad. And Betsy must help her two friends—Tib to find a husband and Tacy to have a baby. Readers much younger than those in the recommended grade levels will want to read the entire series.

120 MC CORMICK, DELL J. *Tall Timber Tales, More Paul Bunyan Stories;* illus. by Lorna Livesley. Caldwell, Idaho: Caxton, 1939. (4-6) #
Minnesota rightfully lays claim to Paul Bunyan since it was Paul who fashioned the Mississippi from six small rivers, helped Jim Hill lay railroads, felled the state's trees in one mighty stroke and used Minnesota gophers to dig his fencepost holes. Unfortunately Babe, the Blue Ox, was so frightened by the backfiring of an automobile in a circus parade in Minneapolis, that he left the state and headed for the Rockies.

These and other tall tales told with robust humor are
accompanied by lively illustrations. Easy and enjoyable reading.

121 MC DERMOTT, JOHN FRANCIS. *Seth Eastman's Mississippi: A Lost Portfolio Recovered.* Urbana,
Ill.: University of Illinois Press, 1973.
(6-) P
When Captain Seth Eastman, famed artist of
Indian portraits, was stationed at Fort Snelling from
1841 to 1848, he painted many miniature watercolors of
the Mississippi River from St. Anthony Falls in Minnesota to the mouth of the Ohio River below St. Louis.
The paintings were missing until uncovered in a private
collection in 1970. McDermott writes of the discovery
and of Eastman's work as a painter. There are nine
preliminary sketches and 79 plates of Eastman's watercolors (the first 29 from Minnesota), none unfortunately in color. An art book with historical significance.
Bibliography and index.

122 MASON, MIRIAM E. *The Middle Sister;* illus. by
Grace Paull. New York: Macmillan, 1947.
(2-4) F
When the Glossbrenner family moves from Ohio to
a Minnesota homestead, 8-year-old Sarah Samantha, the
shy middle sister, insists that her favorite apple tree
be brought along on the train. The tree is transplant-
ed, but has difficulty bearing fruit. In the process
of trying to raise apples, Sarah loses her shyness. A
quaint story of the olden days which will appeal to
some young readers today.

123 MAY, JULIAN. *Fran Tarkenton: Scrambling Quarterback.* Mankato, Minn.: Crestwood, 1973.
(4-6) B
A short, factual biography of the Minnesota
Vikings quarterback from his childhood, through high
school and into pro-football in the NFL ending with the
1972 season. There are numerous photographs of Tarkenton and his family. Despite the uninspired writing and
dated information, this book will have a readership
among young football fans.

124 MAY, JULIAN. *The Minnesota Vikings*. Mankato,
Minn.: Creative Ed., 1977. (4-6)
A brief history of the Minnesota Vikings football team from their first NFL game in 1961 to their
defeat in the Super Bowl in 1975. Included are highlights of the seasons, information on coaches and players, the win-loss record and action photographs of
games. Though a short book, it is packed with facts
and information which young sports lovers will relish.

125 MINNESOTA DEPT. OF NATURAL RESOURCES. *Trees of*
Minnesota: How to Know Them; illus. St. Paul:
State of Minnesota, 1977. (6-) R
A small, inexpensive pocket manual which gives
illustrations, common and scientific names, identifying
characteristics, tree distribution and descriptions of
wood of 50 species of trees commonly found in the state.
Included is information on forestry, tree planting,
school projects, forest fires and tree growth. A A
clearly-written, handy field guide for use in Minnesota and adjoining states.

126 MONSERUD, WILMA and OWENBY, GERALD B. *Common Wild*
Flowers of Minnesota; illus. Minneapolis: University of Minnesota Press, 1971. (7-) P R *
Superb botanical illustrations by Monserud of
over 300 species of wild flowers commonly found in
Minnesota and adjoining states. The text, written by
University of Minnesota botany professor Owenby, gives
descriptive information, habitat and area for each
plant. Arranged alphabetically according to plant families, genera and species, the book is designed to be
used easily by the general public, teachers and students.
A guide book in handsome format which includes meticulous drawings and well-organized information for regional use. Glossary and index.

187

127 MORRIS, LUCY LEAVENWORTH WILDER, ed. *Old Rail Fence Corners: Frontier Tales Told by Minnesota Pioneers.* Reprint ed. St. Paul: Minnesota Historical Society, 1976. Paper. (6-)
    A reprint of a 1914 collection of frontier stories from the mid-1800's as told to interviewers from the Minnesota Daughters of the American Revolution. When Lucy Morris edited the volume, she recognized its value as authentic history for future generations. The stories cover a broad spectrum of frontier experiences as told by 62 men and 92 women. The size of this imposing collection may discourage young readers, but each story can be read individually with ease. An extensive index guides readers to specific topics. A valuable book of personal history.

—— MORRISON, DON. *The Face of Minneapolis.*
    See MN 106

128 MOSES, GEORGE. *Minnesota in Focus;* photographs by the *Minneapolis Star and Tribune.* Minneapolis: University of Minnesota Press, 1974. (6-) P *
    An imaginative text in a visually attractive format that views the state, its land and people, industries and recreation. Moses, veteran newsman and faculty member at Macalester College, sees the state as two separate entities—the urban Twin Cities and the rural outstate areas. Over 200 pictures, many in color, represent the work of 30 photographers. The book fulfills its stated purpose—to present a "fresh view of Minnesota."

—— MOYLE, EVELEN W. *Northland Wild Flowers.*
    See MN 129

129 MOYLE, JOHN B. and MOYLE, EVELEN W. *Northland Wild Flowers: A Guide for the Minnesota Region;* illus. Minneapolis: University of Minnesota Press, 1977. (6-) P R *
    A comprehensive guide to over 400 wild flowers of Minnesota and adjoining regions. Identification is simplified since the flowers are arranged by family

groups, with complete descriptions and over 300 color photographs in natural habitat. A 42-page introduction explains the arrangement of the book, gives charts, maps, a glossary, general information on locating seasonal flowers and the medicinal use of plants by early Indians. Author Moyle, a research biologist and supervisor in the Minnesota Department of Natural Resources, and his photographer wife have compiled a high quality guide for amateurs and experts.

130 NUTE, GRACE LEE. *Rainy River Country*. St. Paul: Minnesota Historical Society, 1969. (8-)
This companion to *The Voyageur's Highway* is a history of the 85 mile stretch along the Minnesota-Ontario border from Rainy Lake to the Lake of the Woods. Based on extensive research, historian Nute writes of the early history, exploration, boundary disputes, settlement and industrialization of the area. There are historical photographs, a regional map, bibliography and index. This authoritative adult book will appeal to mature young historians who have an interest in this specific area.

131 NUTE, GRACE LEE. *The Voyageur;* illus. by Carl W. Bertsch. St. Paul: Minnesota Historical Society, 1966. (8-)
A detailed study of the colorful voyageurs who transported furs along the St. Lawrence, Great Lakes and northern Minnesota-Ontario boundary waters in the 18th and early 19th centuries. From her long years of research, Nute draws a vivid picture of these dashing men, their daily routine, costumes, canoes, voyages, fort life, family life and songs. There are black and white woodcuts, a map of routes, an extensive bibliography and an index. A book to be read by mature readers and a reference source for younger students.

132 NUTE, GRACE LEE. *The Voyageur's Highway, Minnesota's Border Lake Land*. St. Paul: Minnesota Historical Society, 1970. (8-)
The colorful history of the Minnesota-Ontario boundary region from Rainy Lake to Lake Superior. The

area's natural resources attracted explorers, fur traders, gold prospectors and loggers. Nute includes other
chapters on famous men, the voyageurs, Indians, immigrants and more recent events. There are historical
maps, photographs, a chronology of significant dates,
a bibliography and an index. A well-organized, readable account of an area rich in history. For adults
and for student research of specific historical events
and people.

133 O'CONNOR, RICHARD. *Sinclair Lewis.* New York:
McGraw-Hill, 1971. (7-10) B
From his unhappy childhood, through a tortured
youth and into adult life, Minnesota's novelist, Sinclair Lewis, was little understood and often misunder-
stood. Sauk Centre, Minnesota, his boyhood home,
became the basis for the novel *Main Street,* causing a
local furor when it was published. O'Connor exposes
Lewis's problems (alcoholism, two unhappy marriages,
ill health) and his distinctions (among them the Nobel
Prize in 1930). This sensitively-written biography
puts Lewis's life together with his novels and the
characters in them. It will whet the appetite of those
who have not read his books and give those who have,
insight into why he wrote them.

134 OETTING, BOB and OETTING, RAE. *Quetico Wolf;* illus.
by Ken Carlson. Fayetteville, Ga.: Oddo, 1966.
(4-7)
The wolf pack, led by the spirited young wolf,
Quetico, struggles to survive in the Quetico-Superior
region in Ontario and northern Minnesota. The wolves
face starvation and are threatened by natural enemies,
trappers and bounty hunters. An enlightening, sympathetic account that emphasizes the balance maintained
in nature if not disturbed by man's interference.
Numerous illustrations, some unfortunately obscuring
the text. Despite a few printing errors, this animal
story provides exciting reading.

—— OETTING, RAE. *Quetico Wolf*. See MN 134

135 OLSON, SIGURD F. *The Hidden Forest;* photographs by
Les Blacklock. New York: Viking, 1969.
(6-) P *
A beautiful volume of nature essays and color
photographs. Though not exclusively of Minnesota this
portrays the spirit of the state's unique wilderness
region. Naturalist Sigurd Olson walks through the
woods and poetically describes the "little things close
to earth" that grow on the forest floor during each
season of the year. Between chapters Les Blacklock captures nature in exciting, full-color photographs from
areas around the country. A book with wide appeal—for
youngsters to enjoy in picture and for older ones to
appreciate for its philosophy and camera artistry.

136 OLSON, SIGURD F. *Listening Point;* illus. by
Francis Lee Jaques. New York: Knopf, 1958.
(6-) *
Minnesota's Sigurd Olson searches for just the
right old cabin to dismantle and rebuild on just the
right spot in the wilderness. He finds both, and he
names his retreat "Listening Point." Here he can
observe and reflect on the world of nature about him.
With keen perception Olson writes of our natural heritage and the need to preserve it. Small black and
white drawings introduce each chapter. A book to be
enjoyed by different ages. Young readers will like
chapters such as "The Laughing Loon", while adults will
appreciate Olson's affinity and concern for nature.

137 OLSON, SIGURD F. *Open Horizons;* illus. by Leslie
Kouba. New York: Knopf, 1969. (7-)
The author reflects on his own childhood, youth
and early manhood as he searched for direction and voca-
tions. He found his true identity in the wilderness
experience and the open horizons of the north. With
spiritual and philosophical contemplation Olson ponders
the essence of life. Black and white drawings of outdoor scenes help set the tone. For thinking young
naturalists who also may be wondering what life is all
about.

138 OLSON, SIGURD F. *Runes of the North;* illus. by
Robert Hines. New York: Knopf, 1963. (7-)
Inspired by the Finnish epic poem "Kalevala",
Olson reflects on life in the wilderness and its sig-
nificance for humanity. The first part deals with the
Quetico-Superior area, the second with northern Canada,
the Yukon and Alaska. Drawings introduce each chapter.
With eloquence and feeling Olson opens up more discover-
ies for readers mature enough to share his appreciation
of the natural world.

139 OLSON, SIGURD F. *Sigurd F. Olson's Wilderness Days;*
photographs by J. Arnold Bolz, drawings and maps
by other artists. New York: Knopf, 1972.
(6-) P *
A collection of Olson's most meaningful writings
from earlier books, arranged by seasons of the year.
Each season is introduced by a new essay and 4 pages of
magnificent photographs by Bolz. Throughout the volume
there are sketches by other artists from Olson's books
and 3 maps of the wilderness area by David Lindroth.
In the prologue the author tells what the wilderness
means to him; in the epilogue he worries about the
future world that man is creating. A beautiful book
which summarizes and memorializes the spirit of this
remarkable man.

140 OLSON, SIGURD F. *The Singing Wilderness;* illus. by
Francis Lee Jaques. New York: Knopf, 1956.
(6-) *
This is Sigurd Olson's first book. In his
search for solitude and the primitive experience, he
discovers them in the area near his Ely, Minnesota,
home. Each season brings new delights which Olson
records with keen observation and contagious enthusiasm.
The drawings by Jaques lend dignity and grace to the
poetic text. Although each of Olson's books stands
alone, this first book serves as an introduction to his
thoughts and passions and sets the stage for succeding
volumes.

141 O'MEARA, WALTER. *We Made It through the Winter: A Memory of Northern Minnesota Boyhood.* St. Paul: Minnesota Historical Society, 1974. (6-)

A veteran author reflects on his boyhood in 1906 at the lumbertown of Cloquet in northeastern Minnesota. In sharp detail O'Meara recalls the duties and activities that marked each changing season. The warmth of family life and the excitement of boyhood adventure are portrayed against the backdrop of the boisterous, logging settlement. And there are the people whose lives touched and shaped his. Written with charm and style, and carefully documented with reference notes, this lighthearted, nostalgic book of how it was in the "olden days" can be enjoyed by today's young readers. Index.

—— OMINSKY, ALAN. *Fort Snelling.* See MN 180

—— OWENBY, GERALD B. *Common Wild Flowers of Minnesota.* See MN 126

142 PEDERSON, KERN O. *The Story of Fort Snelling.* St. Paul: Minnesota Historical Society, 1966. Paper. (6-)

This first booklet in the *Minnesota Historic Sites* series gives the history of Fort Snelling from 1805 to the beginning of its restoration in 1965. The story of Minnesota's oldest military post is told through black and white drawings by cartoonist-author Pederson. Alternate pages of text are excerpts from old journals, letters, army records and diaries. Carefully selected and researched original material presented in a visually attractive format especially useful for students.

143 PEYTON, KAREN. *The World So Fair.* Philadelphia: Chilton, 1963. (7-10) F

When Val and her Aunt Siri move to Duluth, Val longs for her former home on the southern Minnesota prairie. But she grows to admire the big lake, Superior, and acquires new friends and interests. When rich Torrey Ramsey brings glamor and romance to her life, she has to face the realization that there may be no

resolution to their differing stations. Although the
book may have limited appeal, it is a realistic, warm
portrait of Norwegian immigrant life with well-developed characters and natural conversation which includes
Norwegian phrases and mild profanity.

144 POATGIETER, A. HERMINA and DUNN, JAMES TAYLOR, eds.
Gopher Reader. St. Paul: Minnesota Historical
Society, 1966. (4-8) *
   This first volume is a collection of the best
selections from the children's periodical, the *Gopher
Historian*, no longer published. There are signed articles by well-known authors on a wide variety of topics
dealing with Minnesota's past and present. Though some
articles are dated, the book contains information in
greater depth than is in most social studies textbooks.
A complete subject and picture index will aid the young
researcher.

145 POATGIETER, A. HERMINA and DUNN, JAMES TAYLOR, eds.
Gopher Reader II. St. Paul: Minnesota Historical Society, 1975. (4-8) *
   This volume also draws on articles from the
Gopher Historian published by the Minnesota Historical
Society from 1946 through 1972. Volume II includes
information on areas of Minnesota, archeology and geology of the state, ethnic and minority groups, pioneer
life, history of the state and biographies of famous
historical figures. Numerous drawings, maps and photographs illustrate the signed articles. A wealth of
accurate and well-written information presented in an
attractive format. An excellent index.

146 PRICHARD, BARRY and SMITH, ROBERT K. *Seeing Itasca:
A Pictorial Guide*. Detroit Lakes, Minn.: Lakes,
1974. Paper. (5-)
   An attractive booklet to acquaint visitors with
Itasca State Park, the location of the headwaters of
the Mississippi River. There are brief descriptions of
the park's history, main features and wildlife. Handsome photographs, some in color, make this an inviting
pamphlet for park visitors.

147 RAINBOLT, RICHARD. *Gold Glory.* Wayzata, Minn.:
Turtinen, 1972. (7-)
A journalized history of the Golden Gophers of
the University of Minnesota from the early 1880's to
1971. Through the years many football "greats" have
been applauded by loyal fans, among them Bronco Nagur-
ski, Pug Lund, Bruce Smith and Paul Giel. Coaches,
such as Bernie Bierman and Murray Warmath, have their
names engraved in the Gopher's hall of fame. Old photographs from past seasons plus those of more recent vin-
tage add interest. This will have a limited readership,
but fans who want to see where college football has
been will like this large, handsome volume.

148 ROSENFELT, WILLARD E. *The Last Buffalo;* maps and
illus. by Howard Lindberg. Minneapolis:
Denison, 1973. (4-8)
A view of the Dakota Indians who once inhabited
the woodlands and plains of the Midwest. The text
includes: life style, customs and culture of the
Dakotas; treaties and battles in Minnesota and western
states; short biographies and photographs of seven
Dakota leaders. An introduction advises modern man to
return to the Indian philosophy of respecting Mother
Earth. Additional features include bright illustrations, chart of tribal divisions of the Dakota nation,
map of west ward migration, culture vocabulary, chart
of sign language and calendar of moons. Readable and
packed with information. Reading list and index.

149 ROSENFELT, WILLARD E. *Minnesota: Its People and
Culture;* illus. Minneapolis: Denison, 1973.
(4-6)
A student text in a social studies program. The
book includes open-ended chapters on various aspects of
the culture, geography and history of Minnesota. Students are encouraged to do further research on each
topic. The last section includes statistics, information on historic sites, state symbols and references
for additional reading. There are numerous photographs,
maps, charts and graphs as well as an index. This is
best used with adult guidance. Paper or hard-cover
editions.

—— ROSSMAN, BOB. *Bald Eagles of the Chippewa Forest.*
See MN 5

—— ROSSMAN, BOB. *The Loon: Minnesota's State Bird.*
See MN 6

150 RUBIN, BOB. *Minnesota's Vikings: The Scrambler
and the Purple Gang;* photography by Malcolm
Emmons, John and Vernon Biever. Englewood
Cliffs, N.J.: Prentice-Hall, 1973. (6-)
An inside look at the Minnesota Vikings from
their beginning in the NFL in 1961 through the 1972
season, with special coverage on Fran Tarkenton and
the front four "purple people eaters." Sports writer
Rubin assesses the roles of coaches Norm Van Brocklin
and Bud Grant and their differing philosophies. There
are brief sketches of some of the Vikings "greats" and
numerous action-packed photographs. For the sports fan
interested in background material and past performances.

151 RYAN, J. C. *Early Loggers in Minnesota, Vol. I;*
illus. Duluth, Minn.: Minnesota Timber Prod.,
1975. (6-)
The author originally wrote these 20 stories on
"Loggers of the Past" for issues of the *Minnesota Timber Producers Bulletin.* Ryan's entire life until
retirement in 1970 was spent with forest and timber
industries in various parts of northern Minnesota. He
writes of timber cruisers, log loaders, sawyers, cooks,
clerks and scalers. Readers of many states will appreciate the detail, thoroughness and color of these stories of logging days in the early 1900's. Numerous old
photographs from the St. Louis Historical Society and
the author's own collection illustrate each story.

152 RYAN, J. C. *Early Loggers in Minnesota, Vol. II;*
illus. Duluth, Minn.: Minnesota Timber Prod.,
1976. (6-)
The popularity of Vol. I of this same title led
to a second volume of 19 stories, reprinted from the
Minnesota Timber Producers Bulletin. Vol. II includes
stories of other loggers, their equipment and duties—

the camp foreman, blacksmith, road monkey, bull cook,
sky pilot, wood butcher, tie maker, barn boss, man
catcher and swamper. There are chapters on oxen, river
runs, Minnesota cedar and the C.C.C.'s of the 1930's.
Written with expertise and zest, these are stories and
photographs of more uncommon aspects of logging in the
early 1900's.

153 SALMI, JOHN. *Minnesota Lumberjack.* Detroit, Mich.:
Harlo, 1971. (6-)
A Finnish resident writes of his 52 years in a
typical lumbering community, Orr, in northern Minnesota
in the 1920's and 1930's. The first two chapters of
life in a lumber camp and short episodes from the
lives of nine colorful lumberjacks will interest the
general reader. The succeeding chapters deal with more
specific information on places in the area, boating and
fishing techniques, tables of rock formations from Win-
chell's report in 1898. Four pages of old photographs
are included. A homey, chatty book from an author who
finds deep satisfaction in his humble heritage and
roots. Will have limited apeeal.

154 SASSE, FRED A. *The Great Dan Patch;* illus. by
author. Blue Earth, Minn.: Piper, 1972. (7-)
When Minneapolis millionaire, M. W. Savage
bought the record-breaking pacer, Dan Patch, for
$60,000 in the early 1900's, many thought he was crazy.
After building a palatial stable on the Minnesota River
at the town of Savage, the owner brought in the best
caretakers and trainers. Sasse highlights the exciting
story of the inseparable pair and captures the excitement of the races and the pathos of Dan Patch's death
followed one day later by the death of the owner.
Includes numerous small drawings, an appendix of Dan
Patch's 9-year racing record and index. Paper edition
and hard-cover.

155 SEVAREID, ERIC. *Canoeing with the Cree*. St. Paul:
Minnesota Historical Society, 1968. (6-)
In 1930 Eric Sevareid, then 17, and a companion
made a 2250 mile canoe trip from Fort Snelling up the
Minnesota and Red Rivers to York Factory at Hudson Bay.
This includes a log of the trip and newspaper accounts
Sevareid sent back to be published by the *Minneapolis
Star*, sponsors of the trip. The physically grueling
trip, which had never been attempted before, was
fraught with difficulties, but rewarded by scenery of
untold beauty and generous aid from many people. A
dashing adventure from a veteran newsman and commentator,
who even at 17 had a flair for colorful lenguage.

156 SHEPHARD, ESTHER. *Paul Bunyan*; illus. by Rockwell
Kent. New York: Harcourt Brace, 1952. (5-8) #
A collection of 21 tales taking the legendary
Paul Bunyan from Maine to Washington. Two chapters
tell of the lumberjack's logging days in Minnesota.
Here he invents buckskin harnesses, hunts "patridges"
and endures the Winter of the Blue Snow when even Lake
Superior turns into one chunk of ice. In the introduction the author gives information on the origin and significance of Paul Bunyan legends in American frontier
life. Young readers may have difficulty with the lumberjack lingo, but it will make for good storytelling.

157 SMITH, JAY H. *Fran Tarkenton*; illus. by Harold
Henriksen. Mankato, Minn.: Creative Ed., 1974.
(3-6) B
If we need more information for young readers
on the "Scrambler" and how he plays the game, this will
suffice. Most of the text dwells on Tarkenton's playing career, his attitude towards sports and his disputes with Coach Norm Van Brocklin. There is a brief,
impersonal biographical sketch of the veteran player.
Although the text is dull, the information dated and
the illustrations garish, this book will be read by
young sports enthusiasts.

—— SMITH, ROBERT K. *Seeing Itasca.* See MN 146

158 SNEVE, VIRGINIA DRIVING HAWK. *Betrayed.* New York: Holiday, 1974. (5-8) F
The author, originally from the Rosebud Sioux Reservation, bases this story on the Sioux Uprising of 1862 in Minnesota. After being deceived by the U.S. government, the destitute Santee Sioux stage a raid at Lake Shetek, killing and capturing many white settlers. Two white women and six children taken into Dakota Territory by the Santee are later rescued by young braves from the Teton Sioux. The story ends with the hanging of 38 Indians at Mankato, Minnesota. Sneve maintains a detached, unemotional view of the good and evil of both sides. Books for young people based on actual historical events in Minnesota are rare, making this an important contribution to the field of children's literature.

159 SPAVIN, DON. *Chippewa Dawn: Legends of an Indian People;* illus. by Jack Kraywinkle. Bloomington, Minn.: Voyageur, 1977. (3-5)
Eleven short Chippewa Indian legends originally collected by W.P.A. interviewers and writers on the White Earth Indian Reservation in northwestern Minnesota. These tales told around the campfire explain how the rabbit got its long ears, why the weasel's coat turns white, how the birch tree got its marks and other similar "hows" and "whys." Unfortunately the book suffers from printing errors and inadequate illustrations, but the oral origin of the legends makes this a unique collection. Paper and hardcover editions.

160 STONG, PHIL. *Honk: The Moose;* pictures by Kurt Wiese. New York: Dodd, Mead, 1935. (3-5) F
In the 1930's at Birora, fictitious Finnish mining-lumbering town on the Minnesota Iron Range, young Ivar Ketonen and his friend discover that a moose has moved into the horse barn. Honk, the moose, is lured to the city park where he becomes the community mascot and nuisance. Everyone is relieved when Honk finally wanders away, but many hope to see him return comes winter. A spoof with a slight story told with

typically Finnish gusto and tongue-in-cheek humor accompanied by equally funny illustrations. This would be a successful read-aloud by one who can capitalize on the situation and the Finnish background.

161 STUHLER, BARBARA and KREUTER, GRETCHEN, eds. *Women of Minnesota: Selected Biographical Essays.* St. Paul: Minnesota Historical Society, 1977. (8-) B

Biographies of "women achievers' who have made noteworthy contributions in diverse fields in Minnesota and the nation. Each major essay is written by a different author; the last chapter is a compilation of over 100 additional outstanding women of the past and present. Although some women may be unfamiliar, young readers will recognize names such as Maud Hart Lovelace (*Betsy-Tacy* books) and Wanda Gag (*Millions of Cats*). There are photographs, reference notes and an index to names, places and professions. A long overdue volume which gives recognition to *some* women of the state.

162 SWANHOLM, MARX. *Alexander Ramsey and the Politics of Survival.* St. Paul: Minnesota Historical Society, 1977. Paper. (8-)

One of the *Minnesota Historic Sites* pamphlets on the long political career of Minnesota's first territorial governor and second state governor. Ramsey secured land from the Dakota Indians by questionable treaties followed by broken promises which led to the Sioux Uprising of 1862. Although this is for adults, it is one of the few books on the man who helped shape the state which can be read by interested younger readers. Several portraits and photographs and a bibliography are included.

163 SWANHOLM, MARX. *Shadows in the Stillness: Early Man on the Rainy River;* illus. St. Paul: Minnesota Historical Society, 1978. (8-)

This publication in the *Minnesota Historic Sites* series tells of the mound builders, called the Laurel, who lived about 2000 years ago in the Rainy River Valley in northern Minnesota. During the last 40 years

archeologists have tried to learn more of these myster-
ious people whose artifacts are buried in the area.
Photographs and drawings illustrate a high-level text.
Bibliography.

164 SWENSON, GRACE STAGEBERG. *From the Ashes: The
Story of the Hinckley Fire of 1894.* Stillwater,
Minn.: Croixside, 1978. (6-)
On September 1, 1894, a forest fire swept over
the small lumber town of Hinckley, Minnesota, and neighboring settlements devastating 480 square miles of pine
forests and killing over 418 people. This tells of the
fire, dramatic stories of people, rescue of survivors,
burial of the dead, relief efforts and the return to
rebuild burned villages. Based on old newspaper
accounts, original railroad and government records,
historical collections and interviews with survivors,
this gives the complete story of one of the nation's
great fires. A documented account with numerous old
photographs, bibliography and index.

—— TARKENTON, FRAN. *Tarkenton.* See MN 97

165 THOMAS, JANE RESH. *Elizabeth Catches a Fish;* illus.
by Joseph Duffy. New York. Seabury, 1977.
(K-3) F
A warm, gentle story portraying a fine father-
daughter relationship. On her seventh birthday Elizabeth receives fishing equipment and a promise from her
father that just the two of them will go fishing. When
the day arrives, rain threatens, but Elizabeth keeps
fishing until she hooks and lands a four-pound bass.
She also can run the motor and clean her catch.
Thomas's reflective story is inspired by her own childhood experiences and those of her son on Minnesota
lakes. Full-page pen and ink drawings capture the
quiet, misty mood of the story.

166 TIPPLE, BRUCE. *The Land of Minnesota.* Fenton,
Mich.: McRoberts, 1975. (4-6)
A social studies text which deals with general
concepts such as habitat, topography, population, land
use, industry, recreation, planning communities, etc.
Each concept is illustrated by one specific case study,
e.g. farming is shown in the "Land of the Green Giant"
at Le Sueur, Minnesota. There are maps, charts, graphs
and photographs as well as questions to encourage discussion. Although some information may be of interest,
this text, with no index, has limitations for the individual reader. Better coverage of the same material is
found in Rosenfelt's student text, *Minnesota.*

167 TOYE, WILLIAM. *The Loon's Necklace;* illus. by
Elizabeth Cleaver. Toronto, Canada: Oxford
University Press, 1977. (K-3) P
This charming Indian legend from Canada tells
how the loon, Minnesota's state bird, received its
white markings. When an old blind man's sight is
restored, he gives the loon a shell necklace which
turns into beautiful white feathers sprinkled over the
loon's body. The proud loon can sometimes be heard
laughing for joy. Cleaver's richly-colored illustrations are in complete harmony with the Indian character
of the sparsely-worded tale. A beautiful book which
can be used in conjunction with the motion picture of
the same name.

168 TREUER, ROBERT. *The Tree Farm;* illus. by Sandra
Sandholm Reischel. Boston: Little, Brown, 1977.
(7-)
When Treuer forsook city life to move to a run-
down farm near Bemidji, Minnesota, he was searching for
a meaningful life for himself and his family. After 18
years of hard work, they had created a thriving tree
farm, developed an appreciation of the natural world
and found a deeper personal philosophy. Short vignettes in diary form include everyday events as well as
dramatic episodes such as fighting forest fires and
chasing off marauding dogs. Treuer, a master of language, expresses profound thoughts with simple eloquence,

sensitivity and humor. A book to be appreciated for
its sincere message and skillful writing.

169 TURNEY, IDA VIRGINIA. *Paul Bunyan, the Work Giant;*
    illus. by Norma Madge Lyon and Harold L. Price.
    Portland, Ore.: Binford and Mort, 1941. (3-5)
    Paul Bunyan worked in many states, but he and
his crews really left their mark on Minnesota. Here he
felled the mighty white pines, opened an iron mine and
invented a gadget for pulling stumps. Babe, the Blue
Ox, left footprints that became the 10,000 lakes, and
Brimstone Bill's spilled water turned into the Mississippi River. Bold blue pictures enliven the short easy-
to-read chapters which children should relish.

170 TURNGREN, ELLEN. *Listen, My Heart;* decorations by
    Vera Bock. New York: McKay, 1956. (8-10) F
    Fifteen-year-old Sigrid Almbeck, who lives with
her immigrant parents on the family farm near Kramer,
Minnesota, finds herself torn in many directions. She
is caught in the conflict between her spend-thrift
father and her thrifty mother, and when circumstances
force her to manage the farm, she puts aside hopes for
a college education. She also must choose between two
suitors of differing temperaments. The author writes
for older boys and girls from her own farm experiences
in Minnesota. She tells of a way of life of the 1930's,
one which has almost disappeared from the Minnesota
scene.

171 VAN ZEE, RON and KUBISTA, IVAN. *Minnesota;* illus.
    Portland, Ore.: Belding, 1976. (6-) P
    One of the most spectacular of the over-sized
photo-essays on Minnesota. This captures the natural
beauty of the state in all seasons. Full-page and
double-page color photographs by camera artist Van Zee
range from close-ups of wild flowers to broad vistas
of magnificent scenes. In 12 pages of readable, informal text, Kubista introduces small doses of Minnesota
history, geography and local color as he travels
through the state. Though expensive, this "coffee
table" book is of exceptional quality.

172 VIZENOR, GERALD. *The Everlasting Sky: New Voices from the People Named the Chippewa;* illus. New York: Macmillan, 1972. (7-)

Vizenor, from the White Earth Reservation in Minnesota, prefers to be known as a member of the "oshki anishinabe", or the new people of the woodland, instead of "indian", "chippewa", or "ojibway", which are white man's words. He tells of reservation life in Minnesota and Wisconsin, beliefs of his people and problems confronting them as they search for dignity and pride in white America. Although he writes with some degree of detachment, Vizenor is convinced there must be change in American institutions and society. One of the few recent books telling of the "oshki anishinabe" by a member of the tribe. Photographs and index.

173 WARNER, EDYTHE RECORDS. *Cabin for Ducks;* illus. by author. New York: Viking, 1958. o.p. (2-4) F P

Two young brothers join their Grandfather at his northern Minnesota cabin for the fall duck hunt. One boy relates the story as they learn from Grandpa of nature, outdoor life and hunting. Warner's detailed illustrations in brown tones are precisely drawn and share equally with the text. An attractive, oversized book, unfortunately out-of-print.

174 WATERS, THOMAS F. *The Streams and Rivers of Minnesota;* photographs and maps by author. Minneapolis: University of Minnesota Press, 1977. (8-) R *

The most comprehensive source available on the major watersheds of Minnesota. The book covers geology history, physical and biological characteristics of rivers and streams, wildlife and aquatic life, and recreational uses of the area. The author pleads for river and flood management while maintaining rivers and streams in their natural state. Historical and present day canoe routes are mapped. Included are numerous color photographs, black and white pictures and maps, bibliography, index to streams and a general index. A useful book for nature lovers, conservationists, fisher men and canoeists.

—— WATSON, LINDA. *A Gathering of Waters*. See MN 24

175 WILDER, LAURA INGALLS. *On the Banks of Plum Creek;*
illus. by Garth Williams. New York: Harper &
Row, 1953. (4-6) F *
This fourth book in the *Little House* series
finds the Ingalls family moving by covered wagon to a
sod house on Plum Creek near Walnut Grove, Minnesota.
Here they encounter grasshopper plagues, droughts,
fires and blizzards, but the family courageously holds
on. Through it all Laura and her sisters bounce from
one adventure to another. Garth Williams' illustrations capture the pioneer spirit. Plum Creek and
Walnut Grove exist today, and children are better off
because they existed for Laura Ingalls Wilder in the
1870's.

—— WILLIAMS, NEVA. *Patrick DesJarlait*. See MN 51

176 WILSON, BLANCHE NICHOLAS. *Minnetonka Story.*
Wayzata, Minn.: Ross and Haines, 1971. (6-)
Spanning the years from canoes to cruisers, this
tells the story of Lake Minnetonka, one of Minnesota's
most popular residential lakes near the Twin Cities.
The author, a lake-dweller most of her life, writes of
the history, the early settlers, the era of luxury
hotels and excursion boats and the coming of enterprises to the area. A collection of colorful, well-
written stories gathered from interviews, newspapers,
letters and diaries. There are 12 pages of old photographs. This will have more than local interest because it tells of an area well-known in the state.

177 WITHERIDGE, ELIZABETH. *Dead End Bluff;* illus. by
Charles Geer. New York: Atheneum, 1966. o.p.
(5-8) F
In the small town of Scott, fictitious village
on the Mississippi River near Minneapolis, Quig Smith,
14-year old blind boy attempts to do everything his
sighted friends can do, even though it means disobeying
his overly-protective father. He swims in meets,
attends public school, takes a job that involves him in

a theft and ventures down dangerous Dead End Bluff
alone. A fast-paced adventure with strong characters
and the added dimension of a handicapped person dealing
with problems.

178 WITHERIDGE, ELIZABETH. *Just One Indian Boy.* New
York: Atheneum, 1974. (6-9) F
Based on a true story of the author's friend.
When Andy Thunder, a Chippewa youth, walks out of the
local high school, he faces the real world of job-
hunting, racial prejudice and brushes with the law.
Through the encouragement of his mother, a friend and a
teacher, Andy pulls his life together, gets an education, marries and returns to the Lake Vermilion Reservation to work with his people. A fast-moving story of
the times written with empathy and understanding. One
of the few current young people's novels on this social
theme which is based on real places and people in the
state.

179 YATES, ELIZABETH. *With Pipe, Paddle and Song: A
Story of the French-Canadian Voyageurs . . .
Circa 1750.* New York: Dutton, 1968. o.p.
(7-10) F
Guillaume Puissant, 16-year-old French-Canadian,
signs on as a singer with a crew of voyageurs traveling from Montreal to Grand Portage on Lake Superior.
The route is treacherous, and Guillaume is dashed over-
board in rough water near Grand Portage. The injured
lad is rescued by the Chippewa, brought to camp and
nursed by Willow Wand, with whom Guillaume falls in
love. He joins the voyageurs on their homeward trip.
Years later he returns to claim his love. A romantic
adventure by a distinguished author whose beautiful
prose and historical detail of the 1750's will appeal
to some readers.

180 ZIEBARTH, MARILYN and OMINSKY, ALAN. *Fort Snelling,
Anchor Post of the Northwest.* St. Paul: Minnesota Historical Society, 1970. Paper. (6-)
A booklet in the *Minnesota Historical Sites*
series which traces the outpost's 150 year history from

the laying of the cornerstone in 1820 by Josiah Snelling through its restoration up to 1970. Numerous photographs, old maps and drawings illustrate the fort's history and the reconstruction process. An attractive, condensed publication.

OHIO

compiled by **MARILYN SOLT**

Long after the glaciers that covered three-fourths of the state in the Ice Age had receded, prehistoric Indians lived in what is now Ohio. Among the descendants of these early peoples were the Mound Builders who, from 1000 B.C. to A.D. 1300, constructed over 6000 burial mounds and other earthworks throughout the Ohio region.

The Mound Builders were gone before the arrival of the European explorers who found a forest wilderness abounding in game and sparsely settled by about 15,000 Indians. For many years both the French and British claimed the rich lands of the Indians, but, at the close of the French and Indian War in 1763, the Northwest Territory including present-day Ohio, passed to the British who then lost it to the young United States in 1783.

The new nation rapidly began to occupy and develop the wilderness domain. In 1788, the Ohio Company founded Marietta, the first permanent white settlement in Ohio. Other communities close to the Ohio River were soon settled. The rush of settlers into Indian lands provoked the tribes to warfare, forcing the government to deal with them. In 1794, near present-day Toledo, General Anthony Wayne decisively defeated the Indians. The following year, in the Treaty of Greenville, the Indians ceded the United States about two-thirds of the land that is now Ohio.

With peace restored, settlers poured into the area. Many Virginians and Kentuckians settled in the valleys of rivers flowing into the Ohio. New Englanders came in covered wagons to claim land in the northeastern part of the region called the Western Reserve. Soon the territory had sufficient population to become a state, the first one in the Northwest Territory. Ohio became the seventeenth state on March 1, 1803.

Following the War of 1812, in which Ohio took an active part, thousands of people moved to Ohio from eastern states, together with immigrants from Germany and Great Britain. New forms of transportation quick-ened the flow of residents into the state. The first steamboat arrived on the Ohio River in 1811, and *Walk-in-the-Water* in 1818 became the first steamboat on Lake Erie. Soon canals, and, a short time later, railroads were being extended into all parts of the state. The Irish arrived in great numbers to work on these projects as laborers.

Because the canals and railroads made eastern mar-kets easily accessible, they contributed to increased prosperity. Many mills and factories were built between 1830 and 1860.

During the years before the Civil War, many Ohioans felt very strongly about slavery. Some hated it so much they helped slaves escape through the Underground Railroad to Canada. Others had cultural and economic ties with Kentucky and the slave-holding South. When war came, Ohio supplied about 345,000 men to the Union army and the wheels of industry turned unceasingly to provide ambulances, mess kits, uniforms, and cannons. Packing houses provided endless barrels of beef, pork, and lard for the army quartermasters.

Following the Civil War, Ohio's industrial centers flourished. Many workers came to the state from northern Europe and later from southeastern Europe. The shipping of coal and iron ore on Lake Erie increased. In 1870 Benjamin Goodrich began the manufacture of rubber goods in Akron. By 1880 John D. Rockefeller of Cleveland was the oil baron of the world.

Cleveland became a center, not only of industry, but of culture, as well. Today there are located in that city eight of the fifty-six Ohio colleges and universities accredited by the North Central Association.

Although farming continued to be a leading occupation, the movement was toward urbanization and industrialization. In the decades since 1900 this trend has continued, until today Ohio ranks third among the states in the total value of manufactured products. Although farmlands still stretch across many acres of the state, agriculture at present supplies only six percent of the state's total value of all products.

Today Ohio is sixth among the states in population, with about three-fourths of Ohio's eleven million inhabitants living in urban areas. One-third of the people live in the metropolitan areas of Cleveland and Cincinnati. There are five other major cities: Columbus, the capital since 1812; Toledo; Akron; Dayton; and Youngstown. The remaining population is in innumerable bustling towns, small villages, and on farms.

At present about 97 of every 100 Ohioans were born in the United States. Many of the members of Ohio's sizable black population have migrated from the Deep South since 1920. A majority of people born in other countries came from Germany, Great Britain, Hungary, Italy, Poland, and Yugoslavia.

Eight Presidents are among the famous people coming from Ohio. In 1840 William Henry Harrison of North Bend became the ninth President. From the years 1868 to 1900 five Ohio-born Presidents, all Republicans, were elected: Ulysses S. Grant, Rutherford B. Hayes, James A. Garfield, Benjamin Harrison, and William McKinley. William Howard Taft of Cincinnati became the twenty-seventh President in 1909, and in 1921 Warren G. Harding of Marion became the twenty-ninth President. Famous inventors born in Ohio include Thomas A. Edison and Wilbur and Orville Wright. Ohio's leadership in aviation has been upheld by astronauts John Glenn, pioneer of outer space, and Neil Armstrong, first man to walk on the moon.

Many aspects of past and present life in Ohio may be explored through the books that follow.

1   ADOFF, ARNOLD. *Tornado! Poems;* illus. New York:
    Delacorte Press, 1976, 1977. (3-)
    The poet lives only a few miles from the scene
of the Xenia tornado of April 3, 1974. He dedicates
his poetic description of a tornado and its aftermath
"to the people of Xenia, Ohio, who are rebuilding, and
to people everywhere who survive and overcome forces
greater than themselves." Black and white illustrations vivify the fury of the storm and the resulting
destruction.

2   ALLEE, MARJORIE HILL. *Susanna and Tristram;* illus.
    Boston, Mass.: Houghton Mifflin, 1957. (4-8) F
    Sixteen-year-old Susanna Coffin and her younger
brother, Tristram, orphans, make their way from Indiana
to Cincinnnati and to the care of Cousin Levi Coffin,
an actual historical personage. He, like Susanna and
Tristram, is a Quaker, and the unofficial president of
the Underground Railroad. Showing the composure and
courage of her famous cousin, Susanna soon is assisting
in the transportation of slaves. A good presentation
of period details and the various attitudes toward
slavery that existed in pre-Civil War Cincinnati.

3   ALLEN, LE ROY. *Shawnee Lance.* New York:
    Delacorte Press, 1970. (5-8) F
    The year and the exact location of the story are
not given—probably southwest Ohio before 1795. After
killing his father, the Shawnee adopt 14-year-old
Daniel. Envied by his new brother, Black Eagle, and
hated by his new cousin, Buffalo Skull, Daniel does not
find life easy. But because their father is good and
wise, Black Eagle and Daniel come to feel that they are
truly brothers. As Daniel adapts to his new life, the
reader learns about the Indian culture, including the
Shawnee ritual of adoption.

4   ALTSHELER, JOSEPH A. *The Riflemen of the Ohio.*
    New York: Appleton-Century-Crofts, 1937. o.p.
    (6-8) F
    Originally published in 1910, this title contin-
ues the fortunes of Henry Ware and five youthful companions who were the central characters in *The Young*

213

Trailers and several other books. This story focuses
on conflict with the Indians in Ohio territory.
Although Henry is but a boy, he performs heroic feats.
In the woods he is as quick-thinking and competent as
Daniel Boone and Simon Kenton, both of whom show up in
time to aid a beleaguered fort. Although Henry is not
a believable character, the plot is fast-moving and
exciting. The story contains much information about
the Indian tribes and the white renegades who fought
with them in the early days of Ohio.

5   ANDERSON, SHERWOOD. *Winesburg, Ohio.* New York:
      Viking, 1960. (7-) *
      In perhaps the most famous novel ever written
about Ohio, originally published in 1919, Anderson
describes small town life at the turn of the century.
Modeled after Clyde, Ohio, the book takes the form of
a series of interconnected character sketches. Though
written for adults, it could profitably be read, in
whole or in part, by the sophisticated junior high
school reader.

6   AVERY, LYNN. *Cappy and the River;* illus. New York:
      Duell, Sloan & Pearce, 1960. o.p. (4-6) F
      The spring of 1798 finds young Ken McLennon and
his performing dog Cappy journeying with Professor
Alexander Montgomery, an entertainer, and the two young
Canadian boatmen down the Ohio River from Wheeling to
Cincinnati. On the way, they give performances at
settlements and towns. They also have exciting, but
improbable, adventures, besting Black Tom and his Wheeling gang on three different accasions. Ken and Cappy
rejoin Ken's family in Cincinnati and they proceed to
the Miami River valley where they take up land. Authentic information about Ohio and travel on the river in
early days, but falls short as literature.

7   BAILEY, BERNADINE. *Picture Book of Ohio;* illus. by
      Kurt Wiese. Chicago: Whitman, 1963. (3-5)
      An inclusive, simply-written book for younger
readers. Contains a brief history of the state, its
industries, inventions, citizens, art, and literature.

Kurt Wiese's illustrations are as informative as the text. There is a picture on every page; black and white sketches alternate with water-color paintings.

8   BAKER, JIM. *For the Ohio Country;* illus. Marlton, N.J.: Periods and Commas, 1976. Paper. (2-5) (2-5) F

The settling of Marietta and Gallipolis are seen through the eyes of an imaginary frontiersman, Ben Hardy, who has a part in each story. Reprinted from the author's syndicated newspaper feature, *Ben Hardy,* these comic strip stories are authentic. They bring early days in Ohio to life for younger readers.

9   BARRY, JAMES P. *The Battle of Lake Erie, September, 1813;* illus. New York: Watts, 1970. (6-) * #

On September 10, 1813, Oliver Hazard Perry and his American squadron of nine vessels defeated a British squadron of seven in a naval battle that decided a United States boundary: the land lying between the Ohio River and the Great Lakes became a part of the young United States. This book, illustrated with contemporary prints, brings the event into such clear focus that the reader feels he is with Perry preparing for the battle and fighting it. Bibliography. Index.

10   BASKIN, JOHN. *New Burlington: The Life and Death of an American Village;* illus. New York: Norton, 1976. (7-) *

For almost two hundred years, the farming village of New Burlington stood in southwestern Ohio, between Dayton and Cincinnati. Then in the early 1970's, the United States Corps of Engineers began building a dam and, behind it, a lake to cover New Burlington. In the last year of the village's life, John Baskin interviewed the residents and wrote *New Burlington* which he thinks of as a "book of stories and voices in which the characters ponder some of their time on earth. It could be said, then, that it is no more than a book about loneliness." Nonfiction, it has the emotional impact of *Winesburg, Ohio.*

215

11 BEARD, CHARLES A. *The Presidents in American History.* (brought forward since 1948 by William Beard). New York: Messner, 1969. (7-8) B

Each President's portrait and signature precede a brief, clear, and unbiased discussion of the circumstances surrounding his selection, his qualifications, and the events of his administration. Eminent historian Beard also provides an interesting and provocative introduction and a biographical digest giving basic facts of personal and public life, cabinet members, and the popular and electoral votes of each presidential election. Eight presidents, because of birth or long-time residency, are associated with Ohio.

12 BENNETT, EMERSON. *Forest Rose; A Tale of the Frontier.* Athens, Ohio: Ohio University Press, 1975. (6-) F

First published in Cincinnati in 1850, *The Forest Rose,* based upon a true incident, is a tale of romantic adventure set in the Hocking Valley in the early 1790's. The author assigns the leading roles to the famous Indian fighter, Lewis Wetzel, and two virtuous young adults. Albert Maywood, with Wetzel's help, finds and rescues from the Indians, his fiancée, the lovely Rose Forester. Interesting to today's reader for the attitude expressed toward the Indians. Introductory essay discusses nineteenth century "western" literature.

13 BIESTERVELD, BETTY. *Run, Reddy, Run;* illus. New York: Nelson, 1962. o.p. (3-6) F

Henrilee's father is a sawyer on a logging crew that travels from place to place to harvest the mature trees from the forest. Henrilee loves the woods, especially the animals living there. Still, she longs to remain in one place, on a farm. Her wishes come true in southeastern Ohio, a land of pleasant farms as well as forests, where Henrilee raises an orphaned fox, Reddy, and finally makes friends with pesky Jiggers Thompson. Nice appreciation of wildlife.

14 BJORKLUND, KARNA L. *The Indians of Northeastern America;* illus. New York: Dodd, Mead, 1969. (4-)

Very attractive illustrations by the author's father increase the appeal of this well-written and authentic account of the Woodland Indians. One chapter discusses the cultural exchanges that took place between the Indians and the colonizers: ". . . what the white man received from the natives made possible his very existence in the New World. . ." By contrast, the Indian lost "an ancient way of life." Contains a bibliography, index, and a list of museums with Woodland Indian collections.

15 BLEEKER, SONIA. *The Delaware Indians;* illus. by Patricia Boodell. New York: Morrow, 1953. (3-6)

The first four chapters describe the daily life and religious ceremonies of the Delawares in their villages along the Atlantic coast in areas that are today in New Jersey, Pennsylvania and Delaware. Chapter 5 recreates the signing of the treaty between the Delawares and William Penn. The final chapter tells of the Delawares' displacement, first by Penn's sons, and subsequently by other colonists. In the push westward that continued for two hundred years, they were forced into the Ohio territory and then out of it. Simple style; written objectively.

16 BLOCH, MARIE HALUN. *Marya;* illus. New York: Coward-McCann, 1957. o.p. (4-6) F

Marya Palenko left the Ukraine with her parents when Marya was two. Until her ninth year, Marya was happy in a Ukrainian neighborhood in Cleveland, but now she feels out of place. Her teacher Anglicizes her name and because of her Eastern Orthodox faith, Marya doesn't celebrate Christmas and Easter in the same way as her classmates. Understanding does come in this good re-creation of an ethnic neighborhood where the author spent her childhood.

17 BOESCH, MARK. *Beyond the Muskingum;* illus. Phila.
  delphia, Pa.: Winston, 1935. o.p. (6-) F
    After his father is killed by Indians, young
Jonathan Hale, hoping to avenge his death, goes on a
scouting expedition with the great woodsman, Lewis
Wetzel, beyond the Muskingum into the Ohio country
the Delawares. "The-only-good-Indian-is-a-dead-Indian"
philosophy espoused by Wetzel may shock the reader;
still it is a true reflection of an accepted attitude
of that time. Besides the excitement engendered by pursuing—and being pursued—there is a nice appreciation
of the beauty of the wild Ohio country.

18 BOWMAN, JAMES CLOYD. *Mike Fink;* illus. Boston:
  Little, Brown, 1957. (5-8)
    The truth and legend of Mike Fink, American
frontiersman and keelboatman on the Ohio and Mississippi Rivers in the early 1800's, is related in tall-
tale tradition. This lively book contains the brags
and songs of the river boatmen, as well as stories of
Mike's prowess. The author notes that his interest in
the riverboatmen began in childhood when his imagination was kindled by tales his grandparents told of
their trek down the Ohio.

19 BRANDENBERG, ALIKI. *The Story of Johnny Appleseed;*
  illus. Englewood Cliffs, N.J.: Prentice-Hall,
  1963. o.p. (1-3) B
    A very simple account of Johnny's journeying
through the country planting appleseeds and being
friendly and helpful toward whites, Indians, wild animals, and children. Alternate full-page color and
black and white illustrations.

20 BRANLEY, FRANKLIN M. *Man in Space to the Moon;*
  illus. by Louis Glanzman. New York: Crowell,
  1970. (4-8) *
    "In the summer of 1969, man's age-old dream to
set foot on another world was fulfilled . . . . Astronaut Neil Armstrong, Commander of the Apollo 11 mission
. . . stepped . . . onto the surface of the moon."
That historic event involving an Ohioan is described in

this well-written account by astronomer Dr. Franklyn M.
Branley, who has written many excellent science books
for young readers. Very good illustrations. Table of
manned space flights. Index.

21 BROMFIELD, LOUIS. *The Farm*. New York: Harper,
      1933. (7-) F *
      The Farm is a panoramic novel based on four gen-
erations of the author's family history. The Colonel,
Johnny's great-grandfather, settled in Richland County
in 1815 and from the wilderness carved a farm and a
good life for himself and his family. During the
mature years of Johnny's grandparents, the farm became
very productive and profitable. Gradually, the old
life became harder and harder until, finally, in 1914,
the farm was sold. Though lacking in dialogue and con-
ventional plot elements, a number of well-realized
characters are seen against a realistic social background.

22 BROWN, JOE E. and HANCOCK, RALPH. *Laughter Is a
      Wonderful Thing;* illus. New York: Barnes, 1956.
      o.p. (6-) B
      Born in Holgate, a small northwestern Ohio town,
Joe E. Brown moved with his family to Toledo in 1902
before he was seven. At ten he was an acrobatic per-
former in circuses. By the time he was fifteen he had
added comedy to the acrobatic routine and also played
semi-pro baseball. Mr. Brown was sixty-four when he
wrote *Laughter Is a Wonderful Thing*. Includes details
of life in the Toledo area in the first two decades of
this century. Photographs. Index.

23 BUEHR, WALTER. *1812: The War and the World,* illus.
      Chicago: Rand McNally, 1967. o.p. (6-)
      Much of the fighting on land during the War of
1812 took place in the state of Ohio, the territory of
Michigan, and on the Canadian frontier that is now a
part of the province of Ontario. Many of the naval
engagements were fought on two of the Great Lakes,
Ontario and Erie. Reading almost like a suspense story,
this accurate account places all of the events of the
war in a broad historical context. Index.

24 BURCHARD, MARSHALL. *Sports Hero: Pete Rose;* illus.
New York: Putnam's, 1976. (3-6) B
This large print biography gives an excellent
portrait of the Cincinnati Red's Pete Rose. It follows
his career through his team's victory in the 1975 World
Series.

25 BURCHARD, MARSHALL and BURCHARD, SUE. *Sports Hero:*
Johnny Bench; illus. New York: Putnam's, 1973.
(2-5) B
In 1970, at the age of twenty-three, Johnny
Bench of the Cincinnati Reds was the youngest player
ever to receive the National League's Most Valuable
Player Award. This readable large-print biography
covers his life and career to that point. Illustrated
with photographs.

— BURCHARD, SUE. *Sports Hero: Johnny Bench.*
See OH 25

26 BUTLER, MARGARET MANOR. *A Pictorial History of the*
Western Reserve, 1796 to 1860. Cleveland:
World, 1963. (4-) P *
Three hundred fifty illustrations, each accurately and fully described, provide a pictorial record
of the development of the Western Reserve from the
early pioneer days of Moses Cleveland to the beginning
of modern industrialism just before the Civil War.
This very attractive book deepens the reader's appreciation for the rich American heritage of the Western
Reserve. Bibliography. Index.

27 BYARS, BETSY. *The House of Wings;* illus. New
York: Viking, 1972. (4-7) F *
Sammy, ten, is disconsolate when his parents
leave him with his grandfather, whom he has not seen
since he was a baby, at Grandfather's farm in Northern
Ohio, while they go on to Detroit to get settled into a
new job and home. But, by the second day, after he has
helped Grandfather rescue and care for an injured sandhill crane, his attitude has changed. He now looks forward to spending the summer with Grandfather and his

220

pets—a parrot, an owl, a gaggle of geese—in the house
of wings. The scene is not really important but the
big white house—ramshackle, 70-80 years old—is typical of many in northern Ohio.

28 CAMERON, ELEANOR. *To the Green Mountains.* New
York: Dutton, 1975. (7-) F *
Kathryn Rule, fourteen, and her mother, Ellen,
have lived in a small town hotel near Springfield for
eight years. Her mother, the hotel manager-housekeeper,
practically supports her ne'er-do-well husband, who
lives on a farm. Eventually, Kath and her mother leave
both the hotel and her father to live with Ellen's
mother in the Green Mountains of Vermont. Characterization is good with changes in relationships logically
motivated. The time is World War I, although the war
is not important to the story, which evokes life in a
small town of that time.

29 CAMPEN, RICHARD N. *Ohio—An Architectural Portrait;*
illus. Chagrin Falls, Ohio: West Summit Press,
1973. (6-) P
A forty page essay, "The Architecture of Ohio"
introduces over 500 photographs, each with an informative caption. The author, an authority on architectural history, took all the pictures. Collectively,
the photographs show the whole range of Ohio's architecture—residential, governmental, commercial, and
institutional—from the early 1800's to the present.
The author declares the architecture of Ohio important
because over the years "building in the State reflects
the succession of styles which mark the development of
the building art in the Nation at large." This enjoyable and attractive book is printed in folio. Bibliography and indices.

30 CARPENTER, ALLAN. *Ohio: From Its Glorious Past to
the Present;* illus. by Phil Austin. Chicago:
Children's Press, 1963. (4-8)
Concise and interesting story of Ohio including
its history, resources and people. Attractive illustrations in color supplement the text. Handy Reference

221

Section at the back gives basic data including significant dates in Ohio history and well-known men and women
of Ohio. Index. *Enchantment of America* series.

31 CARPER, JEAN and DICKERSON, GRACE L. *Little Turtle;*
     illus. Chicago: Whitman, 1959. (4-8) B #
     When he was only twenty, Little Turtle became a
Miami Chief. He left his home in Kekionga (site of
present-day Fort Wayne) to lead the Indian forces to
victory over the whites on battlegrounds in western
Ohio in 1790 and 1791. William Wells, Little Turtle's
adopted white son, fought with the Indians in these two
battles, but became a scout for Anthony Wayne before his
defeat of the Indians at Fallen Timbers. After the
Treaty of Greenville, Little Turtle acted as an agent
between the whites and the Indians. Told in story form,
this is a good account of a great Indian leader.

32 CAVANAH, FRANCES and CRANDALL, ELIZABETH L. *Meet
     the Presidents;* illus. Philadelphia: Macrae
     Smith, 1962. (4-8) B
     Eight of the thirty-five presidents whose lives
are recorded here were Ohioans by birth or long-time
residencey. In a chapter devoted to each President,
there is a fictionalized account of the President in
his youth, followed by an account of a high point in
his career. A factual summary of the significant
events and dates in his lifetime concludes the chapter.
A pen and ink drawing of each president appears at the
beginning of the chapter. The incidents are chosen to
reveal the personalities of the Presidents.

33 COLLETT, RITTER. *The Cincinnati Reds;* illus. Vir-
     ginia Beach, Va.: Jordan-Powers, 1976. o.p. (4-)
     This book, subtitled "A Pictorial History of
Professional Baseball's Oldest Team," records the evolution of "pro" baseball in clear prose and with many
fine action photographs. The history begins with the
Red Stockings winning all the games played in their
first year, 1869, and concludes with their winning the
1975 World Series. The author, Sports Editor for the
Dayton *Journal Herald,* has been following the Cincinnati
Reds for nearly thirty years.

222

34 COLLIER, EDMUND. *The Story of Annie Oakley;* illus.
New York: Grosset & Dunlap, 1956. o.p.
(3-7) B
The first half of this fictionalized biography
covers Annie's life as a child in Darke County in the
years following the Civil War. The second half records
her meeting with Frank Butler, who became her husband,
and their professional life together as stars in the
Buffalo Bill Wild West Show. Although fame came before
she was twenty, Annie experienced hardships earlier,
especially between the ages of ten and twelve when she
worked for the cruel people she named "The Wolves."
A well-written, readable biography.

35 COLLINS, CHARLES W. *Ohio, an Atlas.* Madison, Wis.:
American Printing & Publishing, 1975. (5-) *
The Atlas is divided into four parts: Physical
Geography, Population, Agriculture, and Economy.
Statistical maps provide a great variety of information
on topics ranging from population per square mile to
acres of various crops planted in each county. The
author states that the geographer finds Ohio an especially interesting state because "it displays great
variety in its physical and human resources as well as
in the distribution of those resources."

36 COLLINS, WILLIAM R. *Ohio, the Buckeye State;* illus.
5th ed. Englewood Cliffs, N.J.: Prentice-Hall,
1974. (6-8)
A comprehensive well-written text for junior
high use covering Ohio history, geography, and government. The history extends from prehistoric times to
the present. The final unit discusses notable men,
women, events, and anecdotes of Ohio. An annotated
list of relevant books, films, and filmstrips appears
at the end of each unit. The state consitution is
included. There are many good illustrations, maps, and
an index.

37 COLVER, ANNE. *Yankee Doodle Painter;* illus. New
York: Knopf, 1955. o.p. (4-8) F *
A very good fictional account of the circumstances surrounding the painting of the famous picture,
The Spirit of '76. The artist, Archibald Willard, was
the author's great-uncle. When Uncle Arch made the
painting, the author's father, Will Colver, was a boy
of twelve living with the Willards in Cleveland. They
had recently moved there from Wellington. The story is
told from Will's viewpoint. Good period details and an
excellent view of the Philadelphia Centennial Exposition of 1876 where the painting was exhibited.

38 COOKE, DAVID C. *Tecumseh, Destiny's Warrior.* New
York: Simon and Schuster, 1959. (6-8) B *
"In history's record is eternally written the
magnificence of Tecumseh of the Shawnee . . . . Enemy
of Americans . . . but a noble American . . . he set an
example for honesty, for plain speaking, for generosity
and humane behavior never equaled by any other North
American Indian." This book explicates these state-
ments taken from the conclusion. Besides giving an
excellent portrait of Tecumseh, it also vividly depicts
westward expansion in the young United States from the
Revolutionary War to the War of 1812. Bibliography and
index.

— CRANDALL, ELIZABETH L. *Meet the Presidents.*
See OH 32

39 CRAWFORD, PHYLLIS. *Hello, the Boat;* illus. New
York: Holt, Rinehart & Winston, 1938, 1966.
o.p. (5-8) F
In the spring of 1817, the Doak family—mother,
father, sixteen-year-old Susan, fourteen-year-old Steve,
and ten-year-old David—operate a storeboat on the Ohio
River while traveling from their old home in Pittsburgh
to a new home in Cincinnati. As they progress downstream and sell their goods in response to the cry,
"Hello, the boat," the reader learns of the river craft,
the towns, and the people of that region and time.

The riverboatmen use slangy river talk. The book
relates two encounters with General William Henry
Harrison. Newbery Honor Book, 1939.

40 CROUCH, TOM D. *The Giant Leap;* illus. Columbus,
      Ohio: The Ohio Historical Society, 1971. (4-)
      This is a chronology of Ohio aerospace events
and personalities from 1815, when a Mr. Gaston released
a hot air balloon at a fireworks exhibition in Cincinnati, to 1969 when Neil Armstrong walked on the moon.
With Ohioans Wilbur and Orville Wright, Eddie Rickenbacker, Jimmy Doolittle, and John Glenn making history
in the pages between, there is some exciting reading.
Illustrated with photos and old prints. Good bibliography.

41 CROUT, GEORGE and MC CALL, EDITH S. *Where the Ohio
      Flows;* illus. Chicago: Benefic, 1960. o.p.
      (3-7) #
      The aim of the author was to show the part the
Ohio River Valley played in making America great.
Covering glacial times to the present, this book is
appropriate for classes in Ohio history. The facts are
accurate and the writing is competent. Many pictures
and maps illustrate the text. There are study questions and suggested activities at the close of each
chapter.

42 DAUGHERTY, JAMES. *Daniel Boone;* illus. by author.
      New York: Viking, 1939. (4-8) B NA
      In the early days of Kentucky, the Shawnees from
the Ohio country frequently crossed the Ohio River to
raid the settlements and kill the whites. Daniel Boone
fought them often and was captured more than once. On
one occasion he was taken to the Indian village of
Chillicothe, adopted by Chief Black Fish, and marched
to Detroit as an exhibit for the British. Daugherty's
non-fictionalized narrative and epic pictures bring
alive pioneer days and the heroic figure of Daniel
Boone. Original lithographs in color. Newbery Award,
1940.

43 DE LEEUW, ADELE. *Civil War Nurse, Mary Ann Bicker-dyke*. New York: Messner, 1973. B *
An interesting biography about the woman who cared for hundreds of soldiers wounded in nineteen Civil War battles. After the war she worked to obtain pensions for veterans and Civil War nurses. A native of Knox County, Ohio, Mary Ann lived in Ohio until she was in her thirties, when she moved with her husband and children to Galesburg, Illinois. Possessed of tremendous energy and courage, and with a genius for organization, Mother Bickerdyke often ignored red tape, and, on several occasions, went over all heads straight to General Grant or General Sherman. Bibliography. Index.

44 DE LEEUW, ADELE and DE LEEUW, CATEAU. *Hideaway House;* illus. Boston: Little, Brown, 1953. o.p. (4-6) F
In 1791 the Titus family travels by flatboat to Cincinnati where they proceed north to the 360 acres they have purchased near the Big Miami River. This is before the Treaty of Greenville and there is still conflict with the Indians. The Tituses vow to stay but another family, the Whipples, leave following an Indian scare during which the families hide in a cave the children had discovered while playing. The characters are semi-stereotyped, but the dangers of pioneering at that time are realistically portrayed. Rights of the Indians are defended.

45 DE LEEUW, CATEAU. *Fear in the Forest;* illus. New York: Nelson, 1960. o.p. (4-7) F
Twelve-year-old Daniel overcomes an almost morbid fear of the forest he has felt since his father "got kilt" by the Indians in 1791, three years earlier. He conquers the fear while working on a pack-horse train that carries supplies to the string of forts General Anthony Wayne built at twenty-five mile intervals north of Cincinnati. Provides a good picture of pack-horse trains, the forts, and the settlers' fear of Indian raids.

46 DE LEEUW, CATEAU. *Give Me Your Hand.* Boston:
Little, Brown, 1960. o.p. (4-8) F
    With the death of her mother, seventeen-year-old
Ellen Spencer, who had lived all her life with her
parents on a farm near Hamilton, takes over the care of
her five younger brothers and sisters and the many
tasks that occupied the housewife in 1819 in Ohio.
While much of the everyday life of the time is well
portrayed, Ellen is the only well-developed character.
Her two suitors—Horace Estabrook, a handsome stranger
from Philadelphia, and Jethroe Parrish, a steady, hard-
working young neighbor,—are not well delineated.

— DE LEEUW, CATEAU. *Hideaway House.* See OH 44

47 DE LEEUW, CATEAU. *The Proving Years;* illus. New
York: Nelson, 1962. o.p. (5-8) F
    The Proving Years chronicles the part played by
the Army of the Northwest under General William Henry
Harrison during the War of 1812. The reader experiences the events through the eyes of young Jason who
tags along when his older brother joins the militia.
An expert woodsman, Jason spies with the Rangers. He
is also skillful in caring for the sick and wounded and
serves as the doctor's assistant. The action includes
a march through the Black Swamp and the building and
defense of Fort Meigs. Although Jason as a character
seems a little too good to be true, the story effectively recreates the historical events.

— DICKERSON, GRACE L. *Little Turtle.* See OH 31

48 DOBRIN, NORMA. *Delawares;* illus. Chicago:
Melmont, 1963. o.p. (2-3)
    When the colonists came to America, the Delaware
Indians lived in the mid-Atlantic states including
Delaware. The Treaty of Fort Stanwix (1768) forced
them across the Ohio River. This book does not detail
the encounters between the colonists and Indians but
describes certain aspects of their mythology and their
daily life including the Doll Dance and a boy's finding
his protecting spirit. The large print, attractive

illustrations, and easy text make this appropriate for
early elementary pupils.

49 DOWNES, RANDOLPH C. and SIMONDS, CATHERINE G. *The
Maumee Valley, U.S.A.;* illus. Toledo: Historical Society of Northwestern Ohio, 1955. (7-8)
Written for seventh and eighth grade pupils,
this book relates the local history of Ohio and particularly of Northwestern Ohio and the Maumee Valley to
national history. It begins with the coming of the
Indians and French to the Maumee Valley and carries the
story through World War II. Aspects of daily living,
science, literature, art, and architecture are treated,
as well as politics and economics. At the end of each
unit there are study aids, unit activities, visual aids,
and a booklist. Index.

50 DU JARDIN, ROSEMARY. *Showboat Summer.* Philadelphia: Lippincott, 1955. o.p. (5-8) F
The story is contemporary with the time it was
written. Penny and Pam Howard, twins who have completed their Freshman year in college, enroll in a
summer drama course being taught on an Ohio River showboat. The characters, including the twins, are stereo-
types, and the plot has been overused (after problems,
the lovely twins are both engaged at summer's end).
Still, the story has some good points: the description
of the showboat is authentic, the Captain tells tales
of earlier showboats, and the college troupe enacts the
melodramas performed in early showboat days.

51 EAGER, EDWARD. *Half Magic;* illus. by N. M. Bodecker.
New York: Harcourt Brace Jovanovich, 1954.
(3-7) F *
The setting of Toledo, Ohio, in the 1920's
firmly roots this lively fantasy in reality. By means
of a magic coin they find and wish on, Jane, Mark,
Katharine, and Martha transform a humdrum summer into
their **most** exciting one. Since the coin grants only
one-half of the expressed wish, it is necessary to wish
double. Accordingly, Katharine carefully wishes "that
we may go back twice as far as the days of King
Arthur"—and lo!—they are in Camelot.

52 ECKERT, ALLAN W. *Blue Jacket: War Chief of the Shawnee.* Boston: Little, Brown, 1969.
(6-) B *

Marmaduke Van Swearingen was seventeen when he was captured by the Shawnee Indians in 1771, adopted into the tribe, and named Blue Jacket, because of the blue shirt he was wearing when captured. Blue Jacket took to his new life as if he had been born to it, becoming a great warrior who led raids into Kentucky from the Ohio country. He was an important commander at the defeats of Harmar and St. Clair and the commander-in-chief of the Indian forces when they met defeat at Fallen Timbers. A very well-written fictionalized biography by a well-known literary historian.

53 ECKERT, ALLAN W. *The Frontiersmen.* Boston: Little, Brown, 1967. (8-) *

A panoramic re-creation of the period between 1755 and 1815 when the all-out struggle for supremacy between the whites and the Indians occurred on the frontier of the old Northwest. The locale is frequently the area that is Ohio today. Two important historical lives unify, but do not dominate, the narrative. Simon Kenton, born in 1755, gives the viewpoint of the advancing whites. The brilliant Shawnee, Tecumseh, the Indians' last great native leader east of the Mississippi, symbolizes the Indians' defending spirit. Researched for seven years, *The Frontiersmen* provides fascinating reading for both general readers and historians, for both younger and older people.

54 ECKERT, ALLAN W. *Tecumseh!* (A Play.) Boston: Little, Brown, 1974. (6-) B *

Tecumseh!, an outdoor drama performed annually at the Sugarloaf Amphitheater in Chillicothe, Ohio, recreates the struggle for America's Northwest Territory. In this moving drama, the conflict comes to a climax with Tecumseh, the Shawnee Indian with great love for his land and people, opposing General William Henry Harrison, governor of the Indian Territory. Author Eckert is a four time nominee for the Pulitzer Prize.

55 ECKERT, ALLAN W. *A Time of Terror;* illus. Boston:
Little, Brown, 1965. (5-) *
   Using diaries, logs, interviews and newspaper
records, Allan Eckert reconstructs, with the impact of
an eye-witness account, the Dayton Flood of 1913, one of
the most disastrous floods in American history. Maps
and photographs highlight the absorbing text.

56 EDDY, MARY O., collector. *Ballads and Songs from
Ohio;* illus. Hatboro, Pa.: Folklore Associates,
1964. (4-)
   Originally printed in 1939, these songs and
ballads were collected by Miss Eddy principally in the
environs of Perrysville, in Ashland County, her home,
and Canton, where she was a teacher. She recorded
tunes for about half of the texts. Variants of many of
the traditional ballads appear here, along with ballads relating events of Ohio history, such as the burning at the stake of Colonel Crawford. Dramatic local
events—murders, for example—have also been recorded
in ballads. Comments about the contributors and the
ballads are informative and interesting. A correct
folklorist, she includes a bibliography for the separate ballads.

— EPSTEIN, BERYL. *The Andrews Raid or the Great
Locomotive Chase.* See OH 58

57 EPSTEIN, BERYL. *Lucky, Lucky, White Horse;* illus.
New York: Harper & Row, 1965. o.p. (3-5) F
   In two big moving wagons Ellen Evans and her
family move from Marysville to Columbus in 1916. The
first night in her new home Ellen learns how to play
"Lucky, lucky, white horse." She is told that after
she has counted one hundred white horses she is to
walk straight around the block without stopping and she
will find something. What Ellen finds is far nicer
than she had anticipated. Period details evoke pre-
World War I Columbus.

58 EPSTEIN, SAMUEL and EPSTEIN, BERYL. *The Andrews Raid or The Great Locomotive Chase;* illus. New York: Coward-McCann, 1956. o.p. (5-8) *

This is an authentic and dramatic account of a Civil War raid. In April, 1862, a Northern spy, James Andrews, and twenty-two volunteers from Ohio regiments went south posing as Kentuckians on their way to enlist in the Confederate Army. In Georgia, they stole an unguarded locomotive, *The General,* and three box cards and headed north toward Chattanooga. Because the Confederates soon pursued them, they had little time to damage the railroad track and the bridges and tunnels it passed over and through. Finally, after six hours, the raiders abandoned the locomotive.

59 EVATT, HARRIET. *The Secret at the Old Coach Inn;* illus. Indianapolis, Ind.: Bobbs-Merrill, 1959. o.p. (3-6) F

Serena Adair, 10, lives with her grandparents in the early 1900's, near Delaware, Ohio. She loves her Grandmother's stories about the long-closed old coach inn, formerly a station on the Underground Railroad. She is delighted the day Mr. Meredith, the owner, and his daughter, Crystal, arrive in a "new-fangled horse-less carriage." The girls become friends and after their house is damaged by fire, the Adairs move into the inn with the Merediths. Among the discoveries the girls make is a secret passageway. In spite of the passageway, this is a slight, only mildly interesting story.

60 EVERSON, FLORENCE M. and POWER, EFFIE. *Early Days in Ohio;* illus. New York: Dutton, 1928. o.p. (3-6) F

In May of 1800, after traveling from Vermont by covered wagon and in open batteaux, the Clark and Spafford families arrive at the new settlement of Cleveland in the Western Reserve. The book covers their first two years in the country. Little emphasis on characterization and the style is outmoded. Chief merit is that it authentically describes almost all aspects of daily life.

61 FEIS, RUTH S. B. *Mollie Garfield in the White House*. Chicago: Rand McNally, 1963. o.p. (4-8) B

Molly Garfield was fourteen in 1881 when her father became President. He was shot by an assassin the following July and died in September. The author, Mollie's daughter, has used family anecdotes and letters as well as the diaries of the President, his son Jim and daughter, Mollie, to reconstruct the White House life of the Garfields. Quotations from the children's diaries reveal the effect of the shooting on the family. Family life in America in the late nineteenth century is nicely portrayed in scenes set at Mentor Farm, the Garfields' Ohio home. Family photographs add to the word picture.

62 FIFE, DALE. *Walk a Narrow Bridge*. New York: Coward-McCann, 1966. o.p. (5-8) F

By 1910 Lisalea Vogel's parents, natives of Alsace, have lived for many years on their productive farm in Huron County. Still Papa Vogel refuses to mingle with his Yankee and German neighbors. When Lisalea and Tony Enright, a second generation American of German descent, begin to go together, Papa informs her that they do not marry outside their group. The conflict that develops because Lisalea loves both her family and Tony is not resolved until the end of the story. Believable characters and excellent depiction of early twentieth century farm life, especially as lived by hard-working immigrant families. The author received the Ohioana Award for this book.

63 FISHER, AILEEN. *A Lantern in the Window*; illus. New York: Nelson, 1958. o.p. (4-8) F *

Peter is twelve in 1851 when he goes to help Uncle Eb and Aunt Ellie on their farm fronting on the Ohio River. His excitement over seeing steamboats every day fades in the new excitement of helping runaway slaves to freedom. As Quakers, Uncle Eb and Aunt Ellie believe that the Fugitive Slave Law violates God's laws, so they do not obey it. A lantern placed in the attic window facing the river is a beacon for

escaping slaves. Beliefs of the Quakers, opposition to
the Fugitive Slave Law, and life on a pre-Civil War
farm are integrated into this well-written story.

64 FOSTER, MARTHA S. *A Red Carpet for Lafayette;*
      illus. Indianapolis, Ind.: Bobbs-Merrill, 1961.
      o.p. (3-6) F
      There is great excitement in May of 1824 in the
French settlement of Gallipolis on the Ohio River. The
great General Lafayette is coming to visit. Before he
arrives, Nicky Michaux, his cousin Claude, and Grand-
père have a memorable ride on one of the new steamboats
to Marietta in quest of a magnificent red carpet that
will be unrolled for *le bon général* to walk on. The
events of the story leading up to Lafayette's visit are
contrived, but there is a good picture of early
Gallipolis, particularly of the tavern which is eleven-
year-old Nicky's home.

65 FRADIN, DENNIS B. *Ohio: in Words and Pictures;*
      illus. Chicago: Children's Press, 1977. (2-4)
      This brief book gives an overview of the seven-
teenth state to be admitted to the union: its history,
people, industry, cities, and natural resources.
There are also maps, a pronunciation guide, historical
dates and an index. Many colored photographs and pictures supplement the simple text.

66 FRANCHERE, RUTH. *The Wright Brothers;* illus. by
      Louis Glanzman. New York: Crowell, 1972.
      (3-6) B *
      The author admires people who use "intelligence,
imagination, and great perseverance to reach the high
goals they have set for themselves." She finds these
qualities in Wilbur and Orville Wright and develops the
book around that theme. The non-fictionalized text is
concise and well-written. Accurate illustrations contribute to recreating the world of the Wright brothers.

67 FRANK, RALPH W.; HAYES, BEN; and RODABAUGH, JAMES H.
"Ohio, the Buckeye State." *The World Book
Encyclopedia*, XIV, 516-534. Chicago: World
Book, 1975. (4-)
A comprehensive and excellent article with many
photographs, maps, and tables. At the end is a listing
of ninety other related articles appearing in *World
Book*.

68 FRIERMOOD, ELISABETH HAMILTON. *Promises in the
Attic*. Garden City, N.Y.: Doubleday, 1960.
(5-8) F
Energetic Ginger O'Neal, a senior at Steele High
in Dayton in 1913, aspires to be a writer. Her dream
is realized when a magazine purchases a long story she
wrote while she and her Grandpa were marooned in the
attic of their home watching the flood waters rise to
their second story windows. Ginger is an engaging
heroine. The small events of her home and school life
provide contrast with the drama of the flood. The
title comes from a slogan used after the flood to rally
the citizens to raise $2,000,000 for permanent flood
control.

69 GARBER, D. W. *Water Wheels and Millstones: A
History of Ohio Gristmills and Milling*; illus.
Columbus, Ohio: The Ohio Historical Society,
1970. (6-)
The author, a descendant of millers on both
sides of his family, has, from childhood, been interested in gristmills and milling. Since 1923 he has
actively collected mill records, photographs, milling
manuals and related data. He writes of millers and
milling with authority and with fondness for an occupation that is now as passé as the horse and buggy. A
glossary defines technical terms. Many excellent
photos.

70 GEORGE, MARY KARL (Sister). *The Rise and Fall of
      Toledo, Michigan . . . The Toledo War!;* illus.
      Lansing: Michigan Historical Commission, 1971.
      Paper. (6-) #
      A lively account of the boundary dispute between
Michigan and Ohio that climaxed in the events of 1835
known as the Toledo War. Quotations from newspapers of
the time and recollections written later by partici-
pants add authenticity and human interest, as do contemporary pictorial materials. The author's mock-epic
tone and titles—*e.g.* "Drums along the Maumee"—add
humor. Although each side mobilized a few hundred
troops for a brief time, there were no casualties.
Index.

71 GISH, LILLIAN. *Dorothy and Lillian Gish;* illus.
      New York: Scribner's, 1973. o.p. (4-) B P *
      Lillian Gish was born in Springfield, Ohio, in
1876 and Dorothy Gish in Dayton in 1898. They made
their stage debuts at the ages of four and six in
Rising Sun, a small town in northwestern Ohio. This
folio contains nearly 300 pages of captioned photographs covering their six decades on the stage and in
motion pictures. Interesting for both general readers
and students of drama and film. Stageography and film-
ography for each sister is included.

72 GLINES, CARROLL V. *The Wright Brothers, Pioneers
      of Power Flight.* New York: Watts, 1968. o.p.
      (6-) B *
      A very complete, non-fictionalized biography of
the Wright brothers for older readers. Besides recording the events of their lives to their historic flight
in 1903, this biography also covers in detail the part
of their lives often neglected in biographies for young
people, the years after Kitty Hawk. That event changed
their lives completely. Gradually they becam   so
occupied with their financial affairs that they had
little time for the research and experimentation they
loved. Immediacy is gained by quotations from their
correspondence and their father's notes. Chronology,
brief bibliography, and index.

73 GOOD, HOWARD E. *Black Swamp Farm;* illus. Columbus:
    Ohio State University Press, 1967. (5-)
    A factual account of farm life in Van Wert County
in the old Black Swamp region of the Maumee Valley
(Northwestern Ohio) as experienced and witnessed by
the author, who was born there in a log house on a farm
late in the 1800's. The material is treated topically
as "The Well-Fed Farm Family," "Ani al Companions and
Aids," and "Language of Everyday Communication." Many
of the anecdotes and examples are taken from his
family's experiences. The author is objective, describing the disadvantages as well as the advantages of life
in the "good old days."

74 GOODROUGH, DAVID. *Pontiac's War, 1763-1766;* illus.
    New York: Watts, 1970. o.p. (6-8)
    This "Focus" book contains a detailed and accu-
rate account of the causes, the battles, and the significance of Pontiac's War, especially its effects on
the settlers of the area west of the Appalachian mountains. Illustrations include both old and present-day
maps and pictures. Selected bibliography and index.

75 GOULD, JEAN. *That Dunbar Boy;* illus. New York:
    Dodd, Mead, 1958. o.p. (5-8) B
    Ohio's outstanding Black poet, Paul Lawrence
Dunbar, was born in Dayton in 1872. Both of his parents
had lived in slavery. Paul wrote poems from the time
he was seven and gained recognition at an early age,
but died from tuberculosis at 34. Recreates both Paul's
life, and also Dayton of that time. Although fictionalized, the book gains authenticity from the many quotations from Paul's writing, especially his poetry.
Given the Thomas Alva Edison Foundation Children's Book
Award for its "Special Excellence in Contribution to
the Character Development of Children." (1959)

76 GOULDER, GRACE. *Ohio Scenes and Citizens.* Cleve-
    land, Ohio: World, 1964. (6-) B *
    The Ohio years of 17 citizens chosen because
they were born or lived in the state are the subject of
this collective biography. The subjects range from

Marshall Field's romantic first wife, Nannie Scott of
Mount Vernon Furnace, to Wayne Wheeler of Cleveland,
who was instrumental in bringing Prohibition to the
nation. Includes an excellent essay on Warren G.
Harding. The author, a student of Ohio history all her
life, writes interestingly and supplies much detail.
Maps of Ohio and the United States, with points of reference marked, add to the book's usefulness. Notes at
the end credit sources. Reprinted in paperback by
Landfell Press (1973) under author's married name,
Izant.

77 *The Governors of Ohio;* illus. Columbus: The Ohio
Historical Society, 1954. o.p. (6-) B
Portraits from the paintings of the governors
which hang in the State Capitol accompany brief biographical sketches of Ohio's first 57 governors.
Authors of the sketches were selected because of special study they have done on the subjects; most of the
biographies are very well-written. The governors are
viewed against a background of the events that occurred
during Ohio's first one hundred and fifty years of
statehood.

78 GRAVES, CHARLES. *The Wright Brothers;* illus. New
York: Putnam's, 1973. (3-5) B *
A well-written, factual biography for young
readers. Besides giving information about the Wrights,
with a few details the author suggests the world they
lived in; for example, in 1878 there were "no airplanes
and not even any cars. People traveled by train, ship,
horse and buggy, and bicycle." He takes care to show
that the airplane was not just a lucky invention, that
years of work preceded the Wright brother's actual
flight. In their third summer of gliding they flew the
glider "more than a thousand times." Key words are
listed in a table. Authentic illustrations.

79 GREENE, LETHA C. *Long Live the Delta Queen;* illus.
New York: Hastings House, 1973. (6-)
From its home port in Cincinnati, the *Delta Queen,* one of the last of the old-time riverboats, departs on cruises to all parts of the Ohio and Mississippi Rivers. The author and her husband acquired the *Delta Queen* in 1946. After her husband's death in 1950, Mrs. Greene managed the boat until 1973. She recalls these years: memorable cruises, land excursions to sights and cities on the river, minor and major mishaps. Although the style is undistinguished, the book is informative.

80 GRIDLEY, MARION E. *Pontiac;* illus. New York:
Putnam's, 1970. (2-4) B #
The author, an adopted member of two Indian tribes, in a brief and simple text, presents Pontiac's whole life, together with the effect the white man had on the Indian way of life. She explains why the Indians favored the French over the English. Vigorous illustrations. A *See and Read, Beginning-to-Read* biography.

81 HAINES, MADGE and MORRILL, LESLIE. *The Wright Brothers, First to Fly;* illus. Nashville, Tenn.:
Abingdon, 1955. (3-5) B
Written in story form, twelve of the fourteen chapters deal with the Wright brothers' lives prior to the time they began to fly. The thirteenth chapter relates their experiments with gliders and the last chapter describes their successful flight in 1903.

82 HAMILTON, VIRGINIA. *Arilla Sun Down.* New York:
Morrow, 1976. (6-8) F *
In a contemporary story set in a small town near Dayton, Virginia Hamilton effectively uses the devices of stream-of-consciousness and flashbacks as twelve-year-old Arilla Sun Down Adams tells her own story of her search for identity and an understanding of her interracial background. Arilla's father is part-Black and part Indian; her mother is Black. Her brother, Jack Sun Run, a few years older than Arilla, rides a

horse everywhere and looks "like the first Indian . . . or the last." While making her characters well-rounded and distinctive, she also deals with basic universal problems.

83 HAMILTON, VIRGINIA. *The House of Dies Drear.* New York: Macmillan, 1968. (5-8) F *
Thomas Small, a Black boy, is thirteen the day he moves with his family from North Carolina to a community in southwestern Ohio very like the author's native Yellow Springs. Thomas's father, who is to teach history at the local university, has rented the house of Dies Drear, which has been occupied for only short intervals for the past 100 years. The house is said to be haunted since Drear and two escaping slaves he was concealing were murdered in it. Suspense is sustained through strange and frightening happenings. Mystery Writers of America Edgar Award, 1968.

84 HAMILTON, VIRGINIA. *M. C. Higgins, the Great.* New York: Macmillan, 1974. (6-8) F NA *
From a perch atop his 40-foot pole on Sarah's Mountain (named for his great-grandmother, a runaway slave who found refuge there in 1854), 13-year-old M. C. Higgins, the Great (self-proclaimed) can see the Ohio River. He can also see, on the mountain directly behind his family's home, the huge spoil heap left by the strip-miners, which seems to be slowly oozing down the hillside toward the Higginses' home. These elements, his family, and two outsiders contribute to M. C.'s growing up on three oppressively hot, humid summer days. This original and memorable book won both the Newbery Award and the National Book Award in 1975.

85 HAMILTON, VIRGINIA. *Zeely;* illus. by Symeon Shemin. New York: Macmillan, 1967. (4-7) F *
Elizabeth Perry, an imaginative 11-year-old, and her younger brother, John—renamed Geeder and Toeboy by Elizabeth—go to Uncle Ross Perry's farm for the summer. There Geeder fantasizes that a young neighbor woman, Miss Zeely Tayber "more than six and a half feet tall, thin and deeply dark as a pole of Ceylon ebony," is a

Watusi queen and Geeder her trusted friend. Crystal, the nearby town, is reminiscent of Miss Hamilton's home-town of Yellow Springs, Ohio, where her mother's family, the Perrys, have lived since pre-Civil War days. The author evokes the atmosphere of a rural Ohio summer.

— HANCOCK, RALPH. *Laughter is a Wonderful Thing.*
    See OH 22

86 HARNISHFEGER, LLOYD. *Hunters of the Black Swamp;*
    illus. Minneapolis, Minn.: Lerner, 1971.
    (5-8) F
        The story of a boy's coming of age in prehistoric North America. His father is severely wounded by a charging grizzly while the two of them are hunting in the part of Ohio later known as the Black Swamp. The boy cares for his father until aided by a tribe of mastodon hunters. A dramatic story that gives an excellent idea of the life of these prehistoric people. The author lives in the area of which he writes.

87 HARNISHFEGER, LLOYD. *Prisoner of the Mound Builders;* illus. Minneapolis, Minn.: Lerner, 1973. (5-8) F
        This story takes place in prehistoric North America in the area that became Ohio. O-Ta-Wah, a young Indian hunter with a crippled leg, strays outside his tribe's hunting grounds and is captured and enslaved by the culturally advanced but cruel Mound Builders. On the eve of the day he is to be killed and buried with a great chief, he escapes. Later he becomes a wise leader and founder of a new tribe of Indians, the Ottawa. The Ohio author's special interest is American prehistory and, although his characters are not completely believable, he has provided an accurate background.

88 HATCHER, HARLAN. *The Western Reserve.* Rev. ed.
Cleveland, Ohio: World, 1966. o.p. (7-) R *
First published in 1949, this is a comprehensive
survey of the Western Reserve from its beginnings as
New Connecticut in 1796 to the present time. Very well
written, with appropriate illustrations. Index.

89 HAVIGHURST, MARION BOYD. *Strange Island.* Cleveland, Ohio: World, 1957. o.p. (6-8) F
Pretty Faith Arnold of Marietta was sixteen in
1806 when Margaret Blennerhassett hired her to come to
her beautiful home on an island in the Ohio River as a
governess for her two young sons. Then, to the island
came Aaron Burr who succeeded in interesting the Blennerhassetts in his grandiose scheme for establishing an
independent state in the West. As the story closes,
the Blennerhassetts are departing down the river and
Faith has returned to Marietta. Evokes the atmosphere
of mystery that has surrounded the relationship between
the Blennerhassetts and Aaron Burr.

90 HAVIGHURST, MARION BOYD. *The Sycamore Tree.*
Cleveland, Ohio: World, 1960. o.p. (5-8) F
The central incident is Confederate General John
Hunt Morgan's (1863) raid into Indiana and Ohio. Among
his volunteer cavalrymen is Tom Rogers of Kentucky, an
Ohio native who had spent most of his life on a farm
near Belpre. When he is injured while scouting in that
vicinity, he is hidden and cared for by former neighbors. Besides Tom, there are a number of attractive
young people in the story. The issues of the Civil War
are presented from both northern and southern viewpoints. Farm and small town life of that period is
interestingly and authentically portrayed.

91 HAVIGHURST, WALTER. *The First Book of Pioneers;*
illus. New York: Watts, 1959. (3-6) * #
Slightly fictionalized text tells of the settl-
ing of the Stone family in Butler County, Ohio, in 1817.
The Indians were gone, but there was still dense forest.
By 1850, not only Ohio, but all the Midwest was settled.

Mr. Havighurst writes of the necessary activities of
pioneer life in readable, uncondescending language.
Index.

92 HAVIGHURST, WALTER. *The Heartland: Ohio, Indiana,
Illinois;* illus. Rev. ed. New York: Harper &
Row, 1974. (6-) R * #
    Mr. Havighurst regards Ohio, Indiana, and Illi-
nois as a unit. "The Ohio-Indiana and Indiana-Illinois
boundaries are," he states, "political only." Almost
framed by the Great Lakes and the Ohio and Mississippi
Rivers, this area is "the heartland, the center of
America's population and the source of important currents
of its political, economic, and cultural life." In
vigorous prose, he describes and assesses the area from
the coming of the pioneers to the present time.
Vignettes of Simon Kenton, Ulysses S. Grant, Little
Turtle, and others bring these people alive. Bibliography. Index.

93 HAVIGHURST, WALTER. *Ohio: A Bicentennial History;*
    illus. New York: Norton, 1976. (7-) *
    One of a series of fity-one books—a volume on
every state, plus the District of Columbia—published
for the bicentennial. Each author was asked for a sum-
ming up of what seemed significant about his state's
history. The author of *Ohio,* Walter Havighurst, had
already written several distinguished books about the
state before he began this assignment. In a sensitive,
thoughtful book that is well-written and readable, he
has interpreted Ohio's past and present. The epilogue
looks to the future. A photographer's essay by Joe
Clark presents his perceptions of the state's contemporary flavor. Bibliography and index.

— HAYES, BEN. "Ohio, the Buckeye State." See OH 67

94 HAYS, WILMA PITCHFORD. *Pontiac: Lion in the Forest;* illus. by Lorence Bjorklund. Boston: Houghton Mifflin, 1965. o.p. (4-8) B #

This excellent biography presents Pontiac's entire life, from his birth in 1720 in an Ottawa village on the Maumee River, to his assassination in 1769 while visiting a tribe in Illinois. There is some fictionalizing particularly in the scenes recreating Pontiac's childhood, but many of the speeches are based on records written by interpreters who sat in council with the Indians and white men. Pontiac's five-month siege of Detroit in the war with the colonists—known in history as Pontiac's Conspiracy—is covered in detail, although other engagements of the war are not discussed. The British called him "that lion in the forest." Pronunciation key.

95 HEUMAN, WILLIAM. *Famous American Indians;* illus. New York: Dodd, Mead, 1972. (5-8) B *

Each of the nine well-known Indians whose lives are recorded in this book resisted the white man's usurpation of Indian homelands. Two of the nine, Pontiac and Tecumseh, were born and lived much of their lives in the area that today is Ohio. These dramatically-written biographies vividly show the white-red conflict. They also reveal the Indians, not as wild savages, but as men of character who loved their people and their homeland and who were determined to protect them. Illustrated with photographs and old prints. Index.

96 HICKMAN, JANET. *The Stones;* illus. by Richard Cuffari. New York: Macmillan, 1976. (4-7) F

Although the setting is probably Ohio, there is nothing in the text to identify it positively. The author, a native Ohioan, still resides there. Springtown, close to the small town in which the story is set, appears to be Springfield. The weather is typical of Ohio. The time is World War II. While his father is fighting in Europe, eleven-year-old Garrett McKay and several friends carry on a war game at home. When the boys learn that an old man of the town has a German name, they begin to harass him. Their misguided patriotism almost brings tragedy.

97 HICKMAN, JANET. *The Valley of the Shadow*. New York: Macmillan, 1974. (5-8) F *
   In the massacre of the Christian Indians of Gnadenhutten and Salem (62 adults and 34 children), in March 1782, two boys miraculously escaped; they passed through the "valley of the shadow." These boys, Tobias and Thomas, are the protagonists of a well-written story that makes real the life the converted Indians lived with their Moravian teachers, Daniel Zeisberger and John Heckewelder. A shameful chapter in American history is authentically and vividly recreated.

98 HOWARD, ELIZABETH. *The Courage of Bethea*. New York: Morrow, 1959. o.p. (5-8) F
   Bethea is almost sixteen in the fall of 1859 when she enters the newly-established Western Female Seminary (later Western College for Women) in Oxford, Ohio. The idea of a college for women was revolutionary, and those who enrolled in this earliest women's college in Ohio were indeed courageous. Authentic history of the college and the town of Oxford is interwoven into the narrative.

99 HOWE, HENRY. *Historical Collections of Ohio;* illus. (3 vol.) Columbus, Ohio: Henry Howe, 1889, 1891. o.p. (7-) *
   Henry Howe made extended journeys over the state in the 1840's and again in the 1880's. He talked with people, sketched scenes, and recorded the passing era, contrasting the Ohio of 1846 with 1886-88. The work is organized by counties. Invaluable for the historian, these collections provide engrossing reading for anyone over twelve. Over 2000 pages and 700 engravings.

100 HOWELLS, WILLIAM COOPER. *Recollections of Life in Ohio from 1813 to 1840;* illus. Gainesville, Fla.: Scholars' Facsimiles and Reprints, 1963. (6-) B *

Originally published in 1895, this is an inform- ally-written, first-hand account of life in Ohio from 1813 to 1840. William Cooper Howells was six the year he moved to Ohio with his English family. The family moved frequently and both William and his father en- gaged in a variety of occupations. The various locali- ties and occupations are described, as well as such un- like activities as drying peaches and attending public executions. Introduction and conclusion by author's son, William Dean Howells, and an essay written in 1962 by Indiana University English professor Edwin H. Cady. Photographs.

101 HOWELLS, WILLIAM DEAN. *Stories of Ohio;* illus. New York: American Book, 1897. o.p. (5-) *

"In the following stories, drawn from the annals of Ohio," wrote William Dean Howells in his preface more than eighty years ago, "I have tried to possess the reader with a knowledge, in outline at least, of the history of the State from the earliest times." Howells drew his materials from his own observations and from books written shortly after the events occurred. These stories, with old illustrations, still provide engrossing reading.

102 HOYT, EDWIN P. *James A. Garfield;* illus. Chicago: Reilly & Lee, 1964. o.p. (6-) B

An interesting account of the life of the twen- tieth President. Although he was shot less than four months after taking office and died two and one-half months later, James Garfield was a central figure in American government from the early 1860's until his death in 1881. "A politician's politician," Garfield, a Dark Horse, was nominated by the Republicans in 1880 on the thirty-sixth ballot. The complexities of his character revealed in his public and political life are delineated, but there is little about his private life. Bibliography and index.

103 HOYT, EDWIN P. *William McKinley;* illus. Chicago:
Reilly & Lee, 1967. o.p. (7-8) B
This biography emphasizes the political and public activities of the twenty-fifth President. The
author's explanation of political issues and legislation is clear and objective. He does not, however,
include many details of contemporary events. Nor,
except for commenting several times on McKinley's devotion to his invalid wife, does he reveal much of the
President's personality and personal life. Photographs.
Bibliography. Index.

104 HUNT, IRENE. *Trail of Apple Blossoms;* illus. by
Don Bolognese. Chicago: Follett, 1968. o.p.
(4-8) B *
In prose as graceful as the blossoming apple
trees that grew from the seeds Johnny Appleseed planted
in northern Ohio and Indiana, Irene Hunt recounts events
from his life. They reveal his philosophy of self-
denial and love for all living things. Like the text,
Bolognese's illustrations, in black and white and color,
evoke the spirit of the gentle, kindly man known as
Johnny Appleseed.

105 HUNT, MABEL LEIGH. *Better Known as Johnny Apple-
Seed;* illus. by James Daugherty. Philadelphia:
Lippincott, 1950. (6-) B #
"In the rich, beautiful country of Ohio and
Indiana there has been slowly growing for more than a
century a legend not very different from that of St.
Francis of Assisi. It concerns a humble man regarded
in his day as an eccentric but a man who was univer-
sally loved in the frontier wilderness country by
Indians and white settlers alike." (From Foreword by
Louis Bromfield.) The author recreates the country
Bromfield speaks of and the man he describes, using
known biographical facts and legends that have grown up
around him. Map of the Ohio country. Newbery Honor
Book, 1951.

106 HUSTON, ANNE. *The Cat Across the Way;* illus. New
York: Seabury Press, 1968. o.p. (3-5) F
Lacey Lewis, a fifth grader, hates her new home
in Cleveland. She longs to return to her small town
home, her best friend, and her beloved pony. When Mon-
day comes, she goes to school reluctantly. At week's
end, after some difficult days, she has a friend,
Rosette Di Nalli, owner of the big yellow cat across
the way. Both girls are believable characters. A convincing presentation of problems that confront children
after moving. Simple black and white sketches complement the text.

107 ICHENHOWER, JOSEPH B. *Tecumseh and the Indian Confederation 1811-1813;* illus. New York: Watts,
1975. (5-8) #
A straightforward recital of the events that
transpired from the establishment of the Proclamation
Line of 1763 (a limiting line beyond which no whites
could legally settle) to the death of Tecumseh on a
battlefield in Canada in 1813. With his death Indian-
white strife east of the Mississippi and north of the
Ohio ended. Even though it is brief, the author succeeds in portraying the admirable character and remarkable achievements of the Indian some have regarded as
the greatest Indian chief in American history. Good
nineteenth century pictures. Bibliography, index, and
a map.

108 IZANT, GRACE GOULDER. *This is Ohio;* illus. Cleveland, Ohio: World, 1953. o.p. (4-) *
In exact yet flowing language, the author presents a panorama of Ohio, told in sketches of each of
Ohio's 88 counties with an accompanying photograph.
The information given about each county includes: year
of organization, origin of the name, highlights from
its growth and development, and the county in the
1950's, when his was written. Although the book contains much useful information, it would be even more
helpful if it were brought up-to-date. Contains index,
bibliography, and a list of Ohio colleges and universities.

109 JACKSON, C. PAUL. *Two Boys and a Soap Box Derby;*
illus. New York: Hastings House, 1958. o.p.
(3-5) F
Seventh-grader Dee Dee Hoad, with support from
younger Burr Head Douglas, builds a soap box derby
racer that wins in his city's competition and qualifies
him to enter the All-American and International Soap
Box Derby that is held each August in Akron, Ohio. Dee
Dee's home city is not named—it could be almost any
medium-sized American city. Although the characters
are stereotyped, the plot predictable, and the dialogue
somewhat stilted, the book is interesting because it
details the step-by-step procedure one boy follows in
building a racer, and also provides information about
the Akron race.

110 JACOB, HELEN PIERCE. *The Diary of the Strawbridge
Place.* New York: Atheneum, 1978. (4-8) F
In the 1850's the Strawbridge family of Ashta-
bula County, who are Quakers, operate a station on the
Underground Railroad in defiance of the Fugitive Slave
Law. From a cave on their farm on the southern shore
of Lake Erie, the slaves are taken directly to Canada.
Thirteen-year-old twins, Faith and Victory, are the
leading characters of this novel. Victory records
their activities in a diary and the events are seen
from her viewpoint. A readable story although some of
the minor characters are not altogether believable and
a few of the episodes seem artifically devised to main-
tain suspense.

111 JAGENDORF, MORITZ A. *Sand in the Bag and Other
Folk Stories of Ohio, Indiana, and Illinois;*
illus. New York: Vanguard, 1952. (4-) #
One-third of the volume consists of tales collected by Dr. Jagendorf in Ohio. They range from the
story told in Bellaire about Jake and his little mule
Jack, to an account of the only witch trial ever held
in Ohio. There are legends about real people and a
story about a tapping ghost. The tone is brisk, often

humorous; the characters speak in the vernacular of the region of each story. A closing essay describes the research and names those who contributed stories.

112 JOHNSON, GRACE TRACY and JOHNSON, HAROLD N.
Courage Wins; illus. New York: Dutton, 1954. o.p. (5-8) F
This book chronicles the Cobb family's migration in 1812 from Connecticut to the Western Reserve and their first year there. They make the trip in 46 days, traveling by sleigh for 100 miles across frozen Lake Erie. They settle near Kinsman. In a short while the father leaves with the militia to fight in the War of 1812. The family bravely carries on at home. Contains many details of pioneering well-integrated into the story.

—— JOHNSON, HAROLD N. *Courage Wins.* See OH 112

113 JOHNSTON, JOHANNA. *The Indians and the Strangers;* illus. by Rocco Negri. New York: Dodd, Mead, 1972. (3-6)
Brief chronicles of twelve Indians from Squanto in the early 1600's to Sitting Bull in the late 1800's— and their encounters with the white strangers. Pontiac and Tecumseh, two of the Indians whose stories are recorded here, lived on land that is part of Ohio today. Expressive woodcut illustrations in black and white.

114 JUDSON, CLARA INGRAM. *Michael's Victory;* illus. Boston: Houghton Mifflin, 1946. o.p. (6-8) F *
Michael O'Hara, fourteen in 1854, works with his father on the construction gang that is building the railroad between Toledo and Fort Wayne. During the months this story takes place, the O'Hara family is in Defiance. The canal passes through the town and there is animosity between the canalers and railroaders. A feud with the canal boys is resolved when Michael repays mischief with kindness. The author uses little Irish brogue, but includes Irish customs such as a May

Day Eve dance. There are few good stories about the many immigrants who came to Ohio. This one is memorable.

115 KETCHAM, BRYAN E. *Covered Bridges on the Byways of Ohio;* illus. Oxford, Ohio: Oxford Printing, 1969. (4-) P
This interesting book contains over 200 photographs of covered bridges taken by the author in Ohio. Below each picture he gives the name of the bridge, the year it was built, its exact location, and technical data such as length, width, type of roof, and load limit. This is followed by a history of the bridge and immediate locality. Ketcham notes that there was little bridge data recorded and that word-of-mouth was the chief method used in procuring much of the material.

116 KLEIN, ISABELLE H. *Wild Flowers of Ohio and Adjacent States;* illus. Cleveland, Ohio: The Press, Case Western Reserve University, 1970. (4-) *
The diversity of geographical situations and soil compositions found in Ohio and adjacent states results in a great variety of wild flowers. In this valuable handbook the flowers are grouped according to plant family and each flower is sketched for identification. Bibliography. Index.

117 KNEPPER, GEO. W. *An Ohio Portrait;* illus. Columbus, Ohio: Ohio Historical Society, 1976. (5-) P *
Over 600 black and white illustrations and photographs and nearly 150 colored plates expand the meaning of Mr. Knepper's historical narrative of Ohio's change from an almost unoccupied wilderness to a populous industrialized state. He records how Ohio developed agriculturally, industrially, culturally, educationally, politically, and socially. Author does not bypass or gloss over undesirable aspects.

118 KNOPF, RICHARD C. *Indians of the Ohio Country;*
illus. Modern Methods, 1959. o.p. (2-4)
This brief but informative book, divided into 12
chapters with questions and "words to remember" following each, is intended for a grades 2-4 social studies
unit on Indians of the Ohio country. It covers the
daily life of the Indians (including games), the tribes
in Ohio, Indian leaders, and contact with the white man.
Illustrations add interest.

119 LAFFOON, POLK, IV. *Tornado;* illus. New York:
Harper & Row, 1975. (6-) P *
The author recreates the day the killer tornado
struck Xenia, Ohio,—April 3, 1974—and the days, weeks,
and months that followed. He has recorded here the
experiences told him by dozens of victims of the storm.
He has recorded, also, information and insight gained
from talking to persons involved in the rehabilitation,
including doctors who instructed him in the psycholog-
ical effects of a natural catastrophe. The result is a
dramatic, detailed chronicle of one of Ohio's worst
natural disasters. Excellent photographs.

120 LAWRENCE, MILDRED. *Peachtree Island;* illus. by
Mary Stevens. New York: Harcourt, Brace, 1948.
(3-5) F
Orphaned Cissie, ten, goes to live with Uncle
Eban and his housekeeper, Mrs. Halloran, on Peachtree
Island in Lake Erie, which is reached only by ferry
from Port Angelo (Port Clinton). Because she loves it
there and wants to stay permanently, she tries to show
Uncle Evan that she is as useful as a boy would be in a
peach orchard. Through Cissie's eyes the reader learns
about fruit farming. There are also chapters on apple
butter making and ice fishing. A pleasant story recall-
ing life in the 1930's or 1940's in a particular locale.

121 LAWRENCE, MILDRED. *The Questing Heart.* New York:
Harcourt, Brace, 1959. o.p. (5-8) F
When hail destroys the peach crop, there is not
enough money for Dinny Bracken to leave her island home
off the sourthern shore of Lake Erie (Kelley's Island?)

251

to go to college. So that there will be money for certain the following year, Dinny's mother takes a job on
the mainland and Dinny, doubting her ability to manage,
is left to keep house for her father and younger brother.
During the year, as she acquires new skills and new
friends, Dinny's self-confidence increases and the year
she dreaded becomes a happy one. Island life in winter
is well-portrayed.

122 LEISH, KENNETH V. *The American Heritage Pictorial
History of the Presidents of the United States;*
illus. (2 vols.) New York: American Heritage,
1968. (5-) B P *
This outstanding two-volume work devotes twenty
to thirty pages to each president. A full page portrait is followed by a biography revealing the character of the man and his times. A picture portfolio follows, featuring much fresh material: cartoons, newspaper headlines, and campaign memorabilia. "Facts in
Summary" includes a chronology, biographical facts, and
facts about the elections and administrations. An
excellent source book for teachers and for children
seeking information about presidents from Ohio.

123 LENGYEL, CORNEL ADAM. *Presidents of the United
States;* illus. New York: Golden Press, 1961.
(2-7) B P *
Seven natives of Ohio have become President:
Ulysses S. Grant, Rutherford B. Hayes, James A. Garfield,
Benjamin Harrison, William McKinley, William H. Taft,
and Warren G. Harding. An eighth, William H. Harrison,
spent most of his adult life in Ohio. Well-written
two-page biographies include personal as well as public
events. In addition to a portrait of each president,
there are family pictures and scenes from public life.
Most of the pictorial material, which is exceptionally
good, is from the collections of the Library of Congress. Index.

124 LENSKI, LOIS. *A Going to the Westward;* illus. by
author. New York: Stokes, 1937. o.p.
(4-8) F *
In a foreword the author states that "to the
westward" was the phrase commonly used to describe the
early migration to Ohio. Description of conditions met
on the journey are based, she notes, on a study of
actual eye-witness accounts left by travelers of the
period. It is apparent that Miss Lenski was thorough
in her research. The story tells of the Bartlett
family, including Aunt Matilda, the most memorable
character in the book, who migrated from Connecticut to
Franklin County in 1811. Author Lenski uses characteristic speech and includes many factual details. A far
better book on pioneering than most.

125 LENSKI, LOIS. *The Story of Mary Jemison;* illus. by
author. Philadelphia: Lippincott, 1941. o.p.
(4-8) B
Recounts the early years of Mary's captivity
among the Seneca Indians, first in Ohio and later in
New YYork State. At the close of the story when the
opportunity comes for her to return to the white people,
Mary decides that since her own family is all dead she
will remain with the Indians who have adopted her.
When Mary was eighty years old, she repeated her memories of her experiences to a doctor who made a book
from them. Although fictionalized, this biography is
based on that record. Newbery Honor Book, 1942.

126 LE SEUR, MERIDEL. *The Mound Builders;* illus. New
York: Watts, 1974. o.p. (3-8)
This brief, scholarly, and interestingly-written
book describes the four major ancient mound-building
cultures from the evidence found in surviving mounds
and their contents. The center of the second and third
major groups, the Adenas and Hopewells, was the area
around Chillicothe, Ohio. Many photographs of both the
mounds and the artifacts taken from them supplement the
text. This material is enthusiastically presented in a
way that arouses interest in these cultures. Bibliography and index.

127 LIBBY, BILL. *Pete Rose: They Call Him Charlie Hustle*. New York: Putnam's, 1972. (4-8) B
   Pete Rose, a native of Cincinnati, has been a hometown hero of the Cincinnati Reds' fans since 1963. Dubbed "Charlie Hustle" in his first major league training session because of his habit of running out walks and sliding into base headfirst, Pete Rose has never slowed down. A good look at what makes Rose run and at baseball as played by the Reds from 1963 through 1971.

—— MC CALL, EDITH S. *Where the Ohio Flows*. See OH 41

128 MC CLOSKEY, ROBERT. *Centerburg Tales;* illus. by author. New York: Viking, 1951. (3-7) F *
   Grandfather Hercules tells Homer and his friends tall tales about the way life never was in the early days of Centerburg, Ohio, and Homer has more outsize adventures. The hilarious illustrations are a perfect accompaniment to the stories.

129 MC CLOSKEY, ROBERT. *Homer Price;* illus. by author. New York: Viking, 1943. (3-7) F *
   Episodes from the life of Homer Price, an enterprising boy of the 1920's, who lives in Centerburg, a fictional town like those McCloskey knew in his youth in Butler County, Ohio. Homer and his friends go fishing, but often they're engaged in more exciting activities—such as capturing robbers. (Homer's pet skunk, Aroma, has an important role in that adventure.) The humorous stories and illustrations have made this book popular since it was first published.

130 MC CLOSKEY, ROBERT. *Lentil;* illus. by author. New York: Viking, 1940. (1-4) F *
   "In the town of Alto, Ohio, there lived a boy named Lentil." The time is not given, but the illustrations suggest an Ohio small town of the 1920's. Because he wanted to make music, but could neither sing nor whistle, Lentil learned to play the harmonica. He became so expert that he was able to lead the great Colonel Carter's homecoming parade. The humorous text comes alive in author-artist McCloskey's realistically-detailed illustrations.

131 MC KAY, ROBERT. *Dave's Song.* New York: Meredith
  Press, 1969. (5-8) F
    A contemporary story set in fictional Tylerton,
a small town in central Ohio about an hour's drive from
Columbus. In alternating chapters, two high school
seniors record their reactions to the events of that
fall. Dave Burdick, who lives on a chicken farm with
his parents, decides he wants to be an ethologist.
Kate Adams learns she dislikes Tylerton less than she
thought she did. The characters are not very believable
and the story is only mildly interesting.

132 MC MILLEN, WHEELER. *Ohio Farm;* illus. by John D.
  Firestone & Assoc. Columbus, Ohio: Ohio State
  University Press, 1974. (5-) *
    Author McMillen, for many years editor of the
Farm Journal, recalls his family's daily life on a
farm from about 1890 to 1920. With sentiment but not
sentimentality, he vividly describes what went on in
field, barn, house, and the rural neighborhood.
Although the family farm on which McMillen grew up was
located in Hardin County, Ohio, the way of life he
recreates so well was lived by most of the people
throughout the Midwest.

133 MARGOLIS, ELLEN. *Idy the Fox-Chasing Cow and Other
  Stories;* illus. by Kurt Werth. Cleveland, Ohio:
  World, 1962. o.p. (3-7)
    Seven stories collected in Ohio are retold in
folk dialect by an experienced storyteller. In addition
to the tale of Idy, the cow who hunts like a hound,
there are two about Lazy Tom; also, a ghost story; and
another about Hiram who, on his way home from courting
Sabrina, beats off a pack of wolves with an umbrella.
Black and white drawings capture the humorous tone of
the text.

134 MARTIN, ANAMAL. *Columbus, the Buckeye Capital;*
  illus. Columbus, Ohio: Merrill, 1966. o.p.
  (4-8)
    The first unit in this textbook contains back-
ground material applicable to other parts of the state

as well as Columbus. The remaining five units record
the founding and growth of the city of Columbus. The
final chapter describes the cultures of the various
groups of people who settled in Franklin County. Some
fictionalized incidents, such as Jeremiah's captivity
and life with the Wyandot Indians, add interest. Many
good illustrations, including art works by Columbus
children, complement the readable text. Glossary.

135 MEADER, STEPHEN W. *Boy with a Pack;* illus. by
Edward Shenton. New York: Harcourt, Brace,
1939. (5-8) F
    With a peddler's pack on his back, 17-year-old
Bill Crawford, in the spring of 1837, starts out from
his New Hampshire home for Ohio. Several months later,
after his "Yankee notions" are all sold, Bill decides
to stay in the new country. There are a number of
exciting parts: one of the best is Bill's forwarding
an escaping slave two stations on the Underground Railroad. A far better written book than many others
written in the 1930's. Newbery Honor Book, 1940.

136 MEADOWCROFT, ENID LA MONTE. *By Wagon and Flatboat;*
illus. by Ninon MacKnight. New York: Crowell,
1938. (3-5) F
    In 1789, shortly after George Washington was
elected President, the Burd and Mathews families travel
by Conestoga wagon and flatboat from Pennsylvania to a
new home in Cincinnati, at that time a settlement of
twenty log houses. Contains a great deal of information, but some of it is not closely related to the
story. The characters are flat and the incidents of
plot are not original. The book continues to appear on
recommended reading lists, probably because it is accurate and fills a need for fiction in this area for the
lower elementary grades.

137 MEDARY, MARJORIE. *Buckeye Boy.* New York: Longmans, Green, 1944. o.p. (4-8) F
    Orphan Tom Kenyon is only fourteen in the spring
of 1854 when he runs away from his Uncle Andy's home
where he is badly treated. He works for a year on the

canal, then becomes an apprentice printer. While carefully authentic—one of her sources is *Reminiscences* of
her grandfather—author Medary tells an interesting
story of life in northeastern Ohio in the 1850's.

138 MELTZER, MILTON. *Langston Hughes: A Biography.*
New York: Crowell, 1968. (5-) B *
An illuminating biography of the Black writer
who portrayed Black life and interpreted it for innumerable people in the United States and abroad. His poems
first made him known and Meltzer quotes from them gener-
ously, but also gives meaningful excerpts from his
prose works. Hughes lived in Cleveland during his high
school years, and returned there during the years his
mother made her home there. His grandmother, with whom
he lived until he was twelve, was the first Black woman
to attend Oberlin College. Bibliography includes books
by and about Langston Hughes.

139 MELVIN, RUTH W. *A Guide to Ohio Outdoor Education
Areas;* illus. 2d ed. Columbus, Ohio: Ohio
Department of Natural Resources and the Ohio
Academy of Science, 1974. (4-) *
An attractive book on Ohio's park lands, nature
centers, trails, camps, caves, and other outdoor spots.
The places are arranged geographically by counties.
Illustrated with photographs in color, the guide is use-
ful for both the general reader and those who use the
outdoors as classroom and laboratory. Bibliography and
index.

——MORRILL, LESLIE. *The Wright Brothers, First to Fly.*
See OH 81

140 MOSER, DON. *A Heart to the Hawks.* New York:
Atheneum, 1975. (6-) F
From the woods and a pond situated near his
Cleveland suburban home, Mike Harrington happily collects biological specimens. He cares for an injured
red-tailed hawk and teaches it to hunt. He is also
responsible for the labeling of three enormous white
oaks as Moses Cleaveland trees, signifying that they
were standing "as part of the original forest when

Moses Cleaveland landed at the mouth of the Cuyahoga
River, July 22, 1796." Mike's wonderful world collap-
ses when workmen arrive to cut the woods and drain the
pond for a shopping center. A plea for conservation
of the natural world.

141 MOYER, JOHN W. *Famous Frontiersmen;* illus. by
James L. Vlasaty. Northbrook, Ill.: Hubbard
Press, 1972. (3-8) B
Two of these ten frontiersmen are closely associated with Ohio. Daniel Boone fought for years the
Indians who came into Kentucky from present-day Ohio.
Once he was captured and taken across the Ohio River to
the Shawnee village of Old Chillicothe. After having
been marched through the wilderness to and from Detroit,
he was adopted by the Indians, but later managed to
escape. The second frontiersman, George Armstrong
Custer, was born in Harrison County. He left Ohio in
1858 to attend West Point, but returned to visit his
parents who had moved to Wood County. A slightly romanticized full-page portrait in color precedes each biography.

142 MUSGRAVE, FLORENCE. *Merrie's Miracle;* illus. by
Mary Stevens. New York: Hastings, 1962. o.p.
(4-8) F
Merrie Hilliard is fifteen in 1837 when she and
her family journey from Connecticut to take up land
close to Mentor in the Western Reserve. During the
next year and a half Merrie experiences the hardships
of pioneering, but also finds new friends and romance.
Many details are included as a natural part of Merrie's
new life. She attends a barn-raising and a corn-
husking, goes to school in Painesville and plays a part
in an Underground Railroad episode. The difficulties
of the Hilliards are perhaps solved too easily, but
Merrie's maturation is convincing. When Merrie realizes
that the lame foot she has had all her life is not a
handicap unless she lets it be, she feels as if she has
experienced a miracle.

143 MUSGRAVE, FLORENCE. *Robert E.;* illus. by Mary
Stevens. New York: Hastings, 1957. o.p.
(4-6) F
After Granny's death in the 1950's, Robert E., a
ten-year-old mountain boy, and his doughty Grandpap
reluctantly go up north to live with Melinda, Robert E's
mother and Grandpap's daughter, in Willoughby, Ohio.
Robert E's father had been killed during World War II
shortly before his son's birth. Although Robert E.
finds it difficult at first, he does make friends and
by Christmas is happy in his new home. A fictional but
realistic account of life in a northern Ohio town.

144 MYERS, ELIZABETH P. *Rutherford B. Hayes;* illus.
Chicago: Reilly & Lee, 1969. o.p. (6-) B
Born in Delaware, Ohio, Hayes lived most of his
life in his native state. This biography covers his
public life very thoroughly, but only glances at his
private life and the era of which he was a part. Con-
sequently, Hayes does not come alive as a person.
Photographs, bibliography, index.

145 MYRON, ROBERT. *Shadow of the Hawk: Saga of the
Mound Builders;* illus. New York: Putnam's,
1965. o.p. (4-8)
A complete and well-organized account of the
origins, development, and the achievements of the Mound
Builders, the Hopewell and Adena Indians, and the
theories that explain their decline. Special emphasis
is placed on the artifacts as works of art and as testi-
mony of the culture of their creators. The most common
of the many living creatures portrayed in their sculpture was the hawk which is appropriately included in
the title. Both author and illustrator have studied
the Mound Builders intensively over a long period of
time. Includes: index; selected bibliography; chronology relating the Ohio prehistoric people to the
Mexican and South American and European and Mediter-
ranean civilizations.

—— NEIMARK, PAUL G. *The Jesse Owens Story.*
    See OH 150

146 NOLAN, JEANNETTE (COVERT). *John Brown;* illus. by
    Robert Burns. New York: Messner, 1950.
    (6-8) B *
    The radical Abolitionist whose actions at Har-
per's Ferry, Virginia, in 1859, helped to bring on the
Civil War, lived about half of his fifty-nine years in
north-eastern Ohio. In 1805, when John was five, his
family migrated from Connecticut to Hudson, his home
until the middle 1820's, when he moved his own wife and
children to Pennsylvania. During the next thirty years
they lived in Ohio again for varying periods of time:
four years in Franklin Mills, in Hudson, several years
in Akron. This very good fictionalized account is
unbiased and reveals all sides of Brown's temperament.
Bibliograpny. Index.

147 NORMAN, GERTRUDE. *Johnny Appleseed;* illus. by
    James Caraway. New York: Putnam's, 1960.
    (1-3) B
    A pleasant, elementary biography that tells how
Johnny Appleseed traveled about planting appleseeds and
offering friendship to both whites and Indians. Dates
and places are not given, but a map shows his travels
through the states. Attractive pictures in brown and
green.

148 NORTON, ANDRE and STEMM, BERTHA. *Bertie and May;*
    illus. Cleveland, Ohio: World, 1969. o.p.
    (4-8) F *
    A delightful fictionalized story of Bertie, 8,
and May, 10, real girls of the 1880's. When roller-
grinding made stone-grinding obsolete, their miller
father moved his family into nearby Loudonville (Ashland County), where he learned the new methods. Frightened at first, the girls soon loved town life. This
story, like the *Little House Books,* excels in its portrayal of day-to-day living within a close-knit family
group. Bertie grew up to become the mother of well-
known children's author Andre Norton.

—— NORTON, BERTHA STEMM. *Bertie and May.* See OH 148

149 OVERMAN, WILLIAM D. *Ohio Town Names.* Akron, Ohio:
Atlantic, 1959. o.p. (4-)
The author accomplishes his aim to supply "the
facts, the color, and the lore" of Ohio's towns and
cities. In the preface he discusses how and why Ohio
towns got their present names. Includes a list of
place names which have changed, and a selected bibliography. Concise and interesting explanations.

150 OWENS, JESSE with NEIMARK, PAUL G. *The Jesse Owens
Story.* New York: Putnam's, 1970. (3-7) B
Jesse Owens tells his own moving story, from his
birth in Alabama in 1913 until he was nearly sixty.
His family moved to Cleveland when Jesse was eight, and
his athletic ability was noticed almost at once. Even
in grade school he ran exceptionally fast. He set new
records at Cleveland's East Technical High and Ohio
State University. He won four gold medals at the 1936
Olympics in Berlin, where Hitler refused to shake hands
with him because he was Black. The reader sees him not
only as one of the century's great athletes, but also
as an admirable man. Index.

151 PARISH, PEGGY. *Let's Be Indians;* illus. by Arnold
Lobel. New York: Harper & Row, 1962. (2-6) *
Easy-to-follow instructions for making the kinds
of things Indians of the woodlands, plains, and desert
used. Some items are child-sized: moccasins, jewelry,
cradle boards. Others are small models for building
Indian villages: wickiups, canoes. Illustrations are
integral to and clarify the text.

152 PARSONS, GEORGE A. *Put Her to Port, Johnny;* illus.
New York: Holt, 1957. o.p. (5-8) F
John Hancock Honeycutt's father gives up farming
to follow his dream of making a living on the river.
On *Noah's Ark,* a large houseboat, the Honeycutts float
down the Ohio, trading queen's ware dishes for scrap
metal and other junk. There are both dangerous and
pleasant times, but Johnny, at eleven, thrives on both.

The time is the early 1900's and steamboats and showboats are still a part of the colorful river scene.
The author says that many of the incidents are biographical and that "a boyhood spent on the river is a thing
to be remembered."

153 PERRY, DICK. *Ohio, A Personal Portrait of the 17th
State;* photography by Bruce Goldflies. Garden
City, N.Y.: Doubleday, 1969. o.p. (5-) P *
The author and photographer, native Ohioans,
spent months traveling Ohio's roads and highways, visiting its cities and towns, and studying its history and
geography. They call this large, fact-filled work a
personal portrait because this is the way the state
looked to them. The casual, often humorous, style makes
the text pleasurable reading; the full-page photographs
are stories without words. Geographical index.

154 PERRY, DICK. *Raymond and Me That Summer.* New York:
Harcourt, Brace & World, 1963, 1964. o.p.
(5-8) F
Cincinnatians George and Raymond were ten and
eleven in the Depression summer of 1933. Even though
their fathers were out of work and money was very
scarce, the boys had more happy days than sad. George
relates, in a series of episodes, the events of the
summer: Raymond read Faith Baldwin novels from the
library; George paid a two cent toll and walked across
the bridge to visit his grandfather in Kentucky. Together they listened to Orphan Annie on the radio,
explored empty warehouses, and spent all of one Sunday
riding the street car for a quarter. Gives an excellent sense of a particular period and place.

155 PIERCE, PHILIP N. (Lt.Col., USMC) and SCHUON, KARL.
John H. Glenn, Astronaut; illus. New York:
Watts, 1962. o.p. (5-) B
Although one chapter sketches briefly his boy-
hood and school days, the emphasis is on John Glenn's
flying career from World War II through February 20,
1962, when he orbited the earth three times in the
Mercury Capsule, Friendship 7. The account is detailed

and factual. Appendices contain Glenn's message delivered to a joint session of Congress after his historic flight, a chronology of Mercury test launchings, and a glossary of space terms. Informative drawings and official photographs. Index.

156 POTTER, MARTHA A. *Ohio's Prehistoric People;* illus. by William Turner. Columbus: The Ohio Historical Society, 1968. (4-8)

Softbound book written in nontechnical language describes the living habits, the artistic accomplishments, the religious customs, the physical characteristics, and the interrelation of all of the prehistoric Indian groups that inhabited Ohio more or less continuously for over 10,000 years. Original two-color illustrations portraying the life of each culture, a bibliography, and chronology of Ohio's prehistoric Indians contribute to making this an attractive and useful book. Potter is Assistant Curator of Archaeology of the Ohio Historical Society.

—— POWER, EFFIE. *Early Days in Ohio.* See OH 60.

157 QUACKENBUSH, ROBERT. *Take Me Out to the Airfield;* illus. by author. New York: Parents, 1976. (3-7) B *

Captivating, full-page colored pictures and a simple text tell "how the Wright brothers invented the airplane." There are also instructions for building a model Wright flyer using toothpicks and a styrofoam meat tray. Authentic and entertaining narrative of "possibly the greatest single invention in the history of mankind."

158 REEDER, RED (Col.). *Sheridan: The General Who Wasn't Afraid to Take a Chance.* New York: Duell, Sloan & Pearce, 1962. o.p. (6-8) B

This good biography covers an eighteen year period in Sheridan's life from 1847, when he was fifteen, to the close of the Civil War, when he had become one of the four greatest Union commanders. The author depicts "Phil's" childhood in Somerset, Ohio. Later,

at West Point he shows how Phil's fiery temper got him
into trouble, but this trait may have contributed to
his being one of the most daring battlefield leaders in
history. Excellent cameos of Lincoln, Confederate
general Jubal Early, and fellow Ohioans Grant, George
Armstrong Custer, and William MacPherson, the highest
ranking Union officer to die in battle. Bibliography,
index.

159 REEDER, RED (Col.). *Ulysses S. Grant: Horseman
    and Fighter;* illus. by Ken Wagner. Champaign,
    Ill.: Garrard, 1964. o.p. (2-4) B
    Easy-to-read biography covering Grant's whole
life. Some incidents are fictionalized, particularly
those that reveal Grant as an exceptional horseman.
For many children these episodes will have more appeal
than those that show Grant the strategist and fighter.

160 RENICK, MARION. *States of the Nation: Ohio,*
    Donald P. Gavin, Consultant; illus. New York:
    Coward, McCann, 1970. o.p. (4-8) *
    A survey of the history, resources, present-day
economy, and people that have called the Buckeye State
home. A large amount of information is presented in a
lively manner by an author who is obviously enthusiastic about her subject. The Ohio Profile section at the
end of the book gives a concise summary of physical
characteristics, leading products, government, history,
and outstanding Ohioans. Many photos and maps, a pronunciation guide, and index.

161 RENICK, MARION. *Steve Marches with the General;*
    illus. by Pru Herric. New York: Scribner, 1962.
    o.p. (3-6) F
    Grantville, Ohio, named for General Grant who
was President at the time of its founding, is celebrat-
ing its centennial. Young Steve Dixon, who identifies
with young Ulysses Grant because he, too, is small for
his age, hopes to play the part of young Grant in the
pageant. After a number of realistic complications in
which Steve makes mature decisions which reveal that he

has become like Grant in character as well as stature, he is given the coveted role. Authentic historical and biographical facts, and also information on the theater, are well-integrated into the story.

162 RENICK, MARION and TYLER, MARGARET C. *Buckskin Scout and Other Ohio Stories;* illus. by Paul Galdone. Cleveland: World, 1953. o.p.
(3-8) B
Twenty interestingly-told stories about a variety of people who helped make history in Ohio. Except for Tecumseh, the only Indian, less-well-known persons are the subject. Included are Daniel Drake, recipient of the first doctor's diploma given west of the Allegheny Mountains, and "Mad Anne" Bailey who rode a hundred miles at night through the woods to bring aid to a fort besieged by the Indians.

163 REYNOLDS, QUENTIN. *The Wright Brothers: Pioneers of American Aviation;* illus. by Jacob Landau. New York: Random, 1950. (3-8) B
The story opens when Wilbur is eleven and Orville seven. It closes after they have made a successful exhibition of their flying machine in the east. They are to have dinner with President Theodore Roosevelt before taking the midnight train home to Dayton. A well-written fictionalized account that does not cover their entire lives.

164 RHODES, JAMES. *Teenage Hall of Fame;* illus. Indianapolis: Bobbs-Merrill, 1960. o.p.
(4-8) B
Brief biographies of twenty-five Ohioans who achieved something noteworthy before their twentieth birthdays. The author believes "the achievements of great teenagers can be an inspiration to the youth of today and of the future." Artist's sketches picturing the subjects as they looked in their youth hang in the Ohio State Capitol, visited annually by thousands of junior and senior high school students. Among them are Joe E. Brown, Dorothy and Lillian Gish, Roy Rogers, Eddie Rickenbacker, and the Wright brothers.

165 RICHTER, CONRAD. *A Country of Strangers.* New York:
 Knopf, 1966. o.p. (6-) F *
 A companion novel to *The Light in the Forest.*
Like True Son of that story, Stone Girl, born Mary
Stanton, was captured when young, adopted, and raised
by the Lenni Lenape in an Indian village in what is
today southeastern Ohio. Following the death of her
Indian husband, Stone Girl and her son are returned to
her white father in Pennsylvania. He rejects her as an
imposter. Tragedy follows tragedy in Stone Girl's life.
At length she meets True Son and they set out for the
West again, exiles, wanderers "banished to live in a
country of strangers." A story that grips the heart.

166 RICHTER, CONRAD. *The Fields.* New York: Knopf,
 1945. o.p. (7-) F *
 The Fields, showing the life of the early farmer,
is volume two of Richter's trilogy (OH 169, 168) which
records the experiences of one family in the settlement
and growth of an Ohio community. Sayward and Portius
set about clearing the gigantic trees from their land.
After Ohio becomes a state, Portius' time is divided
between teaching school and practicing law. But Sayward, calm and efficient, continues to clear the land.
She plows, plants, and harvests the crops. She gives
birth to and cares for four sons and six daughters. As
the years pass, a town begins to grow around Sayward's
cabin.

167 RICHTER, CONRAD. *Light in the Forest;* illus. by
 Warren Chappell. New York: Knopf, 1963.
 (6-) F *
 "True Son," born John Butler in a pioneer settlement in Pennsylvania, was captured by the Lenni Lenape
Indians (the Delawares) when he was four years old and
adopted into the tribe. Until he was fifteen, he lived
happily with his foster family in a village on the
Tuscarawas. Then, although he did not want to go,
because of a treaty he was returned to his flesh-and-
blood white family. After a year he ran away to his
Indian family in the Ohio forest, but learned he did
not really belong there anymore, either. Authentic,

thought-provoking, very well-written. Companion novel
to *A Country of Strangers.*

168 RICHTER, CONRAD. *The Town.* New York: Knopf, 1950.
(7-) F *
The Pulitzer Prize was awarded to Conrad Richter
for *The Town,* the concluding title in his triology
(OH 169, 166) about Sayward Luckett Wheeler and her
family. In this volume, the fictitious town of Ameri-
cus grows up on Sayward's farm. Portius, now a judge,
and Sayward, still thinking of herself as a "woodsy,"
with their family leave their double cabin to live in a
fine mansion. The children marry and Sayward becomes a
grandmother. Many loose strands of story from the pre-
vious books are woven into this narrative. The reader
puts the books down with a feeling of having experienced
life in early Ohio.

169 RICHTER, CONRAD. *The Trees.* New York: Knopf,
1940. (7-) F *
First volume of a trilogy (OH 166, 168) that
traces, through one family, life in the Scioto River
valley from territorial days to the late 1850's. In
the 1790's, Jary and Worth Luckett and their five children, with their possessions on their backs, tramp into
the wilderness of Ohio. The story is told from the
point of view of Sayward, fifteen, the oldest child.
Worth, a hunter, is at home here where "the whites are
as scarce as birds' teeth and the Indians plentiful as
dogberries." But Jary, lonely for the settlements, sick-
ens and dies. After her death, Worth leaves, but
steady, dependable Sayward, now in her late teens,
holds the family together. Later, she marries Portius
Wheeler, a young Bay State lawyer who has been living a
solitary life in the woods.

170 RIVERA, ROBERTA, ed. *Ohio Almanac;* illus. Lorain,
Ohio: Lorain Journal, 1977. (4-) *
Facts of Ohio history, Ohio government, politics,
elections, and Ohio's 88 counties concisely presented.
index.

171 ROBINSON, BARBARA. *Trace Through the Forest;* illus.
by Evaline Ness. New York: Lothrop, Lee &
Shepard, 1965. (4-8) F
"I was fourteen years old that summer of 1796
when we built the road into the wilderness of Ohio."
Thus Jim Fraley begins his story of the road (trace)
Colonel Zane and his eleven men with axes blazed through
250 miles of unbroken forest. The trace began at a
point across the river from Wheeling, ran through
present-day Zanesville, Lancaster and Chillicothe, and
ended opposite Maysville, Kentucky. The story is interesting and exciting, although some of the incidents are
a bit improbable. There is good description of the
forest that was "so thick no sunlight ever showed
through."

—— RODABAUGH, JAMES H. *Ohio, the Buckeye State.*
See OH 67

172 ROSEBOOM, EUGENE H. and WEISENBURGER, FRANCIS P.
A History of Ohio; illus. by James H. Rodabaugh.
Columbus: Ohio Historical Society, 1953.
(6-) *
An excellent one-volume general history of Ohio,
clearly and vigorously written by recognized scholars.
Well-chosen illustrations increase the appeal. Brought
up to date in 1967 by the addition of a chapter titled
"Ohio Moves Toward the Late Twentieth Century." Com-
prehensive bibliography. Index.

173 ROTH, ARTHUR. *The Secret Lover of Elmtree.* New
York: Four Winds, 1976. (5-8) F
Greg, who is adopted, tells his own story. In
the summer between his junior and senior years in high
school, he meets his natural father for the first time.
Greg learns his natural mother is dead but his natural
father is wealthy and lives in New York City. He asks
Greg to come live with him and his wife. Greg agonizes,
but decides to stay with his adoptive family in the
small town of Elmtree, Ohio. (Clues in the text place
this fictitious town in western Ohio somewhere between
Indian Lake and Cincinnati.) The story is readable,
although Greg's monologue occasionally becomes tedious.

174 SCHEELE, WILLIAM E. *The Mound Builders;* illus. by
author. Cleveland: Collins-World, 1960.
(2-6) #
An accurate but simple text, large print, and
the many illustrations and maps showing mound-builder
earthworks in southern Ohio make this a good "first"
book. The author, Director of the Cleveland Museum of
Natural History, focuses on the prehistoric Indians of
the Ohio River valley, especially the Hopewells and
their mound groups near Chillicothe. In addition to
describing their way of life and the construction and
uses of the mounds, he emphasizes their artistry and
the richness of their traditions, Also explained are
the methods used to estimate the age of prehistoric
materials and the procedures followed in opening a
mound for scientific study.

―― SCHUON, KARL. *John H. Glenn, Astronaut.*
See OH 155

175 SCISM, CAROL K. *Secret Emily;* illus. by Donald
McKay. New York: Dial, 1972. (4-7) F *
More than anything in the world, twelve-year-old
Emily longs to be a member of the snobbish Clique-
Claque Club. When she is finally asked to join, the
secret-Emily part of her personality causes her to
reject the invitation because she realizes that she
does not want to limit her friends to a small group.
Emily's home, an old stagecoach inn converted into a
house, is modeled on the author's childhood home and is
situated, as was the author's, in northeastern Ohio.

176 SEIDEL, FRANK. *The Ohio Story.* Cleveland: World,
1950. o.p. (5-) B *
Contains 22 human interest stories about a variety of Ohioans. Famous people such as Annie Oakley and
Mike Fink are portrayed here, but also present are such
less well-known figures as Leslie Peltier of Delphos
who, in the 1930's, gained the reputation of being
America's greatest amateur astronomer. One notorious
Ohioan is included: Lottie Moon Clark, an Oxford resident who served as a Confederate spy during the Civil

War. Several stories focus on the human interest element in famous companies and products like Hoover Vacu-
um Cleaners and Firestone Rubber. Informative and
enjoyable reading.

177 SEIDEL, FRANK. *Out of the Midwest.* Cleveland:
World, 1953. o.p. (5-) B
The author of *The Ohio Story* subtitled his second book *More Chapters in the Ohio Story.* The subjects
of the thirty-one interestingly-told tales are Ohioans
from all parts of the state and all walks of life. Two
of them are Zane Grey of Zanesville, the dentist who
became one of America's most widely-read writers; and
actor Clark Gable in the days when he was Billy Gable.

178 SEVERN, BILL. *William Howard Taft, the President
Who Became Chief Justice.* New York: McKay,
1970. o.p. (7-) B *
Taft's father wrote when his son Will was seven,
"To be Chief Justice of the United States is more than
to be President in my estimation." His son, the only
person to fill both offices, agreed. In a readable and
well-written biography, the author presents Cincinnatian
William Howard Taft's entire life (1857-1930). He
explains clearly the decisions which Taft handed down
from the bench. He makes both Taft and Theodore Roosevelt come alive and traces their relationships in
friendship and enmity. He portrays Taft as a warm
human being. Bibliography and index.

179 SILVERBURG, ROBERT. *The Mound Builders;* illus.
Greenwich, Conn.: New York Graphic Society,
1970. (6-) *
This work is an abridged edition of the author's
*Mound Builders of Ancient America: The Archaeology of
a Myth,* published in 1968. The first half of the book
documents the various theories advanced to explain who
the Mound Builders were. In later chapters the author
discusses the Adena and Hopewell cultures, both of
which centered in Ohio, and the Temple Mound people who
carried on the Hopewellian influence after the collapse

of the Ohio Hopewell. Informative and well-written.
Bibliography. Index. Also published by Ballentine,
1975, paper edition.

180 SIMON, SHIRLEY. *Cousins at Camm Corners;* illus. by
Reisie Lonette. New York: Lothrop, Lee &
Shepard, 1963. o.p. (3-6) F
After her father's death, Marcy Sutton's guar-
dian, bachelor Uncle George, sends the girl to live
with his sister, Aunt Helen Kent, and her family in
Camm Corners, Ohio. Marcy goes against her will—she
had hoped to stay in New York City with her father's
fiancee, actress Alice Deering. Certain she'll hate
her new life, Marcy soon finds herself loving it. In
three months when told that she may choose where she
wants to live, Marcy chooses to stay with the Kents.
A pleasant story, although neither characterization
nor plot are exceptional.

—— SIMONDS, CATHERINE G. *The Maumee Valley, U.S.A.*
See OH 49

—— STEMM, BERTHA. *Bertie and May.* See OH 148

181 STEVENSON, AUGUSTA. *Tecumseh, Shawnee Boy;* illus.
by Clotilde Embree Funk. Indianapolis: Bobbs-
Merrill, 1955. (2-4) B #
Tecumseh, the only hero of the *Childhood of
Famous Americans* series who fought against the United
States, was included because he was truly great in
many respects. This fictionalized biography covers his
life from age nine to eleven (1777-1779). Its principal aim is to show the training of a Shawnee boy and
the Shawnee way of life in old Piqua. Relationships
with other tribes are mentioned. There is contact with
the whites when Daniel Boone is captured and brought to
the camp.

182 STEVENSON, AUGUSTA. *Wilbur and Orville Wright, Boys with Wings;* illus. by Paul Laune. Indianapolis: Bobbs-Merrill, 1951. (3-5) B

A biography in the *Childhood of Famous Americans* series, this fictionalized account emphasizes their childhood, especially their money-making activities. The style of this book which contains invented incidents and conversations, now seems outmoded. Other biographies of Wilbur and Orville Wright for the young reader give pertinent information more concisely.

183 STUART, JESSE. *The Land Beyond the River.* New York: McGraw-Hill, 1973. (7-) F *

Ohio is "the land beyond the river" where Kentucky-born Poppie and Mommie Perkins, and their brood of fourteen children move in search of a better life. There they are able to live more comfortably on welfare and food stamps than many who work for a living. The author effectively fulfills his obvious purpose of exposing loopholes in the welfare system. At the same time, he draws memorable characters: the parents and adolescent children, Cassie-Belle, Pedike (the narrator), Tishie, and Timmie. Although probably written for adults, it can be read easily by junior high students.

184 TEBBEL, JOHN. *The Battle of Fallen Timbers, August 20, 1794;* illus. New York: Watts, 1972. (6-)

Subtitled *President Washington Secures the Ohio Valley,* this *Focus* book examines the battle which occurred in the Ohio wilderness in the context of Washington's western policy and the events leading up to the battle. General Anthony Wayne's decisive victory there ended Indian and British control of the Ohio valley. Clearly and concisely written. Illustrated with photographs and contemporary prints. Selected bibliography and index.

185 THOMAS, HENRY. *Ulysses S. Grant.* New York:
Putnam, 1961. o.p. (5-8) B #
The complete life of the great Civil War general
and eighteenth president. The author relates anecdotes
from Grant's youthful Georgetown years in which he
revealed qualities that were still with him in adulthood:
his ability to size up a situation, his tenacity, and
his talent for handling horses. His failures as well
as his successes are recorded. Bibliography. Index.

186 THOMAS, WILLIAM. *The Country in the Boy.* Nashville, Tenn.: Nelson, 1975. (6-) F
A slightly fictionalized account of the author's
life from age six to seventeen. He lived on a farm
close to Prospect, along the Scioto River in Marion
County, Ohio, in the second decade of this century.
Although written from a boy's viewpoint, there are
girls present: at school and church, on sleigh rides,
at box socials, and, most memorably, at the senior
class picnic. A good re-creation of life in an Ohio
farm family and community.

187 TUNIS, EDWIN. *Frontier Living;* illus. by author.
Cleveland: World, 1961. (4-)
A detailed description of the conditions of
everyday life on the American frontier. Tunis focuses
on the forest frontier east of the Mississippi, which
has received much less attention than the area west of
the Mississippi. His plain and sometimes humorous
style is appropriate to his subject matter. Both text
and the precise black-and-white line drawings reveal
careful research. Section 4, dealing with daily life
in "Caintuck," and Section 5, with road and river transportation, contain much material of value to those
studying the old Northwest Territory, the subject of
Section 6. Index. 1962 Newbery Honor Book.

188 TUNIS, EDWIN. *The Young United States, 1783 to
1830;* illus. by author. New York: World, 1969.
(5-) P *
Like Tunis's other history books, this one shows
meticulous research, is well-written, and contains many

of the author's memorable illustrations. Section 18,
"The Growth of the West," describes specifically life in
the Old Northwest. There are, however, numerous references to the area in other chapters: for example, in
one, a Greek Revival house in Michigan is pictured.
The book is topically organized—*e.g.* "Inventions and
Factories"—and covers both daily life and historical
events. Index.

—— TYLER, MARGARET C. *Buckskin Scout and Other Ohio
Stories.* See OH 162

189 WALKER, ALICE. *Langston Hughes, American Poet;*
illus. by Don Miller. New York: Crowell, 1974.
(3-6) B *
This book is an excellent introduction to the
writer and instructive of Negro life in America during
the years of Langston Hughes' life, 1902-1967. The two
poems reprinted in the text are "When Susanna Jones
Wears Red," written when he was a student at Central
High in Cleveland and "The Negro Speaks of Rivers,"
composed shortly after his high school graduation in
1920. Although many of his poems articulate the despair of blacks over social and economic conditions,
many others, like these, show deep racial pride.
Attractive illustrations.

—— WEISENBURGER, FRANCIS P. *A History of Ohio.*
See OH 172

190 WEISENBURGER, FRANCIS P. *A Students' Guide to
Localized History.* New York: Teachers College,
Columbia University, 1965. (6-)
An introduction tells where to look in the community for information: *e.g.,* the library, county histories, newspaper files. The introduction is followed
by a short history of Ohio. After each chapter there
is a bibliography, a listing of historical museums and
sites, and the names of other institutions from which
the student may acquire information. This brief book
is a good starting place for those interested in studying either local or state history.

191 WELLMAN, PAUL I. *Indian Wars and Warriors (East);*
illus. by Lorence Bjorklund. Boston: Houghton
Mifflin, 1959. o.p. (4-8)
Details of the struggle between the white men
and the Indians on the eastern side of the Mississippi.
In chapter 8 the author describes Little Turtle's defeat of General Harmer in 1790, his rout of General
Arthur St. Clair in 1791, and the defeat of the Indians
by General Anthony Wayne at the Battle of Fallen Timbers
in 1794. In "The Fates Against Tecumseh" he chronicles
the plans and efforts of that heroic warrier to attain
a permanent federation of all the Indians east of the
Mississippi. A map at the beginning of each chapter,
an index, and appealing illustrations in sepia add to
the usefulness of this unbiased, interestingly-written
account of Iroquois, Creeks, Seminoles, Chippewas, and
other tribes.

192 WEST, JESSAMYN. *Leafy Rivers.* New York: Harcourt,
Brace & World, 1967. (7-) F *
As Leafy Rivers labors for two days to give
birth to her first child on a farm in southeastern Ohio
in 1818, she relives in lucid moments her life to that
point. Very well-developed characters and excellent
depiction of the settlers' way of life. For mature
junior high students. Reissued, Avon 1974, paper.

193 WILCOX, ELEANOR REINDOLLAR. *The Cornhusk Doll;*
illus. by Gerald McCann. New York: Hale, 1956.
o.p. (5-8) F
In the spring of 1764, Sally Redpath, 10, and
her parents, leave their friends and their big brick
house in Philadelphia to make a home beyond the Ohio
River, where her adventurous father engages in the fur
trade. In the fall, Sally is kidnapped by Shawnees and
taken to their village deep in the Ohio country. Sally
misses her parents, but grows to love her Indian family.
The next spring, aided by a white woman who has lived
with the Indians many years, Sally is returned home,
taking her cornhusk doll as a token of love from her
Indian family. Even though the plot is contrived,
Sally is an attractive character and the story is
enjoyable.

194 WILCOX, FRANK. *The Ohio Canals;* illus. by author.
Kent, Ohio: Kent State University Press, 1969.
(5-) P
   In the years before the Civil War, two great
canals, the Miami-Erie and the Ohio-Erie, together with
numerous connections and feeders, laced Ohio with a
thousand miles of waterways. Today the canals and the
colorful way of life they supported are all but vanished. This work, a series of paintings, sketches and
essays, restores the Ohio canals to their former activity. Artist-historian Wilcox, for forty years an instructor in the Cleveland Art Institute, personally
researched every mile of the major canals in the state.
Bibliography.

195 WILCOX, FRANK. *Ohio Indian Trails;* illus. by
author. Kent, Ohio: Kent State University
Press, 1970. o.p. (4-) P
   The author-artist studied Indian trails for
thirty years. His many full-page pictures—black-and-
white pen drawings, watercolors, and wash drawings—
supplement the careful descriptions of the trails and
the Indians who used them. Especially interesting is a
map of Ohio showing Indian trails and towns in 1776.
Has bibliography, index, and charts showing the relationship between Ohio rivers and the trails and present-
day Ohio towns and trails.

196 WILKIE, KATHERINE E. *Simon Kenton: Young Trail
Blazer;* illus. by Gray Morrow. New York: Bobbs-
Merrill, 1960. (3-6) B
   The first two-thirds of this fictionalized biography relates Simon Kenton's life on a farm on Bull Run
Mountain in Virginia, from his birth in 1755 until he
was sixteen. The remaining chapters pass over rather
briefly his part in the settling of Kentucky and fighting in the Indian Wars north of the Ohio. The information is accurate, but the book is too consistently opti-
mistic in tone: running the gauntlet and a near-burning
at the stake are regarded as "adventures." The illustrations idealize the characters: backwoods boys wear
the costumes wealthy Williamsburg boys might wear. A
Childhood of Famous Americans biography.

276

197 WILSON, ELLEN. *Annie Oakley;* illus. by Vance Locke.
Indianapolis: Bobbs-Merrill, 1962. (3-5) B
Often the childhood of a famous person is very
like the childhood of one who does not become famous.
Annie Oakley was an exception: she fired her father's
Kentucky rifle for the first time in 1867 when she was
seven, and killed a wolf when she was nine. By the
time she was fourteen Annie practically supported her
family by shooting, in the woods around her native
Greenville, quails and other game for a restaurant in
Cincinnati. The final chapters of this fictionalized
biography in the *Childhood of Famous American* series
touches briefly on Annie Oakley's later career as an
outstanding markswoman.

198 WISE, WINIFRED E. *Harriet Beecher Stowe: Woman
with a Cause.* New York: Putnam, 1965. o.p.
(6-) B *
An admirable portrait of a complex woman.
Although Harriet Beecher Stowe's whole life is chronicled here, there is special emphasis on the Cincinnati
years, 1832-1850. While living there close to slavery
she gathered material that formed the basis for many
characters and incidents in *Uncle Tom's Cabin,* called
by author Wise "the most powerful and influential book
of the nineteenth century and one of the most-discussed
novels of all time."

199 WITTEN, HERBERT. *Escape from the Shawnees;* illus.
by Leonard F. Bjorklund. Chicago: Follett,
1958. o.p. (5-8) F
Whit Martin, 11, and Gabe Stoner, a hunter, are
captured by Indians while hunting for game for Whit's
family and others moving into Kentucky. Their captors
take them to a Shawnee village in Ohio country. They
manage to escape during a blinding blizzard and at
length make their way to a settlement on the Big Sandy
River in Kentucky. The reader learns survival skills
as injured Gabe instructs Whit in hunting and scouting
techniques.

200 WREADE, ESTELLA H. *Ohio Quiz Book;* illus. by Douglas Dean. Toledo: Northern Historical Ohio Pub., 1962. (4-8)

Written by a teacher of Ohio history, *Ohio Quiz Book* is intended primarily as a handbook for elementary school pupils and for teachers of Ohio history. The format is questions with answers supplied. At the end of each unit there is a quiz and references for further reading. Although the writing is not distinguished, the book contains much information covering many aspects of life in present-day Ohio as well as facts of Ohio history. Bibliography and index.

201 WRIGHT, ALICE. *The Seed Is Blown;* illus. by Joan Berg. Chicago: Rand McNally, 1965. o.p. (5-8) F

Separated from their father while traveling by flatboat down the Ohio River, the Lake children—Winthrop, almost 15, Suzanne, a year younger, and Merry, 4—dock their boat at Putnam's settlement, the future Marietta. In the year-and-a-half before their father is able to rejoin them, the children are cared for by a widow. Winthrop and Suzanne contribute their labor to the new settlement. The characters are not well-drawn and the plot is contrived, but there is a fair description of Fort Harmar, and the building of Marietta.

202 YOUNG, STANLEY. *Tippecanoe and Tyler, Too;* illus. by Warren Chappell. New York: Random, 1957. o.p. (5-8) B

A *Landmark* book that tells William Henry Harrison's entire life story from his birth into an aristocratic Virginia family to his death one month after his inauguration as President. He was in Ohio and Indiana territory almost continuously from 1793 to 1840, the years of his life most emphasized in this biography. Little space is devoted to his personal life, nor is there much fictionalizing. Map of Ohio and Indiana territory.

203 ZEHNPFENNIG, GLADYS. *Charles F. Kettering, Inventor and Idealist.* Minneapolis: Denison, 1962. o.p. (6-) B *

Born in Ashland County in 1876, Charles Kettering lived a long and exceptionally productive life until his death in 1958. Although he spent twenty-five years as head of the General Motors Research Corporation, he remained an Ohioan, commuting from his home in Dayton and returning often to Loudonville, where he spent his childhood. A great creative inventor—of the self-starter for cars, the Delco Farm Lighting System, refinements for Diesel engines—Kettering interested himself also in education, solar energy, and cancer research. This exceptionally well-written biography brings to life a scientific genius at work and a truly likable man. In an acknowledgement, the author names sources consulted.

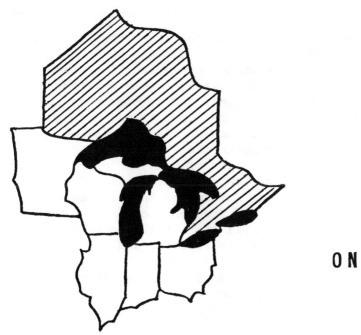

ONTARIO

compiled by **PAT TOMEY**

A place to stand, a place to grow
Ontari-ari-ari o

This refrain from a song promoting the Canadian province at Expo '67 is still familiar today. Certainly there is plenty of room "to stand" in its 412,582 square miles, an area nearly twice the size of France. Perhaps the song should have included "a place to float," because lakes and rivers cover more than one-fifth of the province, excluding the four bordering Great Lakes of Ontario, Erie, Huron and Superior. As for "a place to grow", Ontario's population has expanded from 45,000 Native Indians in the early 1600's to nearly nine million people today, representing many nationalities, religions and cultures.

Before the white man arrived, the Indians who inhabited the area belonged to two linguistic groups. The Iroquoian tribes, including the Hurons, lived in the southern part of the province while the Algonkian-speaking tribes were scattered throughout the Pre-Cambrian Shield in the north.

The first permanent white settlers were the French who located in the Ottawa and Windsor regions in the early 1700's, although French explorers, fur traders and missionaries had used Ontario's waterways for some time. Among them were Etienne Brulé, Samuel de Champlain, Henry Hudson, Radisson, Chouart and de LaSalle. After the American Revolution, a large number of United Empire loyalists moved north from the United States to settle on the northern shores of Lakes Erie and Ontario and along the Upper St. Lawrence River. In 1791, the province of Upper Canada was formed in the area now known as Southern Ontario. The small colony was threatened during the War of 1812-14, but its independence was preserved because of the ability and courage of the the Loyalists.

Fur trading played an important role in the early economy, with the headquarters of the Hudson Bay Company at Fort William. In the mid-nineteenth century, however, lumber trade and small industries increased, with agriculture the principal means of livelihood.

After an unsuccessful rebellion in 1837 against an autocratic administration, Upper and Lower Canada were united in 1841. A national government with four federated provinces—Ontario, Quebec, Nova Scotia and New Brunswick—was later established in 1867.

Ontario today is a prosperous province, blessed with natural resources. With half of its area forested, 94% of that forest land is Crown land, managed by the Ministry of Natural Resources. In the Sudbury basin, one-third of the world's supply of nickel, two-fifths of Canada's copper, and the free world's largest supply of platinum are produced. Uranium, gold, silver and iron ore are also mined in Northern Ontario.

Although Southern Ontario is one of the most productive farming areas in Canada, it is also the industrial core of the country. The province produces half of all the goods manufactured in Canada, with 38% of exports originating in Ontario. Toronto is the provincial capital, as well as the industrial, commercial and cultural centre of Ontario. Hamilton, second city in size, is noted for its steel industry, while Windsor is the center of Canada's automobile industry.

Before World War II, the population of the province
was mostly of British descent, with smaller numbers of
French descent and Indians also present. But large
scale immigrations from Italy, Portugal, Greece—and
more recently, Hong Kong and the West Indies—have
transformed Southern Ontario cities to multi-ethnic and
multi-cultural centres. Toronto, for example, houses
the largest number of Italians outside of Italy.

It has been said that literature for children reflects the culture and concerns of the people of a
region. Titles in the following bibliography have been
selected from that literature to represent the various
aspects of the history and structure of the province as
well as the past achievements and present interests of
its inhabitants.

1   ADAMSON, ANTHONY. *The Gaiety of Gables; Ontario's*
     Architectural Folk Art; photos by John Willard.
     Toronto: McClelland and Stewart, 1974. (7-8) P
     A pictorial tribute to the multiplicity of
designs which flourish on the eaves of gingerbread farm-
houses in Ontario. Beginning with a history of Ontario
architecture and its influences, the author traces the
Ontario method of making barge boards and the evolution
of gingerbread to the peak of the gables in the mid-
nineteenth century. Over one hundred interesting photographs, mostly black and white, form the major part of
this book about one of Canada's unique art forms.

2   ADDISON, OTTELYN. *Early Days in Algonquin Park;*
     illus. Toronto: McGraw-Hill Ryerson, 1974.
     Paper. (7-8)
     Using diaries, anecdotes and experiences of her
Park Ranger father, the author tells the story of the
Algonquin area from its geological beginnings and habi-
tation by Indians to its present use as a provincial
park. Many black and white photographs illustrate
logging activities, camping parties, old lodges and
inns and Canadian artists who painted there. Although
the format and writing style are undistinguished, it
does provide historical background on that area for
interested older students.

3   ADDISON, OTTELYN. *Tom Thomson: the Algonquin*
     Years; illus. Toronto: Ryerson Press, 1969.
     (7-8) B
     The daughter of one of Thomson's closest friends
during his "Algonquin Years" has written this well-
researched account of the man and the artist. Although
the mystery of Thomson's death is not discussed, the
book shows how his love for the Ontario woods influenced his paintings. Only three of his paintings are
reproduced in colour, unfortunately, but there are many
in black and white, plus photographs.

4   AIKENS, JAMES R. *Stratford*. (Jackdaw 33.) Toronto:
       Clarke, Irwin, 1972. Paper. (7-8)
       This folder, containing an interesting collec-
tion of reproduced items, was originally issued to com-
memorate the 20th season of the Stratford Festival.
There are newspaper clippings, copies of correspondence
between Tyrone Guthrie and Canadian promoters, a page
from a prompt book, a poster, plus drawings and photographs. Of special interest to classes planning a trip
to the Stratford Festival and to students interested in
drama.

5   ALLEN, ROBERT THOMAS. *The Violin;* photos by George
       Pastic. Toronto: McGraw-Hill Ryerson, 1976.
       Paper. (2-4) F
       Based on the award-winning Canadian film of the
same title, with a well-known Canadian writer retelling
the story, this picture story-book can be shared by
children and parents. Young Chris saves to buy a
violin in order to play the kind of music he heard at a
concert. An old man teaches him to play the instrument
and a friendship develops. The book has merit apart
from its cinematic prototype, for its setting is
Toronto and Toronto Island.

6   ALLINSON, BEVERLY and O'KELLEY, BARBARA. *Click;*
       illus. Agincourt, Ont.: Methuen, 1976. Paper.
       (4-8)
       One of a set of four attractive booklets which
reflect the multi-culturalism of Toronto. Four children of different origins, Chile, Jamaica, Trinidad and
China, delight in learning and new experiences. In
Click they learn about photography, taking delightful
shots of Toronto's zoo and the Caribbean Carnival.
These are reproduced in full colour on good quality
paper. The back cover provides a brief resumé of the
story in six languages. Excellent for class discussion,
especially with the teacher's guide which is available
separately. *Kids Like Us* series.

7   ALLINSON, BEVERLY and O'KELLEY, BARBARA. *Flashback;*
     illus. Agincourt, Ont.: Methuen, 1976. Paper.
     (4-8)

     Another in the set of booklets with multicultural
theme, and featuring Toronto school children. This
shows four friends trying to teach English to Miguel, a
recent arrival from Chile. He teaches them to dive and
all learn more about Canadian history when they visit a
Canadian book store. Attractive, amusing photographs
complement the text, and a summary of the story is
printed in six languages on the back cover. A teacher's
guide, available separately, adds to its usefulness.
Kids Like Us series.

8   ALLINSON, BEVERLY and O'KELLEY, BARBARA. *Trips;*
     illus. Agincourt, Ont.: Methuen, 1976. Paper.
     (4-8)

     Four Toronto school children with different cul-
tural backgrounds are again featured in the third title
of this series. This time Selwyn from Trinidad goes on
a trip to the west coast. The others dream of far away
adventures, but enjoy pursuing their own activities at
home. Full-colour illustrations that complement the
text are lively and refreshing. Children who read
Italian, Spanish, French or Chinese will like the summary printed in their own language on the back cover.
Suggestions for use of this booklet are included in the
separate teacher's guide. *Kids Like Us* series.

9   ALLINSON, BEVERLY and O'KELLEY, BARBARA. *Wallpaper;*
     illus. Agincourt, Ont.: Methuen, 1976. Paper.
     (4-8)

     Part of a series of four booklets, *Wallpaper*
shows the four friends from Chile, Jamaica, Trinidad
and China engaging in a school newspaper project.
Although they come to realize they lack money to
finance it, they do learn a lot about proof-reading,
typesetting, galleys and paste-ups. Interesting on-
location photographs in black and white enliven the
text. Six-language summaries are printed on the back
cover. Suggestions for use are provided in the teacher's guide for the set, which is an additional purchase.
Kids Like Us series.

10 ALLISON, ROSEMARY. *The Green Harpy at the Corner Store;* illus. by Claire Watson Garcia. Toronto: Kids Can, 1976. Paper. (K-2) F

Imagine a harpy (a mythological creature, part female, part bird) who is lost on a Toronto street and lame from a broken wing. Imagine her moving into a Greek-Canadian home and doing outrageous things like walking across the ceiling. This fanciful picture book with lively illustrations of green and black and white will tickle the funnybone of the small fry from beginning to end, even if they aren't of Greek ancestry.

11 ALLISON, ROSEMARY and POWELL, ANN. *The Travels of Ms Beaver;* illus. Toronto: Women's Press, 1973. Paper. (K-3) F

Ms Beaver has wander-lust. She decides to leave her Ontario lake to travel to Toronto, where she rides on the subway and visits the city hall and museum. But when she builds a dam, creating a lake in Riverdale Park, the authorities are not amused. Luckily, the mayor comes up with a happy but hilarious solution. The line drawings are undistinguished but the ludicrous story has great appeal for young children.

12 ANDRAE, CHRISTOPHER. *The London and Port Stanley Railway, 1856;* illus. Toronto: Ginn, 1974. Paper. (5-8)

Excellent illustrations, large print and quality paper enhance this short history of the building of this central Ontario railway. The author relates how the construction was initiated by local businessmen and municipalities, the problems involved in making the roadbed and laying the track, plus the celebration at its completion. Questions intended for class discussion are placed in boxed inserts, so that they do not distract library readers. Students living near this area will find this booklet of most interest. One of the series *Ginn Studies in Canadian History.*

13 ANDREWS, ELIZABETH. *Ellen Elliott: A Pioneer;*
　　illus. Toronto: Ginn, 1972. Paper. (5-8)
　　A true-life story of a Scottish pioneer family
who experience hardships in starting a new life in the
Guelph area. Colour photographs from Upper Canada Village plus interesting archival paintings and sketches
enhance the brief text. The triple-column format and
questions following each short chapter makes it more
suitable for classroom study than individual reading,
but Guelph area libraries will find it a useful
resource on local history. In the series *Ginn Studies
in Canadian History.*

14 BAINE, RICHARD P. *The Sudbury Region;* illus.
　　Toronto: Holt, Rinehart & Winston, 1969. Paper.
　　(5-8)
　　The world economic situation has affected Sudbury mines since this social studies text was written.
But the author's aim "to provide a better understanding
of the importance of metals in the lives of people who
live in the region" is still valid. Short, simply
written chapters describe the life of a miner in Sudbury, and office worker at Coppercliff, mines and
mining techniques and metal processing. More space is
devoted to questions and suggested activities than to
the text, so that learning by thinking and doing is
actively encouraged. The few photos are disappointing,
but the approach is provocative.

15 BAKER, LAURA NELSON. *O Children of the Wind and
　　Pines;* illus. by Inez Storer. Philadelphia:
　　Lippincott, 1967. (3-4) F
　　How the first Christmas carol on this continent
may have come to be written is the subject of this
story. Using the diaries of Jesuit missionaries who
lived among the Hurons, the author tells of a motherless little Indian girl who is befriended by Father
Jean de Brebeuf. When he persuades her to sing his
carol in front of her Indian school-mates, she gains
the confidence she badly needs. Includes words and
music of the Huron carol.

16 BARNES, MICHAEL. *In the Public Service: The
     Ontario Provincial Police;* illus. Cobalt, Ont.:
     Highway Book Shop, 1974. Paper. (5-8)
     An interesting, informative account of the many
roles of the police force that patrols Ontario highways.
It provides details on their training, weapons, equipment in the patrol cruiser, including the radio code
system. It also describes specialized personnel—scuba
divers, motorcyclists and police dogs—with fictionalized incidents to interest younger readers. Several
black and white photographs of the O.P.P. are included.

17 BASSETT, JOHN. *Elizabeth Simcoe;* illus. Don Mills,
     Ont.: Fitzhenry and Whiteside, 1974. Paper.
     (7-9) B
     Lady Simcoe's own diaries and sketches provide a
wealth of material of her adventures and impressions.
Selection of which details to include in a brief biography of the First Lady of Upper Canada would be difficult, and this book illustrates the author's dilemma.
Many facts of her life are carefully, if tediously,
chronicled, with her sketches and paintings accompanying
the text. Some details inserted into the narration and
invented dialogue are trivial, while other pertinent
details are omitted. The book deserves consideration a
as a simply written reference source on one of the few
women who made history in Early Ontario.
In *The Canadians* series.

18 BASSETT, JOHN. *Timothy Eaton;* Don Mills, Ont.:
     Fitzhenry and Whiteside, 1975. Paper. (6-8) B
     When Timothy Eaton opened the first department
store in Canada on Yonge Street, Toronto, he had three
innovative policies—"cash only," "one price," "satisfaction or money refunded." His success with these
policies revolutionized merchandising and built up
one of the largest department stores in North America
with a huge mail-order business. Illustrations, including pages from old Eaton's catalogues, enhance the text.
This short biography not only provides interesting information about a remarkable Canadian, but also sheds
light on nineteenth century industrial practices, fashions and life-styles. In *The Canadians* series.

19 BASSETT, JOHN and PETRIE, A. ROY. *Allan Napier
    MacNab;* illus. Don Mills, Ont.: Fitzhenry and
    Whiteside, 1974. Paper. (6-8) B
    From a young midshipman in the War of 1812 to a
fighting colonel who suppressed the Rebellion of Upper
Canada in 1832; from a prisoner jailed for debts in
York to proud owner of Dundurn Castle in Hamilton; from
Tory M.P. in the Family Compact to first Prime Minister
of the United Canadas; and finally, entertainer of
Royalty—the story of MacNab's remarkable life is at
last told for younger readers. Better writing would
have made it more enjoyable, but it does fill a need in
Canadian libraries for more background material on
colourful personalities in our history. In the series
The Canadians.

20 BASSETT, JOHN and PETRIE, A. ROY. *Laura Secord:
    A Canadian Heroine;* illus. by Frank Leconte.
    Don Mills, Ont.: Fitzhenry and Whiteside, 1974.
    Paper. (6-8) B
    Details of Laura Secord's historic walk from
Queenston to Beaver Dams form the basis of this short
biography. There is, however, additional information
on the settlement of the Niagara area, events in the
War of 1812 and the Rebellion of 1832. Although the
historical background is authentic, dialogue has been
invented, supposedly to enliven the text. Black and
white illustrations, including drawings by C. W. Jeffreys, diagrams and maps are sprinkled throughout the
book. This is an additional source of reference on
Canadian history for older children. Questions for
discussion may be useful for teachers as well. In the
series *The Canadians*.

21 BASSETT, JOHN and PETRIE, A. ROY. *William Hamilton
    Merritt;* illus. Don Mills, Ont.: Fitzhenry and
    Whiteside, 1974. Paper. (6-8) B
    Merritt is known chiefly as the builder of the
Welland Canal, but this somewhat fictionalized biography
reveals other aspects of his active life. A member of
a Loyalist family who arrived near the present city of
St. Catharines in 1796, young Merritt fought at the

battles of Stoney Creek and Lundy's Lane before settling down as a mill-owner in the Short Hills. It was
his interest in shipping wheat more cheaply that led to
his forming a company to build the Welland Canal. The
text is readable as well as informative, and accompanied by numerous photographs and drawings. Questions for
research and discussion following the chapters makes
this book useful for classrooms as well as individual
reading. In *The Canadians* series.

22 BEAUDRY, LINDSAY. *Kawin: a Book of Indian Crafts*;
       illus. Don Mills, Ont.: Fitzhenry and White-
       side, 1977. Paper. (6-8) *
       A large colourful paperback prepared in conjunc-
tion with Ahbenoojeyug, Inc., a program for native
Indian children living in Toronto. It provides large
clear diagrams and simple instructions for making models
of wigwams and longhouses, for many different items of
Ojibway and Iroquois clothing, dyes, designs, rock
paintings and beading. Crafts range from simple to complex with suggestions for related activities and class
projects. A good addition to a library collection on
native peoples.

23 BENHAM, LESLIE and BENHAM, LOIS. *The Heroine of
       Long Point*; illus. by Vernon Mould. Toronto:
       Macmillan of Canada, 1963. (4-6) F
       In 1854 the schooner *Conductor* ran aground at
Long Point on Lake Erie during a gale. The crew was
rescued by the wife of a trapper living on Long Point,
although the waters were freezing and she couldn't
swim. A fictionalized version of this true incident is
re-told for young readers. The writing is uneven and
stilted at times but the story, told from the viewpoint
of a cabin boy aboard the schooner, has action, suspense and heroism. Large-print format, with simple
vocabulary.

— BENHAM, LOIS. *The Heroine of Long Point*.
       See ON 23

24 BLAKE, VERSCHOYLE and GREENHILL, RALPH. *Rural Ontario;* illus. Toronto: University of Toronto Press, 1969. o.p. (7-8)

A handsome photographic record of the rural Ontario landscape and 19th century architecture that is fast disappearing with urbanization. Greenhill's full page photographs in black and white reflect distinctive buildings, homes and surroundings. The text contains two essays which explain how the characteristic appearance of the Ontario countryside evolved from a social, as well as architectural, viewpoint. Brief, well-spaced annotations explain the pictures. Although most children will find the text too difficult, the photographs and captions make rewarding reading and will enhance the enjoyment of driving through the Ontario countryside.

25 BRADFORD, KARLEEN. *A Year for Growing;* illus. by Charles Hilder. Richmond Hill, Ont.: Scholastic-Tab, 1977. (5-8) F

A warm, appealing story of a city boy who goes to live with his grandfather on a farm near Owen Sound, Ontario. The conflict between the boy's ideals of wildlife conservation and the old man's enjoyment of hunting and fishing is resolved when the two go on a canoe trip to the Temagami region. Although the theme is moralistic, young readers will enjoy the believable characters who demonstrate respect for nature and wildlife amidst the realities of every day life.

26 BRENNAN, TERRENCE. *The Timber Trade in the Ottawa Valley;* illus. Toronto: Ginn, 1971. Paper. (5-8)

A sturdy well-illustrated booklet providing historical material on the logging industry in north-eastern Ontario. It describes the shanties and conditions in the logging camps, the logging operations from axing the trees to getting the log booms downriver to Quebec. A wide variety of illustrative material is used along with the simple text to provide answers to questions asked at the ends of the short chapters. Useful for classroom or independent study. From the series *Ginn Studies in Canadian History.*

27 BRIMACOMBE, PHILIP. *The Story of Oakville Harbour.*
(Halton County Series.) Cheltenham, Ont.:
Boston Mills, 1975. Paper. (6-8)
A brief, but detailed history of what is now the
Oakville area—from an Indian Reserve at the mouth of
the Sixteen Mile Creek to a yacht-building centre today.
Although the few photographs are of poor quality, the
wealth of information provided would be most useful for
detailed studies of the history of Ontario water transportation and early industries, as well as local history studies.

28 BROOKS, BILL. *The Colour of Ontario;* illus.
Willowdale, Ont.: Hounslow, 1977. (4-7)
Writer-photographer Brooks has produced this pictorial essay on his home-province. Impressive colour
photographs, many full-page, are grouped under headings
such as "Frontier," "Breadbasket," "Cottage Country."
Captions describing the photographs include personal
observations and experiences, anecdotes, as well as
suggestions for places to visit. Intended only as a
loving over-view of the province and its character, the
book provides pleasant browsing material and relaxed
reading.

29 BROWN, RON. *Ghost Towns of Ontario;* illus.
Langley, B.C.: Stagecoach, 1978. Paper.
(7-8) R
Each chapter of this book concentrates on a
specific region in Southern Ontario, describing ghost
villages and towns in that region and the stages in
Ontario's history which caused their rise and fall.
With an extensive bibliography, black and white photos
and an index, this is an extra source of reference on
local history for Ontario libraries.

30 BURNFORD, SHEILA. *The Incredible Journey;* illus.
by Masaru Shimizu. Toronto: Hodder and Stoughton, 1976 (c1960). (6-8) F *
An attractive new edition of an animal story
that has become a classic in children's literature. An
old bull-terrier, a Labrador and Siamese cat, leave

their temporary boarding home in Northern Ontario to
return to their real home. The slow perilous journey
of 250 miles is indeed incredible as is the final reunion with their human family. Fine illustrations enhance the text. A Canadian Library Association Book
of the Year (1963).

31 BURNS, FLORENCE M. *William Berczy;* illus. Don
    Mills, Ont.: Fitzhenry and Whiteside, 1977.
    Paper. (6-8) B
    The unpublicized role of William Berczy, as co-
founder of the city of Toronto, is brought to light in
this paperback from *The Canadians* series. The story of
this well-educated German who brought a group of immigrants to York in hope of receiving a land grant, only
to suffer hardships, and disappointments has been well
researched. Accompanied by old portraits, sketches and
paintings, and questions in the margin for further discussion and research, this biography provides good background reading for study of 18th century pioneer life
in Upper Canada.

32 CALLAGHAN, MORLEY. *Luke Baldwin's Vow;* illus. by
    Michael Poulton Toronto: Macmillan, 1974
    (c1948). (5-8) F *
    A re-issue of a story by one of Canada's best-
known authors. Young orphan Luke goes to live with his
childless uncle and aunt in Collingwood on Georgian Bay.
When his uncle decides to destroy an old half-lame and
blind dog, Luke strives to save the dog's life. In so
doing he learns to understand his outwardly-practical
uncle. A moving, poignant story, well-told, with the
universal theme of growing up.

33 CAMPBELL, SUSAN. *Fort William: Living and Working
    at the Post;* illus. Ontario Ministry of Culture
    and Recreation, 1976. Paper. (7-8)
    This large paperback was produced by the Fort
William Archeological Project for the reconstruction of
the Fort, but is also aimed at the general reader.
There is interesting historical information on the early
fur-traders, North-West Company, the role of Fort

William and its management, using anecdotes and diaries. It ends with a description of the city today, renamed Thunder Bay. Black and white illustrations add to its usefulness as a reference source of local history.

34 CANADA-ONTARIO-RIDEAU-TRENT-SEVERN STUDY COMMITTEE. *Optimum Recreational Development in the Quinte-Kingston Area.* Supplementary Report of Courts, Canada-Ontario-Rideau-Trent-Severn, reprinted 1975. R

The appendices in this well-researched report, more than the report itself, provide useful material for teachers and students studying that area. They comprise a concise general history plus excellent fold-out maps, photographs and a bibliography. An inexpensive source of reference for libraries in south-eastern Ontario.

35 CARROLL, JAMES. *Power at Niagara;* illus. Toronto: Ginn, 1971. Paper. (5-7)

This large, slim booklet is one of a series of units in social studies designed for classroom use. The text is in large print and simply written, but the emphasis is on illustration. Coloured maps, diagrams, graphs, tables and photos illustrate how power is generated, power development on the Niagara River, Ontario Hydro's power grid and sources of electrical energy in Ontario. There are questions for discussion, and suggested follow-up activities and additional research. A good teaching aid for this topic.

36 CARROLL, JAMES A. and MILBERRY, LARRY. *Canadian Communities;* illus. Toronto: Ginn, 1975. Paper. (4-6)

Fourteen different communities are featured in this colourful paperback, designed as a social studies text. Black Creek Pioneer Village in Ontario is used as an example of a pioneer community, Toronto as a metropolitan community and Ottawa, the capital city. Emphasis is on pictorial content to stimulate interest and class discussion with photographs, maps, graphs and collages, mostly in colour. The text is minimal, mostly confined to questions, suggested activities and topics for further research. In the series *Ginn World Studies*.

37 CARSON, LORNA. *Assembling Automobiles at Oakville;* illus. Toronto: Ginn, 1968. (5-7)

A large illustrated booklet designed for classroom use. The Ford Motor Company at Oakville provides a case-study in manufacturing where automation is used. It studies Oakville's location and the process of making cars. There are questions for further study arising from the photographs and diagrams as well as the text. From the series *Sample Studies of Canada*, sold in packages of five copies of a title.

38 CLEAVER, NANCY. *How the Chipmunk Got Its Stripes;* illus. by Laszlo Gal. Toronto: Clarke, Irwin, 1973. (2-4) F

A simple but beautiful telling of an Algonkian legend for young readers. Because of her devotion to a small boy, a red squirrel is rewarded by Manitou, who gives her stripes. Thus, she becomes the first chipmunk. Soft, appealing illustrations in brown and white complement the text.

39 *The C.N. Tower Guidebook: The World's Tallest Book about the World's Tallest Free-standing Structure.* Toronto: Greey de Pencier, 1975. (5-8)

This 22 inch tall book, provides an appropriate tribute to the Toronto landmark by folding out to create a tower itself. It gives much information about the construction of the tower, its uses, extra tourist attractions, as well as a history of tall structures from the time of Egyptian pyramids. Awkward for library shelving but worth the effort.

40 COATSWORTH, DAVID. *Farmers of the East: Huron Indians;* illus. Toronto: Ginn, 1975. Paper. (5-8)

An illustrated fictionalized account of a family of Ouendat (Huron) Indians in the 16th century. Facts about family life, farming and other occupations, cere-

monies and legends, are woven into the simple, brief
text. Excellent illustrative material in colour and
black and white, along with questions for discussion
and research, make this slim booklet a good resource
for classroom study and history projects.

41 COLLINS, PAUL. *Hart Massey;* illus. Don Mills,
       Ont.: Fitzhenry and Whiteside, 1977. Paper.
       (6-8) B
       Supposedly a biography of Hart Massey, this
actually covers three generations of a remarkable family who contributed much to Toronto and Canadian life
in the last century. Daniel founded the farm implement
business; son Hart built Massey Hall, Hart House, Fred
Victor Mission; and grandson Vincent became governor-
general. Although the stilted writing style and depar-
tures from chronological sequence may deter some readers, the book is concise, well-researched and provides
additional background material on the economic and
social history of Ontario. In the **series** *The Canadians.*

42 *Come with Us: Children Speak for Themselves;* illus.
       Toronto: Women's Ed. Press, 1978. (3-5) *
       Canadian school children express themselves on a
variety of themes in this fascinating collection of
essays and paintings. Different immigrant children
describe why they came to Canada, and colourful drawings illustrate the places they came from. Other children describe their streets and schools as well as themselves. Most of the writers and artists are children
living in Ontario. The attractive format and contents
will appeal to children, especially those in multi-
cultural areas.

43 CONNOR, RALPH (pseud.). *Glengarry School Days.*
       Toronto: McClelland and Stewart, 1975. (Orig.
       pub. in 1902.) Paper. (7-8) F
       Life in Glengarry was harsh and demanding; so
was the domini; so were the parents. It might seem
that youngsters in this dour small new-world Scottish
community had little time for fun. But like all children everywhere, they found fun and joy in swimming

holes and spelling bees, and all the half-forgotten
kinds of homespun gaiety. They worked hard; they
played hard; and they had a life that many might now
envy. This classic work is a welcome reminder of Upper
Canada's log-cabin past.

44 COOK, LYN. *The Secret of Willow Castle;* illus. by
     Kelly Clark. Toronto: Macmillan of Canada,
     1966. (4-6) F
     The setting is Napanee, Ontario in the year 1834.
Eleven-year-old Henrietta is bored with her sheltered
life until she discovers a secret friend and receives a
precious gift from her cousin, John A. Macdonald. The
historical background is accurate, introducing some of
the social history of the period, but the story moves
from event to event without any real plot or characterization. The idea of a heroine instead of a hero in a
book of Canadian historical fiction is, however, a
pleasant change.

45 COOK, WILLIAM E. *Milton: Welcome to Our Town;*
     illus. Cheltenham, Ont.: Boston Mills, 1977.
     Paper. (7-8)
     Well-researched facts, anecdotes, old photo-
graphs and paintings are combined to trace the history
of Halton County as well as the town of Milton, once
its seat of government. Although the book offers a
glimpse of small town life in Ontario in the 19th century, it would be of most use to students in that area
studying local history. The same publisher has produced other local histories in paperback.

46 CORKUM, NADJA. *How Canada Got Its Capital;* illus.
     by Emma Hesse. Toronto: McClelland and Stewart
     in association with the National Capital Commis-
     sion, 1975. Paper. (4-7) *
     An attractive, well-written account of the his-
tory of Ottawa, Ontario. The author uses fascinating
details to describe Champlain's voyage up the Ottawa
River, a pioneer family's trek to the area, Colonel
By's efforts to build a canal, the lumbering years, and
the choice by Queen Victoria of Ottawa as Canada's

298

capital. The book is well-illustrated with bold
coloured and black and white drawings, and should be in
every Canadian elementary school library.

47 CRAIG, JOHN. *No Word for Goodbye;* illus. by Harri
Aalto. Toronto: Peter Martin, 1969. Paper.
(6-8) F *
There is no happy ending to this story of a summer friendship. Ken is a boy who has just about everything he needs. His friend Paul, an Ojibway, has almost nothing, and what little remains to his people is
threatened by prejudice and "progress." The friends do
all they can to save Paul's home, but they are defeated.
Paul's family slips away in silence, for the Ojibways
have no word for goodbye . . . but Ken, and the reader
remember. Well-written and realistic.

48 CRAIG, JOHN. *The Noronic Is Burning;* illus. Don
Mills, Ont.: General Pub., 1976. Paper. (7-8)
On September 16, 1949, the Noronic, the largest
passenger ship on the Great Lakes, was in Toronto harbour from Detroit. Suddenly, fire broke out and 118
passengers lost their lives. The events surrounding
this disaster are dramatically told, using eye-witness
accounts. The controversy about the captain, the accu-
sations of survivors, and the dismaying facts on safety
equipment and procedures are all carefully documented
by the author. Thirty pages of black and white photographs are included. The book portrays a significant
but tragic chapter in the history of Great Lakes
shipping.

49 CRAIG, JOHN. *Who Wants to Be Alone?* (originally
entitled *Zach*). Richmond Hill, Ont.:
Scholastic-Tab, 1972. Paper. (7-8) F
Three young people have had it with the world
they live in. Zach, a young Indian from Northern
Ontario, wants to find his lost tribe; Matsun, an American black athlete opts out of the society that has
used and abused him; D.J., "a poor little rich girl,"
is running away from a life that gives everything and
nothing. Somehow, half-unwillingly, the three find

that they are becoming a family, and as the title says, nobody "wants to be alone." Although the mood is of the 60's, with communal living the solution, many of the people and places ring true.

50 CRAIG, JOHN. *The Wormburners;* illus. by Alan
      Daniel. Richmond Hill, Ont.: Scholastic-Tab,
      1975. Paper. (6-8) F
      Everybody loves a story of losers who finally come out on top. *The Wormburners* is a term of affectionate mockery given to the Wedley Park Athletic Association, a band of inner-city kids who run fast enough to scorch the worms in the ground. They haven't had much of a chance in life so far, but now they are shooting for the top—to be national champion cross-country runners. The city is really Toronto; the time is more of less now; the kids are any kids.

51 CRAWFORD, MICHAEL. *1837: Mackenzie.* (Jackdaw
      Series) Toronto: Clarke Irwin, 1967. (6-8)
      Designed "to spark a sense of the presence of history," this large folder is filled with facsimiles of despatches, newspaper clippings, broadsheets and lithographs from the period of the Rebellion in Upper Canada. Interesting, non-text book materials for teachers and students.

52 CREIGHTON, LUELLA. *The Hitching Post;* illus. by
      Tom McNeely. Toronto: McClelland and Stewart,
      1969. (4-5) F
      Magic and wishes-come-true are the ingredients of this refreshing tale of a poor little girl and a hitching post in the shape of a horse's head. Cecilia hopes that the horse's magic will somehow bring her mother back to the little Ontario village. But the magic really comes from eccentric old Mr. Merriweather, who bequeaths her the hitching post after his death, producing wondrous results. An improbable plot, yes, but the author has used a little magic herself to create empathy for the heroine and suspension of disbelief for the fairy-tale ending.

53 CUMMING, H. G. *The Moose in Ontario;* illus. Toronto: Ontario Ministry of Natural Resources, 1972. Paper. (6-8)

An information booklet on one of Ontario's greatest wildlife assets. Organized under headings such as, description, history and occurrence, habits, and predators, the text is clear and straightforward. Black and white photos are of poor quality, but tables, graphs, and a map are included. Useful vertical file material for natural science projects.

54 CURNOE, W. GLEN. *Around London 1900-1950; A Picture History;* illus. London, Ont.: Curnoe, 1973. o.p. Paper. (4-7)

Black and white photos and views from old postcards are annotated to recreate the earlier days of this city. The attractive format of cut-out illustrations and large type should appeal to nostalgia buffs and students interested in their local history. It includes information on architecture, transportation, leisure activities, posters and packaging.

55 DAGG, ANNE INNIS. *Mammals of Ontario;* illus. by Roslyn A. Alexander. Waterloo, Ont.: Otter, 1974. (4-8)

A particularly useful book on wildlife in the province. The attractive format provides two pages for each animal. A clear black and white drawing heads one page, with simple concise information below arranged under headings of measurement, weight, characteristics, size of litter, habitat and food. The opposite page gives an outline map showing the animal's geographical location, and interesting additional information on current research concerning the animal. The index lists the topics discussed in the research items. A must for all school and public libraries in Ontario.

56 DAMANIA, LAURA. *Egerton Ryerson;* illus. Don Mills, Ont.: Fitzhenry and Whiteside, 1975. Paper. (6-8) B

A brief straightforward biography of the founder of the educational system of Upper Canada. Methodist minister, first principal of Victoria College, writer,

301

editor, publisher—Ryerson was a driving force in religion, politics and free general education, in mid-
nineteenth century. This slim paperback is liberally
sprinkled with portraits, paintings, archival photographs and reproductions of newspaper clippings and
letters. A useful source of information on an important figure in Ontario's history. From the series
The Canadians.

57 DARLING, CHRISTOPHER and FRASER, JOHN. *Kain &
    Augustyn: A Photographic Study;* illus. Toronto:
    Macmillan of Canada, 1977. Paper. (6-8) P *
    The artistry of Canada's most exciting team of
ballet dancers, Karen Kain and Frank Augustyn, is cele-
brated in this superb collection of photographs. It
includes glimpses of the pair rehearsing, performing,
and relaxing, with quotes on their feelings and opinions
about themselves and their work. This story of the
first international stars of the Canadian Ballet should
be in every school and public library.

58 DAVIDSON, WILLIAM. *Return to Rainbow Country.* Don
    Mills, Ont.: Paperjacks, 1975. Paper. (5-7) F
    This story of wilderness adventure is closely
tied to the successful T.V. series "Rainbow Country"
set in the glorious Ontario woodland. It has the pace
and excitement—and the wild improbability—of a T.V.
segment. A boy's search for his lost father runs a
whirlwind course to a neat, if unhappy, conclusion.
All of it makes for pleasant, if unmemorable, story.

— DOBSON, MURRAY. *The Firefighter.* See ON 150

— DOBSON, MURRAY. *The Policeman in Your Community.*
   See ON 149

— DOWNIE, JOHN. *Honor Bound.* See ON 60

59 DOWNIE, MARY ALICE. *Dragon on Parade;* illus. by
    Mary Lyn Baker. Toronto: Martin, 1974. (1-3) F
    A picture story book of lazy summer holidays in
Bayfield, near Goderich, Ontario. Three sisters dress
up as a dragon and march in the Lions Club Parade.

Their cardboard and curtain creation wins them a special prize. Appealing sepia-coloured illustrations compensate for the somewhat predictable story.

60 DOWNIE, MARY ALICE and DOWNIE, JOHN. *Honor Bound;* illus. by Jean Hoffman. Toronto: Oxford University Press, 1971. (5-8) F *
A Loyalist family, in 1784, forced to leave their comfortable home in Philadelphia, make their painful way to refuge in Canada at Cataraqui, now Kingston. There are plenty of surprises and dangers, including a hair-raising canoe trip on the St. Lawrence River. A vivid picture of a difficult and suspenseful time of divided loyalties. A Canadian award winning book. (C.A.C.L.)

61 DUNHAM, MABEL. *Kristli's Trees;* illus. by Selwyn Dewdney. Toronto: McClelland and Stewart, 1974. Paper. (4-7) F *
A welcome reprint of the 1949 Canadian Book of the Year for Children, this is a warm, intimate portrayal of Mennonite family life near Kitchener in the 1940's. The author, a Kitchener librarian, reveals her knowledge and respect for these people as she related the everyday events in the life of eight-year-old Kristli. The writing style appropriately reflects the simplicity and quiet integrity of the Mennonite way of life.

62 ENGEL, MARION. *My Name Is Not Odessa Yarker;* illus. by Laszlo Gal. Toronto: Kids Can, 1977. (3-5) F
Geraldine is so upset when her nine-year-old brother announces at school that her name is now Odessa Yarker, she is driven to desperate action. A shouted announcement from atop an equestrian statue of Queen's Park, Toronto, plus a written, notarized statement denying the name change satisfied everyone, including herself. A slight, humorous story with appealing pencil drawings.

63 EPP, HENRY. *Agriculture in Southern Ontario;* John
   Koegler, gen. ed.; illus. Don Mills, Ont.:
   Dent, 1972. (7-8)
   Designed for classroom use in social studies
programs, this short book provides brief information,
maps, graphs, tables and charts on the topics of climate, vegetation, and soils, with suggested exercises.
It then examines five case studies of farming—green-
houses, dairy, beef, orchard, and one poor farm, in no
particular location. Exercises for further research
and discussion are also included. No table of contents
or index. Listed in *Canadian Geography Resources*
series.

— FEATHER, DONALD. *Fort York.* See ON 193

64 FILEY, MICHAEL. *Passengers Must Not Ride on
   Fenders;* illus. Toronto: Musson, 1974.
   (6-8) P
   A splendid illustrated history of Toronto and
its streetcars, an important part of the city's transportation. The author has written an informative,
entertaining text combining anecdotes, quotes, newspaper accounts and official reports. He tells the
story of horse-drawn omnibuses operating in 1849 as
private enterprise, to the fleet of "red rockets" still
maintained by the Toronto Transit Commission as the
best transit vehicle ever produced. The numerous,
large sepia-coloured photographs, advertisements and
clippings also reveal the character and growth of the
city itself.

65 FILEY, MICHAEL. *A Toronto Album; Glimpses of the
   City That Was;* illus. Toronto: University of
   Toronto Press, 1970. Paper. (7-8) P
   A selection of black and white photographs from
Filey's collection that illustrate the city's evolution
from 1860 to 1950. Well-written captions provide concise historical information enlivened with quotes and
anecdotes. Many of the pictures deal with transportation and are therefore repetitious, but scenes of mud
streets, beaches, amusement parks and the waterfront

illustrate the changes in the urban fabric. Young and new Torontonians may derive a sense of the city's history by examining these visual archives in the convenient paperback format.

66 FILEY, MICHAEL. *Trillium and Toronto Island;* illus. Toronto: Martin, 1976. Paper. (6-8)
This large paperback, written by a Toronto historian, recounts the early history of Toronto Island, from its origin as a peninsula. Black and white drawings illustrate many successive ferry boats used through the early years, and photographs show later ones, including the Trillium. Brief text and photos describe life and activity in the island and the restoration of the Trillium as a sightseeing vessel.

67 FILEY, MICHAEL. *Wish You Were Here: Great Postcards of Early Toronto;* illus. Toronto: Greey de Pencier, 1977. Paper. (5-8) P
A collection of sixteen postcards, showing Toronto prior to World War I. Perforated for separation, the cards come with extra pages which relate interesting tid-bits of historical information about the subjects depicted. A section, "Here Today," points out the different aspects of the city that make it distinctive in North America. Because of the format, librarians might prefer to place the cards in the vertical file.

68 FORRESTER, JAMES. *Making Steel in Hamilton;* illus. Toronto: Ginn, 1967. Paper. (5-8)
Designed for classroom use, this colourful booklet introduces Canada's steel capital, Hamilton, Ontario. The accent is on illustration, with a minimal text in large print and simple vocabulary. Photographs, mostly small and black and white, are unimpressive but there a are good clear diagrams of furnaces and shaping steel. Following each short section is a set of suggested activities and research ideas. From the series *Ginn Sample Studies of Canada.*

69 FORRESTER, JAMES and OTHERS. *Longhouse to Blast Furnace: Growth of an Industrial Community;* illus. Don Mills, Ont.: Fitzhenry and Whiteside, 1973. Paper. (4-5)
The city of Hamilton, past and present, is examined as an example of industrial growth in this attractive social studies text. Using both printed and visual information on each page, students are asked to answer questions, solve problems or puzzles, do further research, before proceeding to the next units. These include Indian life in the Hamilton area, Hamilton as a mill town, and now as a centre for steel manufacturing. The text is simple and profusely illustrated with paintings, photographs, diagrams, charts and maps. Listed in the series *Man in His World*.

70 FREEMAN, BILL. *Shantyman of Cache Lake;* illus. Toronto: Lorimer, 1976. Paper. (6-8) F *
A fast-moving adventure story of a 14-year-old boy and his younger sister in an Ottawa Valley lumber camp 100 years ago. The plot revolves around the attempt to get a union formed among the Shantymen, and the children's growing awareness that their father's pro-union efforts had been a factor in his "accidental" death at the camp. Details of life at the lumber camp are skilfully woven into the story. If the book reveals a pro-union bias, it is also pro-feminist, for the girl is protrayed taking an equal role with her brother in camp work and activities. Winner of the Canada Council Award for Children's Literature in 1976.

71 FROOM, BARBARA. *Ontario Turtles;* illus. Toronto: Ontario Ministry of Natural Resources, 1975. Rev. ed. Paper. (6-8)
Eight species of turtles native to Ontario are fully covered in this large booklet. There are page-long essays on each species with black and white illustrations on the opposite page. A short, final chapter discusses turtles as pets, and a bibliography follows. Readable and inexpensive.

72 FRYER, MARY BEACOCK. *Escape: Adventures of a Loyalist Family;* illus. by Stephen Clarke. Don Mills, Ont.: Dent, 1976. Paper. (6-8) F
A fictionalized account of a Loyalist family of eight who were forced to flee from Schnectady, New York, to Canada in 1789. The story of their courage and resourcefulness amid constant danger makes exciting reading, especially since the Toronto author is a descendent of that family.

73 GENTILCORE, LOUIS, ed. *Ontario;* (Studies in Canadian Geography Series). Toronto: University of Toronto Press, 1972. Paper. (8-)
An impressive collection of articles by different experts on aspects of Ontario, such as environment, settlement, economy and urban network. Accompanying maps show population, land form, temperatures. Because the approach is scholarly and the vocabulary at a high school level, it could be used only by more mature students capable of in-depth research.

74 GILLARD, WILLIAM and TOOKE, THOMAS. *The Niagara Escarpment: From Tobermory to Niagara Falls;* illus. Toronto: University of Toronto Press, 1974. Paper. (7-8) F R
This history of the escarpment is divided into three parts, the first dealing with the area from Tobermory to Owen Sound; the second, Meaford to Dundas; and the third, Hamilton to Niagara Falls. Although little of the geology is given, it provides details of early settlements, and interesting black and white photographs of scenes, buildings, historic homes. Since the style of writing is ordinary, the book would be of most interest to students who live in or near the Niagara Escarpment area, as well as Bruce Trail hikers.

75 GRAY, MARGARET; RAND, MARGARET and GREEN, LOIS. *A. J. Casson;* illus. Agincourt, Ont.: Gage, 1976. (7-8) R
This Toronto-born artist was a member of both the "blasphemous" Group of Seven and the ultra-conservative Ontario Society of Artists in the crucial years

after 1920. The authors have written an interesting
biography, with quotes from interviews with the artist.
Coloured reproductions of many of his paintings are
included, which feature Ontario settings done in water
colour and oils.

76 GRAY, MARGARET and OTHERS. *Carl Schaefer*; illus.
    Agincourt, Ont.: Gage, 1977. (7-8)
    The works of Carl Schaefer are to be found in
many prestigious collections, both public and private.
He is a regional artist and through him the scenes
familiar to Southern Ontarians have been made available
to the world. Young readers may not be equal to the
text of this slim volume, but the illustrations of
Schaefer's work speak for themselves and will fascinate
students of artistic bent.

— GREEN, LOIS. *A. J. Casson*. See ON 75

77 GREENE, ALMA. *Tales of the Mohawks*; illus. by R. G.
    Miller. Don Mills, Ont.: Dent, 1975. (7-8) F
    Here are some of the stories told on the Six
Nations Reserve near Brantford, Ontario, as recalled by
a Mohawk clan mother. They are divided by subject and
feature beautiful pencil drawings by an Indian artist.
Because the stories show the influence of the white
man's culture and tradition on Indian folklore, the
book would be of particular interest to older students
of folklore.

— GREENHILL, RALPH. *Rural Ontario*. See ON 24

78 GUILLET, EDWIN. *Pioneer Arts and Crafts*; illus.
    Toronto: University of Toronto Press, 1968
    Paper. (7-8)
    Since tourist "pioneer villages" have been devel-
oped, with arts and crafts in action, student interest
in this subject has increased. This reprint of the
author's 1940 publication provides in-depth information
on all kinds of industries and crafts such as spinning
and weaving, maple sugar and soap making, food processing. Quotes from Catharine Trail's valuable source

book, *The Female Emigrant's Guide* (1854), are often
used, as are archival photos and sketches.

79 GUILLET, EDWIN. *Pioneer Days in Upper Canada;*
illus. Toronto: University of Toronto Press,
1964. Paper. (7-8)
A reprint from the author's 1933 book, this
hefty paperback provides a comprehensive social history
of early Upper Canada. Here one finds details of pioneer homes, foods and cooking, maple-sugar making, lumbering, and fishing. Co-operative activities—"Bees,"
amusement and social life in towns and rural districts—
are also described, with comments, anecdotes and quotes.
Black and white reproductions of archival paintings and
sketches are included. Although the approach is scholarly, the vocabulary is not difficult. This has remained one of the definitive sources of reference for
Canadian history.

80 GUILLET, EDWIN. *Pioneer Settlements in Upper
Canada;* illus. Toronto: University of Toronto
Press, 1969. Paper. (7-8)
A reprint of the section "Settlement" from *Early
Life in Upper Canada,* published in 1933. Like the
other two reprinted sections, this noted historian uses
contemporary letters, diaries, newspapers and interviews to recreate the past for younger readers. Six
settlements are traced: Glengarry, Carlton, Peter-
borough, York, Talbot and Detroit River. Numerous archival illustrations add interest to this fine source of
reference on Ontario's social and economic history.

81 GUILLET, EDWIN. *Pioneer Travel in Upper Canada;*
illus. Toronto: University of Toronto Press,
1966. Paper. (7-8)
A section of the book *Early Life in Upper Canada*
by a distinguished historian is reprinted in paperback.
Like *Pioneer Days in Upper Canada* the author uses letters, documents, diaries and newspapers to weave together a detailed but enjoyable account of early travel and
transportation, by water, road and rail. The approach
is scholarly, but the text is aimed toward a student

audience. Authentic portraits, paintings, drawings and
photographs in black and white are included. An indis-
pensable source of reference for teachers and students
of Canadian history.

82 HANCOCK, DAVID and WOODFORD, JIM. *Some Common and
    Uncommon Birds of Ontario and Quebec;* illus.
    Don Mills, Ont.: General, 1973. (3-8)
    Many beautiful colour photographs highlight the
first three parts of this book, which are devoted to
general information on birds, bird groups and bird
watching. Only the final fourth chapter deals with
birds of Ontario and Quebec, illustrated with black and
white photos. It does provide a "life zone" map of the
provinces with brief descriptions of good places for
bird watching, a list of provincial clubs to join and a
check-list of birds of Ontario and Quebec.

83 HARRINGTON, LYN. *Ontario;* illus. Stratford, Ont.:
    Scholar's Choice, 1975. (4-6)
    A general over-view of the history, geography,
resources, industry and people of the province, designed
for younger readers. Because the information is brief
on a wide range of topics, there are a few over-general-
izations, but the text is readable and attractive with
wide margins, and sub-headings, interspersed with numerous colour photographs. There is a handy reference section at the back and a good index.

84 HAWKES, CHRISTOPHER. *Sainte Marie among the Hurons;*
    illus. Toronto: Ginn, 1972. Paper. (5-8)
    A story of a Huron Indian boy at Sainte Marie
serves as an introduction to this brief account of the
French Jesuit settlement, and its tragic ending. The
final chapter "Sainte Marie in the 20th Century" features colour photographs of the restored fort. Although
inserted questions about the text and illustrations are
intended for classroom use, this attractive booklet may
also be used for library reading. From the series *Ginn
Studies in Canadian History.*

85 HAYES, JOHN F. *Wilderness Mission: The Story of Sainte-Marie-Among-the Hurons;* illus. Toronto: Ryerson, 1969. (6-8) *

Well-researched, well-written, well-illustrated, this book does justice to the historical significance of Sainte Marie. It describes the Huron culture prior to the fouding of the mission; its conception and construction which were amazing architectural and engineering achievements; and the tragedy of its short existence. A final chapter details the painstaking research that went into the reconstruction so that visitors to the site near Midland can visualize life in Canada's first European community. Numerous black and white photos enhance the simple, straightforward text.

86 HERAPATH, THEODORA. *Journey into Danger;* illus. by William Wheeler. Richmond Hill, Ont.: Scholastic-Tab, 1974. Paper. (5-8) F

When young Robert is stranded in Quebec in 1751 after missing this ship back to France, he is sent with voyageurs to Fort Toronto. The book describes his journey to the lonely fort, his adventures which include the rescue of a child kidnapped by Indians, and his reunion with his father in Montreal. The plot is slight, the characters one-dimensional, but the historical background is authentic and readers will gain insight into early life in French Canada. A reprint from the 1966 edition.

87 HEWITT, D. F. *Rocks and Minerals of Ontario;* illus. Toronto: Ontario Dept. of Mines and Northern Affairs, 1972. Paper. (6-8)

First printed in 1964, this revised edition provides comprehensive information on all the common minerals of Ontario. An introductory chapter describes the chemical compositon and different physical properties of minerals. Minerals in each group are then briefly described under headings of Properties, Occurrence, and Ontario localities. There are chapters on the geology of Ontario, mining methods, and a history of the mining of different metals in the province. Although no illustrations are in colour, a deterrent for identification,

there are maps, charts and tables which add to its usefulness as a reference source.

88 HINES. R. and OTHERS. *Ontario Fishing Guide;* illus.
   Kitchener, Ont.: Outdoor Pub., 1975. Paper.
   (7-8)
   An oversize, profusely illustrated, paperback
describing everything about fresh-water fishing in
clear simple language. Chapters deal with fishing techniques, fishing sciences, filleting, first-aid, concluding with descriptions of 35 specific fishing areas in
Ontario, with full-page maps. Informative and practical.

89 *A History of the Toronto Islands;* by students of
   Toronto Island Public School; illus. Toronto:
   Coach House, 1972. o.p. Paper. (5-8)
   Undertaken as a school project, this illustrated
history is professionally produced, well-organized and
fascinating to read. Old photographs, maps, sketches
and newspaper clippings enhance short, interesting
articles on the geology of the Islands, the history of
the Island, the lighthouse, the school and other buildings and landmarks. A series of black and white photos
depicting the present-day Island and its school children, are added at the end. A delightful piece of
local history.

90 HOCKING, ANTHONY. *Ontario;* illus. Toronto:
   McGraw-Hill Ryerson, 1978. (6-8) *
   A comprehensive, well-produced textbook on
Ontario—its history, economy, industries, government,
culture, and recreation. There are full colour illustrations, maps, and charts, with a good index. An
excellent source of reference for libraries as well as
classrooms.

91 HOOPLE, E. L. *Medicine Maid: The Life Story of a
   Canadian Pioneer.* Belleville, Ont.: Mika, 1977.
   (6-8) F
   Written by the great, great granddaughter of
the heroine, this book reconstructs the remarkable life-
story of a young Pennsylvania girl captured by Indians.

Although the Indians killed her parents, and separated
her from her brother, she learned to love the adopted
Indian mother who taught her the use of medicinal herbs.
After living with a French family she travels with voyageurs across Lake Erie and Lake Ontario for a reunion
with her uncle. although the writing is somewhat
uneven, the indomitable character of Sarah shines
through.

92 HOWARD, RICHARD, comp. *The War of 1812;* (Jackdaw
      Series). Toronto: Clarke, Irwin, 1972. (7-8)
      A folder containing a collection of reproduced
contemporary materials connected with the War. There
are newspaper clippings, copies of speeches, engravings,
broadsheets and a map of the land war 1811-1815.
Designed to provide teachers and students with non-text-
book materials on the subject.

93 HUNT, JOHN R. *The Search.* Toronto: Macmillan of
      Canada, 1978. Paper. (7-8) F *
      Adventure, mystery, intrigue and suspense are
skilfully blended in this story of a young Toronto
boy's search for his father missing in the Temagami
bush. The fast-paced plot includes fights, break-ins,
chases, kidnapping—even an interview with the Premier
of Ontario—but it all sounds plausible. It also includes a realistic, sympathetic portrayal of an Indian
family who prove worthy of respect. Exciting, worthwhile reading for all young teenagers. One of the
Topliner series.

94 JAMES, DONNA. *Emily Murphy;* illus. Don Mills,
      Ont.: Fitzhenry & Whiteside, 1977. Paper.
      (6-8) B
      The remarkable achievements of Emily Murphy de-
serve wider recognition. This 60 page biography chronicles her career as author, journalist, founder of
Women's Institute, advocate of women's rights, the
first woman judge in Canada, and almost the first woman
senator. Born in Cookstown, educated in Toronto, she
lived mostly in Edmonton, Alberta, where she died in
1933. Like *Emily Stowe* in the same series, *The*

Canadians, this provides additonal information and questions for discussion on the history of women's rights
in Canada.

95 JEFFREYS, C. W. *The Picture Gallery of Canadian
    History;* illus. Toronto: Ryerson Press, 1942.
    (6-8) P *
    Three volumes of a classic series by Ontario's
outstanding historical artist have been combined into
one book. Called "a treasure house of information on
Canada's past," it contains hundreds of pictures of
people, places, events and artifacts, all painstakingly
researched. Detailed annotations for the illustrations
are located at the back of each section, and a good
index is provided for locating specific illustrations
under city, person or event. An invaluable source of
visual information on the history of Canada, including
Ontario.

96 JUDD, WILLIAM WALLACE and SPIERS, J. MURRAY, eds.
    A Naturalist's Guide to Ontario; illus. by
    Sylvia Hahn. Toronto: University of Toronto
    Press for the Federation of Ontario Naturalists,
    1964. (5-8)
    Intended to assist naturalists planning trips in
the province, this book first provides a general description of Ontario's geology, flora, and fauna followed by regional guides arranged alphabetically by
city, town or county. There are more than 300 directions to general locations and descriptions of wild
life typical to the locale. Older students might use
it to study local areas before nature hikes.

97 KENYON, W. A. *Some Bones of Contention: The
    Neutral Indian Burial Site at Grimsby;* illus.
    Toronto: Royal Ontario Museum, 1978. Paper.
    (7-8)
    A pamphlet reprinted from *Rotunda* the R.O.M.
magazine. A museum architect tells the fascinating
story of his discovery of a Neutral Indian burial site,
his citizens' arrest by the Union of Ontario Indians,

and the problems of a winter excavation. Coloured photographs illustrate some of the impressive array of specimens unearthed.

— KERR, MAVIS. *Canoeing in Ontario.* See ON 165

98 KOCH, EDWARD. *Kitchener: A Meat Packing Centre;* illus. Toronto: Holt, Rinehart & Winston, 1971. Paper. (5-7)
A classroom resource booklet that introduces various aspects of this central Ontario city, including factors that contribute to its importance as a centre for meat processing and packing. The brief text is uneven in approach, but there are numerous photographs, diagrams, maps and charts, along with questions, exercises and suggestions for class projects in social studies. From the series *People and Places in Canada.*

99 KORMAN, GORDON. *This Can't Be Happening at Macdonald Hall;* illus. by Affie Mohammed. Richmond Hill, Ont.: Scholastic-Tab, 1978. Paper. (4-7) F
Amazingly, this hilarious story was written by a grade eight student from Thornhill as part of a school project. It describes the adventures of two high-spirited boys at a fictitious boarding school in Toronto. When they are separated by the head master after a series of hi-jinks, their efforts to get together again create even more havoc. Luck and quick wits save them from being expelled. With two few humorous stories in a Canadian setting available for this age group, this is a welcome addition for the paperback collection in children's libraries.

100 KURELEK, WILLIAM. *Lumberjack;* illus. by author. Montreal: Tundra, 1974. (5-8) * #
The award-winning Canadian artist and author describes his experiences as a lumberjack in Northern Ontario and Quebec. The text is most readable, vividly portraying the every-day life in a lumber camp, and his own reactions. Kurelek's realistic paintings, in rich colour, are outstanding and provide an informative, as

315

well as enjoyable, portrayal not only of lumbering, but
of the lumbercamp atmosphere. *Time* magazine called it
"refreshingly simple, grubby and authentic."

101 LAMONT, GRAHAM. *Toronto and York County: A Sample
Study*. Don Mills, Ont.: Dent, 1970. (5-8)
An attractive, well-organized text for classroom
use. It provides clear, factual information on the
three aspects of the area—physical setting, the people
as related to the natural environment, and a study of
Metropolitan Toronto as an urban area. A historical
outline of the settlement of York County is included.
Numerous maps, graphs, diagrams and black and white
photos enhance the text. There are subheadings for
easy reference, and questions in the margins for discussion and research. Teachers should find this book
useful in the planning of field-trips.

102 LANGDON, EUSTELLA. *Pioneer Gardens: At Black
Creek Pioneer Village;* illus. Toronto: Holt,
Rinehart & Winston of Canada, 1972. (4-8) P *
The information for this beautiful full-colour
book is based on research conducted for the planning of
the gradens at Black Creek Pioneer Village, a restored
area north of Toronto. Not only does it describe the
gardens of the pioneers, the plants they grew and how
they used them, but also includes pioneer recipes such
as candied violets, herbal remedies, botanical paintings, old documents, plus stunning photographs taken at
the Village. A delightful glimpse into Ontario's
social history.

103 LANGFORD, CAMERON. *Winter of the Fisher*. Toronto:
Macmillan of Canada, 1971. (7-8) F *
A warm, sensitive, engrossing story of the first
year in the life of a fisher, an animal who dens in the
Northern forest. In the struggle to survive in a harsh
climate the fisher learns that some men, like the beard-
ed trapper, mean destruction, but other men, like the
old Ojibway, can be trusted. The Toronto author, who
died before the book's publication, wrote it as a plea

for freedom and respect for wild creatures, and it is
now considered a classic of animal fiction. A special
reading experience.

104 LEACOCK, STEPHEN. *Sunshine Sketches of a Little
Town;* illus. by Grant Macdonald. Toronto:
McClelland & Stewart, 1948. (7-8) F
   This well-loved work is the great-grandaddy of
all warmhearted, sunlit nostalgia. No little town anywhere ever, was as beautiful as Leacock's imaginary
turn-of-the-century Orillia; but how lovely if they had
been. All the inhabitants featured in the separate
sketches are 'characters' who are not at all objection-
able—any small larcenous instincts are mere jolly
foibles. "Mariposa," Leacock's sunny town, has given
its name to the frame of mind that produces music, festivals, affection and fun.

105 LEE, DENNIS. *Wiggle to the Laundromat;* illus. by
Charles Patcher. Toronto: New Press, 1970.
Paper. (K-3) *
   The first book of nonsense verse published by
Canada's outstanding poet for children. It includes
the enormously popular "Alligator Pie," the title for
his second best-selling book of Canadian nursery rhymes.
This oversize paperback with its bold, zany black and
white drawings is designed not only to delight the ear
and eye but also to create a feeling of Canada, partic-
ularly Ontario. Place names such as Casa Loma, Ottawa,
Nipigon and Temagami crop up in the rollicking rhymes.
A "must" for all Canadian children's libraries along
with Lee's *Alligator Pie, Nicholas Knock,* and *Garbage
Delight.*

106 LITTLE, JEAN. *From Anna;* illus. by Joan Sandin.
New York: Harper & Row, 1972. (6-8) F
   Little Anna, born in Germany, can do nothing
right; her clever brothers and sisters dismiss her as
an awkward baby. Even Mama and Papa have doubts about
their youngest child. But when her problem is at last
diagnosed in Toronto as impaired vision, Anny surprises
even herself with what she can do after all. In spite

317

of the basic improbability of such poor eyesight remaining undetected for so long, this is a charmingly warm story, and one that children with glasses will welcome.

107 LITTLE, JEAN. *Listen for the Singing.* New York:
Dutton, 1977. (6-8) F *
In this sequel to *From Anna,* Anna is older now, and her problems are growing with her. She is faced with the complicated adolescent world, and with the onset of World War II, her German family is made to feel less welcome in their new country than before. But Anna is as dauntless as ever; her family, under pressure, becomes even more close-knit and supportive. Winner of Canada Council award for juvenile literature in 1978.

108 LOGIER, E. B. S. *The Snakes of Ontario;* illus.
Toronto: University of Toronto Press, 1958.
(5-8) *
Almost everything children have wanted to know of our native snakes is included in this well-organized book. Headings, such as "How Do Snakes Travel," "How Do Snakes Feed," " Reproduction," "Hibernation," are in black type and the articles below are written in a conversational style. Descriptions of individual snakes are divided into "harmless" and "venomous" categories, with black and white photos and maps of their range in Ontario. Appendices include a key to Ontario snakes, collecting and preserving specimens, first-aid for snake-bites, and a glossary.

109 LORIMER, JAMES. *The Ex: A Picture History of the Canadian National Exhibition,* illus. Toronto:
James Lewis & Samuel, 1973. (5-8)
An important facet of Toronto life over the years, this annual late-summer exhibition began in 1879. The author not only provides a history of the "Ex" from its early crystal palaces to its trade-show transformation, but also includes many old photographs to demonstrate the fine buildings, grandstand shows, parades, special events, all of which combined to make it a people's festival. Concludes with a chapter on saving Exhibition Park and the Ex for the future.

110 LUNN, JANET. *Double Spell;* illus. by A. M. Calder.
Toronto: Martin, 1968. (4-7) F
Twelve-year-old twins, Jane and Elizabeth, do
not suspect that the antique doll they bought so cheaply on Yonge Street, Toronto, is due to change their
lives. When they suddenly have memories of events in
the 1830's, including a family tragedy, they are caught
up in the mystery and its final solution. The story
moves slowly at first, but tension mounts as the twins
face a repetition of the tragedy. Good Canadian fantasies are rare, but *Double Spell* is one of the better
efforts written in that genre.

111 MC CRAE, MARION. *The Ancestral Roof: Domestic
Architecture of Upper Canada;* illus. Toronto:
Clarke, Irwin, 1963. (6-8) R *
A large, handsome work that not only demonstrates
Ontario's architectural heritage, but also provides a
social history of 1783-1867 period. Lively stories of
the houses, owners and builders are combined with excellent black and white photographs, line drawings, plans
and elevations to demonstrate the five main styles of
architecture and their adaptations in Upper Canada.
The final section deals with the evolution of the house
plan. Excellent for research in social history, as
well as browsing.

112 MC FADDEN, FRED. *Abby Hoffman;* Don Mills, Ont.:
Fitzhenry & Whiteside, 1978. Paper. (5-8) B
Part of the *Superpeople* series, this large
colourful paperback provides a simple but enjoyable
account of one of Canada's star track athletes. From
a nine-year-old girl who made headlines as a star
defenseman for a boy's hockey team in Toronto, to a
gold medallist runner, Abby's life, career, and views
on women in sport are well-covered. Photographs and
drawings accompany the text.

113 MC FARLANE, LESLIE. *The Last of the Great Picnics;*
illus. by Lewis Parker. Toronto: McCelland &
Stewart, 1974. Paper. (5-7) F
The spirit of small town community life in Perth,
Ontario has been successfully recreated in this account
of a memorable Dominion Day picnic in the 1880's. For
young David and his sister there was the excitement of
a man preparing to float in a balloon, brass bands,
lemonade stands, and the mounds of food to be shared
with relatives. There was also an unexpected meeting
with a special guest, Prime Minister Macdonald. Though
the plot is slight, this is a pleasant story of childhood in a by-gone era told by an author who knows how to
to write for children. Originally published in 1965.

114 MC LAUGHLIN, FLORENCE. *First Lady of Upper Canada;*
illus. Toronto: Burns & MacEachern, 1968.
Paper. (7-8) B
The diary of the wife of Governor Simcoe has
been condensed to form a narrative of her life in Upper
Canada. Dialogue has been invented to appeal to younger readers. Although no subsitute for the original
published diary, it does provide an introduction to
this remarkable pioneer woman. Includes reproductions
from Elizabeth Simcoe's paintings and sketches, plus an
index.

115 MAC LENNAN, HUGH. *Rivers of Canada;* illus.
Toronto: Macmillan of Canada, 1974. (6-8) R *
A distinguished Canadian author, and photographer John De Visser have produced this magnificent volume
to describe and illustrate the importance of Canada's
rivers. Of special interest to Ontarians are the two
chapters "The Niagara" and "The Waters of Ontario."
Although most of the text is more suitable for high
school readers, the information is absorbing and the
full-colour photographs are stunning. The book includes reproductions of old paintings and archival
photos.

116 MC MICHAEL CANADIAN COLLECTION. *A Heritage of Canadian Art: The McMichael Collection;* illus. Toronto: Clarke, Irwin, 1976. (7-8) R *
Canadian works of art on display at the famous McMichael collection in Kleinsburg, Ontario, are featured in this handsome volume. More than a catalogue, it is also a vision of Canada with many full-colour reproductions, as well as black and white. Biographies of sixteen Canadian artists are provided, along with chapters on Eskimo and Indian art. A valuable record of our artistic heritage.

117 MALLORY, ENID. *The Green Tiger: James FitzGibbon, Hero of the War of 1812.* Toronto: McClelland & Stewart, 1976. (7-8) B *
History comes alive in this vivid account of the life of James FitzGibbon, an Irish emigrant, who played crucial roles in the War of 1812 and the Rebellion in Upper Canada. Although records of FitzGibbon's activities in 1812 were destroyed, the author includes a dramatic account of the Battle of Queenston Heights, assuming he would be with his idol, Isaac Brock. But stories of his resourcefulness and courage in later events of the war and ruring the Rebellion in 1832, are based on personal and official records. This biography is as absorbing as fiction in action and characterization. Excellent background reading for more mature students and teachers of Canadian history.

118 MANSON, FRED, ed. *Northern Ontario Anthology I.* Cobalt, Ont.: Highway Book Shop, 1977. Paper. (6-8)
Although collections of short stories and poems are not often chosen by young teen-agers, this one has an attractive format and interesting, well-written essays and poetry. The material was selected from hundreds of entries by writers resident, or formerly resident, in Northern Ontario, who describe personal experiences, emotions and ideas about frontier life. Good read-aloud material to convey the spirit and feeling of the North.

—— MIKA, HELMA. *Historic Belleville.* See ON 120

—— MIKA, HELMA. *Railways of Canada.* See ON 121

—— MIKA, HELMA. *United Empire Loyalists.* See ON 122

119 MIKA, NICK. *Ontario of Yesterday;* illus. Belleville, Ont.: Mika, 1971. o.p. (6-8) P R *
This handsome volume is a pictorial record of Ontario's history, as depicted by artists a century ago. Because the 80 full-page illustrations reproduced from the *Canadian Illustrated News* are all hand-screened there was a limited edition of 1000 copies. Clients of libraries fortunate enough to have this book will enjoy reading the simple, informative annotations in large type, as well as savouring the fine quality of the reproductions. There are scenes of Kingston, London, Hamilton, Chatham as well as Ottawa and Toronto.

120 MIKA, NICK and MIKA, HELMA. *Historic Belleville;* illus. Belleville, Ont.: Mika, 1977. (7-8) R
Produced in honour of the city's centennial in 1978, this handsome book provides a complete account of the Centennial celebrations in 1878 as presented in the newspaper at that time, plus a brief history of the city. The coloured reproductions of drawings and postcards of Belleville, with annotations, present an interesting view of life in the Quinte area in the 19th century. Libraries in that area would find it most useful. The same publishers have produced books on other Ontario cities.

121 MIKA, NICK and MIKA, HELMA. *Railways of Canada: A Pictorial History;* illus. Toronto: McGraw-Hill Ryerson, 1972. (7-8)
A well-illustrated account of the epic story of Canada's railways, and the part they played in Canada's development. The text contains first person incidents, excerpts from newspapers, and is illustrated with photos, drawings, maps and posters. There is one chapter devoted to Ontario railway lines. A useful reference for land transportation, and a handsome book for browsing.

322

122 MIKA, NICK and MIKA, HELMA. *United Empire Loyalists: Pioneers of Upper Canada;* illus. Belleville, Ont.: Mika, 1976. (7-8) R

A comprehensive well-researched history of the Loyalists from 1774, their migration to Canada, their new settlements, particularly the Cataraqui settlement. Richly illustrated and produced, it is designed to stimulate the interest of young people in early Ontario history, as well as serve as a valuable source of reference.

—— MILBERRY, LARRY. *Canadian Communities.* See ON 35

123 MINHINNICK, JEANNE. *At Home in Upper Canada;* illus. by John Richmond. Toronto: Clarke, Irwin, 1970. (8-) R

A large, handsome volume aimed at an adult reader. But the wealth of photographs and drawings provide such detailed views of life in early homes of Upper Canada, that it makes a valuable source of reference for interested students if libraries can afford it.

124 MINHINNICK, JEANNE. *Early Furniture in Upper Canada Village;* illus. Toronto: Ryerson Press, in co-operation with St. Lawrence Parks Commission, 1964. Paper. (7-8)

The author, Curator of Furnishings at Upper Canada Village, Morrisburg, Ontario, describes the furniture she collected to recreate life in a small village in Eastern Ontario during the period 1800 to 1837. She covers furniture in the first shelters and work of early coffin, chair and cabinet makers. Photographs are small and in black and white, but the text is concise and informative for students interested in social history.

125 MOON, BARBARA. *The Canadian Shield;* illus. Toronto: Natural Science of Canada, 1970. (6-8) R

This colourful reference book deals with all aspects of this vast area of Pre-Cambrian rock, of which Northern Ontario is a part. Picture stories,

using vivid art work, coloured maps and diagrams, show
the geological beginnings, plant and animal life of the
area, each followed by a chapter of more detailed information with colour photographs. The book also provides
a geologic time scale, a short list of rocks, plants
and animals of the area, plus a good bibliography and
index.

126 MOWAT, FARLEY. *Lost in the Barrens*. Toronto:
McClelland & Stewart, 1956. (5-7) F *
A classic tale of survival against all but insur-
mountable odds. Two boys, a white, city-bred youngster
from Toronto, and an Indian accustomed to the north and
its ways, are marooned together on the barren north-
lands. When the city boy's impatience and determination to conquer the forces of nature almost lead to
tragedy, the Indian teaches him the great lesson of the
wilderness—not to pit puny human strength against so
mighty an apponent. The story of their dangerous winter is exciting and very readable.

127 MOYER, WILLIAM G. *This Unique Heritage: The Story
of Waterloo County;* illus. Kitchener, Ont.:
CHYM Radio, 1971. (7-8)
The author's aim is "to bring to everyone—student, teacher, or interested layman—a concise, but
interesting, compilation of facts about the county from
the years of the Indians to 1930." Although there are
some errors of fact and spelling, this is a most readable and valuable source of reference for students in
Waterloo County who are studying local history. Drawing from old family manuscripts, diaries, letters,
museum documents, and old newspaper files, Moyer has
woven a history of the farming, homemaking, business
life as well as the political and artistic achievements
of the early settlers. There are chapters on the Scots,
the Germans and the Mennonites. Old photographs, drawings and paintings are included.

128 NEERING, ROSEMARY. *Life of the Loyalists.* Don
Mills, Ont.: Fitzhenry & Whiteside, 1975.
Paper. (4-6)
Written for the British Columbia Social Studies
program, this profusely illustrated text book gives
straight historical information as well as a fictionalized narrative of a Loyalist family. Questions are provided at the end of each section for discussion and further research. Sepia coloured drawings, maps, charts,
plus a glossary at the back add to its usefulness for
teachers and students. *Growth of a Nation* series.

129 NICHOLS, RUTH. *The Marrow of the World;* illus. by
Trina Hyman. Toronto: Macmillan of Canada,
1972. (6-8) F *
A magic land shimmering beneath the waters of
Georgian Bay; a quest for the magic that will save the
life of the evil witch-sister of a frightened earth-
girl; and the opposing forces of good and evil combine
in a superior tale of adventure and fantasy. A Canadian Library Association Book of the Year in 1973.

130 NOBLE, IRIS. *The Doctor Who Dared: William Osler.*
Toronto: Copp Clark, 1959. (7-8) B
The achievements of this physician born in Bond
Head, Ontario are fascinating to read. A leading diag-
nostician of his time, a brilliant teacher of medicine,
he also revolutionized the treatment of patients in
hospitals in the 1880's. This fictionalized biography
is well-written, well-researched, and has a comprehensive index.

131 NORTH, STERLING. *Captured by the Mohawks;* illus.
by Victor Mays. Boston: Houghton Mifflin, 1960.
(6-8) #
History reads like fiction in this exciting narrative of Pierre Radisson, the French Canadian Voyageur
who became one of the founders of the Hudson's Bay
Company. Ontario readers will be interested in the
account of the explorations of Radisson and Groseil-
liers up the Ottawa and Mattawa Rivers, and to the
northern shore of Lake Superior. Excellent maps and
illustrations are included.

132 NOVAK, MILAN. *The Beaver in Ontario;* illus. Rev.
ed. Toronto: Ontario Ministry of Natural
Resources, 1976. Paper. (6-8)
A short booklet that contains up-to-date concise
information on this animal under headings such as,
description, life history, habits, ecology and relationship to man. Small illustrations are not in colour,
but there is a map of all beaver colonies in Northern
Ontario sighted by government helicopters.

133 NOWELL, IRIS. *Cross Country Skiing in Ontario.*
Toronto: Greey de Pencier, 1974. Paper. (7-8)
A simple, practical guide on how and where to
ski in this province. Text and diagrams explain equipment, techniques, tips and suggestions. Includes lists
of books and cross country ski clubs in Southern Ontario,
plus regional maps indicating skiing areas, locations
and types of facilities. Useful for beginners in this
increasingly popular sport.

134 OBODIAC, STAN. *The Leafs: The First Fifty Years;*
illus. Toronto: McClelland & Stewart, 1976.
(4-8) *
For the multitude of school-age hockey fans,
especially those of the Toronto Maple Leafs, this large,
illustrated book is bound to be popular. Reluctant
readers who can't manage the text will enjoy examining
the profuse illustrations in full colour and black and
white featuring famous players of the past and present.
This is not only a history of a club that has become an
international sports legend, but also a chronicle featuring facts and figures about the team, individual
players, coaches, executives, sports writers and broad-
casters. Articles by major hockey writers are included,
along with Maple Leaf Gardens archive material.

135 ONTARIO MINISTRY OF CULTURE AND RECREATION.
Hockey—It's Your Game; illus. 1978. (4-6)
A cartoon story of an Ontario boy on a hockey
team is combined with basic information on equipment,
referee's signals and using a hockey stick. There is
also a crossword puzzle on hockey skills. Produced in

association with the Ontario Hockey Council, this
colourful, inexpensive booklet will interest young hockey players and fans—and they are legion in Ontario.

136 ONTARIO MINISTRY OF CULTURE & RECREATION. CITIZENS
INQUIRY BRANCH. *Ontario.* 1977. Paper. (6-8)
All pertinent facts about this province have
been condensed in this unbound, unillustrated booklet.
Separate chapters provide information on the geography,
population, history to 1867, agriculture, natural resources and manufacturing of the province. There is a
list of all Ontario premiers, page-long summaries of
nine Ontario cities, plus a bibliography of fiction and
non-fiction books for students. Excellent for quick
reference. Inexpensive.

137 ONTARIO MINISTRY OF CULTURE & RECREATION. HERITAGE
CONSERVATION DIVISION. *Historical Sketches of
Ontario;* illus. 1976. Paper. (6-8)
A collection of essays on the historical backgrounds of people, places and events for which the
Ontario Government erected historical plaques in 1975.
Each essay gives the location of the plaque, a copy of
the inscription and concise historical information on
events, individuals, industries and enterprises, settlement, structures and institutions. Some archival
photos in black and white are included. The index
makes this a valuable source of quick reference.

138 ONTARIO MINISTRY OF CULTURE & RECREATION. HERITAGE
CONSERVATION DIVISION. *Ontario Historic Sites,
Museums, Galleries and Plaques.* 1977. Paper.
(6-8)
An annotated listing of over 700 places of historic or cultural interest, in alphabetical order by
county, district and region. Each annotation provides
a brief description, the location or address, and the
hours that buildings are open to the public. A useful
book for all children's libraries in Ontario, as well
as a handy guide for history-conscious travellers.

139 ONTARIO MINISTRY OF CULTURE & RECREATION. HISTOR-
ICAL PLANNING AND RESEARCH BRANCH. *Archeology
and the Law in Ontario;* illus. 1976. Paper.
(7-8)
A general information booklet that describes in
simple terms, archeological sites, why we should preserve them and how they are protected by Ontario's
laws. It explains the Ontario Heritage Act of 1975,
licences and permits required, and opportunities in
archeology.

140 ONTARIO MINISTRY OF INDUSTRY & TOURISM. *Heritage
Highways: Ontario and Quebec;* illus. 1977.
(7-8)
A bi-lingual illustrated guide to the Heritage
Highway route from Windsor, Ontario to Quebec's Gaspe
Peninsula, as well as access routes to it. Points of
interest along the way are described and illustrated
with numerous full-colour photographs. A large centre-
fold map of the highways and access routes is included.

141 ONTARIO MINISTRY OF INDUSTRY & TOURISM. *Ontario/
Canada: How It Was, How It Is, How It Will Be;*
illus. 1974. (4-8) P
Stunning colour photographs of Ontario are featured in this glossy booklet designed to attract tourists. Simple, breezy text in large type mentions
places to see, odd facts and tid-bits in no particular
order. Inexpensive browsing material for children who
have just arrived in Ontario.

142 ONTARIO MINISTRY OF NATURAL RESOURCES. *Birds of
Algonquin Provincial Park;* illus. by Howard
Coneybeare. 1977. Paper. (6-8)
The first section of this inexpensive paperback
contains short, interesting accounts of many common
birds seen in the Park, along with attractive pencil
drawings of representative species. Section Two provides an annotated check list of all orders, families
and species of birds sighted in the Park indicating
whether they are common, have bred there, and average

arrival and departure dates. All names are in Latin,
French and English. Useful reference for studies of
Ontario bird life.

143 ONTARIO MINISTRY OF NATURAL RESOURCES. *Mammals of
Algonquin Provincial Park;* illus. by Howard
Coneybeare. 1976. Paper. (6-8)
An attractive but inexpensive paperback that provides useful information on 43 species of animals known
to live in the Park. Mammals are divided in groups—
(with Man listed under Primates!). The articles are
entertaining as well as informative, with beautiful
pencil drawings of animals, their track marks and scats
for identification.

144 ONTARIO MINISTRY OF NATURAL RESOURCES. *Ontario's
Conservation Authorities;* illus. 1977. Paper.
(6-8)
An attractive little booklet that briefly
describes Ontario's need for water management and flood
control, the Conservation Authorities Act in 1946, and
the setting up of 38 regional conservation authorities.
It also describes provincial aid in preserving historic
and natural sites and creating facilities for outdoor
education. A map of Ontario showing the Conservation
Regions is included.

145 ONTARIO MINISTRY OF NATURAL RESOURCES. *A Pictorial
History of Algonquin Provincial Park;* illus.
1978. (6-8)
Fascinating old black and white photographs with
captions show the importance of the area as a centre
for the lumbering industry in the 19th century; the
changes caused by railway access, then the highway; the
lodge era and finally its conversion to a Provincial
Park. Useful background material for study of Ontario's
resources.

146 ONTARIO MINISTRY OF NATURAL RESOURCES. *Reptiles and Amphibians of Algonquin Provincial Park;* illus. by Howard Coneybeare. 1976. Paper. (6-8)

Another useful inexpensive book in the series on wildlife in Algonquin Park. Articles on 14 reptiles and 14 amphibians are not mere descriptions but interesting accounts of their history and habits. Large pencil drawings and a list of reptiles and amphibians by classes and orders in French, Latin and English are also included.

147 ORR, BOBBY. *Bobby Orr: My Game;* with Mark Mulvoy; illus. Toronto: Little, Brown, 1974. (7-8)

Mark Mulvoy, a writer for *Sports Illustrated,* has used taped interviews with Orr to write this book on the famous hockey player from Ontario. Although most of the book explains his technique in hockey, with excellent advice for young players, the first part provides interesting information from parents, friends and coaches of his early years in Owen Sound when he was courted by top professional teams. Excellent action photographs, many in full colour, illustrate Orr's commentary. It also includes the teaching program of exercises and drills used at Orr's hockey camp in Orillia, Ontario. An interesting, as well as informative book for young hockey players and fans.

148 PETERS, JAMES. *A Guide to Understanding Canada;* illus. Toronto: Guiness, 1968. Paper. (6-8)

An attractive text book that seeks "to guide students in understanding the geography of Canada through their own discoveries." Each page contains both printed and illustrative material in the form of coloured photos, maps, charts, diagrams, plus a series of questions. Answers to these may be found in the text, illustrations on the page, or in additional sources. Two chapters, "The Canadian Shield Region" and "Great Lakes and the St. Lawrence Lowlands," relate to Northern and Southern Ontario. A practical, stimulating learning tool.

149 PETERS, JAMES and DOBSON, MURRAY. *The Policeman in Your Community;* illus. Toronto: Dent, 1973. Paper. (1-3)

Excellent colour photographs combined with a simple, large-type text describe the life of a policeman in the Mississauga Police Department. It shows him in a squad car rushing to an accident, a robbery, giving evidence in court, helping a lost child. An attractive, useful booklet for Canadian community studies at the primary level, as well as for individual reading.

150 PETERS, JAMES; PETERS, JULIE and DOBSON, MURRAY. *The Firefighter: In Your Community;* illus. Toronto: Dent, 1974. Paper. (1-3)

During a visit to a firehall, young children watch firemen answer an alarm, and also learn of their other activities—firedrills, maintaining equipment, giving first aid and visiting schools to teach fire prevention. This slim, attractive booklet features colour photos of the Toronto Fire Department with a brief simple text. Useful for young Ontario children studying community helpers.

—— PETERS, JULIE. *The Firefighter.* See ON 150

151 PETRIE, A. ROY. *Alexander Graham Bell;* illus. Don Mills, Ont.: Fitzhenry & Whiteside, 1975. Paper. (7-8) B

Although it was in Boston that Bell's telephone first worked, it was in Brantford, Ontario that his idea was first conceived. This short, somewhat fictionalized biography tells of his family, his many inventions beside the telephone, and of his aerial experiments at Baddeck, Nova Scotia. Numerous black and white photographs and diagrams supplement the text, with occasional questions in the margins for further research. From *The Canadians* series.

—— PETRIE, A. ROY. *Allan Napier MacNab.* See ON 17

—— PETRIE, A. ROY. *Laura Secord: A Canadian Heroine.* See ON 19

152 PETRIE, A. ROY. *Sam McLaughlin;* illus. Don Mills,
Ont.: Fitzhenry & Whiteside, 1975. Paper.
(6-8) B
The author of the life-story of the first president of General Motors of Canada makes use of taped
interviews with McLaughlin before his death. Mr. Petrie
fills in the gaps with his own narration of events in
McLaughlin's life. Although the transcribed interviews
reveal the man's lively personality and his viewpoints,
the alternation of writing techniques may be confusing
for some young readers. However, the rise from carriage-
maker in Oshawa to owner of the first motor car company
in Canada, and finally president of G.M., is an interesting success story. The book also covers his interest
in sailing, racing horses and fishing, plus his philan-
thropic works. Illustrations include a number of pictures of antique cars. The book is another in the series
The Canadians.

—— PETRIE, A. ROY. *William Hamilton Merritt.*
See ON 21

153 POLK, JAMES. *Wilderness Writers;* illus. Toronto:
Clarke, Irwin, 1972. (6-8) B
With new interest in our vanishing wilderness
comes renewed interest in three Canadian writers who
developed a new, realistic form of animal stories—
Ernest Thompson Seton, Charles G. D. Roberts and Grey
Owl. This book contains short biographies of each, with
an introductory chapter on the new form. The author emphasizes their childhood, interest in nature and backgrounds, of which Ontario plays a part. Enjoyable reading for nature-loving children. Part of the *Canadian
Portrait* series.

—— POWELL, ANN. *The Travels of Ms Beaver.* See ON 11

—— RAND, MARGARET. *A. J. Casson.* See ON 75

154 RAY, JANET. *Emily Stowe;* illus. Don Mills, Ont.:
Fitzhenry & Whiteside, 1978. (7-8) B
Although the first woman school principal in
Canada and one of the first women authorized to practice medicine in Canada, Emily Stowe's chief contribution was to the women's-suffrage movement. More than a
biography of this distinguished Toronto physician, this
book is also a history of the women's-suffrage movement
in Canada. The author traces her leadership in the
Toronto Women's-Suffrage Association to the presidency
of the Dominion Women's Enfranchisement Association,
and how her daughter, Dr. Augusta Stowe-Gullen, succeeded her in that office. A needed source of material
for students doing research in women's rights in Canada.

155 REANEY, JAMES. *The Boy with an R in His Hand;*
illus. by Leo Rampen. Toronto: Macmillan of
Canada, 1965. (6-8) F *
Written by a well-known Canadian author, play-
wright and poet, this tells the story of two young
brothers, newly arrived in muddy little York in 1826.
They seem headed in opposite paths, one to win the
approval of his stuffily correct Tory uncle, the other
to become a trouble-making radical. The type-riot in
which William Lyon MacKenzie's printing shop is wrecked,
brings the brothers together again at the climax of a
satisfying, fast-moving story. First-rate story-telling;
charming illustrations.

156 REID, RAYMOND. *Footprints in Time: A Source Book
in the History of Ontario;* illus. Don Mills,
Ont.: Dent, 1967. (7-8) R
A well-organized collection of old diaries, newspaper and magazine articles, contemporary speeches, old
memoirs that provide "written footprints" of Ontario's
past, as the people of the time experienced it. The
documents are in chronological order, each preceded by
a short explanation placing it in its proper historical
setting. Paintings, drawings, woodcuts and photos in
black and white complement the text which is printed in
large, clear type. A good source of reference for history teachers and students.

157 REPO, SATU and OTHERS. *Marco and Michela*. Toronto:
Lorimer, 1978. Paper. (4-6) F
A book from the series *Where We Live* designed
for classroom use with students of varying cultural
backgrounds. Four short stories tell about different
members of an Italian immigrant family in Toronto—the
children's revenge on a local bully, a folktale told by
their grandmother, the father's struggles as a new immigrant worker and the arrival of relatives from Italy.
The writing is bland but the incidents are recognizable
for Italian-Canadian children, and informative for
other children. Includes photographs, and glossaries of
Italian words.

158 ROBINS, PATRICIA. *Star Maiden: An Ojibwa Legend
of the First Water Lily;* illus. Don Mills, Ont.:
Collier-Macmillan, 1975. (K-2) F
A young Chippewa mother tells her little boy the
legend of the beautiful star-maiden who loved the Indians so much that she wanted to live among them. When
they welcomed her joining them in whatever form she
wished to take, she chose to become a water-lily so
that she could live forever "at the heart of the people
she loves." Vibrant water colours accompany the simple
text, creating a picture-story book which was awarded
the Collier-Macmillan prize for Canadian juvenile literature.

159 RODDICK, ELLIS. *Day Hiking and Backpacking in
Ontario;* illus. by Dennis Noble. Toronto:
Greey de Pencier, 1976. Paper. (7-8)
Written especially for Ontario residents, this
practical little hand-book explains everything an inex-
perienced hiker needs to know before hitting the trails.
There are simply-written explanations, accompanied by
clear drawings on what to pack, how to choose equipment,
clothing, tents, and food. A complete listing of trail
clubs and associations is provided along with well-
mapped suggestions of places to hike in the province.
A useful guide for parents as well as young people
interested in taking up this rewarding, inexpensive,
outdoor pastime.

334

160 ROGERS, EDWARD S. *Algonkians of the Eastern Woodlands;* illus. Toronto: Royal Ontario Museum, 1970. Paper. (6-8)

One of a series of introductory guides to the Indians of Canada produced in association with the National Film Board of Canada. Information in the booklet is readable and concise with sub-headings such as Location, Population, Shelters and Social Organization. Black and white drawings are reproduced from the filmstrip of the same title. Useful vertical file material for libraries.

161 ROGERS, EDWARD S. *Iroquoians of the Eastern Woodlands;* illus. Toronto: Royal Ontario Museum, 1970. Paper. (5-8)

A 16-page booklet of concise information on the Indian tribe that occupied New York State and Southern Ontario. The National Film Board of Canada produced the drawings from the filmstrip of the same title for use as a guide to the filmstrip, or for independent use. The arrangment of information under different headings is helpful for quick reference in children's libraries.

162 RUSSELL, L. S. *Lighting the Pioneer Ontario Home;* illus. Toronto: Royal Ontario Museum, 1966. Paper. (7-8)

One of a R.O.M. series of booklets, entitled *What? Why? When? How? Where? Who?*, this describes types of lighting under the above headings. Small black and white photographs illustrate the concise, factual text. Inexpensive material for a library vertical file.

163 ST. JOHN, JUDITH. *Where the Saints Have Trod;* illus. by Robin Jacques. Toronto: Oxford University Press, 1974. (6-8) F

Methodist parsonages in Ontario almost fifty years ago provide the setting for a story of young childhood. In a less complicated, and in many ways happier, time than the present, the story moves as gently as an untroubled life. This nostalgic account of an imaginative child in an affectionate family leaves behind a glow of contentment.

164 SCOTT, IAN. *Discover Your Neighbourhood Heritage.*
Toronto: Learnxs, 1976. Paper. (6-8)
This is a portfolio with four items—a fact-sheet
describing the Historical Collection at the Toronto
Board of Education; a brochure of information about the
Ontario Archives; a paperback *Ontario Historic Sites,
Museums, Galleries, and Plaques;* plus the paperback
with the portfolio title. This clearly outlines how to
attack a project on local history, beginning with
sources—libraries, maps, organizations, interviews—
and ending with a sample schedule for a project. A
valuable learning tool for history students.

165 SCOTT, IAN and KERR, MAVIS. *Canoeing in Ontario;*
illus. by Elaine Macpherson. Toronto: Greey de
Pencier, 1977. Paper. (7-8)
Since Ontario has excellent waterways for this
sport, the detailed information in this little handbook
will be valuable for all those residents or visitors
who can or wish to paddle their own canoe. Straightforward language and clear drawings describe types of
canoes, paddling techniques, canoeing equipment and
camping. Includes maps and listings of 100 places to
canoe in Ontario, along with titles of books, clubs,
and organized trips available. Checklists of personal
necessities and equipment should be useful for absent-
minded amateurs.

166 SETON, ERNEST THOMPSON. *Two Little Savages;* illus.
by author. Garden City, NY: Doubleday, 1959.
(7-8) F
First published in 1903, this classic nature
adventure is set in Northern Ontario. Sam and Yan are
scarcely savages, but they long to live as the Indians
they so admire might have done. With the help of
friends and neighbours, the boys enjoy a camping vacation that becomes an adventure to remember; one that
has charmed readers of several generations. Not mere-
ly a good story, this is at the same time a veritable
encyclopedia of basic woodcraft. Drawings and illustrations by the author are informative and attractive.

167 SETON, ERNEST THOMPSON. *The Worlds of Ernest Thompson Seton;* ed. by John G. Sampson; illus. New York: Knopf; dist. by Random House, 1976. (6-8) P *

This handsome volume not only features 57 of Seton's remarkable paintings and drawings of wild creatures, 36 in full colour reproductions, but also includes selections from Seton's books, journals and articles to complement them. Many selections include anecdotes of his experiences and observations of animals and birds in the Don Valley and Toronto Bay, as well as in Manitoba. While the text may prove difficult for junior grade readers, the precise detail of his many paintings and sketches could be enjoyed by all young animal lovers. An excellent biography of Seton is provided in the introduction.

168 SHACKLETON, PHILIP. *The Furniture of Old Ontario;* illus. Toronto: Macmillan of Canada, 1974. (7-8) R

A fully illustrated guide to furniture made in Ontario prior to 1860. Detailed captions beside clear photographs taken by the author make this an outstanding book for collectors and heritage buffs. Serious students should enjoy the author's introduction where he describes furniture fashions and the history of furniture-making in Ontario. The variety of designs and shapes shown in this large volume makes for enjoyable browsing.

169 SHAW, MARGARET MASON. *Frederick Banting;* illus. Don Mills, Ont.: Fitzhenry & Whiteside, 1976. Paper. (6-8) B

Alliston, Ontario, was the birthplace of the famous Canadian doctor who discovered insulin. This short, well-written biography chronicles his early life in a strict religious home; his university days in Toronto; his distinguished war service; his discovery of insulin, along with Charles Best; the honour of the Nobel Prize; and finally his untimely death in a plane crash. The book is illustrated with numerous black and white photos and provides questions for discussion and

further research in the margins, as in other books in
The Canadians series.

170 SHEFFE, NORMAN. *Casimir Gzowski;* illus. Don Mills,
Ont.: Fitzhenry & Whiteside, 1975. Paper.
(6-8) B
    The achievements of this brilliant engineer who
arrived as a Polish exile from 1830 Russian revolution
are impressive. He was involved in building Lake Erie
Canal, and roads and bridges in Ontario. His company
built the Grand Trunk Railway and designed the Toronto
waterfront. His greatest triumph was the International
Bridge from Fort Erie to Buffalo. The biography is
well-researched and competently written with numerous
photographs, diagrams, maps, bibliography, and questions
included. This book contributes needed material on the
history of transportation in Ontario.

171 SHOVELLER, JOHN. *Our Theatres;* illus. Toronto:
Simon & Pierre, 1975. Paper. (6-8)
    This is volume 2 of *Toronto We Love You,* describ-
ing and illustrating the 35 different theatres operating in Toronto—an impressive number. Although a few
theatres have folded or changed addresses since publication, the book provides interesting articles on each
theatre group—its history, directors, artistic emphasis, and future goals. Black and white photos of
actors, on and off stage, as well as of theatre buildings are liberally sprinkled throughout the book. Of
most interest to drama students around Metro Toronto.

172 SINGER, YVONNE. *Sara and the Apartment Building;*
illus. Toronto: Kids Can, 1975. Paper.
(K-2) F
    Children who live in high-rise apartments will
identify with Sara, who copes with the advantages and
disadvantages of living in an apartment building in
mid-Toronto. Her friend watches her push the buzzer
before accompanying her up in the elevator, and delights in the view from the balcony. The story is
simple and easy to read, complemented by whimsical
crayon drawings in colour.

173 SLAIGHT, ANNABEL, ed. *Exploring Toronto;* illus.
Toronto: Toronto Chapter of Architects; Greey
de Pencier, 1977. Paper. (6-8) R
A comprehensive guide-book to the city, describing twelve walking tours through different districts.
Each chapter describing a particular walk is written by
a different Toronto architect. All convey not only a
sense of history, but also a feeling for the atmosphere
of the city and the people and places which creates it.
Many maps and black and white photos. Student visitors
to Toronto, as well as residents, will find it most
useful and appreciate its pocket-book size for easy
carrying.

174 SLOAN, GLENNA DAVIS. *Spotlight on Liz.* Toronto:
Macmillan of Canada, 1977. Paper. (7-8) F
One of the few contemporary teenage novels with
a Canadian setting which has the ingredients for success. It has a likable teenage heroine whose acting
talent and ambition lead to conflict with her mother,
temptations to cheat, and a frightening adventure in
downtown Toronto. It also involves a friendship with
an Irish Setter dog and a young professional actor.
This simple but sensitively-written story will appeal
to even reluctant teenage readers anywhere. From the
Topliner series.

175 SMITH, JAMES K., ed. *Ottawa: A Portrait of the
Nation's Capital;* illus. Willowdale, Ont.:
Hownslow, 1973. Paper. (5-8)
Prefaced by a short history of the capital city
located in Ontario, this book is comprised mostly of
photographs in colour and black and white, with captions. They depict the Parliament Buildings, historic
sites and statues, views of the city, and activities
for tourists and residents. Useful for students contemplating a visit to Ottawa or for browsing.

176 SMUCKER, BARBARA. *Underground to Canada;* illus. by
Tom McNeely. Toronto: Clarke, Irwin, 1977.
(6-8) F *
A thoroughly absorbing story of the escape of
two Black slave girls from Mississippi to St. Catharines,
Ontario, via the Underground Railway. Julilly makes a
memorable heroine who befriends a mistreated orphan
girl at the plantation. With the aid of a Quaker abo-
litionist, the girls embark on the long perilous journey
north to freedom. Although written as fiction, the
book is based on actual histories and narratives. The
book reveals the tragedy of slavery for broken family
members and the triumph of the human spirit.

177 STACEY, C. P. (Col.) *The Battle of Little York;*
illus. Toronto: The Historical Board, 1963.
Paper. (7-8) R
Although the format of this booklet is intimidat-
ing—poor paper quality, solid text, small sparse sketches as illustration—the well-researched account does
provide more in-depth information on the history of
York, and the people who played a significant part in
the battle in 1813, than other sources. Librarians
would find it useful in providing background material
for teachers and for research by serious students of
Canadian history.

178 STAFFORD, ELLEN. *Stratford, Around and About;*
illus. Stratford, Ont.: Fanfare Books, 1972.
Paper. (6-8)
An excellent source of information on the city,
the Shakespearian Festival held there, and the surrounding area. The author provides a lively account of the
history of the Festival from 1951, a fascinating portrait of "Tiger" Dunlop, who surveyed the Huron Tract,
and an interesting history of the city. There is information on shopping, eating, sleeping, walking and driving around Stratford and nearby areas, enlivened with
comments and anecdotes. Includes photos, a map of
Stratford, plus a listing of all Festival productions
to 1972. Enjoyable reading for local historians, and
visitors to the area.

179 STEPHENSON, WILLIAM. *The Great River Hunt;* illus.
by Maria Jursic and Louise Sheppard. Toronto:
Burns & MacEachern, 1967. (6-8) F
A fast-moving mystery set in contemporary Ottawa.
The implausible plot conerns the kidnapping of an
Ottawa boy, and two boys' successful attempt to find
him, aided by 200 youngsters from the foreign embassies
in Rockliffe. But young readers will admire the resourcefulness of the children and be caught up in the
spirit of their great "treasure hunt" as they close in
on the kidnappers' hideaway. Unfortunately, the map on
the end-papers seems inconsistent with the story.

180 STEWART, DARRYL. *Point Pelee: Canada's Deep
South;* illus. Toronto: Burns & MacEachern,
1977. Paper. (7-8)
This pocket-sized handbook would be of most use
before and after a visit to this national park. But
older interested students would enjoy reading about the
park located as far south as Northern California, which
is, therefore, a refuge for birds, rare or unknown in
the rest of Canada. Includes a short history of Point
Pelee and life zones, with examples of birds, mammals,
reptiles, fish and insects found there. Illustrations,
some in colour, are only fair.

181 STEWART, DON. *A Guide to Pre-Confederation Furniture of English Canada;* illus. Don Mills, Ont.:
Longmans Canada, 1967. o.p. (7-8) R
Clear, black and white photographs show numerous
authentic pieces of Canadian antique furniture. Captions provide a description of each item, its use, origin, time period. Of most use to collectors and would-
be collectors, the book could also be useful for student research on early life in Upper Canada.

182 STEWART, RODERICK. *Bethune.* Don Mills, Ont.:
Paperjacks, 1973. Paper. (8-) B
A detailed, fascinating biography of Norman
Bethune. This Canadian doctor-revolutionary is revered
by millions in China, but was, until recently, almost
unknown in Ontario, his birthplace. The author used

primary source material, including many quotes, to create a scholarly account of the doctor's life and achievements in Canada, U.S., Spain, England and finally China. Rebel, renegade, fighter, hero—opinions still differ, but the legend of Bethune can no longer be ignored. Recommended for better readers in Grade 8.

183 STOKES, PETER JOHN. *Old Niagara on the Lake;* illus. by Robert Montgomery. Toronto: University of Toronto Press, 1971. (6-8) P R *

Superb drawings of a selection of early buildings illustrate different aspects and periods of this historic town and its social background. The author, consulting restoration architect since 1961, provides a brief history of the town in the introduction, and captions describing historical background for each drawing. The order of presentation was designed for walking or driving tourists—one tour to show the old town, then the New Survey, and finally historic sites. An excellent book on early Ontario architecture, and a "must" for visitors to the town.

184 STURGES, JAMES. *Adam Beck;* illus. Don Mills, Ont.: Fitzhenry & Whiteside, 1978. Paper. (7-8) B

At the time of Adam Beck's funeral in 1925, Ontario's electricity was turned off, a fitting tribute to the creator and chairman of the Hydro-Electric Power Commission of Ontario. Details such as these are contained in the 60 page biography of the "Hydro-Knight," illustrated with photographs that include the statue of him in downtown Toronto. New title, *The Canadians* series.

185 SWAYZE, FRED. *The Rowboat War on the Great Lakes, 1812-1814;* illus. by Paul Liberovsky. Toronto: Macmillan of Canada, 1965. (6-8)

The Great Lakes was the scene of many battles during the War of 1812. This fictionalized history concerns Robert Livingstone, a fur trader and Indian agent, who played a major role in defending Michilimackinac for Canada. He and a small band of men in rowboats defiantly ran the American blockade of the Upper Lakes and fought against U.S. warships. The story is

well-researched but the writing is uninspired, and some
young readers may find it difficult to keep all the
details straight. But it does prove the futility of
this war, since ownership of all lands and forts remained the same as before 1812.

186 TENNANT, VERONICA. *On Stage, Please;* illus. by
Rita Briansky. Toronto: McClelland & Stewart,
1977. (4-7) F
The author, a principal ballerina of the National Ballet of Canada, has written this story of a little
girl who begins the training that will prepare her for
the world of professional ballet dancing. Although not
Canada's answer to Noel Streatfeild, Ms. Tennant proves
a competent writer on a subject she knows well. The
result is an acceptable and readable story, set in
Toronto, which portrays a young dancer's world with
accuracy, realism and compassion.

187 TOMKINS, D. M. and OTHERS. *Northern Ontario: Land
of Buried Treasure.* (Regional Studies of Canada)
Agincourt, Ont.: Gage, 1970. Paper. (6-8)
An overview of the geography of Northern Ontario
designed for classroom use. Describes the city of
Kenora, mining areas for nickel, copper, iron ore, farming in the clay belt, forest industries and how glacia-
tion has affected the character of Northern Ontario.
Provides maps, charts and black and white photos,
along with questions for discussion and further research.

—— TOOKE, THOMAS. *The Niagara Escarpment.* See ON 74

188 TURNER, D. HAROLD. *To Hang a Rebel;* illus. by
Merle Smith. Agincourt, Ont.: Gage, 1977.
(5-8) F
William Lyon Mackenzie is one of the most colourful characters in Canadian history. His role in the
1837 Rebellion comes to life for young readers through
the story of 15-year-old Doug sent to Toronto to live
in Mackenzie's home. As a spy for the man, he becomes
involved in many of the events preceding and during the
brief rebellion. Better than average writing, accurate

historical background, and good illustrations compensate for the contrived plot. A welcome addition to the
few books of historical fiction about this period for
middle-grade readers.

189 WALKER, DIANA. *Never Step on an Indian's Shadow.*
Toronto: Fitzhenry & Whiteside, 1973. (7-8) F
The legends say that an Indian's shadow is his
spirit; if you step on it, you may crush his soul. A
young visitor to Moosonee, in Northern Ontario, realizes that her friend Michael is suffering from the
weight of unsympathetic feet upon his shadow. He needs
some help and understanding if he is to break out of
the circumscribed life that is all most of his people
know. A warm story of friendship and generosity.

190 WALKER, DIANA. *The Year of the Horse.* Don Mills,
Ont.: Fitzhenry & Whiteside, 1975. (6-8) F
Fifteen-year-old Joanna, vacationing on her
grandmother's farm in rural Ontario, discovers that she
loves horses and has a natural talent for championship
riding. Despite some stereotyped characters, this is a
warm, entertaining story with enough elements of young
love, mystery and humour to appeal to young girls who
aren't even horse-lovers. It also presents an accurate
picture of contemporary life in south-western Ontario.

191 WALLACE, IAN. *The Christmas Tree House;* illus.
Toronto: Kids Can, 1976. Paper. (2-4) F
A pleasant story of a boy and girl who meet at
Riverdale Zoo in Toronto, and find a treehouse. When
they begin decorating it as a Christmas treehouse, they
discover it belongs to "Don Valley Rose," an old lady
they'd been led to believe was a witch. This book has
the right ingredients for the age-group—a little adventure, a little fear, and a satisfying conclusion. The
soft-pencil drawings are effective. Good for reading
aloud.

192 WALLACE, IAN and WOOD, ANGELA. *The Sandwich;* illus.
Toronto: Kids Can, 1975. Paper. (K-2) F
A delightful little picture story-book about a
small Italian-Canadian boy who eats his lunch at his
Toronto school for the first time, only to discover
that his classmates can't stand his "stinky" sandwich.
The story has a happy ending when Vincenzo's friends
taste his sandwich. Illustrated with simple, but expressive, line drawings of blue on white. Useful for
discussion on respecting cultural differences.

193 WATERS, GEORGE and FEATHER, DONALD. *Fort York;*
illus. Toronto: Ginn, 1972. Paper. (5-7) *
One of the series *Ginn Studies in Canadian History,* this slim, colourful booklet is designed for individual reading as well as classroom use. Using
quotes from diaries, the author tells the story of the
capture of Fort York during the War of 1812, the founding of York and the life of soldiers at the Fort.
Coloured photographs taken from a film about Fort York
are used as illustrations, along with archival paintings and sketches. A bibliography is included along
with questions for discussion and research. A well-
produced interesting source of historical information.

194 WHITE, H. H. *The Forest Trees of Ontario;* illus.
(revised by R. C. Hosie) Toronto: Ontario
Ministry of Natural Resources, 1968. Paper.
(7-8)
This booklet provides not only descriptions of
trees, but also a methodology for identifying types of
trees in Ontario and interpreting the descriptions.
Because of this more mature approach, not all trees are
illustrated and none in colour. The introduction provides information on the distribution of forest trees
in Ontario with an accompanying map.

195 WILSON, MARY CAROL. *Marion Hilliard;* illus. Don
Mills, Ont.: Fitzhenry & Whiteside, 1977.
Paper. (6-8) B
Chief in obstetrics at the Women's College Hospital in Toronto, prior to retirement in 1957, Marion
Hilliard was a beloved physician, teacher, and humani-
tarian until her untimely death in 1958. This biography
not only covers the facts of her remarkable career, but
also provides the flavour of the times for those in
medicine during the depression and war years. Black
and white photos are undistinguished. Questions in
the margins suggest further research or discussion.

196 WOOD, ANGELA. *Kids Can Count;* illus. Toronto:
Kids Can, 1976. Paper. (K-1) P
This is a multi-lingual counting book presenting
the numbers one to ten in four languages as well as in
English. It was prepared as a teaching aid for children of French, Italian, Chinese and Greek origin. The
author uses black and white photographs taken around
Toronto to demonstrate the numbers written in five
languages on the opposite page. The addition of a pronunciation guide would have made it more useful, but
the concept is good.

—— WOOD, ANGELA. *The Sandwich.* See ON 192

—— WOODFORD, JIM. *Some Common and Uncommon Birds of
Ontario and Quebec.* See ON 82

197 WRIGHT, J. V. *Ontario Prehistory; An Eleven-
Thousand-Year Archeological Outline;* illus.
Scarborough, Ont.: Van Nostrand, Reinhold, 1972.
Paper. (7-8) R
Creating a popular account of prehistoric Indian
cultures was the aim of the National Museum of Man,
Ottawa, in producing *The Canadian Prehistory* series.
This one, on Ontario, is impressive in format and con-
tent. It deals with four periods in time—The Palaeo-
Indian, the Archaic, Initial Woodland and Terminal Wood-
land—and shows the culture artifacts that have been
found from each period. The numerous photographs are

clear and well-labelled, although only four are in
colour. The large print, wide margins and suggested
reading list make this a good introduction to Ontario's
archeology for senior elementary students.

—— WYSE, ALEX. *The One to Fifty Books*. See ON 198

198 WYSE, ANNE and WYSE, ALEX. *The One to Fifty Books;*
 illus. Toronto: University of Toronto Press,
 1973. Paper. (K-1)
 A fascinating, illustrated counting book that
actually goes up to 50. The authors have compiled drawings by Indian children in south-western Ontario, Eskimo
children on Baffin Island and others. Children also
designed the lettering, and assisted in lino-cutting
and printing. The result is imaginative and highly
appealing to children. Most of the drawings are black
and white, with occasional splashes of colour. The
poor binding on a book destined for heavy use by small
children is unfortunate, but still worth the purchase.

199 YEO, DOUGLAS. *Mining in the Shield: Timmins;*
 illus. Toronto: Ginn, 1968. Paper. (4-6)
 Intended as a teaching unit for social studies,
this booklet provides a brief overview of the geography,
history and principal industry of the Northern Ontario
city. The emphasis, however, is on illustration, with
photos, graphs, charts and diagrams, mostly in colour.
Questions and suggestions for activities and research
under the heading "Do," are placed at the end of each
short chapter. A vivifying approach to the topic for
teachers and students. Part of the series *Ginn Sample
Studies of Canada*.

WISCONSIN

compiled by ERNESTINE MOKEDE

To the reader of children's books, Wisconsin is a fair land, with her woods, rivers, and lakes; her bluffs on the west, the long Lake Michigan shoreline on the east, cold Lake Superior on the north, and her lush dairy and farm land in the south. Her natural resources and the diverse nature and history of the people who have used them provided rich soil in which the seeds of literature have flourished.

The first to use her woods, water, soil, animals, and lead were the Indians. As their land was discovered, explored, and found rich in furs by the Europeans, these Indians were deprived of their aboriginal culture and left in a badly depressed economic situation. Those remaining in Wisconsin today are the Chippewa, Potawatomi, Stockbridge-Munsee, Winnebago, Menominee, and Oneida, one-third of whom live on eight reservations. The struggle of the Indians to regain their ethnic identification offers interesting and worthwhile subjects for older children's books.

349

The defeat of Black Hawk in 1832, marked the last
of the Indian uprisings and opened the area to a flood
of settlers. The Four Lakes region, where Black Hawk
had sought refuge, was chosen as the site of the future
capital. Milwaukee rapidly developed as a population
center. Prairie du Chien and Green Bay had already
been settled. Two other settlements, Superior, and its
neighbor, Duluth, Minnesota, today run their total
annual harbor tonnage up close to New York's in spite
of being closed down during the coldest winter months.
These towns, along with many others, grew up on the
waterways for which Wisconsin is famous. In fact, some
say that her name is the French version "Ouisconsin" of
the Chippewa word "Meskousing," meaning gathering of
waters.

News of the area's extensive waterways and fertile
land spread far. In 1850, more than a third of the
total population of Wisconsin was foreign-born. Today,
97% of Wisconsinites were born in the United States.
In the early days the largest group came from the
British Isles: Cornish miners; Scots, including John
Muir; Welsh; and Irish. Then came Norwegians and
Germans, including the advocate of freedom, Carl Schurz,
and his wife, who started the first kindergarten in the
United States. Swiss, Danes, Swedish, Polish, Czecho-
slovakians, Greeks, Lithuanians, Hungarians, Yugoslavs,
and Italians soon followed.

Early immigrants found work in farming, dairies,
fishing, mining, sailing, lumbering and factories. It
was the early lead miners who, by their habit of digging shelters into the sides of hills, gave Wisconsin
the nickname of the Badger State.

By 1970, Wisconsin ranked 16th in population in the
United States. With major ethnic groups of German,
Norwegian and Italian, there were 96% white, 3% black
and 1% other races. While so many early settlers found
their livelihood on the farm, the mechanization of the
twentieth century forced the over-supply of farm
workers into the city. The resultant problems of
Wisconsin urban areas, where two-thirds of the population live, are the typical ones of poverty, housing
deterioration, increased crime, and the flight of

business and residential taxpayers to the suburbs. The
state is faced with ever-increasing costs for education,
welfare, and control of water pollution caused by the
industrial growth.

In spite of the problems accompanying urbanization
Wisconsin has profited from the heavy industrialization
of her major cities. The principal manufacturers pro-
duce pulpwood and paper products, machinery, foods,
fabricated metals, and equipment for the transportation, electric and electronic industries. To encourage
tourism, another major source of income, Wisconsin has
committed itself to the purchase of land with scenic
and recreational attractions before its engulfment by
the megapolis spread. The deep forests and natural
lakes provide fishing, hunting, and winter recreation.

Along with industry and tourism, agriculture
remains vital to Wisconsin's economy. As in the past,
dairying continues to provide the greater volume of
agricultural income. However, livestock products and
livestock, such as cattle, hogs, sheep, mink, and
poultry, are rapidly becoming the basis of the state's
agriculture. Corn, hay, and oats are increasingly
important crops used for cattle feed, but of gradually
diminishing economic importance are potatoes, beans,
beets, soybeans, cabbage, and fruits grown for human
consumption.

Although Wisconsin's official programs must of
necessity emphasize economic development, the people of
the state have always nurtured a strong literary heritage. Whether long-time Americans or newly arrived,
the settlers of Wisconsin brought their songs and customs which in time found their way into children's fiction. For example, with the felling of trees came the
Paul Bunyan stories, where many old-world motifs were
fitted into the yarns.

In the field of children's literature, the University of Wisconsin has been an outstanding patron. It
opened in 1849, the same year that John Muir left his
native Scotland. Many writers of children's books have
taught there or attended classes. The University has
been one of the sponsors of the Wisconsin Book Confer-
ence, which has brought children's authors and

illustrators to the state. It gives the Lewis Carroll
Shelf Award to those books deemed worthy to sit on the
shelf with *Alice in Wonderland.*

In 1963, the University helped the Wisconsin Free
Library Commission and others set up the Cooperative
Children's Book Center. Three of the purposes of this
center are to provide a collection for the study of
significant books of past and current output, to
heighten awareness of the long-time value of quality
books, and to assist Wisconsin writers and illustrators
in their creative work.

Wisconsin has had her share of award winners in the
field of children's literature, and has even appeared
as the setting for Newbery Award winners. Writers who
left their native state carried with them a framework
in which to express their theme. Their best work,
regardless of where it was written, has Wisconsin roots
and personality.

Among well-known Wisconsin writers are Lawrence
Keating, James Summers, William Gault, Roy Chapman
Andrews, Virginia Kahl, Maureen Daly, Walter Havighurst,
James Kjelgaard, and Opal Wheeler. Fine writing has
been done by Bernice Carlson, Eleanor Clymer, Loula
Grace Erdman, Helen Ferris, Marguerite Henry, Rita
Ritchie, Mari Sandoz, Charlotte Zolotow, Adolph Regli,
and Keith Robertson. The prolific August Derleth, John
and Jean George and Ruth and Richard Holberg, are
steeped in Wisconsin lore and history.

These and many other authors help to preserve the
history and life of the people of Wisconsin through
their books for children. The individuality, energy,
and progressive spirit which have always marked the
state are found in the books which follow.

1   ADAMSON, WENDY WRISTON. *Who Owns a River? A Story of Environmental Action.* Minneapolis: Dillon, 1977. (7-8) #
A treatise on environmental protection which traces the history of the St. Croix River in Minnesota and Wisconsin, the pollution of the river and steps taken to save it. Bibliography.

2   AMES, MERLIN MC MAIN. *Canthook Country;* illus. by Harvey Kidder. Boston: Houghton, 1941. o.p. (6-8) F
When his older brother disappears from the lumbercamp, Steve leaves the family to fill his place and search for him.

3   AMES, MERLIN MC MAIN. *The Fork in the Trail;* illus. by Henry Pitz. New York: McKay, 1948. o.p. (5-8) F
Against a background of fur trapping, farming and lumbering, young people get involved and solve a mystery in the Wisconsin frontier of 1865. Good characterization.

4   ANDRUS, VERA. *Black River, a Wisconsin Story;* illus. by Irene Burns. Boston: Little, Brown, 1967. o.p. (4-6) F
Successfully developing the first modern creamery in north-central Wisconsin, in the early 1900's, Mr. Garrett is envied and hated by a rival whose threats hang over the otherwise happy Garrett family life. The creamery is set on fire, but that horror is offset by the support of the farmers and townspeople. Told mainly from the viewpoint of the two mischeivous young daughters. Certain stereotyped views, but a good picture of the time and area.

5   ARCHER, JULES. *Famous Young Rebels.* New York: Messner, 1973. (7-8)
Biographies of twelve individuals, including Robert LaFollette, governor of Wisconsin, U.S. Senator, and leader of political reforms which became models for other states.

6   ARCHER, JULES. *Indian Foe, Indian Friend: The Story of William S. Harney;* illus. New York: Crowell-Collier, 1970. (7-8) B
Biography of a man who performed his duty as soldier but respected the Indian in his fight for his lands. Fifteen pages are devoted to the Black Hawk War and to an amusing sidelight on Harney's race with a Menominee Indian. Bibliography and index.

7   ARCHER, MARION F. *Nine Lives of Moses on the Oregon Trail;* illus. by George Armstrong. Chicago: Whitman, 1968. (5-7) F
Exciting historical fiction, mainly about the Van Antwerps' journey on the Oregon Trail. Also depicts their life on a farm near Oshkosh with many homey details, before they started toward the west. Story revolves around 12-year-old Charlotte and her cat, Moses, who saves her life.

8   ARCHER, MARION F. *Sarah Janes;* illus. Chicago: Whitman, 1971. (5-8) F
A teen-age girl and young brother leave an orphanage in Liverpool, England, in 1852 to live with their father on a farm in a Welsh settlement near Oshkosh. Sarah Jane is surprised to find a step-mother and it takes love, patience, and common sense for the latter to overcome the girl's unwillingness to accept her. Good characterization and historically authentic.

9   ARCHER, MARION F. *There Is a Happy Land;* illus. by David Cunningham. Chicago: Whitman, 1963. (5-7) F
In 1865, when their tailor shop and home in Norway burn, Signe's parents seek their fortune in America, settling in Wisconsin near Oshkosh. The girl stays behind with relatives for a year on their farm waiting for her broken leg to mend, experiencing a wedding, a summer in the seters, and Christmas. Joining her parents, she finds her father feeble and blind and her distraught mother struggling to pay bills. Signe works at improving their home and curing her father. A plus for human relations in her friendship

with Irish neighbors. Followed by *Keys for Signe*
(Whitman, 1965.)

10 BAILEY, BERNADINE. *Picture Book of Wisconsin;*
    illus. by Kurt Wiese. Rev. ed. Chicago:
    Whitman, 1966. (3-6) P *
    A brief overview which manages to give the atmos-
phere of the state while high-lighting its geography,
history, cities, people, industries, schools, and fun.
First edition was 1951.

11 BARNOUW, VICTOR. *Dream of the Blue Heron;* illus.
    by Lynd Ward. New York: Delacorte, 1966.
    (6-8) F
    An anthropologist tells a story of conflict
between the old and the new ways of the Chippewas in
northern Wisconsin, in 1905. The Indians argue over
the question of 12-year-old Wabus' attending the white
man's school. Good factual material on the culture but
limited character development.

— BEARDWOOD, VALERIE. *Trails of His Own; The Story
    of John Muir and His Fight to Save Our National
    Parks.* See WI 104

12 BECKHARD, ARTHUR J. *Black Hawk.* New York:
    Messner, 1957. o.p. (6-8) B *
    A compelling story of a Sauk chief's son, who
saw no reason for senseless killing but later fought
long and vigorously to save his nation. Although he
failed in his desire for peace as the white man continued to break treaties, he ended his life in peace, with
time to write his autobiography.

13 BIERHORST, JOHN, ed. *Songs of the Chippewa,*
    adapted from the collections of Frances Densmore
    and Henry Rowe Schoolcraft and arranged for
    piano and guitar; illus. by Joe Servello.
    New York: Farrar, Straus & Giroux, 1974.
    (4-8) P * #
    Seventeen brief songs found near the western
shores of the Great Lakes, include lullabies, ritual

chants, medicine charms, and love songs. An important
addition to collections of music of the American Indian,
and the Ojibway in particular. A handsome full-page
illustration accompanies each selection.

14 BIEVER, JOHN. *Young Sports Photographer with the
Green Bay Packers.* W. W. Norton, 1969. o.p.
(6-8)
The author, in conjunction with George Vecsy of
the *New York Times*, candidly relates his own experiences as a Wisconsin high school student who became the
official photographer for the famous Wisconsin football
team. Much exciting play and personality material.

15 BLAIR, WALTER. *Tall Tale America: A Legendary
History of Our Humorous Heroes;* illus. by Glen
Rounds. New York: Coward, 1944. (5-8)
A university professor presents a very humorous
collection of heroes, including Paul Bunyan. Lively
drawings in the typical Rounds' style. Print is small.

16 BLEEKER, SONIA. *The Chippewa Indians; Rice Gather-
ers of the Great Lakes;* illus. by Patricia
Boodell. New York: Morrow, 1955. (4-7) R P #
Semi-fictional depiction of ways of life of early
Chippewas in the persons of the Crane family: birth
customs, rice gathering, becoming a medicine man,
tanning hide, making maple sugar. Brief account of
present day Chippewas.

17 BOLTON, MIMI DUBOIS. *Merry-Go-Round Family;* illus.
by Oscar Liebman. New York: Coward-McCann,
1954. (4-6) F
In the summer of 1910, when the factory closed,
ten-year-old Marie Turner's father bought a merry-go-
round. She and her mother traveled with him and made
it profitable, even after Mr. Turner's accident caused
him a lengthy stay in the hospital.

18 BOWMAN, JAMES CLOYD. *Winabojo, Master of Life;*
       illus. by Armstrong Perry. Chicago: Whitman,
       1941. o.p. (4-8) * #
       Winabojo was the son of a god and a mortal
mother. With the help of a magic arrow and pocket
canoe, he brought squash and corn to his people and
taught them to bind themselves together in a confederacy. Folklore based on sound research.

19 BRENT, STUART. *Mr. Toast and the Secret of Gold
       Hill;* illus. by George Porter. Philadelphia:
       Lippincott, 1970. (4-6) F
       Toast, a huge golden retriever, once again looks
after his family of parents and eight children. During
spring vacation, they look for the gold stolen by bandits from a government repository in Superior, Wisconsin in the 1860's. Both money and men had disappeared
near Bark Point, site of the Brent family's present-day
cottage. Very good for local color, but slow-moving
and a bit dull in spite of exciting happenings.

20 BRENT, STUART. *Mr. Toast and the Woolly Mammoth;*
       illus. by Lilian Obligado. New York: Viking,
       1966. o.p. (4-6) F
       While the Brent family spend the summer on a
lake shore in northern Wisconsin, the older boys dig
for prehistoric bones at the site of a quarry landslide.
Mr. Toast, their golden retriever, finds the largest
bone he had ever seen—the woolly mammoth. Happy story
with some excitement.

21 BRINK, CAROL RYRIE. *Caddie Woodlawn;* illus. by
       Kate Seredy. New York: Macmillan, 1935.
       (5-7) F NA *
       In Wisconsin of 1864, red-headed Caddie, just
turned twelve, has a glorious time "running wild" with
her brothers but shows evidence of becoming a splendid
woman. Also in new edition (1973) illustrated by Trina
S. Hyman, and paperback edition revised (1970).
Newbery Medal Award 1936.

22 BRINK, CAROL RYRIE. *Caddie Woodlawn, A Play:*
    Dramatization of the Newbery Medal Book, Caddie
    Woodlawn. New York: Macmillan, 1945. o.p.
    (5-7)
        School or library groups may perform this three-
    act play without charge. Includes music.

23 BRINK, CAROL RYRIE. *Magical Melons: More stories*
    about Caddie Woodlawn; illus. by Marguerite
    Davis. New York: Macmillan, 1944. (5-7) F
        Stories are not in sequence but are still highly
    entertaining and filled with the flavor of family life
    on the Wisconsin frontier.

24 BRINK, CAROL RYRIE. *Winter Cottage;* illus. by
    Fermin Rocker. New York: Macmillan, 1968.
    (4-7) F
        In the depression years, 13-year-old Minty's
    father is a dreamer, not a provider. He and his two
    daughters are on their way to live with an aunt when
    they are forced to spend the night in an unoccupied
    lakeside cottage. Deciding to make this their home,
    Minty takes charge and helps the others, including a
    runaway boy, to a sense of responsibility. Seeking a
    way to pay the rent, the children try to find their
    father's secret pancake recipe for a contest. Good
    characterization. Also in paperback.

25 BROCK, EMMA LILLIAN. *Then Came Adventure.*
    New York: Knopf, 1941. o.p. (5-7) F
        Two children find an intruder on their own
    secret island in Lake Superior. She turns out to be
    Pamela Botts, the Botany Lady, and they become enthusi-
    astic Foresters under her tutelage. Nicely sprinkled
    with songs with music, Scandinavian legends, and Paul
    Bunyan lore. Some of the story takes place in Michigan.

26 BROWN, CHARLES E. *Bear Tales: Wisconsin Narra-*
    tives of Bears, Wild Hogs, Honey, Lumberjacks
    and settlers. Madison: Wisconsin Folklore
    Society, 1944. o.p. Paper. (5-)
        Brief accounts, some seemingly factual, some

humorous, some tall tales. Not necessarily written for children, but interesting to them. Pamphlet.

27 BROWN, CHARLES E. *Ben Hooper Tales: Settler's Yarns from Green and LaFayette Counties, Wisconsin.* Madison: Wisconsin Folklore Society, 1944. o.p. Paper. (5-)
Tall tale anecdotes, many of them very familiar in content.

28 BROWN, CHARLES E. *Bluenose Brainerd Stories.* Madison: Wisconsin Folklore Society, 1943. o.p. Paper. (5-)
Ten tales about the cantankerous Mr. and Mrs. Brainerd. He was a sawyer in a lumberjack camp.

29 BROWN, CHARLES E. *Brimstone Bill, Famous Boss Bull Whacker of Paul Bunyan's Camps: Tall Tales of His Exploits.* Madison. Wisconsin Folklore Society, 1942. o.p. Paper. (5-)
Twelve yarns.

30 BROWN, CHARLES E. *Johnny Inkslinger: Deacon Seat Tales of Paul Bunyan's Industrious Camp Clerk at His Sawdust River Camp in Wisconsin.* Madison: Wisconsin Folklore Society, 1944. o.p. Paper. (5-)
More folk tales.

31 BROWN, CHARLES E. *Paul Bunyan Classics.* Madison: Wisconsin Folklore Society, 1945. o.p. Paper. (5-)
Ten yarns.

32 BROWN, CHARLES E. *Winabozho, Hero-God of the Indians of the Old Northwest: Myths, Legends and Stories.* Madison: Wisconsin Folklore Society, 1944. o.p. Paper. (5-)
Seventeen brief tales, many whimsical. Winabozho is often tricked in these tales.

— BROWN, DOROTHY L. *Little Wind.* See WI 40

33 BURCHARD, PETER. *Jed: The Story of a Yankee Soldier and a Southern Boy;* illus. by author. New York: Coward, McCann & Geoghegan, 1960. o.p. (5-8) F *
Jed, a sixteen-year-old Union soldier, befriends and defends a Mississippi farm boy and his family after the Battle of Shiloh. From Elkhorn in southeastern Wisconsin, Jed often reminisces about his small home-town and the man he worked for as a printer's devil. Well-drawn characters; easy for the reader to empathize with them.

34 BURLINGAME, ROGER. *General Billy Mitchell, Champion of Air Defense;* illus. New York: McGraw-Hill, 1952. o.p. (6-8) B
A straightforward telling of the life of an individualist who fought unsuccessfully for his idea of an independent air force. Only two pages are devoted to his early life in Wisconsin, but an entire chapter recounts the Mitchell family's Wisconsin dynasty.

35 BURT, OLIVE. *The Ringling Brothers, Circus Boys;* illus. by Raymond Burns. Indianapolis: Bobbs-Merrill, 1958. (3-7) B
Informal, easy-reading biography of the producers of the Ringling Brothers Circus with emphasis on their early life. About half of the text is devoted to their years in Wisconsin tracing their career from boy-hood acts, to adding a wild animal to the show, and finally to a full-blown circus in Baraboo.

36 BUTLER, BEVERLY. *Feather in the Wind.* New York: Dodd, Mead, 1965. (6-8) F *
During the summer of 1832, when Black Hawk's warriors were raiding frontier settlements in Wisconsin territory, young Dr. David Reade persuades independent, nineteen-year-old Mary Alexia to accept his help in moving her irrascible, crippled father to Ft. Winnebago. Later, after the latter's death, they recognize their

love for each other. Historical fiction of substance
and good characterization.

37 BUTLER, BEVERLY. *A Girl Named Wendy*. New York:
Dodd, Mead, 1976. (7-8) F *
When her parents separate, 15-year-old Wendy and
her young sister leave the Indian mission school to
stay with her Milwaukee aunt, who appears to be trying
to deny her Indian heritage. Though treated well, the
girls flee to the Menominee Reservation to be with
their mother and grandmother. Eventually, Wendy comes
to terms with herself and her aunt, keeping her Indian
pride while seeking advancement in the modern world.
Well-developed characterization. Subject handled with
integrity.

38 BUTLER, BEVERLY. *The Silver Key*. New York: Dodd,
1961. o.p. (7-) F
Pioneer story of the Welsh in Wisconsin of 1860.
Alwyn's shyness made her hope for solitude on her
father's new farm, but instead she becomes involved in
intrigue and conflicts with her sick step-mother, her
roving young step-uncle, and the villainous Mr. Haines.

39 BUTLER, BEVERLY. *Song of the Voyageur*. New York:
Dodd, 1955. o.p. (7-) F
Sixteen-year-old Diane leaves her Massachusetts
home to live in Wisconsin of the 1830's, even though
she is appalled by its hardship. Good character study.

40 BUTTERFIELD, MARGUERITE and BROWN, DOROTHY L.
Little Wind. Des Moines, Iowa: Meredith, 1942.
(2-4) F #
Follows the doings, the fun and the work of a
small Ojibway (Chippewa) boy and his people from summer
through spring.

41 CAMPBELL, SAMUEL ARTHUR. *How's Inky? A Porcupine
and His Pals;* illus. by Bob Kuhn. Indianapolis:
Bobbs-Merrill, 1943. o.p. (4-5)
Inky, along with a ground hog, twin raccoons,
and a fawn, all live in the author's home, Sanctuary of

Wegimind in the Nicolet National Forest of northern
Wisconsin. Although moralistic and pedagogical in
intent, it is told with sympathy and some humor.
Parents and teachers might find it useful.

42 CAMPBELL, SAMUEL ARTHUR. *Too Much Salt and Pepper;*
    illus. Indianapolis: Bobbs-Merrill, 1944.
    o.p. (4-6)
    Accounts of the pranks of two porcupines in and
around the author's home in northern Wisconsin. As the
language is difficult for the interest level, it is
more suitable for reading aloud to the child.

43 CARPENTER, ALLAN. *Wisconsin;* illus. by Phil Austin.
    Chicago: Children's Press, 1964. (4-6) *
    Starting with the exploration of Wisconsin, the
author gives a brief history and description including
natural, industrial, and human resources, enlivened
with anecdotes such as that of Old Abe, the war eagle
mascot of a Civil War regiment. Appendix with instant
facts, dates, people, events, and governors. Index.
Enchantment of America series.

44 CONE, MOLLY. *The Ringling Brothers;* illus. by
    James & Ruth McCrea. New York: Crowell, 1971.
    (2-5) B
    Account of the seven Ringling Brothers, whose
early home was in Baraboo, Wisconsin. With a lively
style, made-up dialogue, and colorful, bold illustrations, it deals with their story from childhood
through merger with Barnum and Bailey in 1918.

45 CONRADER, CONSTANCE STONE. *Blue Wampum.* New York:
    Duell, 1958. (6-8) F * #
    The great Winnebago Indian chieftain, Red Bird,
was one of Paul Duval's heroes. Paul, son of a French-
Indian fur trader and his American wife, closely
watched and listened as the Indians' restlessness
increased over the white man's invasion of the Wisconsin lead country. Filled with beauties of nature.

46 DALY, MAUREEN. *Seventeenth Summer*. New York:
    Dodd, 1948. (7-) F *
    The story of a girl's first love told with charm
and delicacy and a sensitive appreciation of youthful
emotions. Also in paperback (Archway).

47 DAVIS, BETTE J. *Freedom Eagle;* illus. by author.
    New York: Lothrop, Lee & Shepard, 1972.
    (3-7) F
    Based on fact, this is the story of Old Abe, the
eagle who became the regimental mascot for the Eighth
Wisconsin Volunteers in the Civil War. Originally
saved from death by an Indian near Lake Superior, he
served his time in the war and then remained on view in
the state capitol. A real part of Wisconsin heritage.

48 DAVIS, SUSAN B. *Old Forts and Real Folks;* illus.
    Madison, Wisc.: Zoe Bayliss and Susan Davis,
    1939. o.p. (4-7)
    The forts are Fort Howard, Fort Crawford, and
Fort Winnebago.

49 DAVIS, SUSAN B. *Wisconsin Lore for Boys and Girls;*
    illus. Eau Claire, Wisc.: Hale, 1931. o.p.
    (4-7)
    Contains folklore of Wisconsin.

50 DEARN, JILL and SMITH, SUSAN, eds. *Wisconsin: A
    State for All Seasons;* illus. Madison: Wiscon-
    sin Tales and Trails, 1972. (1-8) P *
    About 290 photographs and many articles about
the beauty of the state's changing seasons. Lovely
volume. The pictures can be appreciated by all ages,
although the text is aimed at the older reader.

51 DERLETH, AUGUST. *The Beast in Holger's Woods;*
    illus. by Susan Bennett. New York: Crowell,
    1968. o.p. (6-8) F
    Rick and Banny know the hodag is a myth invented
fifty years ago by a practical joker, but when a real
hodag is reported roaming Holger's Woods, they try to
match wits with the monster. The boys succeed in

unmasking the monster but need to be rescued by a girl.
Humorous and exciting.

52 DERLETH, AUGUST. *Bright Journey.* New York:
   Scribner, 1940. (7-8) F *
   Historical novel of the fur trade in the old
Northwest, 1812-1840. The first part deals with
Hercules Dousman's boyhood on Mackinac Island; the
second takes him to Prairie du Chien in his connection
with the American Fur Company. Dousman was a real
person; his mansion, Villa Louis, still stands. Good
story telling, poetic feeling and good characterization.

53 DERLETH, AUGUST. *The Country of the Hawk;* illus.
   by L. F. Bjorklund. New York: Duell, Sloan &
   Pearce-Meredith Press, 1952. o.p. (6-8) F
   Emigrating from Vermont to what was Michigan
Territory in 1830, David Howe and his family unwitting-
ly join the tide of settlers pushing the Indians from
their Prairie du Sac land. David becomes friends with
an Indian boy, who later saves the Howes from a Sioux
raid. Written with zest.

54 DERLETH, AUGUST. *Ghost of Black Hawk Island.*
   Des Moines, Iowa: Meredith, 1961. o.p.
   (6-8) F
   Steve and Sim encounter a "real ghost" and un-
earth a mysterious necklace while camping in the
Wisconsin Dells.

55 DERLETH, AUGUST. *Land of the Sky-Blue Waters;*
   illus. by Frank Hubbard. New York: Dutton,
   1955. o.p. (6-8) F #
   In 1832, Governor Lewis Cass sent Henry Schoolcraft through Michigan and Wisconsin territories to
find the source of the Mississippi in Minnesota.

56 DERLETH, AUGUST. *The Mill Creek Irregulars:
   Special Detectives.* Des Moines, Iowa: Meredith,
   1959. o.p. (6-8) F
   Steve and Sim get involved in an improbable plot
as they are in and out of Sac Prairie and the farm of

Steve's Uncle Joe. They and a number of other well-characterized people are trying to save the almost eighteen-year-old Molly from her mean stepfather's attempt to marry her to his criminal nephew and get her money.

57 DERLETH, AUGUST. *The Moon Tenders*. Des Moines,
   Iowa: Meredith, 1958. o.p. (6-8) F *
   The village of Sac Prairie and the Wisconsin River are the background of this story. Steve Grendon and Sim Jones, in the summer of 1922, use a raft to float some 40 miles to Bogus Bluff, in search of lost Winnebago tressure. Instead, they found counterfeiters who made prisoners of them. First of the Steve and Sim books.

58 DERLETH, AUGUST. *The Pinkertons Ride Again*. Des
   Moines, Iowa: Meredith, 1960. (6-8) F
   No one believes that Steve and Sim overheard a plot of sinister bandits to hold up a train, so they are duty-bound to foil the evildoers with their own ingenuity.

59 DERLETH, AUGUST. *Wisconsin;* illus. New York:
   Coward-McCann, 1967. (5-8) *
   Rich in historical and biographical lore, filled in with facts of politics, industry, scenery, and ethnic groups. This account by a man proud of his state, is immensely readable. Pronunciation guide, outline of important facts in "Wisconsin Profile," index, photographs, maps on endpapers. *States of the Nation* series.

60 DOUGLAS, WILLIAM O. *Muir of the Mountains;* illus.
   by Harve Stein. Boston: Houghton, 1961. o.p.
   (7-) B
   Douglas imports something of Muir's deep attachment to nature, primarily by quoting the great conservationist whenever possible. Narrative begins in Scotland, on to the Middlewest and the Pacific coast.

61 DUNCAN, MARION. *On the Farm: A Photographic
Picture Book;* illus. New York: McKay, 1940.
o.p. (1-3) P
Brief text and photographs describe adventures
of two real boys on a Wisconsin farm.

62 DUNHAM, MONTREW. *John Muir, Young Naturalist;*
illus. by Al Fiorentino. Indianapolis: Bobbs-
Merrill, 1975. (3-7) B
Among the boyhood to young manhood experiences
of this Scottish-born naturalist in Wisconsin, are an
encounter with an Indian, getting blacked-out in well-
digging, his inventions, and nature walks at the University of Wisconsin. His father does not appear as
dour as he does in other biographies.

63 ECKERT, ALLAN W. *Wild Season;* illus. by Karl E.
Karalus. Boston: Little Brown, 1967. o.p.
(5-7)
A non-scientific, but accurate and objective
account of the ecological community of a glacial lake
in the spring in southern Wisconsin. Animals involved
are a bull snake, bass, raccoon, bull frogs, owl, deer
mouse, and shrew. Predators and the preyed on receive
equal consideration.

64 EIFERT, VIRGINIA. *Louis Jolliet, Explorer of
Rivers.* New York: Dodd, Mead, 1961. o.p.
(7-8) B *
Traces the Jolliet family history from one of
the first settlers of Quebec through the widow of Jean
Nicolet. The author gives an understanding of the
times and, in particular, how the youth gave rise to
the man; *i.e.,* Louis' training in map making from a
Jesuit priest. Jolliet's exploration through Wisconsin
with Father Marquette is seen through their eyes as
something bigger than the commercial venture it
appeared to be. An interesting sidelight is reference
to the Menominee's belief in evil powers in the Mississippi. An erudite presentation. Maps.

65 ELLIS, MEL. *Flight of the White Wolf.* New York:
     Holt, Rinehart & Winston, 1970. (5-7) F *
     Infuriated by taunts of a showdog, Gray, a white
wolf captive since puppyhood, breaks his leash and
kills the dog. Then, in October, begins the northward
trek of Gray and Russ, son of kennel owners who are
remarkably understanding parents. The two journey from
the Kettle Moraine Forest near Milwaukee to a wildlife
reserve (Nicolet National Forest). There Gray can join
a wolf pack and be free of the posses, hunters, blood-
hounds, traps, and threats of poison which pursue him.
Good picture of Wisconsin countryside and dignity of
the wolf. An exciting and plausible account of
survival.

66 ELLIS, MEL. *Ghost Dog of Killicut;* illus. by Dick
     Amundsen. New York: Four Winds Press, 1969.
     o.p. (6-8) F *
     Eighteen-year-old Guy Hardin dreams of the time
when fishing would again be bountiful in Lake Michigan,
and he would own a fleet of boats sailing out of Killicut at the tip of the Door Peninsula. His only chance
to make payments on the boat he has is in collecting
the reward for the champion black Labrador dog, lost
among the desolate Raspberry Islands. With his own
small Labrador, he battles the sea, ice, fire and fog.
The champion is lost, but not before he sired progeny
with Guy's dog. A tale of maturing and survival.

67 ELLIS, MEL. *Hurry Up Harry Hanson.* New York:
     Four Winds Press, 1972. o.p. (5-8) F
     In 1937, smoke from a forest fire is pervading
a north woods community reluctant to leave their homes.
In this setting is 10-year-old Harry Hanson, who likes
feeding the giant muskie living under the family pier.
When the fish kills his pet fox, he develops an obses-
sion to gain revenge to the extent of using a dynamite
bomb and barely destroying the muskie in time to save
his family's life. The shock of that danger and the
race against the encircling fire seem to act as cathar-
sis for the hate in him. First part of book has a
folksy quality.

68 ELLIS, MEL. *Run, Rainey, Run;* illus. by Mel
      Kishner. New York: Holt, Rinehart & Winston,
      1967. o.p. (7-8) *
      An account of the adventures in the life of the
author's dog, a German short-haired Pointer, whose
love of hunting led him to overcome obstacles. No
sentimentality. Paperback ed. in print: Tempo, 1972
(Grosset & Dunlap).

69 ELLIS, MEL. *Sad Song of the Coyote.* New York:
      Holt, Rinehart & Winston, 1967. o.p. (6-8) F
      In order to earn college money, Mark, the son of
a game warden, hunts and collects coyote bounties.
After killing a baby coyote, he goes against his
father's wishes and changes his pursuits to setting up
a money-making zoo.

70 ELLIS, MEL. *Sidewalk Indian.* New York: Holt,
      Rinehart & Winston, 1974. (7-8) F *
      Charley Nightwind, raised in Milwaukee and
falsely accused of murder, seeks refuge on a far northern reservation. The law follows, with harassment and
disrespect by whites. Aided by Betty Sand, an educated
inhabitant of the reservation, and others, Charley has
an idyllic existence. He learns how to survive in his
hiding place in the woods and becomes acquainted with
the ways of his ancestors. In the manner of classic
tragedy, as his fate becomes certain and his desire to
help his people overpowering, he blows up the dam covering their fertile valley and loses his life in the
doing.

71 ELLIS, MEL. *This Mysterious River.* New York:
      Holt, Rinehart & Winston, 1972. (7-8) F
      Twelve-year-old Ham takes ten dollars from the
church collection basket and spends the summer of 1932
trying to earn restitution money. Eventually, he looks
for pearls in river clams near his family's cottage
close to Greenville. Awareness of nature and Ham's
beginning sexuality play a part in this story for the
mature reader.

72 EMERSON, DONALD. *Span across a River.* New York:
   David McKay, 1966. o.p. (7-9) F
   Seventeen-year-old John Holland's classmates
believe his father, a business agent for longshoremen,
is a Communist. In helping to save his father, after
his disappearance, John learns a lot about Communist
double-dealing, bigotry, and the problems of his black
friend. Perhaps the author's desire to teach morals
decreases the quality of this story, but it is fast-
paced, holds the reader's interest, and provides
material in an area little written about for young
people.

73 ENRIGHT, ELIZABETH. *Thimble Summer;* illus. by
   author. New York: Holt, 1938. (4-6) F NA *
   Finding the thimble brought luck to Garnett and
her dry Wisconsin farming community. Rain came, she
and Citronella got locked in the library, she made a
trip by herself to New Conniston, and Timmy won a prize
at the fair. Newbery Award 1939.

— EPSTEIN, BERYL. *Dr. Beaumont and the Man with the
   Hole in His Stomach.* See WI 74

74 EPSTEIN, SAM and EPSTEIN, BERYL. *Dr. Beaumont and
   the Man with the Hole in His Stomach;* illus. by
   Joseph Scrofani. New York: Coward, McCann &
   Geoghegan, 1978. (3-6) B #
   On Mackinac Island in 1822, a voyageur, Alexis
St. Martin, was shot in his stomach. Dr. William
Beaumont, the local army surgeon, saw the advantage of
the fistula that remained after his patient had healed
and started the series of fascinating experiments which
taught him much about the process of digestion. Chapter 5 deals with his stay in Fort Howard at Green Bay,
and Fort Crawford at Prairie du Chien.

75 ERICKSON, PHOEBE. *Black Penny;* illus. by author.
   New York: Knopf, 1951. o.p. (4-6) F *
   Though Emily's Swedish parents warned her not to
get too attached to the colt because they would have
to sell him, she trained him and named him Black Penny.

Eventually Emily did get to keep him, but not until the
city folks who bought the colt and the neighboring farm
decided he was unsafe for their son. Fine family feeling. The place is the tip of Door County.

76 ERNST, JOHN. *Escape King: The Story of Harry
Houdini;* illus. Englewood Cliffs, N.J.:
Prentice-Hall, 1974. (2-5) B
Brief, introductory biography of the immigrant
boy, Erich Weiss. Portrays his determination to succeed as a master magician and escape artist, incidents
in his childhood which influenced him, and his greatest
performances.

77 ERWIN, BETTY K. *Where's Aggie?* Boston: Little,
Brown, 1967. (3-5) F
Aggie, Maggie and Tish, energetic and determined
old ladies, go to Tibet in search of a recipe and leave
their magical objects with the careful Eliot children.
On their way back to Wisconsin, Aggie is captured by
gypsies, but with the aid of mental telepathy manages
to escape. A funny fantasy.

78 ERWIN, BETTY K. *Who Is Victoria?;* illus. by Kathleen Anderson. Boston: Little, Brown, 1973.
(4-6) F
One spring day in the 1930's, Victoria appears
in a small Wisconsin town, wearing a Scottish skirt and
boots and possessing unusual powers. Strange happenings occur in this blend of fun, fantasy and realism.

79 ETTER, LES. *Vince Lombardi, Football Legend;* illus.
Champaign, Ill.: Garrard, 1975. (4-6) B
Easy reading biography of the man who coached
the Green Bay Packers to be winners. Includes his
coaching secrets and special qualities.

80 EUNSON, DALE. *The Day They Gave Babies Away;*
illus. by Douglas Gorsline. New York: Farrar,
Strauss & Giroux, 1970. (4-) F
Based on actual happenings to the author's
father, son of Scottish immigrants. This Christmas

story tells how young Robbie Eunson carried out his
responsibility for finding homes for his orphaned
brothers and sisters, in a small Wisconsin town, Christmas of 1868. Told without sentimentality, with appeal
for children and adults.

81 FALK, ELSA. *Shoes for Matt;* illus. by Tom O'Sullivan. Chicago: Follett, 1960. o.p. (4-6) F
Eleven-year-old Matt Howard works with his
father at farming and making a home at Frenchman's Camp,
on the Mississippi River, in Wisconsin Territory.
Caring for a runt pig and companionship with the son of
a German shoemaker provide some diversion. When a
school opens in the settlement, Matt hopes to become a
lawyer some day.

82 FASSETT, NORMAN C. *Spring Flora of Wisconsin.*
Madison: University of Wisconsin, 1931.
(6-) R
Can be understood by anyone with a real interest
in botany.

83 FELTON, HAROLD W. *Legends of Paul Bunyan;* illus.
by Richard Bennett. New York: Knopf, 1947.
(7-)
A vigorous telling.

84 FENDERSON, LEWIS H. *Daniel Hale Williams, Open-
Heart Doctor;* illus. by Don Miller. New York:
McGraw-Hill, 1971. (6-8) B
This biography deals almost totally with
Williams' medical career, his successes and his frustra-
tions, as when he was called before a Congressional
Committee to defend his administration of Freedman's
Hospital in Washington, D.C. Attention is given to
racial problems. The first thirteen pages are devoted
to Williams' apprenticeship under Doc Palmer in Janes-
ville, Wisconsin.

85 FERRIS, ELMER E. *Jerry at the Academy;* illus. by
    Everett Shinn. New York: Doubleday, 1940.
    o.p. (6-8) F
      The story of Jerry's efforts to get an education
at Wayland Academy in spite of his father's attitude,
is partly autobiographical.

86 FERRIS, ELMER E. *Jerry Foster, Salesman.*
    New York: Doubleday, 1942. o.p. (7-8) F
      Hero of *Jerry of Seven Mile Creek* becomes a
coffee salesman. While learning techniques and rou-
tines of that business, he debated whether to pursue it
or a college career.

87 FERRIS, ELMER E. *Jerry of Seven Mile Creek;* illus.
    by Thomas J. Fogarty. New York: Doubleday,
    1938. o.p. (5-8) F
      As a boy in a small Wisconsin town in the 1880's,
Jerry finds excitement in the circus coming to town, a
political parade, or the thought of being a drummer.
Well-written story with many allusions to nature.

88 FERRY, CHARLES. *Up in Sister Bay;* illus. by Ted
    Lewin. Boston: Houghton Mifflin, 1975.
    (7-9) F
      Hoping to start farming with friends in Sister
Bay in Door County, 17-year-old Robbie Van Epp finds
instead the year 1939 filled with turmoil. A retarded
friend is accused of burning the tannery, another
friend joins the Army, and three well-liked townspeople
die. All this to be handled by Robbie's own confused
emotions of adolescence and maturation. Helping him
over the rough spots are the close relations with the
town's inhabitants. Although the plot is a bit contrived, small town life and the beauty of the land are
well depicted.

— FERSLEV, HELEN L. *It Happened Here: Stories of
    Wisconsin.* See WI 108

372

89 FEUERLICHT, ROBERTA STRAUSS. *Joe McCarthy and McCarthyism, the Hate That Haunts America;* illus. New York: McGraw-Hill, 1971. (7-9)
Account of the Senator from Wisconsin, who, as chairman of various investigating committees, accused or cast suspicions of being communists on people from many walks of life. The author believes that this type of smear attack is still alive. Concise and readable. Photographs.

90 FORSEE, AYLESA. *Frank Lloyd Wright: Rebel in Concrete;* illus. with photographs. Philadelphia: Macrae Smith, 1959. o.p. (7-) P B
Pedestrian account of a creative, controversial genius, highlighting his individuality and insistence on integrity in architecture and that it be wedded to its site. Much takes place in Wisconsin, especially his apprentice Fellowship at Taliesin. Little emphasis on his two divorces and three marriages.

91 FRADIN, DENNIS B. *Wisconsin in Words and Pictures;* illus. by Robert Ulm. Chicago: Children's Press, 1977. (2-5)
With a brief, straightforward text and pictures assuming equal importance, and overall survey of the state is given. Highlights historical events, folklore, land formations, cities, well-known sites, and industries.

92 FRANCHERE, RUTH. *Carl Sandburg, Voice of the People;* illus. by Victor Mays. Champaign, Ill.: Garrard, 1970. o.p. (4-6) B
Objective but sympathetic account of the poor boy born of Swedish parents: his boyhood; his life as a hobo and soldier; his philosophy of working for the underprivileged; his careers of poet, newspaperman, lecturer, folklorist, writer of children's stories, and biographer of Lincoln. The time Sandburg spent in Wisconsin in the early 1900's, when he met and married the sister of Edward Steichen, the photographer, and when he worked for the Social Democratic Party in Appleton and Milwaukee gives a good picture of the progressive spirit of the state.

93 GARA, LARRY. *A Short History of Wisconsin.*
        Madison: State Historical Society of Wisconsin,
        1962. o.p. (8-) P R *
        Readable and compact survey. Contains excerpts
from source materials.

94 GARD, ROBERT and SORDEN, L. G., eds. *Wisconsin
        Lore: Antics and Anecdotes of Wisconsin People
        and Places.* **Madison, Wis.:** Wisconsin House,
        1971. (6-) *
        A collection of stories, proverbs, sayings, etc.
from Wisconsin about Indians, lumberjacks, early medicine, circus, practical jokes, ghosts, hexes, and other
superstitions. Appendix with locale information.

95 GARTNER, JOHN. *Rock Taylor: Football Coach.* New
        York: Dodd, 1951. o.p. (6-8) F
        Newly appointed as coach at Center City, in
Pierce County, Rock Taylor believes that building character is more important than winning, but builds a winning team anyway.

96 GARTNER, JOHN. *Sons of Mercury: A Rock Taylor
        Sports Story.* New York: Dodd, 1956. o.p.
        (6-8) F
        Taylor stands to lose the track and field meet
when he suspends a prize vaulter caught smoking mari-
juana. Others on the team overcome their problems to
help win the championship.

97 GAULT, WILLIAM C. *Speedway Challenge.* New York:
        Dutton, 1956. (5-8) F
        A summer spent on the auto-racing circuit gives
courage to Steve Mallot, just out of college and maybe
a little too careful. Maturity comes to his younger,
brilliant brother, Johnny.

98 GAULT, WILLIAM C. *Through the Line.* New York:
        Dutton, 1961. (5-8) F
        Mark's mathematics teacher believed that the
Wisconsin farm boy's potential was higher than his low
grades. This netted him a football scholarship at an

education-oriented college, whose big triumph was eventually beating the all-for-football school. Nice sprinkling of ethnic group names on the team.

— GEORGIADY, NICHOLAS P. *Exploring Wisconsin.*
   See WI 169

99 GEORGIADY, NICHOLAS P. and ROMANO, LOUIS G.
   Wisconsin's First Settlers—the Indians; illus.
   by Buford Nixon. Milwaukee, Wis.: Franklin,
   n.d. o.p. (4-6)
   A few pages of matter-of-fact narration are
devoted to each topic: ancient Indians and their way
of life, relations with the white man, and the situation of the Indian today. The Fox, the Sauk, and Jean
Nicolet are highlighted.

100 GEORGIADY, NICHOLAS P. and ROMANO, LOUIS G.
   Wisconsin Historical Sights; illus. by Bernard E.
   Merritt, Jr. Milwaukee, Wis.: Franklin, n.d.
   o.p. (4-6)
   Brief historical sketches and anecdotes about
the Ringling Brothers circus; Abraham Lincoln's three-
day stay in the Tallman House in Janesville; the restoration of Stonefield, an 1890 village; and the restored mansion, "Villa Louis," built in the 1830's.

101 GOLDSTON, ROBERT. *The American Nightmare: Senator
   Joseph R. McCarthy and the Politics of Hate;*
   illus. Indianapolis: Bobbs-Merrill, 1973.
   (6-8) B
   Concise, clearly written biography of the junior
Senator from Wisconsin in the 1950's. Recounts his
election campaigns, the Army-McCarthy hearings, and the
climate in America which helped him in his witch-hunt
against communists. Photographs.

102 GRAVES, CHARLES. *John Muir;* illus. by Robert
   Levering. New York: Crowell, 1973. (3-5) B
   Interesting events in the life of the great
naturalist and conservationist. The Wisconsin part
showing his feeling for nature, his hard work, his time

at the University of Wisconsin, and the severity of his father who thought John's interest in plants was a waste of time. Large print.

103 GRAY, JAMES. *Pine, Stream, and Prairie: Wisconsin and Minnesota in Profile;* illus. with photographs. New York: Knopf, 1945. o.p. (7 -) R
Informal anecdotal history of Wisconsin from pioneer days to present. Good description and interpretation.

104 GROSSMAN, ADRIENNE and BEARDWOOD, VALERIE. *Trails of His Own: The Story of John Muir and His Fight to Save Our National Parks;* illus. by Larry Toschil. o.p. (7-) B
Fictionalized biography.

105 GURKO, MIRIAM. *Indian America: The Black Hawk War;* illus. by Richard Cuffari. New York: Crowell-Collier, 1970. o.p. (6-8)
A thoughtful history of the tragedy of the Indians' relations with the white man from colonial days through the 1960's. The struggle of Black Hawk, in the 1830's, against settlers dispossessing his people of their land is used as an example of the Indian's treatment. Maps; bibliography.

106 HAVIGHURST, WALTER. *Song of the Pines;* illus. by Richard Floethe. Philadelphia: Winston, 1949. o.p. (6-8) F *
Fifteen-year-old Nils Thorson, knife grinder in Norway, is fired by persuasive little Cleng Peerson with the urge to go to America. On the boat Nils makes friends with the Svendsens with whom he travels to Wisconsin. After helping them get their farm started, Nils starts out on his own, ending up making a niche for himself by fashioning canthooks for the lumbermen. He successfully meets two problems of the emigrant: learning the language and avoiding being cheated.

107 HEMSCHEMEYER, JUDITH. *Trudie and the Milch Cow;* illus. by Nancy Grossman. New York: Random, 1967. (3-5) F

A little farm girl loves the family's cow, Kuh, who has a bad habit of wandering. She solves the problem in a commonsense way in this warm, nostalgic story based on the childhood of the author's mother in Wisconsin fifty years ago.

108 HENDERSON, MARGARET; SPEERSCHNEIDER, ETHEL D. and FERSLEV, HELEN L. *It happened Here: Stories of Wisconsin;* illus. Madison: State Historical Society of Wisconsin, 1949. (4-8) R

A collection of true stories giving a well-rounded picture of the development of Wisconsin since the days of Jean Nicolet.

109 HILL, MARJORIE W. *Look for the Stars.* New York: Crowell, 1957. o.p. (6-8) F

Latvian refugees from the Russians, the Mitrevic family found life equally hard in Wisconsin. The picture brightened when music helped Elina out of a state of shock, the mother became a caretaker hostess in an historical museum, and sixteen-year-old Marta left behind her bitterness at being different, to take up life with a creative zest. Good character development.

110 HOLBERG, RUTH L. *Hester and Timothy: Pioneers;* illus. by Richard A. Holberg. Garden City: Doubleday, 1937. o.p. (3-4) F

Describes in story form the journey of a pioneer family from Chicago to Milwaukee in 1835 and their daily life after they reached their destination.

111 HOLBERG, RUTH L. *Mitty on Mr. Syrup's Farm;* illus. by Richard A. Holberg. Eau Claire: Hale, 1936. o.p. (2-3) P

Mitty performs farm chores and sees cheese being made, near Greenfield, Wisconsin, in 1890.

112 HOLBERG, RUTH L. *Tansy for Short.* Garden City:
   Doubleday, 1951. o.p. (4-6) F
   A warm, humorous story about Norwegian family
life in pioneer Wisconsin.

113 HOLLING, HOLLING C. *Minn of the Mississippi;* illus.
   by author. Boston: Houghton, 1951. (4-6) P #
   In Chapters 9-11, Minn, the three-legged snapping
turtle, travels through Wisconsin on her way down the
Mississippi. She sees evidences of Paul Bunyan, early
explorers and traders, and mound builders. Fascinating
details of maps, charts, realia, etc., in the margin.

114 HUNT, MABEL LEIGH. *Cupola House;* illus. by Nora
   Unwin. Philadelphia: Lippincott, 1961. o.p.
   (4-6) F #
   What the Hudson children like best about their
new home in the little college town in central Wisconsin is the cupola. When it burns, the whole family contribute toward replacing it, resulting in interesting
money making schemes. Fun and warm family feeling with
a realistic touch.

115 HUZARSKI, RICHARD. *Brushland Bill;* illus. by Bob
   Kuhn. New York: Crowell, 1943. o.p. (6-8) F
   A boy's trapping and hunting adventures in
northern Wisconsin.

116 HYLANDER, CLARENCE J. *American Inventors.* New
   York: Macmillan, 1964. (6-8) B
   Includes a chapter about the invention of the
typewriter by Christopher Sholes.

117 JACKSON, JACQUELINE. *Paleface Red Skins;* illus.
   Boston: Little, Brown, 1958. o.p. (4-6) F
   One summer four Potawatomi children wage war
against Boy Scouts along their lakeside camp. Often
funny and exciting, with good description, but the
story goes on a bit too long.

118 JACOBS, HERBERT. *Frank Lloyd Wright: America's Greatest Architect.* New York: Harcourt, Brace Jovanovich, 1965. o.p. (7-8) B
A scholarly and interesting biography which gives a broad picture of this inner-directed man and his work. Respect and understanding of the subject and an objective viewpoint enhance the value of this book.

119 JORDAN, HOPE DAHLE. *Take Me to My Friend, a Novel of Suspense.* New York: Lothrop, Lee & Shepard, 1962. o.p. (7-8) F
In this well told story, sixteen-year-old Julie Jameson, a nervous new driver, has to take her grandmother from Florida to Wisconsin over dangerous winter roads. Excellent characterization and full of suspense.

120 JORDAN, HOPE DAHLE. *Talk about the Tarchers.* New York: Lothrop, Lee & Shepard, 1968. (7-8) F
When mother decides to finish her high school education, her school-mate daughter is discomfited. But the former is popular with other students, is tutored in French by the council president, and gets involved in school radio. The uneasy situation with her daughter is resolved when the latter successfully substitutes in an important broadcast for her indisposed mother. Unlikely but possible circumstances.

121 KENDALL, LACE. *Houdini: Master of Escape.* Philadelphia: Macrae Smith, 1960. (6-8) B
Warm and intimate account of the Appleton, Wisconsin boy, born Erich Weiss. The son of a poor Hungarian rabbi and later known as Harry Houdini, he gained his reputation of great escape artist through determination and hard work. First quarter of the book deals with the Wisconsin years when Erich performed in a circus at the age of nine, worked for a locksmith and developed the ability to open any lock, and finally left home on a freight train in his 12th year, to seek his fortune.

122 KJELGAARD, JIM A. *The Explorations of Pere Marquette;* illus. by Stephen J. Voorhies. New York: Random, 1951. (4-6) #

This intelligent, loving, and dedicated man comes vibrantly alive, as does his companion, Louis Jolliet, in this account of their exploration of the Mississippi River: the land, the game, the Indians, and the demons and monsters reported to dwell in it. As a Jesuit priest, he brought Christianity and care to the Hurons and Ottawas at site of Ashland, Wisconsin, and to the Illinois at DePere and other areas. Maps.

123 KJELGAARD, JIM A. *The Spell of the White Sturgeon.* New York: Dodd, 1953. o.p. (6-8) F * #

Much of Wisconsin along the shore of Lake Michigan, as well as the tannery where Ramsay Carton was to work, were owned by Devil Chad in 1866. Chad resented the boy's resistance to his bullying, but Ramsay was befriended by a Dutch farmer and his wife. Along with a shipwrecked Dutch captain, they and Ramsay profitably netted white fish, but had to be alert for sabotage.

124 KOHLER, JULILLY H. *Daniel in the Cub Scout Den;* illus. by R. M. Powers. New York: Dutton, 1951. o.p. (3-5) F

Nine-year-old Daniel successfully completes his first year of cubbing with humorous incidents, the strong support of his family, and making a friend of an unhappy, bitter boy.

125 KOHLER, JULILLY H. *Razzberry Jamboree;* illus. by Henry C. Pitz. New York: Crowell, 1957. o.p. (4-6) F

Razz Berry, after being disqualified from attending the Boy Scout Jamboree in California because he is just under twelve, gets to go as a substitute at the last minute. He makes the most of it trading his accumulation of Wisconsin products for a horned toad, etc.

126 KRASKE, ROBERT. *Harry Houdini, Master of Magic;*
illus. by Victor Mays. Champaign, Ill.:
Garrard, 1973. (3-6) B
Fast-moving biography of the man born Ehrich
Weiss in 1874 in Hungary and who immigrated shortly
after birth with his family to Appleton, Wisconsin.
There he spent the first 13 years of his life as the
son of a poor rabbi, helping with odd jobs and practicing tricks. At 16, he changed his name to match that
of a French magician, Robert Houdin, and went on to
become a famous escape artist.

127 LAPP, ELEANOR J. *The Mice Came in Early This Year;*
illus. by David Cunningham. Chicago: Whitman,
1977. (1-2) F
Although the state is not mentioned, it is evident that the author is drawing on her own Wisconsin
locale in this small picture book of preparations for
winter by both people and small animals.

128 LARSEN, EGON. *Men Who Shaped the Future;* with 44
plates and drawings. New York: Roy, 1954.
o.p. (7-) P B
Chapter 7 tells of the exciting events leading
up to the invention of the typewriter by Christopher
Sholes, Wisconsin journalist, senator, and inventor,
who sold his rights to the Remington Company for
$12,000.

129 LAWSON, MARION. *Maggie Flying Bird;* illus. by
Miriam Schottland. New York: Morrow, 1974.
o.p. (5-7) F
Set during the nineteenth century, this somber
story of the daughter of a white trader and a Potawa-
tomi-Chippewa mother is told in the first person.
Kidnapped as a child, she later marries a Chippewa,
who is killed by her white half brothers. With her
two children, she experiences difficult periods of
adjustment as she struggles to reconcile her two
identities. Limited appeal.

130 LAWSON, MARION. *Proud Warrior: The Story of Black Hawk;* illus. by W. T. Mars. New York: Hawthorn, 1968. o.p. (6-8) B

Sauk rites and customs are clearly presented in this sympathetically told story of Black Hawk's life from his wilderness fast, through his fight against the white man, to his death. Well-researched.

131 LAWSON, MARION. *Solomon Juneau, Voyageur;* illus. by Robert Hallock. New York: Crowell, 1974. o.p. (5-7) B

Lively biography of a big, vigorous man born a French Canadian, who became a voyageur and trader, friend of the Indians, loving family man, U.S. citizen, and one of three founders of Milwaukee. He was the first to lay claim to much of the land on which the city was built and became its first mayor. Sometimes, Indian and benevolent white man are portrayed in traditional stereotyped roles.

132 LEAVITT, JEROME E. *America and Its Indians;* illus. by Robert Glaubke. Chicago: Children's Press, 1962. o.p. (4-6)

In the chapter on Indians of the eastern woodlands, there are articles on the Chippewa, Menominee, Ottawa, Potawatomi, Sauk, and Fox, all of whom lived in Wisconsin area. Featured are interesting beliefs and customs, homes, methods of making their living, and famous members.

133 LEEKLEY, THOMAS B. *The World of Manabozho: Tales of the Chippewa Indians;* illus. by Yeffe Kimball. New York: Vanguard, 1965. o.p. (4-8) #

Fourteen legends of Manabozho, the part supernatural being who was a trickster and also helper of his people. Told simply and with charm.

134 LENT, HENRY B. *Men at Work in the Great Lakes States;* illus. New York: Putnam, 1971. o.p. (4-6) #

A sense of immediacy is imparted to evoke interest in the various industries of the Great Lake states.

For example, paper making and the dairy industry are highlighted for Wisconsin. Index.

135 LE SUEUR, MERIDEL. *Sparrow Hawk;* illus. by William
    Moyers. New York: Knopf, 1950. o.p.
    (7-8) F #
    A white boy is befriended by a Sauk Indian youth
at the time that Black Hawk is making raids against
white settlers in an attempt to hold tribal lands. An
experience in tolerance.

136 LIERS, EMIL E. *An Otter's Story;* illus. by Tony
    Palazzo. New York: Viking, 1953. o.p.
    (5-8) *
    Based on the observations of a naturalist author,
this is an entertaining and factual account of the
lives of two otters as they lived, frolicked, and
fought for survival in and around the waterways of
Wisconsin.

137 LIFFRING, JOAN. *Dee and Curtis on a Dairy Farm;*
    illus. Chicago: Follett, 1957. o.p.
    (2-4) F P
    With photographs and brief text, two children
are followed as they watch cows being milked, milk
being made into cheese, and the farmer mending fences
and doing other chores. Although dated, this picture
of rural life could be useful.

138 LINDOP, EDMUND. *War Eagle: The Story of a Civil
    War Mascot;* illus. by Jane Carlson. Boston:
    Little, Brown, 1966. o.p. (3-5)
    Factual account of Old Abe, the hardy pet eagle
who became the mascot of a Wisconsin regiment. Large
blue print and blue illustrations. High interest, low
vocabulary.

139 MC CORMICK, DELL J. *Tall Timber Tales: More Paul
    Bunyan Stories;* illus. by Lorna Livesley.
    Caldwell, Idaho: Caston, 1939. (4-6) #
    Includes: "The Six Mississippis," "The Story of
Pea Soup Shorty," "Paul Invents Calked Shoes," and "The
Log Jam on the Big Auger." All refer to Wisconsin.

140 MC GOLDRICK, RITA C. *The Corduroy Trail;* illus. by
Raul Browe. Garden City, N.Y.: Doubleday, 1934.
o.p. (6-8) F
The adventures of five young people who spent a
summer vacation riding Indian ponies over a corduroy
road in the forests of northern Wisconsin.

141 MC GOWEN, TOM. *The Spirit of the Wild.* Boston:
Little, Brown, 1976. (6-7) F
When a bulldozer accidentally dislodges the rock
door to the world of Indian elves, the spirit of Ween-
digo is freed and threatens to destroy civilization
unless a young girl lures it back to the mound. Skillful build-up in this short fantasy, but characterization
is poor.

142 MC NEER, MAY. *The American Indian Story;* illus. by
Lynd Ward. New York: Farrar, Straus & Giroux,
1963. (4-7) P
Dramatically told stories of Indian heroes and
important events in the history of their people.
Included is Black Hawk with two pages of text dealing
mostly with his raids and the reasons behind them.
Accompanying the account is a full-page colored litho-
graph of Black Hawk, one of fifty such illustrations.

143 MASON, MIRIAM E. *Frances Willard: Girl Crusader;*
illus. Indianapolis: Bobbs-Merrill, 1961.
(3-7) B
Early in life, Willard submitted to but chafed
against her father's benevolent but male chauvanistic
role. She resolved to help people, became a teacher,
and was a forceful champion of women's rights. Over
half of this book is devoted to her tom-boyish growing
up years in Wisconsin at a time when it was becoming a
state, forming agricultural societies and school systems, building railroads west from Milwaukee and a
canal to join the Mississippi River. Style is a bit
condescending to the reader, but the biography provides
worth-while interesting information to this age group.
Childhood of Famous Americans series.

144 MAULE, TEX. *Bart Starr, Professional Quarterback;*
illus. New York: Watts, 1973. (5-8) B
Born in Alabama, Bart Starr went from throwing
balls with his father, to college football, to the
training camp of the Green Bay Packers in 1956. By
1961, he was the complete quarterback. In 1972, he
left playing to coach the young quarterbacks. The book
adequately shows his developing skills and know-how by
application and perserverance and provides good descriptions of game situations. The players' reaction to the
severe Wisconsin winters is mentioned.

145 MAXWELL, WILLIAM. *The Heavenly Tenants;* illus. by
Ilonka Karasz. New York: Harper, 1946. o.p.
(4-6) F
When the Marvel family left their Wisconsin farm
for a vacation, the people and creatures of the zodiac
came down from the sky to take care of things.

146 MEANS, FLORENCE C. *A Candle in the Mist: A Story
for Girls;* illus. by Marguerite de Angeli.
Boston: Houghton, 1931. o.p. (7-) F
A story of pioneering days in Wisconsin and
Minnesota. Janey, at fifteen, taught school, experienced a blizzard, a grasshopper plague, a prairie fire
and other adventures on that frontier of the 1870's.

147 MERIWETHER, LOUISE. *The Heart Man, Dr. Daniel Hale
Williams;* illus. by Floyd Sowell. Englewood
Cliffs, N.J.: Prentice-Hall, 1972. (2-4) B P
This brief biography with sepia sketches on
every other page captures interest as it relates how
the black physician moved to Janesville, Wisconsin in
1873, at the age of seventeen. He worked as a barber,
played in a band, finished high school at twenty-one,
and then worked and learned with a doctor until he
could go to medical school in Chicago. Among his many
accomplishments were setting up the first hospital that
trained black nurses and performing first open-heart
surgery.

148 MOONEY, BOOTH. *General Billy Mitchell;* illus.
Chicago: Follett, 1968. o.p. (6-8) B
This biography of the man who was ahead of his
time in fighting for an independent Air Corps, is
written in an informal style and includes much of his
early life in Wisconsin. Index; photographs.

149 MUIR, JOHN. *The Story of My Boyhood and Youth;*
illus. Madison: University of Wisconsin Press,
1965.
In this autobiography, Muir tells of his childhood in Scotland, farm work and encounters with small
creatures in Wisconsin, and his studies at the
University.

150 NAYLOR, PHYLLIS REYNOLDS. *To Make a Wee Moon;*
illus. by Joe and Beth Krush. Chicago: Follett,
1969. o.p. (4-6) F
Two children find themselves in a miserable situation on a Wisconsin farm until their parents can join
them. They are confronted with a superstitious Scottish grandmother, a mannish aunt, and various preachers,
teachers, and carnival barkers. This moralistic, probably realistic tale, is not very interesting but might
provide a certain ambience for understanding a facet of
Wisconsin experience.

151 NELSON, MARY CARROLL. *Robert Bennett: The Story
of an American Indian;* illus. Minneapolis:
Dillon, 1976. (5-8) B
Simple, clearly written biography of the Wisconsin Oneida Indian who was the only native American to
hold the post of Commissioner of Indian Affairs.
Although he had faith in the white man's education and
economic system, he fought paternalism and sought to
preserve Indian dignity. Map; photographs.

152 NORMAN, CHARLES. *John Muir: Father of Our
National Parks.* New York: Messner, 1957. o.p.
(6-8) B
Account of his brief beginnings in Scotland,
hard work on a Wisconsin farm, his inventions, his 1000

mile walk to the south, adventures with Stickeen and
his fight for national parks. Includes many anecdotal
incidents with good story-telling qualities.

153 NORTH, STERLING. *Captured by the Mohawks, and
    Other Adventures of Radisson;* illus. by Victor
    Mays. Boston: Houghton, Mifflin, 1960.
    (5-7) B #
    Biography of a French-Canadian voyageur who, in
his youth, was captured and adopted by the Mohawks.
Years later, after his escape, he went west and southwest of the Great Lakes, through the Wisconsin area,
and eventually became one of the founders of the
Hudson's Bay Company. Interesting history. *North Star
Books* series.

154 NORTH, STERLING. *Greased Lightning;* illus. by Kurt
    Wiese. Minneapolis: Winston Press, 1941.
    (4-5) F P
    Nine-year-old Zeke saves the runt pig and makes
a pet of him in this lively, humorous tale, remembered
from the author's Wisconsin boyhood.

155 NORTH, STERLING. *Little Rascal;* illus. by Carl
    Burger. New York: Dutton, 1965. (3-5) P *
    The author re-tells for younger readers the
story of the fun, joys, and troubles in his boyhood
year with a pet raccoon, from feeding him through a
wheat straw to releasing him eventually on Lake Koshlo-
nong. Excellent illustrations.

156 NORTH, STERLING. *Rascal: A Memoir of a Better Era;*
    illus. by John Schoenherr. New York: Dutton,
    1963. (6-8) *
    The author was eleven, in 1918, the year he
found and made a pet of a baby raccoon. He recalls the
comic and endearing qualities of Rascal in such episodes
as the animal's accompanying him on a camping trip,
riding in his bicycle basket, and helping him win a pie-
eating contest. Good father-son relationship. Winner
of the Aurianne Award, 1965.

157 NORTH, STERLING. *The Wolfling; A Documentary Novel of the Eighteen-Seventies;* illus. by John Schoen-herr. New York: Dutton, 1969. (7-8) F

Based on the letters written by the author's father about his boyhood, this is the story of twelve-year-old Robbie Trent who crawls into a wolf's den and takes one of her cubs to raise as his pet. Other aspects of the story are Robbie's hard work on his father's farm and his association with There Kumlien, a famous naturalist who had emigrated from Sweden. Good characterization.

158 OBERMEYER, MARION B. *The Listening Post.* New York: McKay, 1957. o.p. (7-) F

Dan goes to the University of Wisconsin, famous for radio research, and, during World War I, he and his sister do important radio work.

159 PLATT, DORIS H. *Wisconsin Reader.* Madison: Wisconsin State Historical Society, 1960. o.p. (4-6) R

A spritely collection of articles from *Badger History,* including material written by children as well as adults.

160 RANSOHOFF, DORIS. *Living Architecture: Frank Lloyd Wright.* Chicago: Encyclopedia Britannica, 1962. o.p. (6-8) P B

Told in waves of retrospect, this biography carries the young reader along in Wright's ideal of being truly oneself. Particularly exciting are the building of the Imperial Hotel in Tokyo and the apprentice set-up at Taliesin, Wisconsin. Little emphasis on his three marriages.

161 REELY, MARY K. *The Blue Mittens;* illus. by Kurt Wiese. Eau Claire, Wisc.: Hale, 1935. o.p. (4-5) F

Stories of a little girl's life on a Wisconsin farm of 1900: the farm animals, starting to school, Decoration Day celebrations, the books she read, and finally leaving the farm and moving to the city.

162 REELY, MARY K. *Seatmates;* illus. by Eloise Wilkin.
New York: Watts, 1949. o.p. (4-5) F
Kate did not realize she no longer hated living
in the town of Spring Green, in 1900, until she was
helping the minister's new daughter get acquainted.
A seatmate in school and the library helped.

163 REYNOLDS, BARBARA LEONARD. *Pepper;* illus. by
Barbara Cooney. New York: Scribner, 1952.
o.p. (4-6) F
Amusing story of a small boy with a problem:
should he keep his mischievous baby raccoon or give him
to a zoo? Delightful drawings.

164 RIETVELD, JANE. *A B C Molly;* illus. New York:
Norton, 1966. o.p. (3-5) F
Molly Conybeare, living in a Wisconsin mining
town, was supposed to stay at home and do housework.
But she wanted to learn to write the poems she composed;
so she went to school disguised as her twin brother.
Tender, wholesome picture of early days in America.

165 RIETVELD, JANE. *Great Lakes Sailor;* illus. by
author. New York: Viking, 1952. o.p.
(4-6) F #
Twelve-year-old Tom Corbin, in Milwaukee of 1844,
persuades his carpenter father to let him sign on as a
cabin boy to a lead-carrying sailcraft. Storm damage
forces his return from Buffalo on a passenger steamboat,
confirming his preference for the sails and the strong,
rough sailors with their sea songs and legend of a sea
serpent.

166 RIETVELD, JANE. *Nicky's Bugle;* illus. by author.
New York: Viking, 1947. o.p. (2-5) F
True-to-life adventures of a small boy who lived
at Fort Winnebago over a hundred years ago.

167 RIETVELD, JANE. *Rocky Point Campers;* illus. New
York: Viking, 1950. o.p. (3-4) F
A Nebraska family vacation near a lake in Door
County. Father and mother get a job picking cherries
on a nearby farm; one of the children decides to help.
A simple, happy story.

168 ROGERS, W. G. *Carl Sandburg, Yes: Poet, Historian,
Novelist, Songster.* New York: Harcourt Brace
Jovanovich, 1970. o.p. (7-9) B
This biography serves as a useful introduction
to Sandburg, depicting well the environment which
inspired his philosophy of exalting the common man and
emphasizing his attention to details of the American
scene. Included are his years in Wisconsin where he
married Paula Steichen, and worked as a newspaperman
and for the Social Democratic Party.

—— ROMANO, LOUIS G. *Wisconsin Historical Sights.*
See WI 100

—— ROMANO, LOUIS G. *Wisconsin's First Settlers—the
Indians.* See WI 99

169 ROMANO, LOUIS G. and NICHOLAS P. GEORGIADY.
Exploring Wisconsin; illus. Rev. ed. Chicago:
Follett, 1970. o.p. (4-6) R
Treatment of the history, geography, and civics
of the state with good material on conservation. Maps.

170 ROUNDS, GLEN. *Ol' Paul, the Mighty Logger;* illus.
by author. New York: Holiday, 1976. (4-6) #
A good reading-aloud book; humorously illustrated.

171 RUSSELL, JOHN M. *Caddie Woodlawn: A Pioneer Girl
on Wisconsin's Frontier;* illus. Menomonee, Wis.:
Dunn County Historical Society, 1970. (5-8)
This pamphlet describes the locale that was the
scene of Carol R. Brink's *Caddie Woodlawn,* the story of
her grandmother's youth. Furnishes interesting background for the book.

172 SCACHERI, MARIO. *Winnebago Boy.* New York:
Harcourt, 1937. o.p. (4-6) P *
At the annual Winnebago camp meeting at the Wisconsin Dells, Landing Hawk spent a delightful summer
learning the crafts, ceremonial dances, and tribal
customs of his people.

173 SCHEELE, WILLIAM E. *The Mound Builders;* illus.
Cleveland: World, 1960. (4-6) #
This discussion of the way archaeologists dis-
covered how the mounds were built and the part they
played in the lives of the builders is limited to the
Hopewell Indians.

174 SCHICK, ALICE. *The Siamang Gibbons: An Ape Family;*
illus. by Joel Schick. Milwaukee: Raintree
Children's Books, 1976. (6-8)
Caught in the jungles of Sumatra and finally
acquired by the Milwaukee Zoo, a pair of gibbons raise
a family, in keeping with the zoo philosophy of breeding endangered species. Limited appeal.

175 SCHOOR, GENE. *Football's Greatest Coach: Vince
Lombardi;* illus. Garden City, N.Y.: Doubleday,
1974. (6-8) B
Fast-moving biography, sprinkled with dialog.
Vince Lombardi coached his Green Bay Packers amost to
the end of his life in 1970. Photographs; index.

176 SHAPIRO, IRWIN. *Paul Bunyan and Other Tales;* illus.
by Al Schmidt. New York: Golden, 1958. o.p.
(4-6)
One yarn after another, including the time Paul
went to Wisconsin and straightened out Round Howlin'
River.

177 SHEPHARD, ESTHER. *Paul Bunyan;* illus. by Rockwell
Kent. New York: Harcourt Brace Jovanovich,
1924. (7-8) #
Tales of the fabulous lumber jack told in the
vernacular.

178 SHERWAN, EARL. *Bruno, the Bear of Split Rock
Island;* illus. New York: Norton, 1966. o.p.
(5-7) F
  With his mother killed by hunters, Bruno becomes
the object of the chase by a guide who wants to use
him as a lure for other hunters. Drawings surpass the
fairly well-constructed text.

179 SHERWAN, EARL. *Mask, the Door County Coon;* illus.
New York: Norton, 1963. o.p. (4-7) F
  A raccoon, living in the woods and lake shores of
Wisconsin, engages in a contest of wits with an unsym-
pathetic trapper. The animal is well-portrayed, but
the man in his vengeance is a bit overdrawn.

180 SHERWOOD, LORRAINE. *"Old Abe," American Eagle;*
illus. by K. Milhous. New York: Scribner,
1946. o.p. (5-7)
  Rescued as a baby by Flambeau Indians in Chippewa country, this eagle served as a mascot and morale
builder for the Eighth Wisconsin Regiment during the
Civil War, and afterwards raised huge sums for veterans
by personal appearances. He was killed by complications
from the fire in the Capitol Building of Wisconsin in
1880.

181 SILBERBERG, ROBERT. *John Muir, Prophet Among the
Glaciers.* New York: Putnam, 1972. (6-8) B
  The life of the Scottish-born conservationist,
with a generous portion of the text devoted to his
youth in Wisconsin, emphasizing his hard work, studies,
inventions, and mentions the temporary loss of sight in
his right eye. Frontispiece.

182 SMITH, FREDRIKA SHUMWAY. *The Sound of Axes;* illus.
by Albert Orbaan. Chicago: Rand McNally, 1965.
o.p. (6-8) F
  Historical fiction about Wisconsin in the 1830's
with settlers in sites of Green Bay, Milwaukee, and
Sheboygan. Story centers about David Harper who spends
two years in the exciting lumbering industry, goes east
to study medicine and returns in 1845 to find his old
lumbercamp turned into a busy village. Endpaper maps.

—— SMITH, SUSAN, ed. *Wisconsin: A State for All Seasons*. See WI 50

183 SMUCKER, BARBARA C. *Wigwam in the City*. New York: Dutton, 1966. o.p. (5-7) F #
A Chippewa family leaves the reservation hoping for a better life in Chicago. Instead, mother and daughter find adjustment difficult in the slum section where the Indian Bureau found them an apartment. With pride in her heritage, the daughter takes a bus back to Wisconsin and finds her brother, who had gone off on his own, camping in a park. Characters are believable.

—— SORDEN, L. G. *Wisconsin Lore: Antics and Anecdotes of Wisconsin People and Places*. See WI 94

—— SPEERSCHNEIDER, ETHEL D. *It Happened Here: Stories of Wisconsin*. See WI 108

184 STEVENS, JAMES. *Paul Bunyan;* woodcuts by Allen Lewis. New York: Knopf, 1948. o.p. (7-8) #
A lengthy introduction giving one explanation of the origin of Paul Bunyan precedes the tales. Also in paperback, Ballantine, 1975, in print.

185 STEWART, JOHN. *Winds in the Woods: The Story of John Muir;* illus. Philadelphia: Westminster, 1975. (5-8) B
The life of the pioneer conservationist, made interesting through the quantity and quality of details. The Wisconsin years show his delight in the 160 acres of the family homestead in Kingston as he and his brother explored the woods and rode horses, his joy in reading, losing consciousness in a well-digging incident, building a four-dialed clock and other inventions.

186 STILL, BAYRD. *Milwaukee: The History of a City*. Madison: Wisconsin State Historical Society, 1948. o.p. (7-) R
A one-volume history of urban development from frontier days to the present industrial center. Nationality backgrounds, commercial foundations, urban services, and political issues are considered.

187 SWIFT, HILDEGARDE. *From the Eagle's Wing: A Biography of John Muir;* illus. by Lynd Ward. New York: Morrow, 1962. o.p. (7-) B *
A distinguished biography of the great naturalist. Deals sensitively with his hard work of making the Wisconsin wilderness into a farm with his brother and dour Scottish father, his stay at the University of Wisconsin, his travels, and his wife.

188 TERRIS, SUSAN. *Whirling Rainbows.* New York: Doubleday, 1974. (5-8) F
At a summer camp in Wisconsin, Leal Friedman, fat and blue eyed, tries to understand her ethnic heritage. Although she was adopted by Jewish parents, her real mother is Chippewa. The story lacks character development, but gives a believable and amusing picture of camp life.

189 TUTT, CLARA L. *Carl Schurz, Patriot;* illus. Madison: Wisconsin State Historical Society, 1960. (5-8) B
The story of the German-born American patriot is written in a fast flowing, exciting style.

190 VANCE, MARGUERITE. *Leave It to Linda;* illus. by Dorothy B. Morse. New York: Dutton, 1958. o.p. (4-6) F
Ten-year-old impulsive, intensive Linda spends the summer on her aunt's dairy farm in Wisconsin, in a Norwegian community, and succeeds in matchmaking with her editor-mother and a famous author.

191 WADSWORTH, WALLACE C. *Paul Bunyan and His Great Blue Ox;* illus. by Will Crawford. New York: Doubleday, 1926. o.p. (4-6) #
Includes "Paul's Bad Luck" about Big Onion Camp from which central location Paul worked all the Lake States, logging off most of the white pine forests of Minnesota, Wisconsin, and Michigan.

192 WARNER, EDYTHE R. *The Fishing River;* illus. by
    author. New York: Viking, 1962. o.p.
    (3-6) P R *
    The author's two sons learn about trout, flora
and fauna, sportsmanship, and conservation in the companionship of their grandfather as they fish in the
Kinnikinick River in western Wisconsin.

193 WHEELER, OPAL. *The Miracle Dish;* illus. by Floyd I.
    Webb. New York: Dutton, 1957. o.p. (3-4) F
    The scene is northern Wisconsin in the early
1900's. How a little girl earned the money for a
Christmas gift for her mother and the miracle which
saved the fragile dish.

194 WHITEHOUSE, ARCH. *Billy Mitchell, America's Eagle
    of Air Power.* New York: Putnam, 1962. o.p.
    (7-8) B
    With warmth and understanding, the author tells
the story of the crusader for a separate air force and
unified control of air power. Devotion to this cause
cost him his rank and career. Bibliography, index.

195 WHYTE, BERTHA K. *Wisconsin Heritage;* photographs
    by author and from other sources. Boston:
    Branford, 1954. o.p. (7-) P R *
    The state's history in text and pictures.
Features illustrations of museum pieces, historically
significant items, and points of interest.

196 WILDER, LAURA INGALLS. *Little House in the Big
    Woods;* illus. by Garth Williams. New York:
    Harper, 1953. (4-6) F *
    First title in an outstanding series about the
daily life of a real pioneer family.

197 WILKINS, MARNE. *The Long Ago Lake: A Child's Book
    of Nature Lore and Crafts;* illus. by Martha
    Weston. New York: Scribner, 1978. (4-8) P *
    Recounting experiences of her childhood summer
months at a Wisconsin lake, the author tells in lively
fashion such things as foraging in fields and woods;

iceboating; playing with Chippewa Indians; and how to make a rope swing, bone and shell jewelry, and lichen dyes. Excellent black and white illustrations. Bibliography and index. A Sierra Club selection.

198 WILLARD, CHARLOTTE. *Frank Lloyd Wright: American Architect;* illus. New York: Macmillan, 1972. (7-8) B

Biography of the individualistic architect who defied tradition in forming and implementing his highly original designs, and who gathered about him a loyal group of followers. Written with clarity. Photographs of his buildings.

199 WORK PROJECTS ADMINISTRATION. *Wisconsin: A Guide to the Badger State;* illus. New York: Hastings, 1954. o.p. (7-) P R *

A general survey of the state, giving historical, current, and geographical background and its social and economic development. *American Guide* series. Reprinted under title, *Wisconsin: A State Guide,* by Somerset Pub.

200 YOUNG, PATRICK. *Old Abe: The Eagle Hero;* illus. by John Kaufmann. Englewood Cliffs, N.J.: Prentice-Hall, 1965. o.p. (2-4)

Brief account for young readers of the famous eagle who served as the mascot of the Eighth Wisconsin Infantry Volunteers for three years during the Civil War. Bold illustrations in two and three colors.

GREAT

LAKES

—

GENERAL

compiled by   ELVIA CARLINO   ERNESTINE MOKEDE
                 LOIS CURTIS   MARILYN SOLT
              DIANE M. GUNN   GRACE STAGEBERG SWENSON
                                       PAT TOMEY

Many books provide valuable general information
which may be applicable to several or all of the areas
of the heartland of the North American continent.
Some of these books concentrate on the Lakes which
constitute the largest body of fresh water in the world.
Others describe Indian tribes which at various times
lived throughout the region. There are books about the
explorers who discovered and charted the vast wilderness, and the fur trappers and hunters who made their
living from its wildlife. Included also are accounts
of the settlers who carved their homes out of that
wilderness, developing at the same time a life style
essential for survival in the new frontier land. Their
expanding needs prompted the widespread development of
the early lumbering industry in the Great Lakes region.
Much of all this rich heritage of the heartland
comes alive because of the efforts of authors whose
books are included in this general bibliography.

397

1   ALLEN, ROBERT THOMAS. *The Great Lakes;* illus.
    Toronto: Natural Science of Canada, 1970.
    (6-8) R *
    A reference work in natural history outstanding
not only for its authenticity, clarity in writing style
and comprehensive coverage, but also for its extensive
use of colour photographs, specially commissioned art
work, diagrams and paintings. Full-colour maps illustrate important aspects of the natural history of the
Great Lakes Canadian region at the beginning of the
book. Fascinating picture stories precede sections on
the geology, plant life, animal life of the area. The
final section on conservation is informative and provocative. Also provides a short list of rocks, plants and
animals of the region for amateur naturalists. Good
index, bibliography.

2   ANDERSON, ELIZABETH STANTON. *Great Lakes Steam
    Vessels;* illus. Meriden, Conn.: Meriden
    Gravure, 1962. (4-) P
    "The verve and flavor of steamboat days lives on
in Samuel Ward Stanton's meticulous drawings of steamers of all types . . ."(Foreword). This book contains
nearly fifty of his drawings of Great Lakes steamers
made in the late nineteenth century when there were
still many steamboats on the lakes. A small amount of
information is included about each vessel: the name,
origin, and fate.

3   AULT, PHIL. *These Are the Great Lakes;* illus. New
    York: Dodd, Mead, 1972. (5-) *
    A most readable overview of the history of the
five Great Lakes with the region being treated as one
area having mutual origin, history and development.
Livened with action-packed anecdotes and human interest
sidelights, it provides a kaleidoscopic view of life,
past and present, in different American and Canadian
locales. The reader sees French explorers living among
the Indians, students digging up a mastadon's bones from
from a suburban Chicago lawn, and a daredevil crossing
Niagara Falls on a tightrope. Ault examines man's

responsibliity for upsetting and correcting the ecological balance of these unique bodies of fresh water.
Includes photographs, a map, bibliography and index.

4   BARRY, JAMES P. *The Battle of Lake Erie, September,
     1813: The Naval Battle That Decided a Northern
     United States Boundary;* illus. New York: Watts,
     1970. (4-8) #
     A *Focus Book* which recounts the naval battle
engaged in by British and American forces to gain control of Lake Erie in 1813. Excellent illustrations.
Bibliography and index.

5   BARRY, JAMES P. *The Fate of the Lakes: A Portrait
     of the Great Lakes;* text and photographs by
     author. Grand Rapids, Mich.: Baker Book House,
     1972. (5-) P
     A large book in superior format which presents
the current status and ecological problems facing the
Great Lakes. Included are sections on the ships that
navigate to the ocean, harbors and shipyards, power
plants along the way, commercial and sport fishing in
the area and threats of industrial pollution. Barry
suggests that it is possible for citizens of the United
States and Canada to strike a balance between living
the good life and preserving the environment. Well-
written and well-illustrated with color and black and
white photographs. Bibliography and index.

6   BARRY, JAMES P. *The Great Lakes;* illus. with photo-
     graphs by author. New York: Watts, 1976.
     (4-8)
     Beginning at Duluth, Minnesota, the freighter
Red Wing carries a cargo of grain through Lakes Superior, Huron, Erie and Ontario to the Atlantic seaboard.
The function of the navigational locks between lakes is
described. Following chapters deal with the glacial
formations, geology and mineral deposits, history,
Indian tribes, recreation and industry of the area.
The last chapter tells of pollution that threatens the
lakes. A well-organized source of general information
written with clarity and illustrated with well-chosen
photographs. Index. A *First Book*.

7   BARRY, JAMES P. *Ships of the Great Lakes: 300
     Years of Navigation;* illus. Berkeley, Calif.:
     Howell-North Books, 1973.
          The vessels that men used on the Great Lakes
reflect the men themselves and their purposes. The
Indian paddling his canoe evokes a whole culture, the
master of a bulk freighter scanning his radar screen a
completely different one. The story of the people and
the ships that sailed the Great Lakes is the story of
developing America.

8   BLEEKER, SONIA. *The Chippewa Indians: Rice Gather-
     ers of the Great Lakes;* illus. by Patricia
     Boodell. New York: Morrow, 1955. 3-6) #
          Provides the everyday life of this Great Lakes
tribe before the arrival of the white man. In the
final chapter the plight of the Chippewas on reservations in North Dakota, Minnesota, Wisconsin and Michigan is portrayed honestly and sympathetically. The
culture is accurately depicted in the black-and-white
line drawings. Very readable text.

9   BOWEN, DANA THOMAS. *Lore of the Lakes;* illus.
     Cleveland, Ohio: Freshwater Press, 1973. (5-8)
          Folklore and reminiscences of the Great Lake
region.

10 BOWEN, DANA THOMAS. *Memories of the Lakes;* illus.
     Cleveland, Ohio: Freshwater Press, 1969. (5-8)
          Stories are from personal interviews detailing
actual experiences aboard ships on the Great Lakes.
Bibliography and index.

11 BOWEN, DANA THOMAS. *Shipwrecks of the Lakes: Told
     in Story and Picture;* illus. Cleveland, Ohio:
     Freshwater Press, 1971. (5-8)
          Stories of great shipwrecks that have taken
place on the Great Lakes.

400

12 BOYER, DWIGHT. *Ghost Ships of the Great Lakes.*
New York: Dodd, Mead, 1968. (6-)
Seventeen stories of missing "ghost ships" taken
from old journals, newspapers, letters and shipping
records. The author writes vividly of phantom ships
and illusionary crews that once travelled the Great
Lakes. Sixteen pages of photographs give proof that
the ships actually did exist. Compelling reading for
the mature reader. Bibliography and index.

13 BOYER, DWIGHT. *Great Stories of the Great Lakes;*
illus. New York: Dodd, Mead, 1966. (6-)
Boyer, an expert story-teller, relates 14 true
tales of Great Lakes ships and men who battled storms,
severe weather, accidents and disasters to keep cargo
and people afloat. Tragedy, humor and heroism dot the
well-documented text which is illustrated by 8 pages of
photographs and maps. Bibliography and index.

14 BOYER, DWIGHT. *Ships and Men of the Great Lakes;*
illus. New York: Dodd, Mead, 1977. (6-)
This volume is dedicated to the men of the big
steamer, *Edmund Fitzgerald,* which disappeared in Lake
Superior during a raging storm on the night of November
10, 1975, apparently only moments after her skipper
reported by radio to another vessel, "I am holding my
own. We are going along like an old shoe. No problems
at all." Most of the other eleven stories also describe
the misadventures of vessels and their crews and the
fierceness of Great Lakes storms.

15 BOYER, DWIGHT. *Strange Adventures of the Great
Lakes;* illus. New York: Dodd, Mead, 1974.
(6-)
A collection of true tales of disappearing ships
collisions at sea, bold rescues, severe lake storms,
perils of winter ice, dangers of running aground,
legends and ghosts. The author relates these documented
stories with gusto and a spirit of suspense and adventure. There are 16 pages of photographs, including
several from the Armistice Day storm of 1940.
Bibliography and index.

16 BOYER, DWIGHT. *True Tales of the Great Lakes;*
  illus. New York: Dodd, Mead, 1971. (6-)
  More strange stories of accidents that defy explanation, lost ships that dropped out of sight, thiev-
ery and deception, gallantry in heroic salvages and
rescues. Six of the thirteen stories concern the "Big
Blow" of 1913, a four-day weather convulsion, in which
twelve ships and their crews numbering about three hundred sailors were lost on Lakes Superior, Huron, Michigan and Erie. A well-organized, documented collection
told with authority and vitality. There are 14 pages
of photographs as well as a bibliography and index.

17 BUEHR, WALTER. *Ships of the Great Lakes;* illus.
  New York: Putnam, 1956. o.p. (3-5)
  The story of the Great Lakes shipping from canoe
to shipping fleets. Actual ships of various lines are
illustrated and discussed.

18 BURT, WILLIAM H. *Mammals of the Great Lakes Region;*
  illus. Ann Arbor, Mich.: University of Michigan, 1972. (6-) R #
  Valuable reference tool for identification and
distribution of species.

19 CARSE, ROBERT. *The Great Lakes Story;* illus. New
  York: Norton, 1968. o.p. (6-8)
  The lakes from the point of view of its sailors.
Includes much seamanship and some history and local
information. Photographs; index.

20 CARUSO, JOHN ANTHONY. *The Great Lakes Frontier;*
  illus. Indianapolis, Ind.: Bobbs-Merrill, 1961.
  o.p. (6-)
  Recounts the saga of the acquisition of the
territory which became the states of Ohio, Indiana,
Illinois, Michigan and Wisconsin. Exploration, coloni-
zation, and the events leading to statehood are recorded
for each state. "Pioneer Days and Ways" are re-created
in detail. The informal writing of this carefully documented book makes it a good reference source for upper
grades. Notes, bibliography, and index.

402

21 CLYMER, THEODORE, comp. *Four Corners of the Sky:
Poems, Chants and Oratory;* illus. by Marc Brown.
Bosoon: Little, Brown, 1975. (3-8) P *
Lavishly illustrated with bold drawings on
colored background, this is a collection of fifty-seven
brief verses and songs from many North American Indian
tribes. Includes eight from the Chippewa dealing with
life, death and nature. Other titles with fewer selections from the Chippewa are:
> JONES, HETTIE, comp. *The Trees Stand Shining;*
> illus. New York: Dial, 1971.
> HOOD, FLORA, comp. *The Turquoise Horse;* illus.
> New York: Putnam, 1972.

22 CROUT, GEORGE and MC CALL, EDITH S. *Where the Ohio
Flows;* illus. by Berthold Tiedemann. Chicago:
Benefic, 1960. o.p. (4-6) #
The part the Ohio River played in the development of mid-western United States. The text accurately
covers the glacial period to the present, and is accompanied by many illustrations and maps. Study questions
and suggested activities are included.

23 DEWDNEY, SELWYN and KIDD, KENNETH E. *Indian Rock
Paintings of the Great Lakes.* 2nd. ed. Toronto:
University of Toronto Press, 1973. (8-) P *
After travelling thousands of miles by canoe
through the Canadian Shield, the Boundary Waters and
Superior National Forest, Dewdney has recorded and
photographed the Indian rock paintings believed to be
over 150 years old. Anthropologist Kidd surveys the
background of Indian culture, mainly the Ojibwa that
inhabited the area. Illustrated by excellent photographs and scale drawings of pictographs. Includes
pronunciation and spelling of Ojibwa words, bibliography, list of sites and index. A provocative,
in-depth study.

— DREW, WAYLAND. *Superior: The Haunted Shore.*
See GL 41

24 ELA, JONATHAN. *The Faces of the Great Lakes;*
    illus. by B. A. King. San Francisco: Sierra
    Club, 1977. (6-) P R
    Following naturalist Sigurd Olson's preface, is
a presentation of the common origin, the historical
changes incurred by traders, missionaries, settlers
and industrialists, and the peculiar characteristics
and problems of each of the five Great Lakes. Included
are Indian lore (mostly Ojibway), the fur trade, rise
and fall of copper country, and pollution and ecology.
The history and social commentary by Ela may be beyond
the grasp of any but very serious students, but King's
100 or more photographs in color and black and white
are quite magnificent. They should thrill readers of
any age capable of appreciating the fragile beauty of
the threatened Great Lakes. An oversize, handsome book
in superior format.

25 ELLIS, WILLIAM DONOHUE. *Land of the Inland Seas:
    The Historic and Beautiful Great Lakes Country;*
    illus. Palo Alto, Calif.: American West, 1974.
    (6-) P *
    A striking book in the *Great West* series. Ellis
treats the Great Lakes area as one region with similar
origin, development and future. The facile text covers
geology, coming of man, struggle for domination, immigration and settlement, industrial and recreational
development and future problems. There are handsome
photographs in intense color, excellent reproductions
of artists' paintings, maps, bibliography and index.
A valuable source of general information for both children and adults.

26 ELMS, F. RAYMOND. *Let's Explore the Great Lakes:
    Stories and Pictures of the Great Lakes;* illus.
    Chicago: Whitman, 1953. o.p. (2-5)
    A fine introductory description of the Great
Lakes region followed by separate accounts of each lake,
its past and present importance, its history and its
physical characteristics. Mineral deposits in the area,
industry, transportation on the lakes and the St. Lawrence Seaway are included. The maps of the entire lake
region and each individual lake are helpful.

404

27 FOLSOM, FRANKLIN. *America's Ancient Treasures:*
Guide to Archaeological Sites and Museums;
illus. New York: Rand McNally, 1974.
(5-8) R *
Prefaced with a general survey of ancient North
American culture and a brief, pithy history for each of
seven divisions, this guide then describes sites in
each state. A pleas is made for amateurs not to dig
and ruin sites from which archaeologists could derive
knowledge of ancient life. All areas in this bibliography, including Ontario, are included. Bibliography
and index.

28 GILCHRIST, MARIE E. *The Story of the Great Lakes;*
illus. by C. H. DeWitt. New York: Harper & Row,
1942. o.p. (2-6) #
All Great Lakes areas are woven into this still
useful, simply written text of the history and geography
of the Lakes. Indians, fur trade, iron ore and lumber
industries and grain shipping are some of the topics.
Lovely lithographs.

29 GRINGHUIS, DIRK. *Open Door to the Great Lakes;*
illus. by author. New York: Duell, Sloan and
Pearce, 1966. o.p. (4-8) #
A fairly complete book about the Great Lakes for
upper elementary students. The opening chapters
describe the Ice Age and the animals and people that
migrated into the area after the ice receded. This is
followed by the age of exploration and the coming of
the settlers. The closing chapters contain tall tales
and portraits of each of the states. Photographs and
illustrations by the author increase the value of the
book. Index.

30 HATCHER, HARLAN and WALTER, ERICH A. *A Pictorial*
History of the Great Lakes; illus. New York:
Bonanza Books, 1963. o.p. (4-8) P *
Encyclopedic coverage of the history of the
Great Lakes area and man's part in its growth and

development. A running commentary connects the photographs and diagrams of everything relating to this
waterway, including reconstructed mastodons, forts,
maps, portraits, lighthouses, harbors, industries, and
churches. Bibliography and index.

31 HAVIGHURST, WALTER. *The First Book of Pioneers:
Northwest Territory;* illus. by Harve Stein.
New York: Watts, 1959. o.p. (3-6) #
General, easy-reading account of the settling of
the five state area: Wisconsin, Illinois, Ohio, Indiana,
and Michigan.

32 HAVIGHURST, WALTER. *The Heartland: Ohio, Indiana,
Illinois;* illus. by Grattan Condon. New York:
Harper & Row, 1962. (6-) R * #
The history and life pulse of America's heartland is revealed in a scholarly blending of history,
people, and times. Havighurst uses vigorous prose to
describe and assess the area from the coming of the
pioneers to the present time. Vignettes of the people
who participated in the developing history. Definitive
table of contents and index. Bibliography.

33 HAVIGHURST, WALTER. *The Long Ships Passing: The
Story of the Great Lakes;* illus. New York:
Macmillan, 1975. (6-)
Dramatic account of three centuries of the Great
Lakes and the men and ships that sailed them. Every
type of craft from canoes to ore boats is discussed.

34 HAVIGHURST, WALTER. *The Midwest;* illus. Grand
Rapids, Mich.: Fideler, 1960. o.p. (4-6)
Photographs and brief text describe the Midwest
in general terms, and then move to each of the eight
states in turn.

35 HENRY, VERA. *Ong, The Wild Gander;* illus. Philadelphia: Lippincott, 1966. o.p. (2-4) F
Fictionalized account of a goose on the Canadian
shores of Lake Superior.

36 Holling, Holling C. *Paddle-to-the-Sea;* illus. by
author. Boston: Houghton Mifflin, 1941.
(4-8) F * #
Carved and launched by an Indian boy, a wooden
canoe is the means by which readers are introduced to
the shore life and the lakes and rivers of the Great
Lakes area from Canada's Nipigon country to the St.
Lawrence River and on to the Atlantic Ocean. Full-
color paintings and detailed black and white sketches
beautifully illustrate the events used to make geography palatable.

37 HOWARD, ELIZABETH. *Summer Under Sail.* New York:
Morrow, 1947. o.p. (6-8) F
Young girl spends the summer on a Great Lakes
sailing ship with her grandfather.

38 JUDSON, CLARA INGRAM. *St. Lawrence Seaway;* illus.
by Lorence Bjorklund. Chicago: Follett, 1959.
o.p. (5-8)
The St. Lawrence Seaway began way back in the
glacial age when the Great Lakes were formed. From
there the author takes us quickly to the explorations
of the French, the struggle between the French and
English for control of the area, the conflict between
the English and Americans, the favorable relations
between Canada and the United States, and finally, in
spite of many problems and mishaps, to the completion
of the Seaway. Diagrams, maps and photographs enhance
this study of the region and seaway which makes it
possible for ocean vessels to sail from the Atlantic
Ocean to Great Lakes ports.

— KIDD, KENNETH E. *Indian Rock Paintings of the
Great Lakes.* See GL 23

39 KUBIAK, WILLIAM J. *Great Lakes Indians—A Pictor-
ial Guide;* illus. by author. Grand Rapids,
Mich.: Baker Book House, 1970. o.p. (4-8) P #
Informative volume and graphic survey of the
Indians of the Great Lakes area; interesting aspects of
Indian life, brief surveys of tribal history. Included

are easy-to-read maps which indicate areas inhabited by
each tribe, and lists of synonymous tribal names.
Striking illustrations show physical features, dress,
and cultural aspects of Indian life. Author Kubiak is
a recognized authority on the Great Lakes Indians.
Bibliography and index.

40 LENT, HENRY B. *Men at Work in the Great Lakes*
    States; illus. New York: Putnam, 1958. o.p.
    (3-6) #
    This book covers many kinds of occupations and
industries found in the states surrounding the Great
Lakes. After a brief historical survey, there are
accounts of Chicago stockyards, Minneosta's iron mines,
Gary's steel mills, food processing plants, industrial
machine manufacturing, and several other kinds of work.
A map of the Great Lakes states would be more useful if
the cities mentioned in the text had been included.

41 LITTELJOHN, BRUCE and DREW, WAYLAND. *Superior;*
    The Haunted Shore; illus. Toronto: Gage, 1975.
    (6-) P *
    Based on a 450 mile canoe trip following the
route of the early fur traders on Lake Superior's north
shore from Batchawana, Ontario, to Grand Portage, Minnesota. In 100 magnificent color photographs, Litteljohn
contrasts the power of the lake and landscape with the
frailty of plant and animal life on shore. Author
Drew's articulate, well researched text emphasizes the
brevity of human existence as compared with the geological age of the land. Together they make a plea for
preserving the wilderness. An oversized, expensive
book with aesthetic appeal for browsers and historical
and geographical detail for mature readers.

42 MC CAGUE, JAMES. *Flatboat Days on Frontier Rivers;*
    illus. by Victor Mays. Champaign, Ill.:
    Garrard, 1968. o.p. (4-8) #
    Farmers and frontiersmen built flatboats to move
cargo down the major rivers to New Orleans. Clumsy
crafts to navigate through treacherous rivers, the flatboats were a vital part of transportation and represented

one facet of pioneer living. Description of flatboa s, methods of propelling them, and hazards of the journey are well depicted. Glossary and index.

— MC CALL, EDITH S. *Where the Ohio Flows.* See OH 22

43 MC CORMICK, DELL J. *Paul Bunyan Swings His Axe;* illus. by author. Caldwell, Idaho: Caxton, 1964 (4-6) #
More tales of the giant of the lumber camps from Maine to California; four from the North Woods. Map on end papers locates settings of stories.

44 MC LAUGHLIN, ROBERT. *The Heartland: Illinois, Indiana, Michigan, Ohio, Wisconsin;* illus. New York: Time-Life, 1967. (4-8) * #
A comprehensive view of the Heartland of the United States—from agricultural to urban regions; from the ice age to its present industrial greatness. Excellent illustrations—many in color. The appendix provides references for tours, museums, local festivals and events, wildlife, and statistical information. Bibliography and index. Time-Life *Library of America* series.

45 MAC LEAN, H. J. *The Fate of the Griffon;* illus. Toronto: Griffin House, 1974. (6-8)
The most famous Great Lakes wreck is the *Griffon,* built for La Salle, the explorer. It mysteriously vanished in 1679 sailing through the Straits of Mackinaw. Was the naval carcass found in 1955 off Tobermory, in Georgian Bay, really the *Griffon?* The author provides not only an interesting account of the building of La Salle's ship, but also describes his own efforts to authenticate the wreck. Ehanced by photographs, sketches and an attractive format, this book brings to light an intriguing saga from our past.

46 MC PHEDRAN, MARIE. *Cargoes in the Great Lakes;*
    illus. Indianapolis: Bobbs-Merrill, 1952.
    o.p. (4-6)
        Informative account of Great Lakes shipping,
ships and cargoes, points of interest, and materials
found around the Great Lakes. Index.

47 NOLAN, JEANNETTE COVERT. *Getting to Know the Ohio*
    River; illus. by Charles Sovek. New York:
    Coward-McCann & Geoghegan, 1973. (4-8) #
        The Ohio River played an important role in the
settlement of its surrounding territory. It provided
a means of access for settlers to the heartland of the
United States when the Northwest Territory was opened
to them. It also provided access to the Mississippi
for the movement of surplus crops in the early days,
and today fleets of barges and diesel towboats carry
oil, coal, gasoline, stone, cement, sand and gravel,
lumber, iron and steel, chemicals, and cereal grain.
The story of the Ohio is the story of the states
through which it flows. Helpful index.

48 OUTDOOR WORLD. *The Great Lakes: North America's*
    Inland Sea; illus. Waukesha, Wisc.: Outdoor
    World, 1974. (5-) P
        Details the formation and geologic and geo-
graphic oddities of the lakes. Relates history through
the explorers and pioneers who claimed and settled the
lake land. 150 photographs show the unique beauty of
each lake.

49 PATTERSON, LILLIE. *Lumberjacks of the North Woods;*
    illus. by Victor Mays. Champaign, Ill.:
    Garrard, 1967. o.p. (2-6) #
        Authentic tales of lumbering and the men who
worked at it in old-time camp days in the Great Lakes
region. Good pictures illustrate camp life.

50 PRESCOTT, JOHN B. *Beautiful Ship: A Story of the
   Great Lakes;* illus. New York: Longmans, 1952.
   o.p. (4-6) F #
   An adventure revolving around the fishing
industry in Lake Michigan.

51 QUIMBY, GEORGE IRVING. *Indian Life in the Upper
   Great Lakes: 11,000 B.C. - A.D. 1800.* Chicago:
   University of Chicago Press, 1960.
   (7-) P R * #
   An anthropologist-archeologist records his
research and that of other specialists of Indian culture from the earliest traces to the destruction of
their culture by the advance of the white man's civilization. This period has no written history, but is
studied through artifacts and archeological sites.
Provides insight to the tribal cultures of the Huron,
Miami, Winnebago, Chippewa, Ottawa, Potawatomi, Sauk,
Fox, and Menominee. An articulate, authoritative text
with excellent photographs, maps and sketches, an
extensive glossary and index.

52 RATIGAN, WILLIAM. *Great Lakes Shipwrecks and
   Survivals;* pictures by Reynold H. Weidenaar.
   Grand Rapids, Mich.: Eerdmans, 1969. (6-)
   A collection of several stories for each of the
five great lakes. Ratigan, who inherited an interest
in the Lakes, writes exciting, authentic narratives of
people who have experienced the erratic and often violent nature of these vast inland seas. Each of the six
sections is introduced by a sea chanty or lake ballad
and is illustrated by a painting, sketch or photograph.
This 1969 expanded reprint edition still bears the 1960
Table of Contents, a minor inconvenience. A readable,
well-researched collection of tales to stretch the
imagination. Index.

53 RICH, LOUISE DICKINSON. *The First Book of Lumber-ing;* illus. by Victor Mays. New York: Watts, 1967. (4-6)
This history of lumbering follows the industry from Maine to the Great Lakes region to the West Coast. The lumberjack's rough way of life and his methods for transporting logs from the forests to the sawmills are vividly described.

54 RIETVELD, JANE. *Great Lakes Sailor;* illus. New York: Viking, 1952. o.p. (4-6) F #
Twelve-year-old Tom Corbin, in Milwaukee of 1844, persuades his carpenter father to let him sign up as a cabin boy on a lead-carrying sailing vessel. Storm damage forces his return from Buffalo on a passenger steamboat, confirming his preference for the sails and the strong, rough sailors with their sea songs and legend of a sea serpent.

— RITZENTHALER, PAT. *The Woodland Indians of the Western Great Lakes.* See GL 55

55 RITZENTHALER, ROBERT E. *The Woodland Indians of the Western Great Lakes;* illus. Garden City, N.Y.: The Natural History Press, 1970. o.p. (5-) #
At the time of Columbus's arrival in the New World, the Woodland Indians, the largest of the eight culture groups into which the Indians of North America have been divided, occupied the forested area of east-ern North America. In this detailed book, compiled from the studies of pioneer ethnologists and their own thirty years of field work, the authors describe, by word and photographs, the Woodland Indian Culture. There is a wealth of information about food, life, customs, religions, games, music, folklore, and medi-cine men. Published for the American Museum of Natural History. Contains glossary, bibliography, and index.

56 STEINHACKER, CHARLES. *Superior.* New York: Harper
     & Row, 1970. (6-) P *
     This handsome over-sized book is a collection of
Steinhacker's superb color photographs showing Lake
Superior in its many moods from the shores of Minnesota,
Michigan, Wisconsin and Ontario. The foreword by Senator Gaylord Nelson pleads for the preservation of this
magnificent body of fresh water. The text includes
carefully selected historical writings by explorers,
missionaries, traders and visitors who travelled to
Lake Superior and the Sault from 1650 to 1880. An
enticing visual experience with a text of historical
significance which may be worth the price.

57 STONEHOUSE, FREDERICK. *Wreck of the Edmund Fitz-
     gerald.* AuTrain, Mich.: Avery Color Studios,
     1977. (8-)
     When the S. S. Edmund Fitzgerald disappeared in
a heavy storm on Lake Superior in November, 1975, it
made headlines and shook maritime personnel. With documentation from many sources, Stonehouse has pieced
together the last voyage of the Fitzgerald and draws
his own conclusions as to why the ship broke in half,
why signals were not received and why rescue operations were not at hand. Included is a list of the 28
seamen who were lost, a glossary of nautical terms and
a bibliography. A compelling story written with immediacy and authority and illustrated with numerous photographs, maps and diagrams.

58 WAITLEY, DOUGLAS. *Portrait of the Midwest;* illus.
     New York: Abelard-Schuman, 1963. o.p. (7-8)
     Dramatically written, panoramic view of all the
areas of this bibliography except Ontario. Moves from
the formation of the land, through the glacial period,
Indian life, exploration, seeking of fur and timber and
other natural resources, settlement, and cultural,
industrial and political development. Second half is
devoted to points of interest and a map for each state.
Index.

— WALTER, ERICH A. *A Pictorial History of the Great Lakes.* See GL 30

59 WEXSTAFF, BERNICE C. *Black Panther of the Great Lakes;* illus. Grand Rapids, Mich.: Eerdmans, 1957. o.p. (4-6) F
Story of a boat owned by Old Jake and Benjy and their adventures on Lake Michigan.

60 WEXSTAFF, BERNICE C. *Haunt of High Island;* illus. Grand Rapids, Mich.: Eerdmans, 1958. o.p. (4-6) F
A sequel to *Black Panther of the Great Lakes* involves skin diving adventures in Lake Michigan.

61 WILSON, HOLLY. *Maggie of Barnaby Bay.* New York: Messner, 1963. o.p. (6-8) F
Story of history and adventure during the War of 1812 on Lake Ontario.

62 WOOD, FRANCES E. *Lakes, Hills, and Prairies;* illus. by Tom Dunnington. Chicago: Children's Press, 1962. o.p. (3-8) #
This attractive book in the *Enchantment of America* series focuses on the middlewestern states of Illinois, Indiana, Michigan, Minnesota, Ohio, and Wisconsin. A general discussion of the geography and history of this area is followed by sections on life in the Lake states today. The final section contains a pictorial map of each state, dates important to that state, and a brief discussion of features unique to the state. Detailed table of contents and glossary are helpful, but unfortunately, no index is included.

63 YOUNG, ANNA G. *Great Lakes Saga: The Influence of One Family on the Development of Canadian Shipping on the Great Lakes, 1816-1931;* illus. by Evan MacDonald. Owen Sound, Ont.: Richardson, Bond & Wright, Printers, 1965. o.p. (7-)
As the daughter of a Great Lakes purser who had access to the records of the Gildersleeve family of Kingston, the author had first hand knowledge of this

part of navigation history. She traces the role played
by the family in Great Lakes shipping for three generations. Although the text is detailed and aimed at
senior readers, the many photographs and drawings, plus
the large map attached to the cover make it a good
source of information on the Great Lakes.

MAGAZINES

The selection of magazines which will help children to understand and appreciate the Great Lakes region was a difficult task at best. Unfortunately, few magazines are written specifically for children and even fewer are written for a particular geographic area, on any reading level. Since the concern of the compilers was to identify those magazines which consistently report on the region and its peoples, they excluded general subject matter magazines which only occasionally publish articles on the Great Lakes region.

The selected magazines feature the past and present of Great Lakes life, giving insight into the ordinary as well as the unique. Readers will enjoy a wide range of science, history, and other factual features, as well as stories, poetry, music, creative crafts and mind teasers. Children, teachers and librarians will find the magazines a fertile source of current pictures and articles, invaluable for browsing, for study, for bulletin board displays, and for vertical file material. The magazines can be the bases for imaginative games, as well as aids in building raading readiness and reading skills. They also supply material for scrapbooks, help develop skill in outlining, provide ideas to stimulate creative writing, and encourage study of regional current events by supplementing the less timely information in books.

Many of the magazines dealing with the Great Lakes region have a broad age appeal. Thus, grade level is indicated in the description only if the magazine is written primarily for children with activities and reading level keyed to younger readers. To facilitate subscribing or requesting sample copies, addresses of publishers and prices current in January 1979 are included.

ILLINOIS

1 *Iliniwek.* (5 times a year)
   Iliniwek, Box 2312, East Peoria, IL 61611.
   $6.50
   An eight page periodical in newspaper format
devoted to historical aspects of Illinois. Each issue
deals with just one topic, such as, Ghost Towns, The
French in Illinois, etc. As it provides more detailed
accounts of each subject than the usual children's
reference materials, it is a valuable resource tool.

2 *Illinois History, A Magazine for Young People.*
   (9 times a year)
   Illinois Historical Society, Old State Capitol,
   Springfield, IL 62706.
   Free to Illinois schools. Others: $1.50 single
   sub.; $1 each for ten or more to same group.
   (4-)
   Articles for the magazine are written by Illinois
students, elementary through high school. Pupils write
on some aspect of the theme for the month ranging
widely. Past themes have been Illinois cities and
towns, Abraham Lincoln, Illinois crafts and craftsmen,
historical periods, etc.

INDIANA

3 *Indiana.* (4 times a year)
   Indiana Dept. of Commerce, Room 336 State House,
   Indianapolis, IN 46204.
   Free to domestic and international addresses.
   Historical, economic and commercial interests.
Colorful photographs and articles to interest all ages.

4 *Outdoor Indiana.* (10 times a year)
    Indiana Dept. of Natural Resources, Room 612,
    State Office Building, Indianapolis, IN 46204.
    $3.
Color and black and white photographs enhance
articles about the beauty, history and economy of
natural resources in Indiana.

MICHIGAN

5 *Chronicle.* (4 times a year)
    Historical Society of Michigan, 2117 Washtenaw,
    Ann Arbor, MI 48104.
    $6.
Well-illustrated articles of interest to history
buffs. Listings of recent magazine and journal
articles of Michigan history. Suitable for grades 5-8.

6 *Michigan History.* (6 times a year)
    Michigan History Division, Dept. of State,
    Lansing, MI 48918.
    $8.95.
Colorful articles concerning Michigan history;
scholarly as well as for popular appeal. Book reviews
and News notes.

7 *Michigan Living/Motor News.* (12 times a year)
    Automobile Club of Michigan, Auto Club Drive,
    Dearborn, MI 48126.
    $4.50.
Features articles on travel, entertainment, dining
and events in Michigan; listing of coming attractions.

8 *Michigan Natural Resources Magazine.*
    (6 times a year)
    Michigan Dept. of Natural Resources, Box 30034,
    Lansing, MI 48909.
    $5.
Colorful, easy reading of Michigan wildlife, personalities, conservation, hunting, and products; general
outdoor magazine. Suitable for grades 4-8.

MINNESOTA

9 *Inland Shores.* (4 times a year)
Inland Shores Land Preservation Foundation,
Ltd., 11050 West Bluemound Road, Milwaukee, WI
53226.
$9.
A high quality quarterly with articles on places of
interest in the Great Lakes country. Features attractive color photographs and paintings.

10 *Minnesota History.* (4 times a year)
Minnesota Historical Society, 1500 Mississippi
St., St. Paul, MN 55101.
$7.
Illustrated articles written mainly for adults on
many aspects of Minnesota's past. Includes book
reviews and "news & notes" of current happenings in the
state.

11 *Minnesota Sportsman.* (6 times a year)
Minnesota Sportsman, Inc., P.O. Box 3003,
Oshkosh, WI 54901.
$5.
Articles on seasonal sports and recreation in
Minnesota with maps, color and black and white photo-
graphs.

12 *The Minnesota Volunteer.* (6 times a year)
Minnesota Dept. of Natural Resources, Box 46,
Centennial Office Building, St. Paul, MN 55155.
Free to Minnesota residents.
An attractive publication with interesting articles
on conservation, natural resources and wildlife in
Minnesota. Includes color photographs and paintings.

13 *Naturalist.* (4 times a year)
Natural History Society, 315 Medical Arts Bldg.,
Minneapolis, MN 55402.
$9.
Beautiful photography and high level articles on
Minnesota's natural resources as well as those in other
areas in the country.

14 *Roots.* (3 times a year)
  Minnesota Historical Society, 1500 Mississippi
  St., St. Paul, MN 55101.
  $4 (5-9)
Each issue focuses on one topic pertaining to
Minnesota history, *e.g.*, exploration, immigration,
lumbering, etc. Illustrated with drawings, maps and
photographs.

OHIO

15 *Cities and Villages.* (12 times a year)
  The Ohio Municipal League, Suite 105, 41 South
  High St., Columbus, OH 43215
  $3. per year for officials of member cities and
  villages; non-member subscriptions, $6.
Perhaps half of the articles are of interest to
city and town officials only, but the remainder—covering such topics as "Ohio's Encephalitis Program" and
"Outdoor Sports Clinics"—are of interest to the
general reader also.

16 *Echoes.* (12 times a year)
  The Ohio Historical Society, I-71 and 17th Ave.,
  Columbus, OH 43211.
  Subscriptions available through any Society mem-
  bership. Individual annual $10. Family Annual
  $15.
The newsletter of the Ohio Historical Society.
Among its contents are reports of activities of the
society, book reviews of recent acquisitions of the
Ohio Historical Centery Library, and short articles on
a variety of subjects of historical interest.

17 *Journal of The Ohio Folklore Society.*
  The Ohio Folklore Society, Ohio State University,
  Columbus, OH.
  Contact for current price.
In the past this journal was published on a regular
basis, but at present it is issued only occasionally.

18 *Ohio History*. (4 times a year)
       The Ohio Historical Society, Ohio Historical
       Center, Columbus, OH 43211.
       $5. a year for Historical Society members;
       $8. a year for non-members; single copies $2.
    "The primary purpose of the journal is to publish
articles, documents, notes, and reviews concerning historical and prehistorical Ohio and the Middle West."

19 *Ohio Magazine*. (12 times a year)
       Ohio Magazine, Inc., 40 W. Gay St., Columbus, OH
       43215.
       Ohio residents, one year $12., two years $20.
    A new publication for the general public covering
topics ranging from activities in the state house to
dining places around the state.

20 *Ohioana Quarterly*. (4 times a year)
       The Martha Kinney Cooper Ohioana Library Assoc.,
       1105 Ohio Departments Building, 65 S. Front St.,
       Columbus, OH 43215.
       $6. a year to libraries. Individual subscrip-
       tions only through membership in the association,
       $8.50.
    The publication is devoted to Ohio authors and
books on the Ohio scene. Includes articles by and
about Ohio authors and their works, and reviews and
discussions of books about Ohio.

ONTARIO

21 *Canadian Children's Magazine*. (4 times a year)
       Canadian Children's Magazine, 4150 Bracken Ave.,
       Victoria, B.C., V8X 3N8, CANADA.
       $5.   (5-8)
    An excellent all-around magazine for children, with
attractive format, interesting articles about Canada
and Canadians, poems, cartoons, puzzles and craft ideas.

22 *Chickadee.* (10 times a year) Young Naturalist
Foundation, 59 Front St. E., Toronto, Ont.,
M5E 1B3, CANADA.
$7. (K-3)
A new magazine like *Owl* has been "especially
created to teach children under eight about their world
in a lively and entertaining way." Contains stories,
puzzles, comics and activities in full colour.

23 *Ontario Fish and Wildlife Review.* (3 times a year)
Ministry of Natural Resources, Publications
Service, Ministry of Government Services,
Toronto, Ont., M5S 1Z8, CANADA.
Free. (8-)
Contains up-to-date articles and illustrations
some in colour, on aspects of wild life in Ontario.
Each issue features one theme, *e.g.*, endangered species.
The print is small but the information is useful for
more mature students.

24 *Ontario Naturalist.* (5 times a year)
Federation of Ontario Naturalists, 1262 Don
Mills Rd., Don Mills, Ont., M3B 2W8, CANADA.
$12. (7-8)
A well-illustrated magazine with articles by distinguished Canadian and Ontario naturalists on ecology,
wild life and plant life. Although the reading level
is advanced, teachers and nature students will find it
useful for reference.

25 *Owl.* (10 times a year)
The Young Naturalist Foundation, 59 Front St. E.,
Toronto, Ont., M5E 1B3, CANADA.
$6.
An outstanding Canadian magazine for children,
financially assisted by the Ontario Arts Council,
Ontario Ministry of Education, and Shell (Canada).
Profusely illustrated in full colour, it provides
interesting easy-to-read articles on nature, nature
crafts, puzzles, etc.

WISCONSIN

26 *Badger History.*   (4 times a year)
>   Wisconsin State Historical Society, 816 State
>   St., Madison, WI   53706
> $4.   (4-8)

Wisconsin historical magazine of local and general interest, written for fourth grade but with appeal for older readers. Well-illustrated.

27 *Wisconsin Trails.*   (4 times a year)
>   Wisconsin   Trails, Box 5650, Madison, WI   53705.
> $8.

Essentially an adult magazine printed on glossy stock, promoting the advantages of Wisconsin with articles on events and personalities in the state. Many illustrations contribute to its appeal for younger readers.

Abelard Press
[*See* Abelard-Schuman, Ltd.]

Abelard-Schuman, Ltd.
Div. of Intext Press, Inc.
[*See* Thomas Y. Crowell Co.]

Abingdon Press
201 Eighth Ave. S.
Nashville, TN 37202

Abraham Lincoln Association
Old State Capitol
Springfield, IL 62706

Addison-Wesley Publishing Co., Inc.
Jacob Way
Redding, MA 01867

Aladdin Books
[*See* E. P. Dutton and Co., Inc.
and Follett Publishing Co.]

American Book Co.
[*See* Litton Educational Publishing, Inc.]

American Heritage Publishing Co., Inc.
10 Rockefeller Plaza
New York, NY 10020

American Printing & Publishing, Inc.
2909 Syene Rd.
Madison, WI 53713

American West
Crown Publishers
1 Park Ave.
New York, NY 10016

Appleton-Century
[*See* Prentice-Hall, Inc.]

Appleton-Century-Crofts
[*See* Prentice-Hall, Inc.]

Arco Publishing Co., Inc.
219 Park Ave. S.
New York, NY 10003

Arkham House Publishers
Sauk City, WI 53583

Atheneum Publishers
Subs. of The Scribner Book Companies
122 E. 42d St.
New York, NY 10017

Atlantic Press Printing, Inc.
1902 Manchester Rd.
Akron, OH 44314

A. Thomas Audel Co.
4300 W. 62d St.
Indianapolis, IN 46206

Avery Color Studios
AuTrain, MI 49806

Baker Book House
1019 Wealthy St. S.E.
Box 6287
Grand Rapids, MI 49506

Ball State University
Little Hoosiers
Burris Laboratory School
Muncie, IN 47306

Ballantine Books, Inc.
Div. of Random House
201 E. 50th
New York, NY 10022

A. S. Barnes and Co., Inc.
Forsgate Drive
Cranbury, NJ 08512

Zoe Bayliss and Susan Davis (*The Author*)
[*address unavailable*]

Charles H. Belding
Graphic Arts Center
2000 N.W. Wilson
Portland, OR 97209

J. F. Bell Museum of Natural History
University of Minnesota
17th & University Ave. S.E.
Minneapolis, MN 55455

Benefic Press
10300 W. Roosevelt Rd.
Westchester, IL 60153

Binford & Mort Publishers
2536 S.E. 11th Ave.
Portland, OR 97202

The Black Letter Press
663 Bridge St. N.W.
Grand Rapids, MI 49504

Bobbs-Merrill Co., Inc.
4300 W. 62d St.
Indianapolis, IN 46206

The Bodley Head, Ltd.
9 Bow St.
London, WC2E 7AL, ENGLAND

Bonanza Books
[See Crown Publishers, Inc.]

Bookwalter
[address unavailable]

Boston Mills Press
R.R. 1
Cheltenham, Ont., LOP 1C0, CANADA

Bowen-Merrill
[See A. Thomas Audel Co.]

Brand
[address unavailable]

Charles T. Branford Company
28 Union St. Box 41
Newton Centre, MA 02159

Buffalo Wallow Press
[address unavailable]

Burns & MacEachern, Ltd.
62 Railside Rd.
Don Mills, Ont., M3A 1A6, CANADA

Burris Laboratory School
[See Ball State University]

CHYM Radio Station
305 King St. W.
Kitchener, Ont., N2G 1B9, CANADA

Canada-Ontario-Rideau-Trent-Severn Study
Committee
[See Ontario Government Publications
Centre]

Canadian Women's Education Press
280 Bloor St. W., Ste. 313
Toronto, Ont., M5S 1W1, CANADA

Caxton Printers, Ltd.
P.O. Box 700
Caldwell, ID 83605

Century
[See Prentice-Hall, Inc.]

Children's Press, Inc.
Div. of Regensteiner Publishing
Enterprises, Inc.
1224 W. Van Buren St.
Chicago, IL 60607

Chilton Book Co.
Chilton Way
Radnor, PA 19089

Clarke, Irwin & Co., Ltd.
791 St. Clair Ave. W.
Toronto, Ont., M6C 1B8, CANADA

Coach House Press
401 Huron St.
Toronto, Ont., M5S 2G5, CANADA

Ritter Collett [The Author]
Sports Editor, Dayton Journal Herald
Fourth & Ludlow Sts.
Dayton, OH 45401

Collier-Macmillan Canada, Ltd.
1125 B Leslie St.
Don Mills, Ont., M3C 2K2, CANADA

William Collins + World Publishing
Co., Inc.
2080 W. 117th St.
Cleveland, OH 44111

Comstock Editions, Inc.
Comstock Book Distributors, Inc.
3030 Bridgeway
Sausalito, CA 94965

Copp Clark
517 Wellington St., West
Toronto, Ont., M5V 1G1, CANADA

Coward, McCann & Geoghegan, Inc.
200 Madison Ave.
New York, NY 10016

Creative Educational Society, Inc.
123 S. Broad St.
Mankato, MN 56001

Crestwood House, Inc.
Highway 66 S.
P.O. Box 3427
Mankato, MN 56001

Croixside Press
310 S. Main St.
Stillwater, MN 55082

Thomas Y. Crowell Company, Inc.
10 E. 53rd St.
New York, NY 10022

Crown Publishers, Inc.
1 Park Ave.
New York, NY 10016

W. Glen Curnoe
P.O. Box 4443
London, Ont., N5W 5J2, CANADA

David-Stewart Publishing Co., Inc.
6503-B Park Central Way
Indianapolis, IN 46260

John Day Company, Inc.
[See Harper & Row, Publishers, Inc.]

Delacorte Press
[See Dell Publishing Co., Inc.]

Dell Publishing Co., Inc.
Subs. of Doubleday & Co.
1 Dag Hammerskjold Plaza
245 E. 47th St.
New York, NY 10017

T. S. Denison & Company, Inc.
9601 Newton Ave. S.
Minneapolis, MN 55431

J. M. Dent & Sons (Canada), Ltd.
100 Scarsdale Rd.
Don Mills, Ont., M3A 2R8, CANADA

Dial Press
Subs. of Dell Publishing Co., Inc.
1 Dag Hammarskjold Plaza
245 E. 47th St.
New York, NY 10017

Dillon Press, Inc.
500 S. Third St.
Minneapolis, MN 55415

Dodd, Mead & Co.
79 Madison Ave.
New York, NY 10016

Dodd, Mead & Co. (Canada), Ltd.
25 Hollinger Rd.
Toronto, Ont., M4B 3G2, CANADA

Dorrance & Co.
35 Cricket Terrace
Ardmore, PA 19003

Doubleday & Company, Inc.
245 Park Ave.
New York, NY 10017

Doubleday Canada, Ltd.
105 Bond St.
Toronto, Ont., M5B 1Y3, CANADA

Doubleday, Doran & Co.
[See Doubleday & Company, Inc.]

Dover Publications, Inc.
180 Varick St.
New York, NY 10014

Duell
[See Meredith Press]

Duell, Sloan & Pearce, Inc.
[See Meredith Press]

Duluth Indian Education Advisory
Committee
(Anishinabe Reading Materials)
Independent School District 709
Duluth, MN 55802

Dunn County Historical Society
1619 B Wilson Ave.
Box 437
Menomonee, WI 54751

Dutton (Canada)
[See Clarke, Irwin & Co., Ltd.]

E. P. Dutton and Company, Inc.
Div. of Sequoia Elsevier Publishing Co.
2 Park Ave.
New York, NY 10016

EMC Corporation
180 E. Sixth St.
St. Paul, MN 55101

Carole Eberly [The Author]
CME Publishing Co.
430 N. Harrison
Lansing, MI 48917

Economy Printing Conern, Inc.
[address unavailable]

William B. Eerdmans Publishing Co.
255 Jefferson Ave. S.E.
Grand Rapids, MI 49503

Elgin Press
[address unavailable]

Exposition Press
900 S. Oyster Bay Rd.
Hicksville, NY 11801

Fanfare Books
30 Waterloo St. S.
Stratford, Ont., n5A 4A6, CANADA

Farrar & Rinehart
[See Farrar, Straus & Giroux, Inc.]

Farrar, Straus & Cudahy
[See Farrar, Straus & Giroux, Inc.]

Farrar, Straus & Giroux, Inc.
19 Union Square, West
New York, NY 10003

Federated Publications, Inc.
155 W. Van Buren
Battle Creek, MI 49017

The Fideler Co.
31 Ottawa Ave., N.W.
Grand Rapids, MI 49503

Fitzhenry & Whiteside, Ltd.
150 Lesmill Rd.
Don Mills, Ont., M3B 2T5, CANADA

Fleet Press Corp.
160 Fifth Ave.
New York, NY 10010

Folklore Associates, Inc.
[See Gale Research Co.]

Follett Publishing Company
1010 W. Washington Blvd.
Chicago, IL 60607

427

Four Winds Press
[*See* Scholastic Book Services]

Franklin Publishers, Inc.
9055 North 51st St.
Milwaukee, WI 53223

Gage Educational Publishing, Ltd.
164 Commander Blvd.
Agincourt, Ont., M1S 3C7, CANADA

Gale Research Co.
Book Tower
Detroit, MI 48226

Garden City Books
[*See* Doubleday & Co., Inc.]

Garrard Publishing Company
1607 N. Market St.
Champaign, IL 61820

Gateway Publishing Co.
[*address unavailable*

General Publishing Co., Ltd.
30 Lesmill Rd.
Don Mills, Ont., M3B 2T6, CANADA

Ginn & Company
Xerox Publishing Div.
191 Spring St.
Lexington, MA 02173

Ginn & Co. (Canada)
3771 Victoria Park Ave.
Scarborough, Ont., M1W 2P9, CANADA

Girard & Girard
1019 Fletcher St.
Owosso, MI 48867

Golden Gate Junior Books
[*See* Chihdren's Press, Inc.]

Golden Press
Western Publishing Co.
1220 Mound Ave.
Racine, WI 53404

Grand Rapids Herald-Review
Grand Rapids, MN 55744

Graphic Arts Center Publishing Co.
2000 N.W. Wilson
Portland, OR 97209

Greey de Pencier
59 Front St. E.
Toronto, Ont., M5E 1B3, CANADA

Griffin House
461 King St. W.
Toronto, Ont., M5V 1K7, CANADA

Grosset & Dunlap, Inc.
51 Madison Ave.
New York, NY 10010

Samuel R. Guard
[*address unavailable*]

Guild Press
[*See* Western Publishing Co.]

Guiness Publishing, Ltd.
P.O. Box 35460
Vancouver, B.C., V6M 4G8, CANADA

E. M. Hale & Co.
20 Waterside Plaza
New York, NY 10010

Harcourt, Brace
[*See* Harcourt Brace Jovanovich, Inc.]

Harcourt, Brace and World
[*See* Harcourt Brace Jovanovich, Inc.]

Harcourt Brace Jovanovich, Inc.
757 Third Ave.
New York, NY 10017

Harlo Press
[*See* John Salmi (*The Author*)]

Harlow
532-536 N.W. Second St.
Okalhoma City, OK 73160

Harper & Brothers, Publishers
[*See* Harper & Row, Publishers, Inc.

Harper & Row (Canada)
[*See* Fitzhenry & Whiteside, Ltd.]

Harper & Row, Publishers, Inc.
10 E. 53rd St.
New York, NY 10022

Harvey House Publishers, Inc.
Div. of E. M. Hale & Co.
20 Waterside Plaza
New York, NY 10010

Hastings House Publishers, Inc.
10 E. 40th St.
New York, NY 10016

Hawthorne Books, Inc.
260 Madison Ave.
New York, NY 10016

Herald Press
616 Walnut Ave.
Scottdale, PA 15683

Highway Book Shop
Dobalt, Ont., P0J 1C0, CANADA

Hillsdale Educational Publishers, Inc.
39 North St.
Hillsdale, MI 49242

The Historical Board
[*See* Toronto Historical Board]

Historical Society of Northwestern Ohio
Now: Maumee Valley Historical Society
1031 River Road
Maumee, OH 43537

Hodder & Stoughton
30 Lesmill Rd.
Don Mills, Ont., M3B 2T6, CANADA

Holiday House, Inc.
18 E. 53rd St.
New York, NY 10022

Henry Holt and Co.
[*See* Holt, Rinehart & Winston, Inc.]

Holt, Rinehart & Winston, Inc.
383 Madison Ave.
New York, NY 10017

Holt, Rinehart & Winston of Canada, Ltd.
55 Horner Ave.
Toronto, Ont., M8Z 4X6, CANADA

Houghton Mifflin Canada, Ltd.
150 Steelcase Rd., W.
Markham, Ont., L3R 2M4, CANADA

Houghton Mifflin Company
1 Beacon St.
Boston, MA 02107

Hounslow Press
124 Parkview Ave.
Willowdale, Ont., M5A 1R7, CANADA

House of Illinois
Decatur, IL

Henry Howe and Son
[*address unavailable*]

Howell Book House, Inc.
730 Fifth Ave.
New York, NY 10019

Hubbard Press
[*See* Hubbard Scientific]

Hubbard Scientific
1946 Raymond Dr.
P.O. Box 104
Northbrook, IL 60062

Illinois State Museum
Spring and Edwards
Springfield, IL 62706

Indiana Historical Society
140 N. Senate
Indianapolis, IN 46204

Indiana Natural Resources Dept.
Division of State Parks
State Office Bldg.
Indianapolis, IN 46204

Indiana State Dept. of Conservation
[*See* Indiana Natural Resources Dept.]

Indiana University Press
Tenth & Morton Sts.
Bloomington, IN 47401

Indianapolis Public Schools
120 E. Walnut
Indianapolis, IN 46204

Marshall Jones Company
[*See* Girard & Girard]

Jordan-Powers Corp.
[*See* Ritter Collett (*The Author*)]

P. J. Kenedy & Sons
[*See* Macmillan, Inc.]

Kent State University Press
Kent, OH 44242

Kids Can Press
485½ Bloor St. W.
Toronto, Ont., M6G 1K5, CANADA

Alfred A. Knopf, Inc.
Subs. of Random House, Inc.
201 E. 50th St.
New York, NY 10022

Laidlaw Brothers
Div. of Doubleday & Co., Inc.
Thatcher & Madison
River Forest, IL 60305

Lakes Publishing Co.
Detroit Lakes, MN 56501

Lamplight Publishing, Inc.
559 W. 26th St.
New York, NY 10001

Learnxs Press
115 College St.
Toronto, Ont., M5T 1P6, CANADA

Ed Leary & Associates
Creative & Advertising Consultants
& Publishers
8021 Egret Lane
Indianapolis, IN 56260

Lerner Publications Company
241 First Ave. N.
Minneapolis, MN 55401

James Lewis and Samuel
[*See* James Lorimer & Co.]

Light & Life Press
Winona Lake, IN 46590

Lion's Head Publishing Co.
4415 Karen Ave.
Fort Wayne, IN 46815

J. B. Lippincott Company
E. Washington Square
Philadelphia, PA 19105

J. B. Lippincott Co. of Canada, Ltd.
75 Horner Ave.
Toronto, Ont., M8Z 4X7, CANADA

Little, Brown & Co.
34 Beacon St.
Boston, MA 02106

Little, Brown & Co. (Canada), Ltd.
25 Hollinger Rd.
Toronto, Ont., M4B 3G2, CANADA

Little Traverse Regional Historical
Society
Box 162
Petoskey, MI 49770

Litton Educational Publishing, Inc.
450 W. 33rd St.
New York, NY 10001

Liveright Publishing Corp.
500 Fifth Ave.
New York, NY 10036

Longman Canada, Ltd.
55 Barber Greene Rd.
Don Mills, Ont., M3C 2A1, CANADA

Longmans
[See David McKay Co., Inc.]

Longmans, Green & Co.
[See David McKay Co., Inc.]

The Lorain Journal Co.
Lorain, OH 44052

James Lorimer & Co.
35 Britain St.
Toronto, Ont., M5A 1R7, CANADA

Lothrop, Lee & Shepard Co.
[See William Morrow & Co., Inc.]

Lyons and Carnahan
[See Rand McNally & Co.

McClelland and Stewart, Ltd.
25 Hollinger Rd.
Toronto, Ont., M4B 3G2, CANADA

A. C. McClurg & Co.
[address unavailable]

McGraw-Hill Book Co.
1221 Ave. of the Americas
New York, NY 10020

McGraw-Hill Ryerson, Ltd.
330 Progress Ave.
Scarborough, Ont., M1P 2Z5, CANADA

David McKay Co., Inc.
750 Third Ave.
New York, NY 10017

Mackinac Island State Park Commission
Box 370
Mackinac Island, MI 49757

Macmillan, Inc.
866 Third Ave.
New York, NY 10022

Macmillan Comapny of Canada, Ltd.
70 Bond St.
Toronto, Ont., M5B 1X3, CANADA

Macrae Smith Co.
Rtes. 54 & Old 47
Turbotville, PA 17772

McRoberts Publishing Co.
3103 Thompson Road
Fenton, MI 48430

Marquette County Historical Society, Inc.
213 North Front St.
Marquette, MI 49855

Abe Martin Publishing Co.
[address unavailable]

Peter Martin Associates, Ltd.
280 Bloor St. W., Ste. 305
Toronto, Ont., M5S 1W1, CANADA

Melmont Publishers
1224 W. Van Buren St.
Chicago, IL 60607

Meredith Press
[See Hawthorne Books, Inc.]

The Meriden Gravure Co.
Meriden, CT 06450

Charles E. Merrill Publishing Co.
Div. of Bell & Howell Co.
1300 Alum Creek Dr.
Columbus, OH 43216

Julian Messner
[See Simon & Schuster, Inc.]

Methuen Publications
2330 Midland Ave.
Agincourt, Ont., M1S 1P7, CANADA

Michigan Audubon Society
7000 N. Westnedge
Kalamazoo, MI 49007

Michigan Dept. of Conservation
[See Michigan Dept. of Natural
Resources]

Michigan Dept. of Natural Resources
Geology Divison
Lansing, MI 48909

Michigan Historical Commission
State Archives Library
3405 N. Logan St.
Lansing, MI 48918

Michigan History Divison
Michigan Dept. of State
208 N. Capitol Ave.
Lansing, MI 48918

Michigan School Service
[address unavailable]

Michigan State University Press
1405 S. Harrison Rd.
East Lansing, MI 48824

Michigan United Conservation Clubs
Box 30235
Lansing, MI 48909

Michigan Ventures
20146 Doyle Court
Grosse Pointe Woods, MI 48236

Mika Publishing Co.
P.O. Box 536
200 Stanley St.
Belleville, Ont., K8N 5B2, CANADA

Walter H. Miller & Co., Inc.
1206 Jamestown Rd.
Williamsburg, VA 23185

Ministry of Natural Resources
[See Ontario Government Publications
Centre]

Minnesota Dept. of Natural Resources
Div. of Parks & Recreation
Rivers Section
Centennial Bldg.
St. Paul, MN 55155

Minnesota Historical Society
690 Cedar St.
St. Paul, MN 55101

Minnesota Timber Producers Assoc.
200 Christie Bldg.
Duluth, MN 55802

Lorna Dee Mistele [The Author]
5090 Buckingham Place
Troy, MI 48084

Modern Methods
[address unavailable]

William Morrow & Co., Inc.
Subs. of Scott, Foresman & Co.
105 Madison Ave.
New York, NY 10016

Museum, Michigan State University
East Lansing, MI 48823

Musson Book Co.
30 Lesmill Rd.
Don Mills, Ont., M3B 2T6, CANADA

National Geographic Society
17th & M Sts. N.W.
Washington, DC 20036

Natural History Press
[See Doubleday & Co., Inc.]

Natural Science of Canada
24 Bartley Dr.
Toronto, Ont., M4A 1G4, CANADA

Naylor Co.
P.O. Box 1838
San Antonio, TX 78206

Thomas Nelson, Inc.
407 Seventh Ave. S.
Nashville, TN 37203

New Press
30 Lesmill Rd.
Don Mills, Ont., M3B 2T6, CANADA

New York Graphic Society Books
41 Mount Vernon St.
Boston, MA 02106

News Publishing Co.
[See Lion's Head Publishing Co.]

Nodin Press
519 North Third St.
Minneapolis, MN 55401

North Star Press
P.O. Box 451
St. Cloud, MN 56301

Northern Michigan University Press
607 Cohodas Administrative Center
Marquette, MI 49855

W. W. Norton & Co., Inc.
500 Fifth Ave.
New York, NY 10036

Oddo Publishing, Inc.
Storybook Acres
Beauregard Blvd.
Fayetteville, GA 30214

Ohio Dept. of Natural Resources
Fountain Square
1952 Belcher Drive
Columbus, OH 43224

Ohio Historical Society
Archives-Library Div.
Interstate 71 & 17th Ave.
Columbus, OH 43211

Ohio State University Press
Hitchcock Hall, Rm. 316
2070 Neil Ave.
Columbus, OH 43210

Ohio University Press
Scott Quadrangle
Athens, OH 45701

Ontario Dept. of Mines
[See Ontario Government Publications
Centre]

Ontario Government Publications Centre
880 Bay St. - Fifth Floor
Toronto, Ont., M5S 1Z8, CANADA

Ontario Ministries - Culture, etc.
[See Ontario Government Publications
Centre]

Ontario Outdoor Publications
Box 1414
Kitcheneer, Ont., CANADA

Orange Judd
[See Howell Book House, Inc.]

Otter Press
P.O. Box 747
Waterloo, Ont., N2J 4C2, CANADA

Outdoor Publications
[See Ontario Outdoor Publications]

Outdoor World
Country Beautiful Corp.
24198 W. Bluemound Rd.
Waukesha, WI 53186

Oxford Printing Co.
Oxford, OH 45056

Oxford University Press (Canada)
70 Wynford Dr.
Don Mills, Ont., M3C 1J9, CANADA

Oxford University Press, Inc.
200 Madison Ave.
New York, NY 10016

Packsack Press
P.O. Box 117
Winton, MN 55796

Paperjacks, Ltd.
330 Steelcase Rd.
Markham, Ont., L3R 2M1, CANADA

Parents' Magazine Press
52 Vanderbilt Ave.
New York, NY 10017

Greey de Pencier
[See Greey de Pencier]

Pendell Publishing Co.
1700 James Savage Rd.
P.O. Box 1666
Midland, MI 48640

Periods and Commas
[address unavailable]

Phillips Brothers, Inc.
1555 West Jefferson St.
Springfield, IL 62702

Piper Publishing, Inc.
120 North Main St.
Blue Earth, MN 56012

Plays, Inc.
8 Arlington St.
Boston, MA 02116

Prentice-Hall, Inc.
Englewood Cliffs, NJ 07632

Press of Case Western Reserve University
Frank Adgate Quail Bldg.
Cleveland, OH 44106

Price, Stern, Sloan, Publishers, Inc.
410 N. La Cienga Blvd.
Los Angeles, CA 90048

G. P. Putnam's Sons
200 Madison Ave.
New York, NY 10016

Raintree Children's Books
[distributed by Follett Publishing Co.]

Ramsey County Historical Society
Old Federal Courts Bldg.
75 W. Fifth St.
St. Paul, MN 55102

Rand McNally & Co.
8255 Central Park Ave.
Skokie, IL 60076

Random House of Canada, Ltd.
5390 Ambler Dr.
Mississauga, Ont., L4W 1Y7, CANADA

Random House, Inc.
Div. of RCA
201 East 50th St.
New York, NY 10022

Regents Publishing Co., Inc.
2 Park Ave.
New York, NY 10016

Henry Regnery Co.
180 N. Michigan Ave.
Chicago, IL 60601

Reilly & Lee Co.
[See Henry Regnery Co.]

Richardson, Bond & Wright, Printers
1749 20th St. E.
P.O. Box 550
Owen Sound, Ont., N4K 5R2, CANADA

Rinehart & Co.
[*See* Holt, Rinehart & Winston]

Ross & Haines, Inc.
639 E. Lake St.
Wayzata, MN 55391

Row, Peterson & Co.
[*See* Harper & Row, Publishers, Inc.]

Royal Ontario Museum
100 Queen's Park
Toronto, Ont., M5S 2C6, CANADA

R. H. Russell
[*See* Atheneum Publishers]

Ryerson Press
[*See* McGraw-Hill Ryerson, Ltd.]

St. Martin's Press, Inc.
175 Fifth Ave.
New York, NY 10010

John Salmi [*The Author*]
Ray, MN 56669

Scholar's Choice
50 Ballantyne Ave.
Stratford, Ont., N5A 6T9, CANADA

Scholar's Facsimiles & Reprints
Box 344
Delmar, NY 12054

Scholastic Book Services
50 W. 44th St.
New York, NY 10036

Scholastic-Tab Publications
123 Newkirk Rd.
Richmond Hill, Ont., L4C 3G5, CANADA

Science Museum of Minnesota
30 E. Tenth St.
St. Paul, MN 55101

William R. Scott, Inc.
[*See* Young Scott Books]

Charles Scribner's Sons
597 Fifth Ave.
New York, NY 10017

Seabury Press, Inc.
815 Second Ave.
New York, NY 10017

E. C. Seale & Co.
1953 E. 54th St.
Indianapolis, IN 46220

Sequoia Press
300 W. Kalamazoo Ave.
Kalamazoo, MI 49007

Sierra Club Books
530 Bush St.
San Francisco, CA 94108

Sierra Club (Canada)
[*See* John Wiley & Sons Canada, Ltd.]

Silver Burdett Co.
Subs. of Scott Foresman & Co.
250 James St.
Morristown, NJ 07960

Simon & Pierre Publishing Co.
Box 280, Adelaide St. P.O.
Toronto, Ont., M5C 2J4, CANADA

Simon & Schuster
Div. of Gulf & Western Corp.
1230 Ave. of the Americas
New York, NY 10020

William Sloane
[*See* Holt, Rinehart & Winston, Inc.]

Somerset Publishers
Div. of Scholarly Press, Inc.
19722 E. Nine Mile Rd.
St. Clair Shores, MI 48080

Southern Illinois University
University Graphics and Publications
[*See* Southern Illinois University
Press]

Southern Illinois University Press
P.O. Box 3697
Carbondale, IL 62901

Stagecoach Pub.
P.O. Box 339
Langley, B.C., V3A 4R7, CANADA

State of Illinois
Dept. of Conservation
Stratton Office Bldg.
Springfield, IL 62706

State of Illinois
Dept. of Registration & Education
Spring and Edwards Sts.
Springfield, IL 62706

State of Illinois
Illinois State Historical Library
Old State Capitol
Springfield, IL 62706

State of Illinois
Office of Education
100 North First St.
Springfield, IL 62706

State of Illinois
Office of Superintendent of Public
Instruction
Springfield, IL 62706

State of Illinois
　Secretary of State's Office
　Centennial Bldg.
　Springfield, IL　62706

State of Minnesota, Dept. of Education,
　Division of Instruction
　Capitol Square Bldg.
　550 Cedar St.
　St. Paul, MN　55101

State of Minnesota, Documents Section
　140 Centennial Bldg.
　St. Paul, MN　55155

State Publishing Co., Inc.
　400 Brooks Lane
　Hazelwood, MO　63402

Frederick A. Stokes Co.
　[See J. B. Lippincott Co.]

Sycamore Press, Inc.
　P.O. Box 552
　Terre Haute, IN　47808

Teachers College
　Columbia University Press
　562 W. 113th St.
　New York, NY　10025

Time-Life Books
　[See Little, Brown & Co.]

Toronto Historical Board
　Canadian National Exhibition Grounds
　Toronto, Ont., M6K 3C3, CANADA

Tundra Books of Montreal
　900 Sherbrooke St. W.
　Montreal, Que., H3A 1G3, CANADA

Ralph Turtinen Publishing Co.
　301 First National Bank Bldg.
　Wayzata, MN　55391

University of Chicago Press
　5801 Ellis Ave.
　Chicago, IL　60637

University of Illinois Press
　Urbana, IL　61801

University of Michigan Press
　615 University
　Ann Arbor, MI　48106

University of Minnesota Press
　2037 University Ave. S.E.
　Minneapolis, MN　55455

University of Toronto Press
　St. George Campus
　University of Toronto
　Toronto, Ont., M5S 1A6, CANADA

University of Wisconsin Press
　P.O. Box 1379
　Madison, WI　53701

Urion Press
　P.O. Box 2244
　Eugene, OR　97402

Van Nostrand, Reinhold (Canada), Ltd.
　1410 Birchmount Rd.
　Scarborough, Ont., M1P 2E7, CANADA

Vanguard Press, Inc.
　424 Madison Ave.
　New York, NY　10017

Vantage Press, Inc.
　516 W. 34th St.
　New York, NY　10001

Viking Press, Inc.
　625 Madison Ave.
　New York, NY　10022

The Villager
　[address unavailable]

Voyageur Press
　9337 Nesbitt Rd.
　Bloomington, MN　55437

Henry Z. Walck, Inc.
　[See David McKay Co., Inc.]

Frederick Warne & Co., Inc.
　101 Fifth Ave.
　New York, NY　10003

Ives Washburn, Inc.
　[See David McKay Co., Inc.]

Franklin Watts, Inc.
　Subs. of Grolier, Inc.
　730 Fifth Ave.
　New York, NY　10019

Wayne State University Press
　The Leonard H. Simons Bldg.
　5959 Woodward Ave.
　Detroit, MI　48202

West Summit Press
　27 W. Summit St.
　Chagrin Falls, OH　44022

Western Publishing Co., Inc.
　1220 Mound Ave.
　Racine, WI　53404

Westminster Press
　905 Witherspoon Bldg.
　Philadelphia, PA　19107

Wheeler Publishing Company
　[See Row, Peterson & Co.]

Albert Whitman & Co.
    560 W. Lake St.
    Chicago, IL 60606

Whittlesey House
    [See McGraw-Hill Book Co.]

Wilcox and Follett
    [See Follett Publishing Company]

John Wiley & Sons Canada, Ltd.
    22 Worcester Rd.
    Rexdale, Ont., M9W 1L1, CANADA

Windsor Publications, Inc.
    21220 Erwin St.
    Woodland Hills, CA 91365

John C. Winston Co.
    [See Holt, Rinehart & Winston, Inc.]

Winston Press
    25 Groveland Terrace
    Minneapolis, MN 55403

Wisconsin Folklore Society [dissolved]
contact: State Historical Society of
                Wisconsin Library
          816 State St.
          Madison, WI 53706
[photocopies can be obtained]

Wisconsin Tales and Trails
    [See Wisconsin Trails]

Wisconsin Trails
    Box 5650
    Madison, WI 53705

Women's Education Press
    [See Canadian Women's Educational Press]

The Women's Press
    [See Canadian Women's Educational Press]

Word Books
    Word, Inc.
    4800 W. Wace Dr.
    Waco, TX 76710

World Book Co.
    [address unavailable]

World Book-Childcraft International, Inc.
    510 Merchandise Mart Plaza
    Chicago, IL 60654

The World Book Encyclopedia
    [See World Book-Childcraft
        International, Inc.]

World Publishing Co.
    [See William Collins + World
        Publishing Co., Inc.]

Thomas Yoseloff, Publisher
    [See A. S. Barnes and Co., Inc.]

Young Scott Books
    [See Addison-Wesley Publishing Co.,Inc.]

435

SOURCES CONSULTED

American Book Publishing Record.
New York: R. R. Bowker, 1977.

BAILEY, BERNADINE. *Picture Book of Indians.*
Chicago: Whitman, 1950.

BANTA, R. E. *Hoosier Caravan: A Treasury of Indian Life and Lore.* Bloomington, Ind.:
Indiana University, 1951.

Books in Print, 1977-78. New York: R. R. Bowker, 1977.

BREWTON, JOHN and SARA. *Index to Children's Poetry, First Supplement.* New York: H. W. Wilson, 1954.

BULLOCK, PENELOPE L. *Michigan Bibliographies and Indexes.* Ypsilanti, Mich.: Eastern Michigan
University, 1960.

Canadian Books for Young People; edited by Irma
McDonough. Revised. Toronto: University of
Toronto Press, 1978.

Canadian Books in Print Subject Guide; edited by Martha
Pluscauskas. Toronto: University of Toronto
Press, 1977.

Canadian Materials; edited by Adele Ashby. Ottawa:
Canadian Library Association.

Canadian Publishers Directory. Toronto: Greey de
Pencier.

Canadiana: Publications of Canadian Interest Received by the National Library. Ottawa: Publishing Centre Supply and Services, 1977, 1978.

Children's Catalog; edited by Barbara Dill. 13th ed. New York: H. W. Wilson, 1976.

COLLINS, WILLIAM R. *Ohio, the Buckeye St te.* Englewood Cliffs, N.J.: Prentice-Hall, 1974.

DERLETH, AUGUST. *Wisconsin.* New York: Coward-McCann, 1967.

EGOFF, SHEILA. *The Republic of Childhood: A Critical Guide to Canadian Children's Literature in English.* Don Mills, Ont.: Oxford Unviersity Press, 1975.

FRANK, RALPH W.; HAYES, BEN; and RODABAUGH, JAMES H. "Ohio, the Buckeye State." *The World Book Encyclopedia,* 1975. XIV, 516-534.

HAVIGHURST, WALTER. *Ohio, A Bicentennial History.* New York: W. W. Norton & Co., 1976.

HUNT, MATE GRAYE. *Michigan History for Young People.* Kalamazoo: Western Michigan University, 1948.

"Illinois: A Bibliography," reprinted from *Illinois Libraries* (September, 1960).

In Review: Canadian Books for Children; edited by Irma McDonough. Toronto: Privincial Library Service.

Junior HIgh School Library Catalog. 3rd ed. New York: H. W. Wilson, 1975.

KATZ, BILL and GARGAL, BERRY. *Magazines for Libraries.* New York: R. R. Bowker, 1969.

438

LASS, WILLIAM E. *Minnesota: A Bicentennial History;*
photographic essay by Don Getsug.
New York: W. W. Norton, 1977.

Library Occurant. Vol. I - XXVI. Indianapolis:
Indiana State Library, 1906-78.

LOCKRIDGE, ROSS F. *The Story of Indiana.*
Oklahoma City, Okla.: Harlow, 1951.

Michigamee: Materials on Michigan. Ann Arbor:
Michigan Association for Media in Education, 1978.

Michigan Books for Young Readers.
Lansing: Michigan State Library, 1968.

Michigan in Fiction.
Detroit: Detroit Public Library, 1978.

MINNESOTA DEPARTMENT OF EDUCATION. *Bibliography of
Minnesota Materials.*
St. Paul: State of Minnesota, 1977.

The Minnesota Legislative Manual, 1977-78; compiled by
Joan Anderson Grewe, Secretary of State.
St. Paul: State of Minnesota, 1977.

Minnesota Pocket Data Book, 1975. St. Paul:
Minnesota State Planning Agency, Development
Planning Division, 1976.

Notable Canadian Children's Books; edited by Irene E.
Aubrey. Ottawa: National Library, 1976.

Ohioana Quarterly. Columbus: The Martha Kinney Cooper
Ohioana Library Association.

PEEK, DAVID T. *Indiana Adventure.*
Indianapolis: Brand, 1962.

Recommended Canadian Titles for Elementary School Libraries. Toronto: Board of Education, 1978. (unpublished.)

Sears List of Subject Headings; edited by Barbara M. Westby. 11th ed. New York: H. W. Wilson, 1977.

SHUMAKER, ARTHUR W. *A History of Indiana Literature.* Indianapolis: Indiana Historical Society, 1962.

The Standard Periodical Directory. 5th ed. New York: Oxbridge Communications, 1976.

Subject Guide to Children's Books in Print. New York: R. R. Bowker, 1971-1977.

Subject Index to Poetry for Children and Young People; compiled by Violet Sell and others. Chicago: American Library Association, 1957.

SWENSON, GRACE STAGEBERG. *Minnesota In Books for Young Readers.* Bloomington, Minn.: Voyageur Press, 1975.

VAN ZEE, RON and KUBISTA, IVAN. *Minnesota.* Portland, Oregon: Charles H. Belding, 1976.

WAITLEY, DOUGLAS. *Portrait of the Midwest.* New York: Abelard-Schuman, 1963.

The Wisconsin Exhibit, a Listing of Books about Wisconsin. Madison, Wisc.: Cooperative Children's Book Center, 1973; and Supplement, 1974-76.

Wisconsin Library Bulletin. Vols. 64 - 74. Madison: Wisconsin State Dept. of Public Instruction, Divison for Library Services, 1968-78.

WORK PROJECTS ADMINISTRATION. *Indiana: A Guide to the Hoosier State.* New York: Oxford University Press, 1941.

The World Book Encyclopedia. Vol. 21. Chicago: Field Enterprises Educational Corp., 1976.

INDEXES

Letters and numbers listed refer to
bibliographic entries and not to pages

AUTHOR INDEX

IL (Ill.); IN (Ind.); MI (Mich.); MN (Minn.); OH (Ohio); ON (Ont.); WI (Wisc.); GL (Gen.)

Aaron, Jan. MI 1
Abbott, Ethelyn Theresa. MI 2
Adamson, Anthony. ON 1
Adamson, Wendy Wriston. MN 1, 2; WI 1
Addison, Ottelyn. ON 2, 3
Ade, George. IN 1
Adler, Ir ing. IL 1
Adler, Ruth. IL 1
Adoff, Arnold. OH 1
Adrian, Mary. MN 3
Aikens, James R. ON 4
Aird, Hazel. MI 3
Akers, Sam. MN 4
Akers, Tom. MN 4
Aldis, Dorothy. IN 2
Allee, Marjorie Hill. OH 2; IN 3, 4; IN 5
Allen, George. MN 5, 6
Allen, John. IIL 2
Allen, LeRoy. OH 3
Allen, Merrit. IL 3
Allen, Robert Thomas. ON 5; GL 1
Alley, Hartley. IN 6
Alley, Jean. IN 6
Allinson, Beverly. ON 6, 7, 8, 9
Allison, Rosemary. ON 10, 11
Altsheler, Joseph A. OH 4
Amb, Thomas M. MN 7
Ames, Merlin McMain. WI 2, 3
Anderson, A. M. IL 4
Anderson, Elizabeth Stanton. GL 2
Anderson, Lavere. IL 5
Anderson, Sherwood. OH 5
Andrae, Christopher. ON 12
Andrews, Elizabeth. ON 13
Andrus, Vera. WI 4
Ankenbruck, John. IN 7
Antell, Will. MN 8
Anthony, Barbara. IL 6
Arbuckle, Dorothy Fry. IN 8, 9
Archer, Jules. WI 5, 6
Archer, Marion. WI 7, 8, 9
Armer, Alberta. MI 4
Armour, David. MI 5
Ault, Phillip H. GL 3
Avery, Lynn. OH 6
Ayars, James. IL 7

Bailey, Bernadine. IL 8, 9; IN 10, 11; MI 6; MN 9; OH 7; WI 10
Baine, Richard P. ON 14
Baird, Willard. MI 7
Baker, Elizabeth. IL 10
Baker, Jim. OH 8
Baker, Laura Nelson. MN 10, 11, 12; ON 15
Baker, Nina (Also See next author). IL 11
Baker, Nina Brown. MI 8
Baker, Ronald. IN 12
Baker, W. C. IL 143
Bald, F. Clever. MI 9
Ball, Cable G. IN 13
Bannon, Laura. MI 10
Bare, Margaret. IL 12
Barnes, Marcillene. IL 6
Barnes, Michael. ON 16
Barnhart, John D. IN 14
Barnouw, Victor. WI 11
Barry, James P. MI 11; OH 9; GL 4, 5, 6, 7
Baskin, John. OH 10

Bassett, John M. ON 17, 18, 19, 20, 21
Batson, Larry. MI 12; MN 13, 14
Baxter, Eric. IL 13
Beals, Frank. IL 14
Beard, Charles A. OH 11
Beardwood, Valerie. WI 104
Beatty, John. IL 15
Beaudry, Lindsay. ON 22
Beckhard, Arthur J. WI 12
Benêt, Laura. IL 16
Benêt, Rosemary. IL 17
Benêt, Stephen. IL 17
Benham, Leslie. ON 23
Benham, Lois. ON 23
Bennett, Emerson. OH 12
Bennett, Rowena. IL 18
Bernard, Jacqueline. MI 13
Bierhorst, John. MI 14; MN 15, 16; WI 13
Biesterveld, Betty. OH 13
Biever, John. WI 14
Bird, Dorothy M. MI 15, 16
Bischoff, Julia Bristol. MI 17, 18, 19
Bjorklund, Karna L. OH 14
Blacklock, Les. MN 17
Blair, Walter. IL 19; WI 15
Blake, Verschoyle. ON 24
Blankmeyer, Helen. IL 20
Blatchford, Frances. IL 21
Bleeker, Sonia. MI 20; MN 18; OH 15; WI 16; GL 8
Bliss, Gordon. IL 22
Bloch, Marie Halun. OH 16
Bloemker, Al. IN 15
Boesch, Mark. OH 17
Bolton, Mimi Dubois. WI 17
Bolz, J. Arnold. MN 19
Borland, Kathryn. IL 23
Bowen, Dana Thomas. GL 9, 10, 11
Bowman, James Cloyd. OH 18; WI 18
Boyer, Dwight. GL 12, 13, 14, 15, 16
Boynick, David. IL 24
Bradford, Karleen. ON 25
Brady, Lillian. MN 20
Brandenberg, Aliki. OH 19
Brandt, Sue. IL 25
Branley, Franklyn M. OH 20
Braun, Thomas. MN 21
Bray, Edmund C. MN 22
Breckenridge, Walter J. MN 23
Breining, Greg. MN 24
Brennan, Terrence. ON 26
Brent, Stuart. WI 19, 20
Brill, Charles. MN 25
Brill, Ethel Claire. MI 21
Brimacombe, Phillip. ON 27
Brings, Lawrence M. MN 26
Brink, Carol Ryrie. WI 21, 22, 23, 24
Britt, Albert. IL 26
Bro, Margueritte Harmon. MN 27
Brock, Emma L. MN 28; WI 25
Bromfield, Louis. OH 21
Brookins, Jean A. MN 78
Brooks, Bill. ON 28
Brooks, Gwendolyn. IL 27
Brown, Charles E. WI 26, 27, 28, 29, 30, 31, 32
Brown, Dorothy L. WI 40

443

AUTHOR INDEX

AUTHOR INDEX

448

AUTHOR INDEX

TITLE INDEX

453

TITLE INDEX

TITLE INDEX

TITLE INDEX

TITLE INDEX

TITLE INDEX

467

SUBJECT INDEX

IL (Ill.); IN (Ind.); MI (Mich.); MN (Minn.); OH (Ohio); ON (Ont.); WI (Wisc.); GL (Gen.)

IL (Ill.); IN (Ind.); MI (Mich.); MN (Minn.); OH (Ohio); ON (Ont.); WI (Wisc.); GL (Gen.)

Wisconsin - History. WI 10, 43, 59, 91,
     WI 93, 100, 103, 108, 159, 169, 195
Wisconsin - Immigration and Emigration -
     Fiction. WI 7
Wisconsin - Natural Resources. WI 169
Wisconsin - Pictorial Works. WI 50
Wolves. MN 3, 134
Wolves - Fiction. WI 65, 157
Women's Rights. ON 94, 154; WI 143
Wonder, Stevie. MI 50
Wooden, John - Biography. IN 147
Woodland Indians - Illinois. IL 79
Woodland Indians - Michigan. MI 188
Woodland Indians.- Ohio. OH 14
Wright, Frank Lloyd. WI 90, 118, 160, 198
Wright, Wilbur and Orville.
     OH 66, 72, 78, 81, 157, 163, 182

Xenia (Ohio). OH 119

Younger Brothers. MN 34, 84
Youth - Ohio. OH 164

Zoological Gardens. WI 174

Badger History MA 26

Canadian Children's Magazine MA 21
Chickadee MA 22
Chronicle MA 5
Cities and Villages MA 15

Echoes MA 16

Iliniwek MA 1
Illinois History MA 2
Indiana MA 3
Inland Shores MA 9

Journal of The Ohio Folklore
     Society MA 17

Michigan History MA 6
Michigan Living/Motor News MA 7
Michigan Natural Resources Magazine MA 8
Minnesota History MA 10
Minnesota Sportsman MA 11
The Minnesota Volunteer MA 12

Naturalist MA 13

Ohio History MA 18
Ohio Magazine MA 19
Ohioana Quarterly MA 20
Ontario Fish & Wildlife Review MA 23
Ontario Naturalist MA 24
Outdoor Indiana MA 4
Owl MA 25

Roots MA 14

Wisconsin Trails MA 27

ABOUT THE COMPILERS

Elvia Carlino recently retired after many years as an elementary school librarian in Springfield, Illinois. She had previously taught English and social studies in junior high and elementary schools. She also was an elementary classroom teacher, and teacher of the academically able. She is a member, and former corresponding secretary, of Children's Reading Round Table; American Association of University Women; and Alpha Delta Kappa. Prior to retirement her memberships included, Illinois Library Association, National Education Association, Illinois Education Association, and Springfield Education Association.

Lois Curtis recently retired after many years as an elementary school media specialist in Lamphere, **Michigan**. She also had been a high school librarian in Birmingham, Michigan, and an English and speech teacher at both elementary and secondary levels in Indianapolis, Indiana. She has been a presenter on innovative uses of media at Michigan Association for Media in Education conferences. Her memberships include, Michigan Association for Media in Education, and Women's National Book Association.

Diane Gunn is a media consultant. She reviews books and media for *School Media Quarterly* and *Booklist*. She is a former elementary school library media specialist in Bloomfield Hills, Michigan, and trustee of Baldwin Public Library, Birmingham, Michigan. She coauthored *Michigan Authors,* to be published by Michigan Association for Media in Education. Her memberships include, American Library Association, Michigan Association for Media in Education, Michigan Library Association, Children's Literature Association, and Beta Phi Mu.

Ernestine Mokede at the time of her death was a middle school library media specialist in Detroit, Michigan. She previously had been a librarian for many years in other Detroit schools and the Detroit Public Library. She was chairman of the district's Elementary Book Selection Committee for several years, and served in various capacities in the annual Detroit Children's Book Fair. She co-authored *Reading Road Map: A Guide to Children's Literature.* Other writing was for a local public television program, "Reading Road Quiz," and for "Skeleton's Closet," a local radio program for children. Her memberships included, American Library Association, Michigan Association for Media in Education, and Detroit Federation of Teachers—Librarians' Chapter.

Marilyn Solt is Professor of Children's Literature at Bowling Green (Ohio) University. She has been a high school English teacher. Her doctoral dissertation was *The Newbery Award: A Survey of Fifty Years of Newbery Winners and Honor Books.* She has presented papers on children's literature at professionsl conferences, and has had articles published in *The English Association of Northwestern Ohio Bulletin* and *Illinois English Bulletin.* Her memberships include, Children's Literature Association; National Council of Teachers of English; English Association of Northwestern Ohio; Library Resources and Reading Improvement Program of the International Reading Association; and Ohioana Library Association.

Grace Stageberg Swenson has been an elementary school library media specialist in Wayzata, Minnesota, for many years. Prior to this library work, she taught high school music and directed church choirs. Her published books are *Minnesota in Books for Young Readers* and *From the Ashes, the Story of the Hinckley Fire.* Her professional memberships include National Education Association, Minnesota Education Association, Minnesota Council of Teachers of English, Minnesota Educational Media Organization, and Delta Kappa Gamma.

Donna Taylor is a former Professor of Library Science at Wayne State University and Eastern Michigan University. She has been a school library media specialist in Redford Township, Michigan, and Detroit, Michigan; and a consultant for media and media center development. She co-authored *Michigan Authors,* to be published by Michigan Association for Media in Education; and has contributed articles to professional journals. Her memberships include, American Library Association; Michigan Association for Media in Education; Children's Literature Association; Michigan Council of Teachers of English; Women's National Book Associaton, past vice-president and *Newsletter* co-editor; and Board Member, Friends of Ann Arbor (Michigan) Public Library.

Pat Tomey recently retired as Library Consultant for Elementary Schools in Toronto, Ontario. She has been a Lecturer in Children's Literature at the University of Toronto and the University of Regina. She participated in a research project at Centre for Research in Librarianship, Faculty of Library Science, University of Toronto. The purpose was the compilation of a selective list of non-print materials for Canadian school libraries. She currently reviews children's books for the Canadian periodicals, *In Review* and *Canadian Materials.* She holds memberships in Canadian Lib rary Association, and Alpha Delta Kappa.

481

typeset by   J. E. TAYLOR

in IBM   8 point COURIER
            8 point COURIER ITALIC
            10 point LIGHT ITALIC
            12 point LETTER GOTHIC
            14 POINT ORATOR